This thing that popped into my mind…
It is so tiny and fragile.
If I rush to give it form, it crumbles in an instant.

I carefully guard it in my head and heart so I can display it
when it finally takes shape.
But before I know it…
It is suddenly gone.

How often am I, thus, unable to put it down on paper?

That is what ideas are like.

—Hiroyuki Asada, 2012

Hiroyuki Asada made his debut in *Monthly Shonen Jump* in
1986. He's best known for his basketball manga *I'll*.
He's a contributor to artist Range Murata's quarterly manga
anthology *Robot*. *Tegami Bachi: Letter Bee*
is his most recent series.

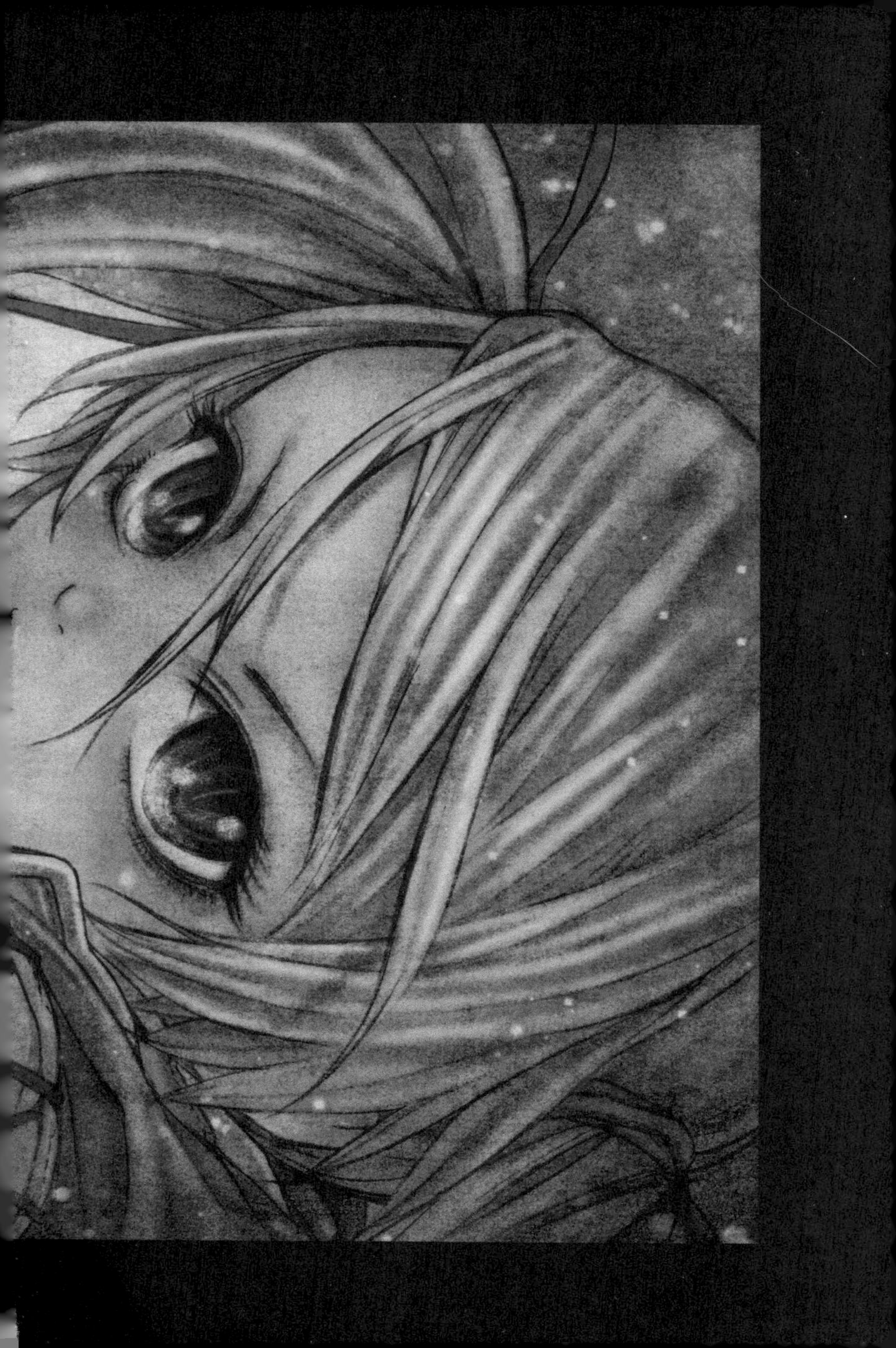

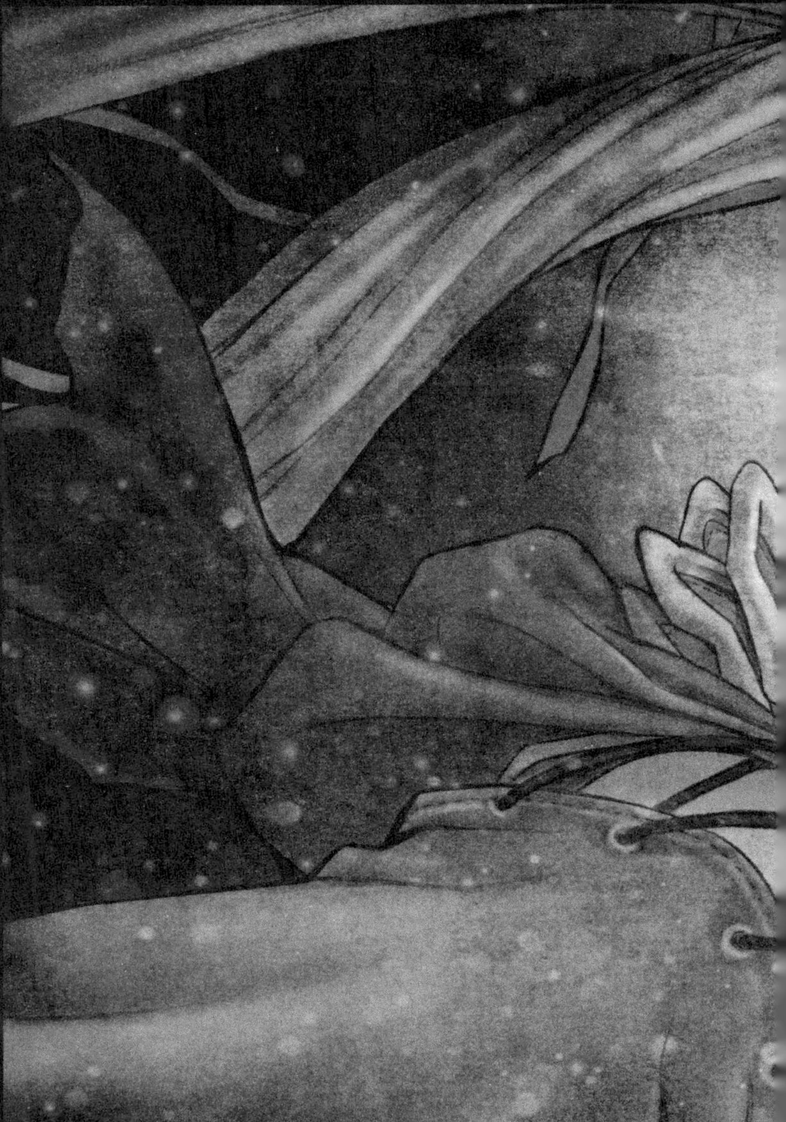

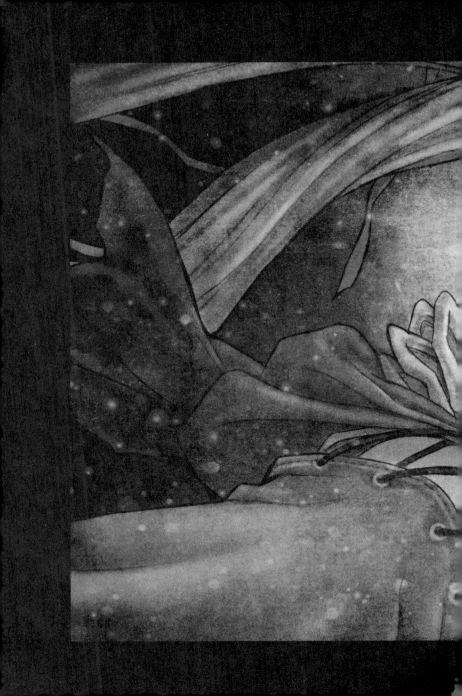

Tegami Bachi
LETTER · BEE

Volume 14

SHONEN JUMP Manga Edition

Story and Art by Hiroyuki Asada

English Adaptation/Rich Amtower
Translation/JN Productions
Touch-up & Lettering/Annaliese Christman
Design/Amy Martin
Editor/Shaenon K. Garrity

Printed in the U.S.A.

Published by VIZ Media, LLC
P.O. Box 77010
San Francisco, CA 94107

10 9 8 7 6 5 4 3 2 1
First printing, August 2013

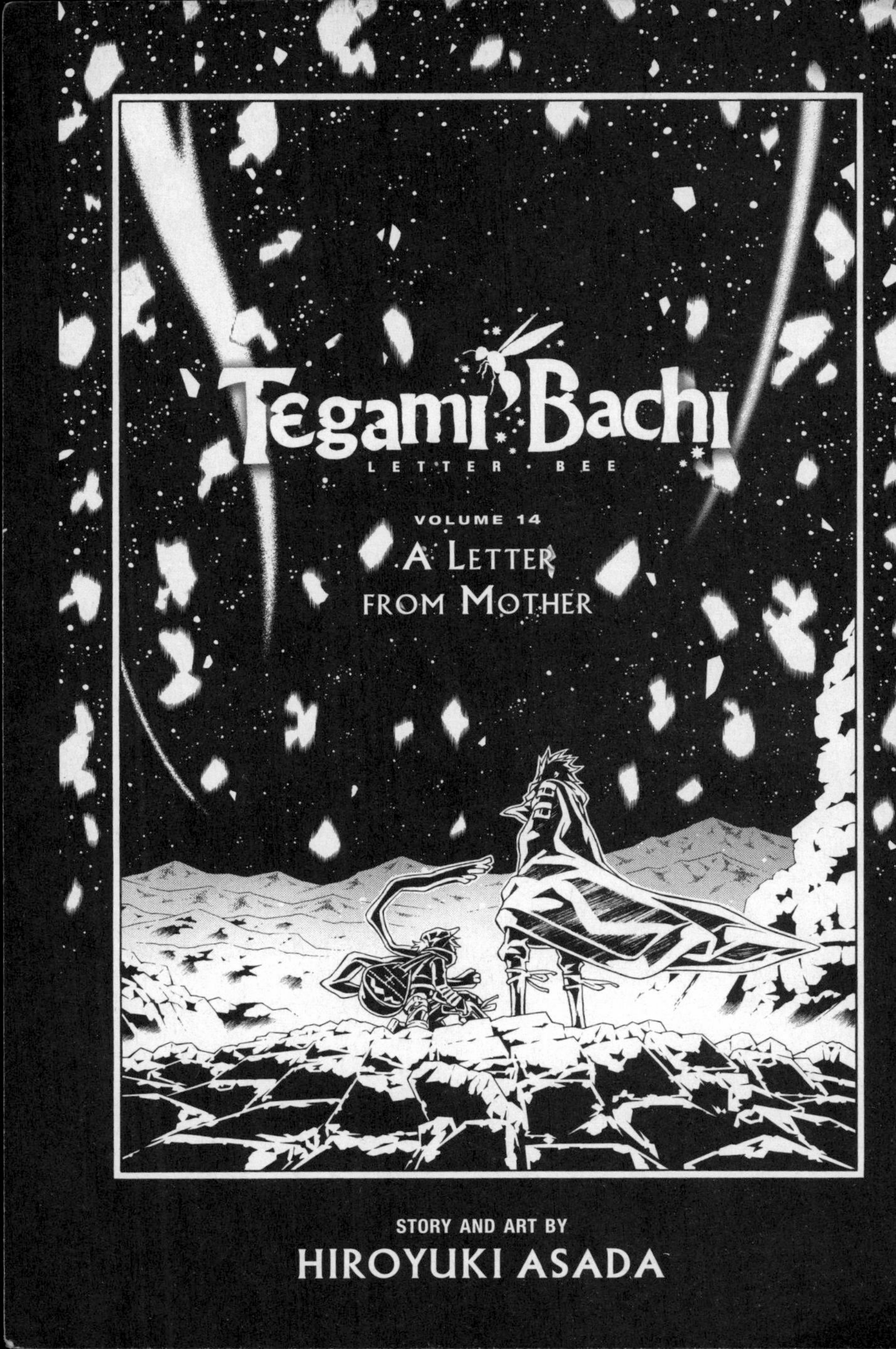

Tegami Bachi

LETTER BEE

VOLUME 14

A Letter from Mother

STORY AND ART BY

HIROYUKI ASADA

This is a country known as Amberground, where night never ends.

Its capital, Akatsuki, is illuminated by a man-made sun. The farther one strays from the capital, the weaker the light. The Yuusari region is cast in twilight; the Yodaka region survives only on pale moonlight.

Letter Bee Gauche Suede and young Lag Seeing meet in the Yodaka region—a postal worker and the "letter" he must deliver. In their short time together, they form a fast friendship, but when the journey ends, each departs down his own path. Gauche longs to become Head Bee, while Lag himself wants to be a Letter Bee, like Gauche.

In time, Lag becomes a Letter Bee. But Gauche has lost his *heart* and become a marauder named Noir, working for the rebel organization Reverse.

Largo Lloyd, former head of the Beehive, joins forces with Reverse, claiming to seek "revolution." He reveals that his father, the powerful politician Jick Barrol, is behind the experiments on human subjects performed in the secret labs of Kagerou. Largo himself is a rejected experiment, "one who could not become spirit."

Meanwhile, in Yuusari, the Bees battle a massively powerful Gaichuu called Cabernet. Unable to find Cabernet's weak spot, they fight a desperate battle to keep Cabernet out of the city, while Zazie and Jiggy Pepper race to join them...

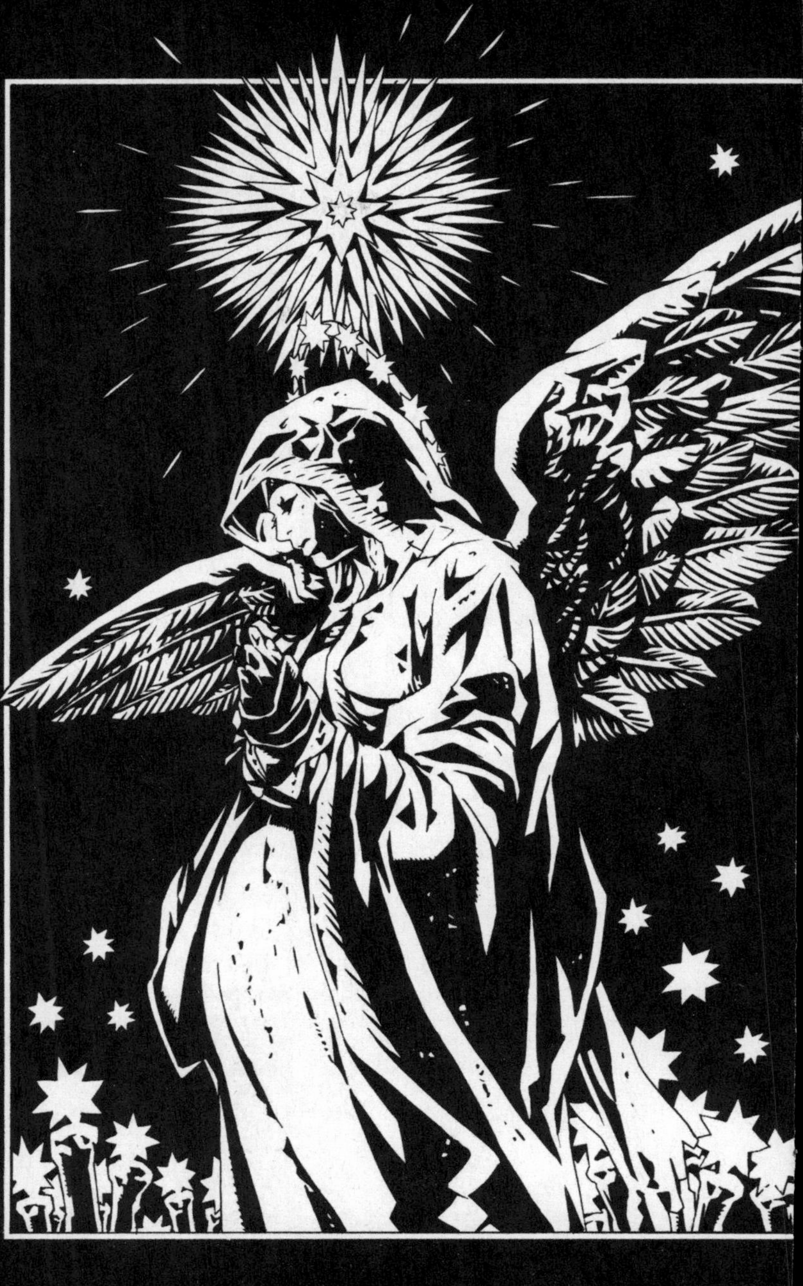

List of Characters

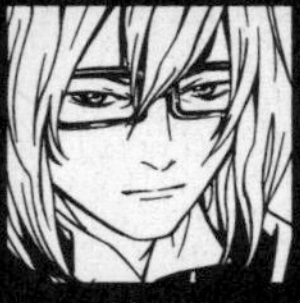

LARGO LLOYD
Ex-Beehive Director

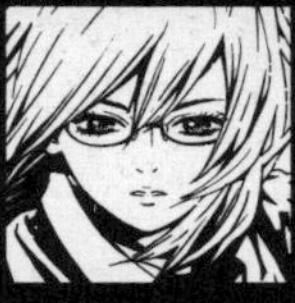

ARIA LINK
Section Chief of the Dead Letter Office

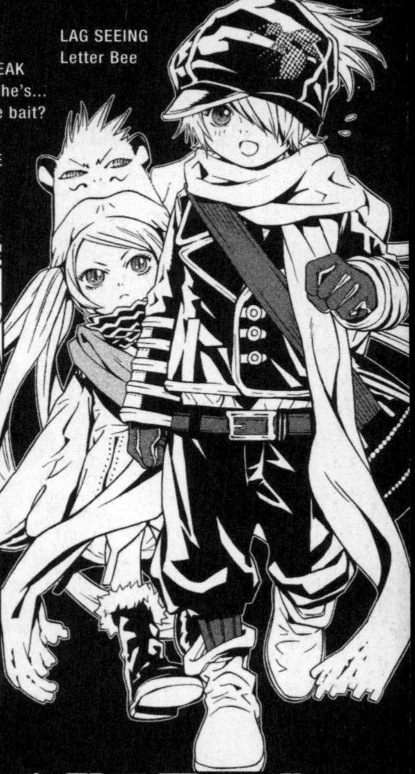

LAG SEEING
Letter Bee

STEAK
Niche's... live bait?

NICHE
Lag's Dingo

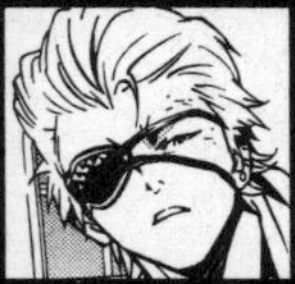

DR. THUNDERLAND, JR.
Member of the AG Biological Science Advisory Board, Third Division and head doctor at the Beehive

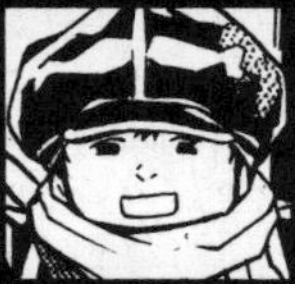

CONNOR KLUFF
Letter Bee

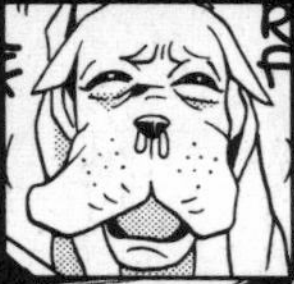

GUS
Connor's Dingo

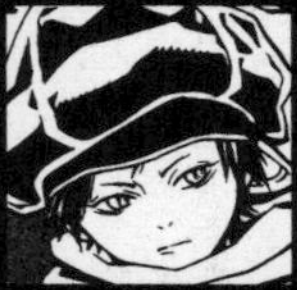

ZAZIE
Letter Bee

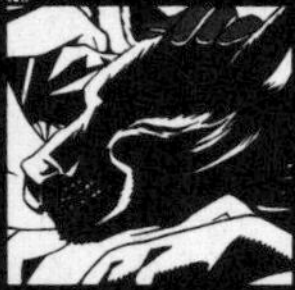

WASIOLKA
Zazie's Dingo

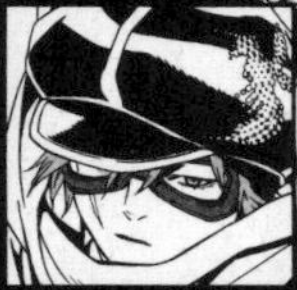

JIGGY PEPPER
Express Delivery Letter Bee

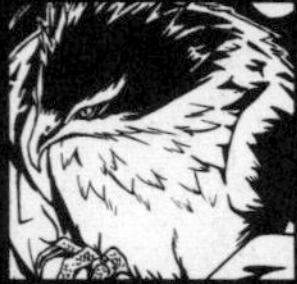

HARRY
Jiggy's Dingo

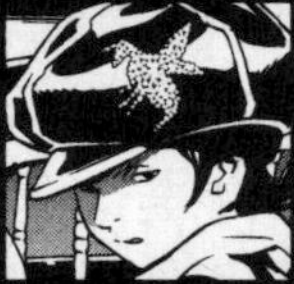

MOC SULLIVAN
Letter Bee

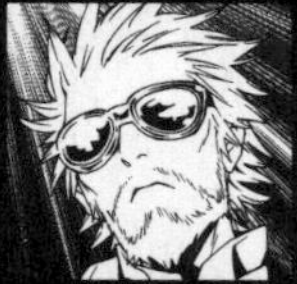

CHALYBS GARRARD
Inspector and ex-Letter Bee

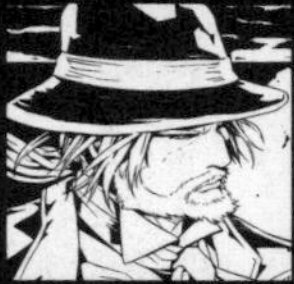

HAZEL VALENTINE
Inspector and Garrard's ex-Dingo

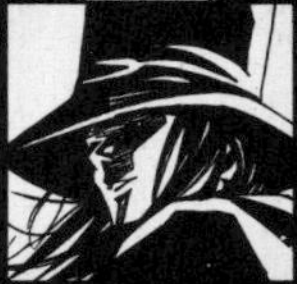

LAWRENCE
The ringleader of Reverse

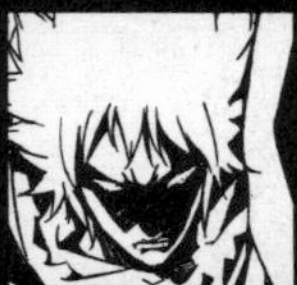

ZEAL
Marauder for Reverse

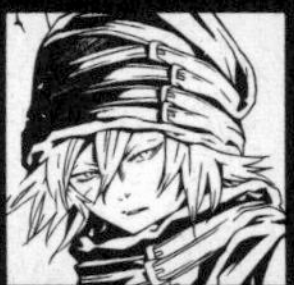

NOIR (FORMERLY GAUCHE SUEDE)
Marauder for Reverse and an ex–Letter Bee

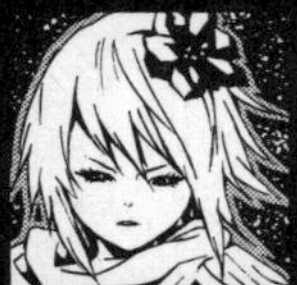

RODA
Noir's Dingo

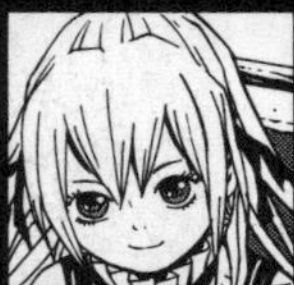

SYLVETTE SUEDE
Gauche's Sister

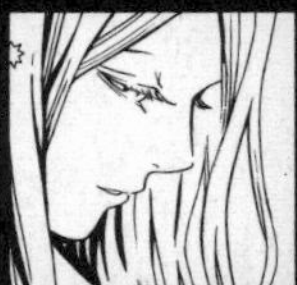

ANNE SEEING
Lag's Mother (Missing)

Tegami Bachi
LETTER · BEE

VOLUME 14
A Letter from Mother

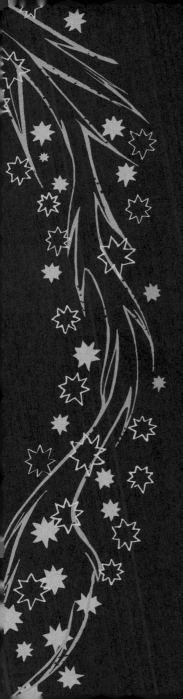

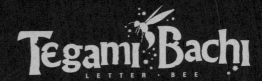

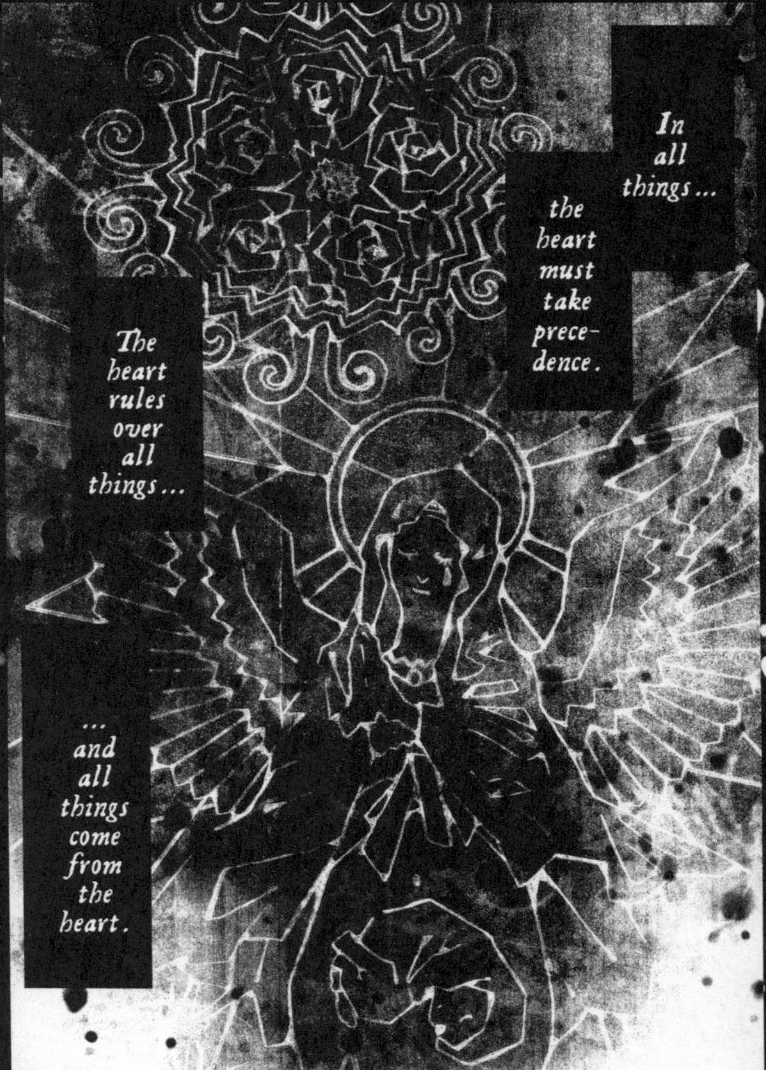
In all things...
the heart must take precedence.
The heart rules over all things...
... and all things come from the heart.

–THE SCRIPTURES OF AMBERGROUND, 1st verse

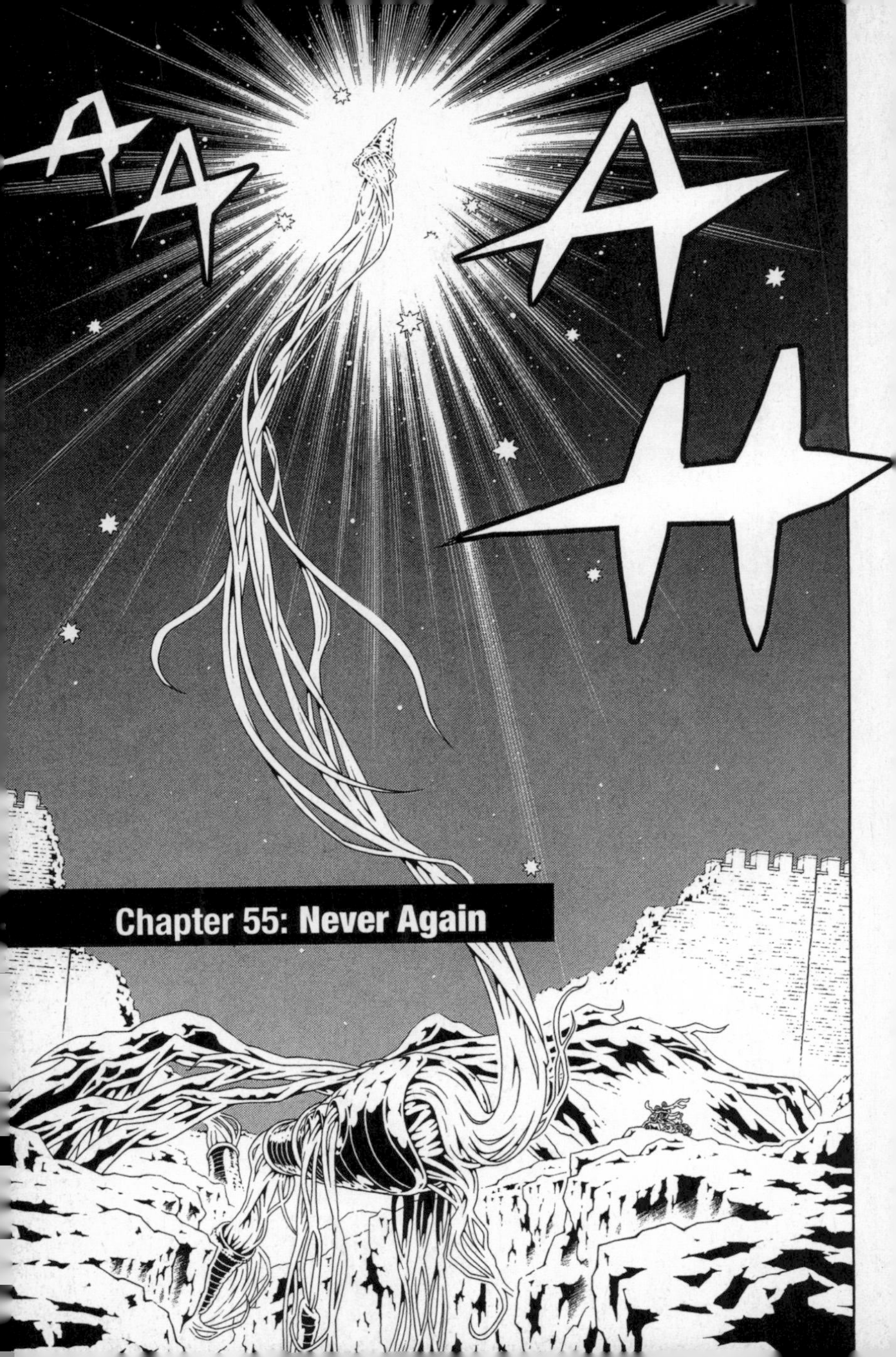
AAAAH
Chapter 55: Never Again

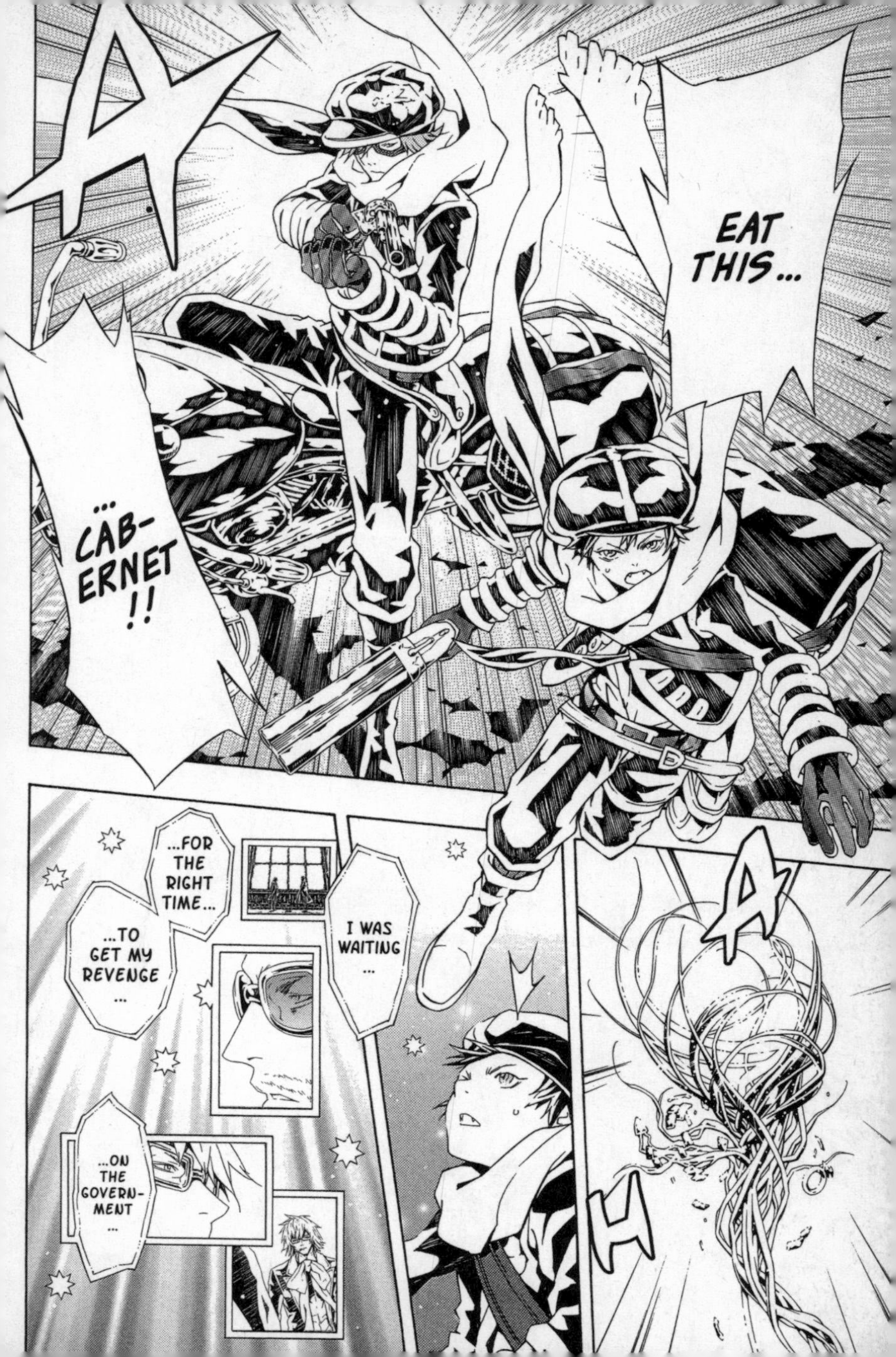
EAT THIS...
...CABERNET!!
I WAS WAITING ...
...FOR THE RIGHT TIME...
...TO GET MY REVENGE ...
...ON THE GOVERNMENT ...

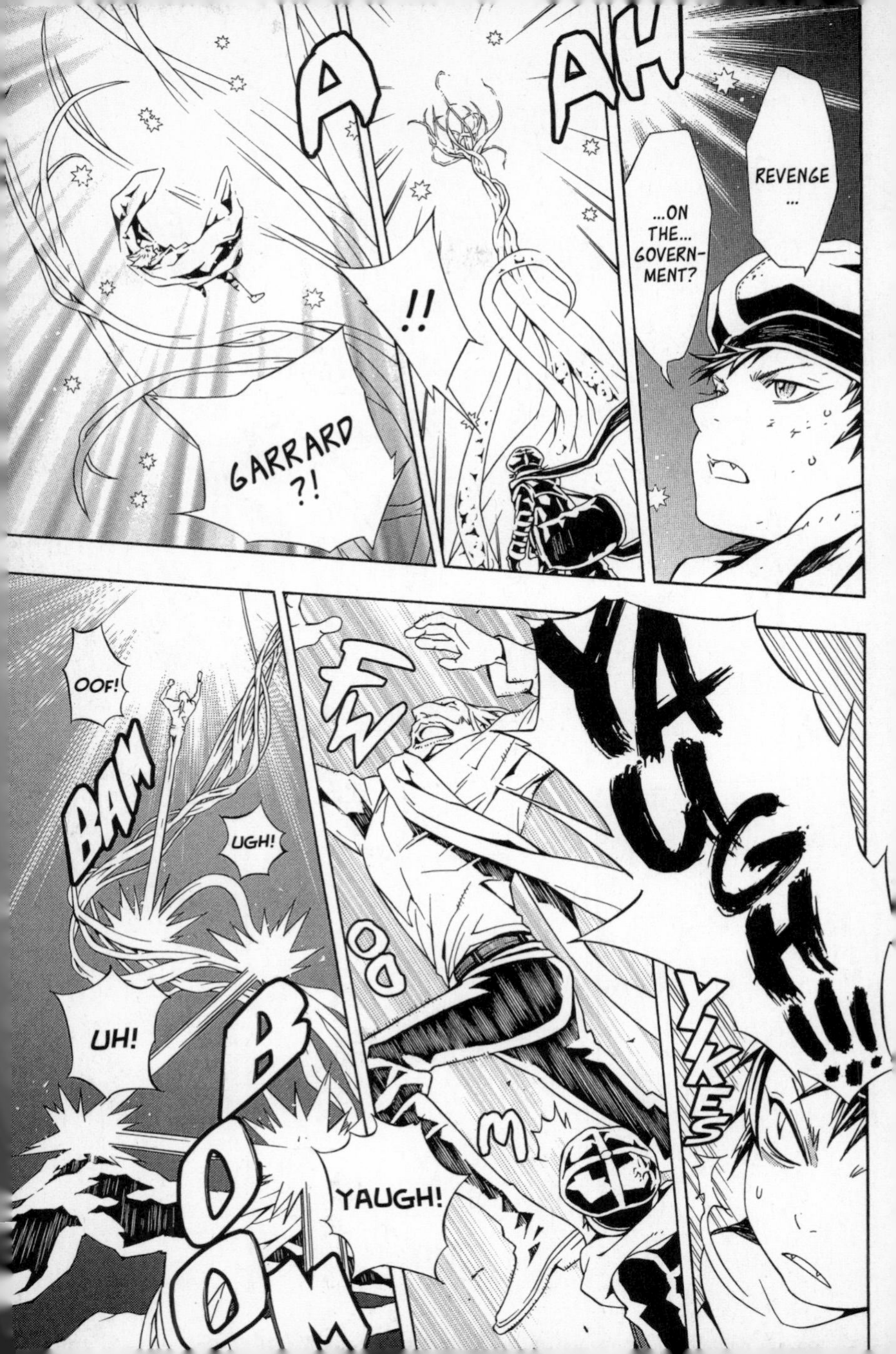
REVENGE ...
...ON THE... GOVERNMENT?
AH
!!
A
GARRARD ?!
YAUGH!!!
YIKES
FW
DOOM
YAUGH!
OOF!
BAM
UGH!
UH!
BOOOM

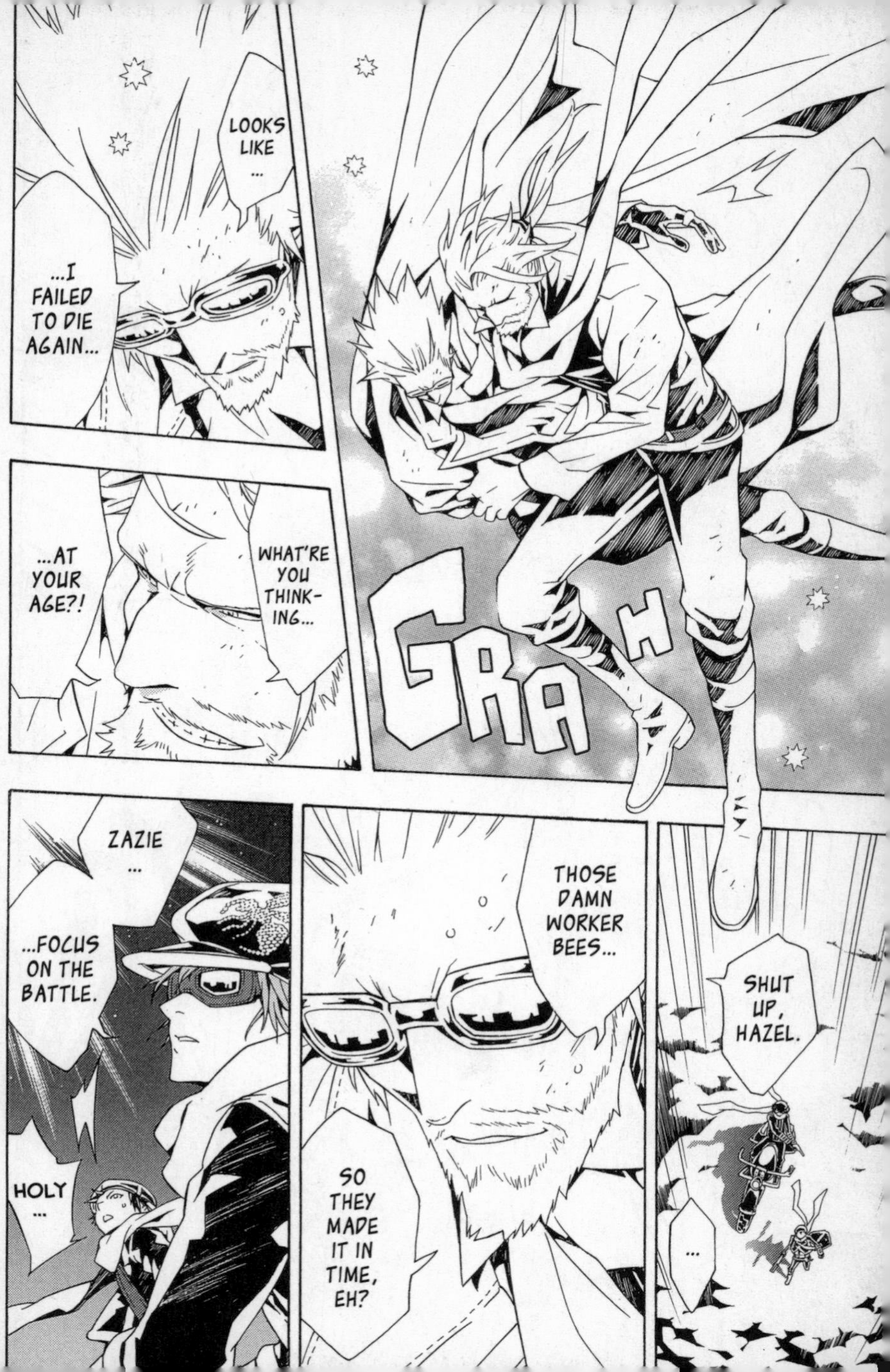
GRAH
LOOKS LIKE ...
...I FAILED TO DIE AGAIN...
WHAT'RE YOU THINKING...
...AT YOUR AGE?!
SHUT UP, HAZEL.
...
THOSE DAMN WORKER BEES...
SO THEY MADE IT IN TIME, EH?
ZAZIE ...
...FOCUS ON THE BATTLE.
HOLY ...

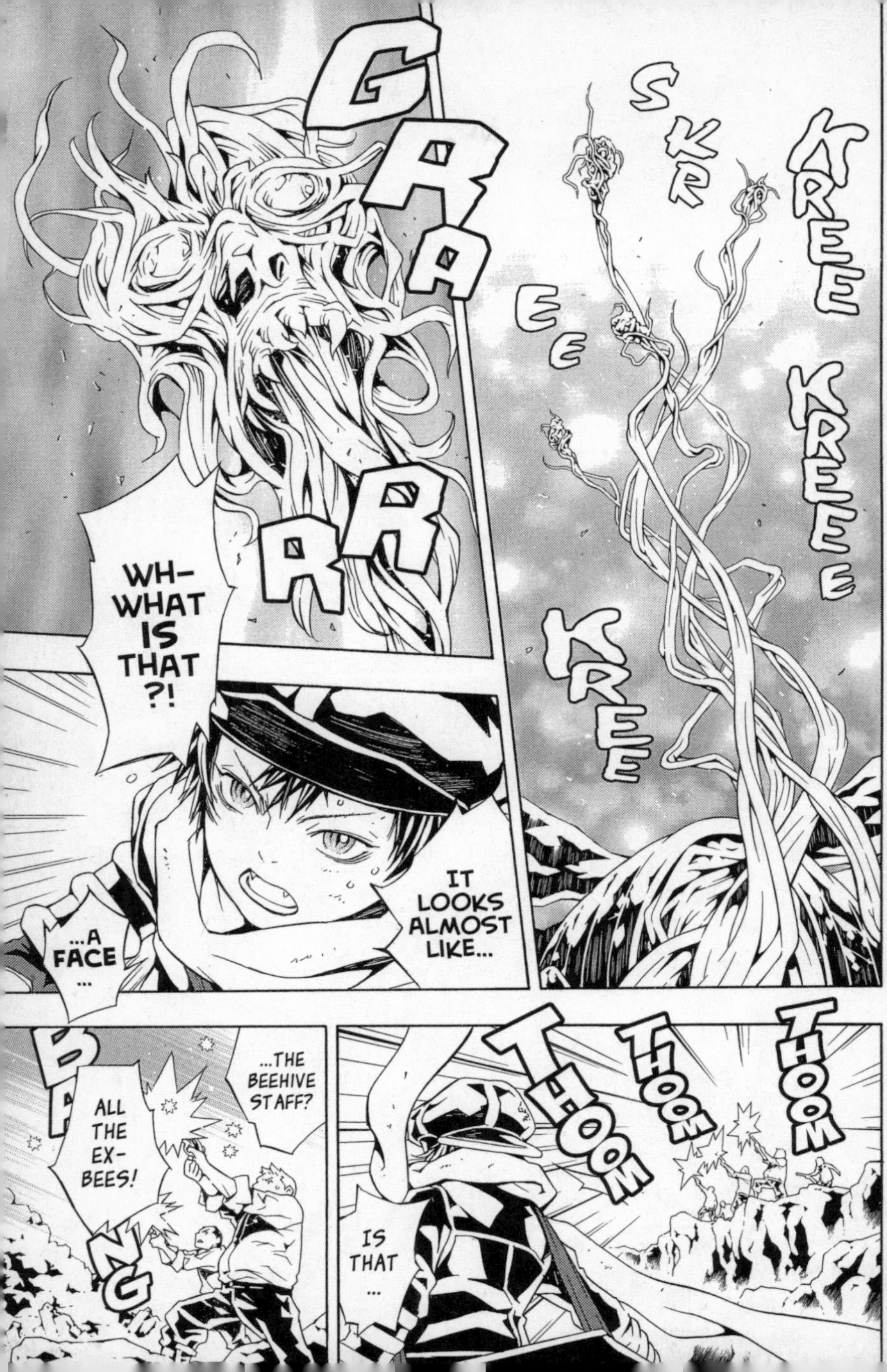
KREE
SKR
KREEE
KREE
GRAAEERR
WH-WHAT IS THAT?!
IT LOOKS ALMOST LIKE...
...A FACE ...
THOOM
THOOM
THOOM
IS THAT ...
...THE BEEHIVE STAFF?
ALL THE EX-BEES!
BANG

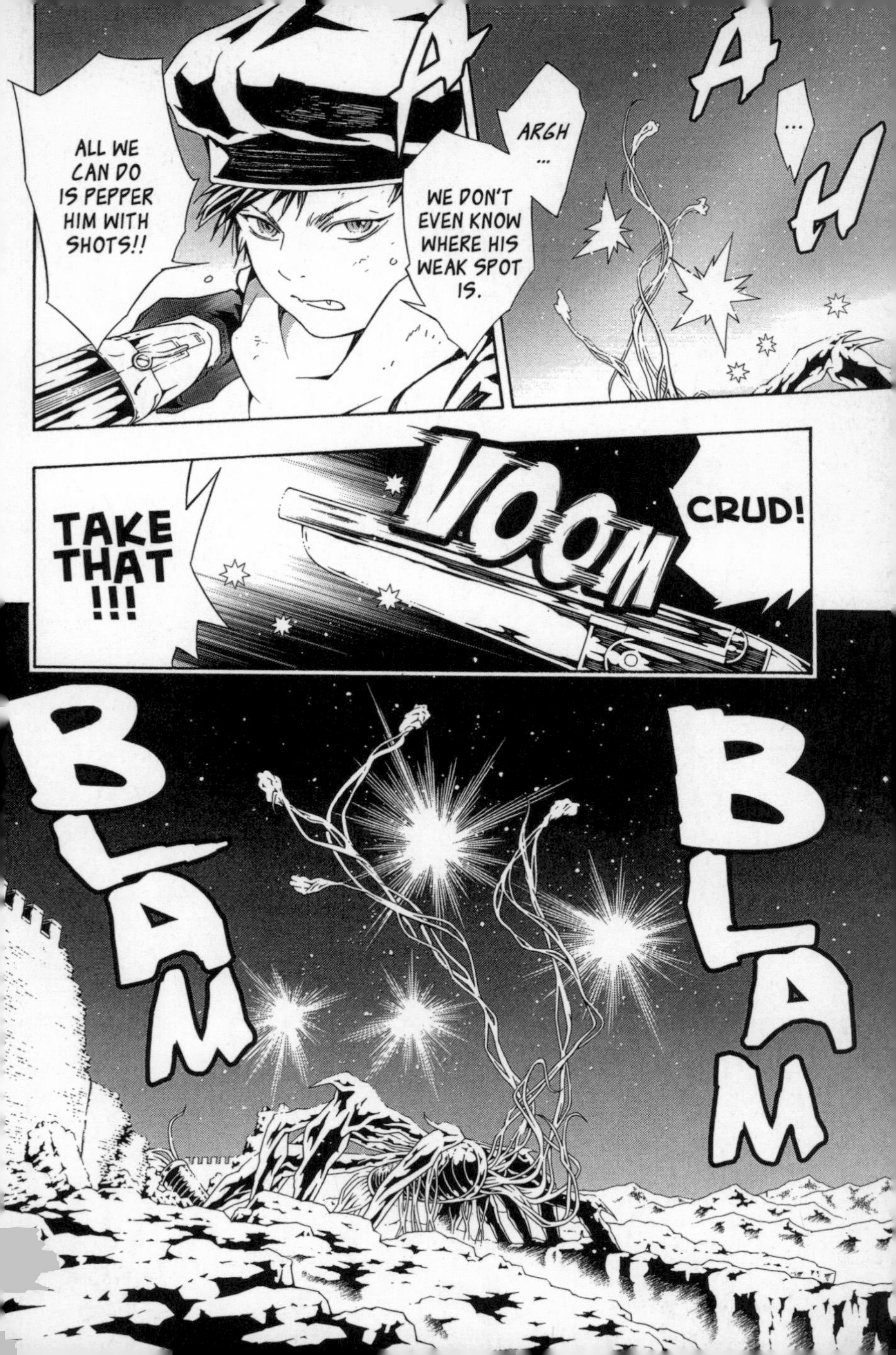
AH
...
ARGH ...
WE DON'T EVEN KNOW WHERE HIS WEAK SPOT IS.
ALL WE CAN DO IS PEPPER HIM WITH SHOTS!!
CRUD!
VOOM
TAKE THAT !!!
BLAM
BLAM

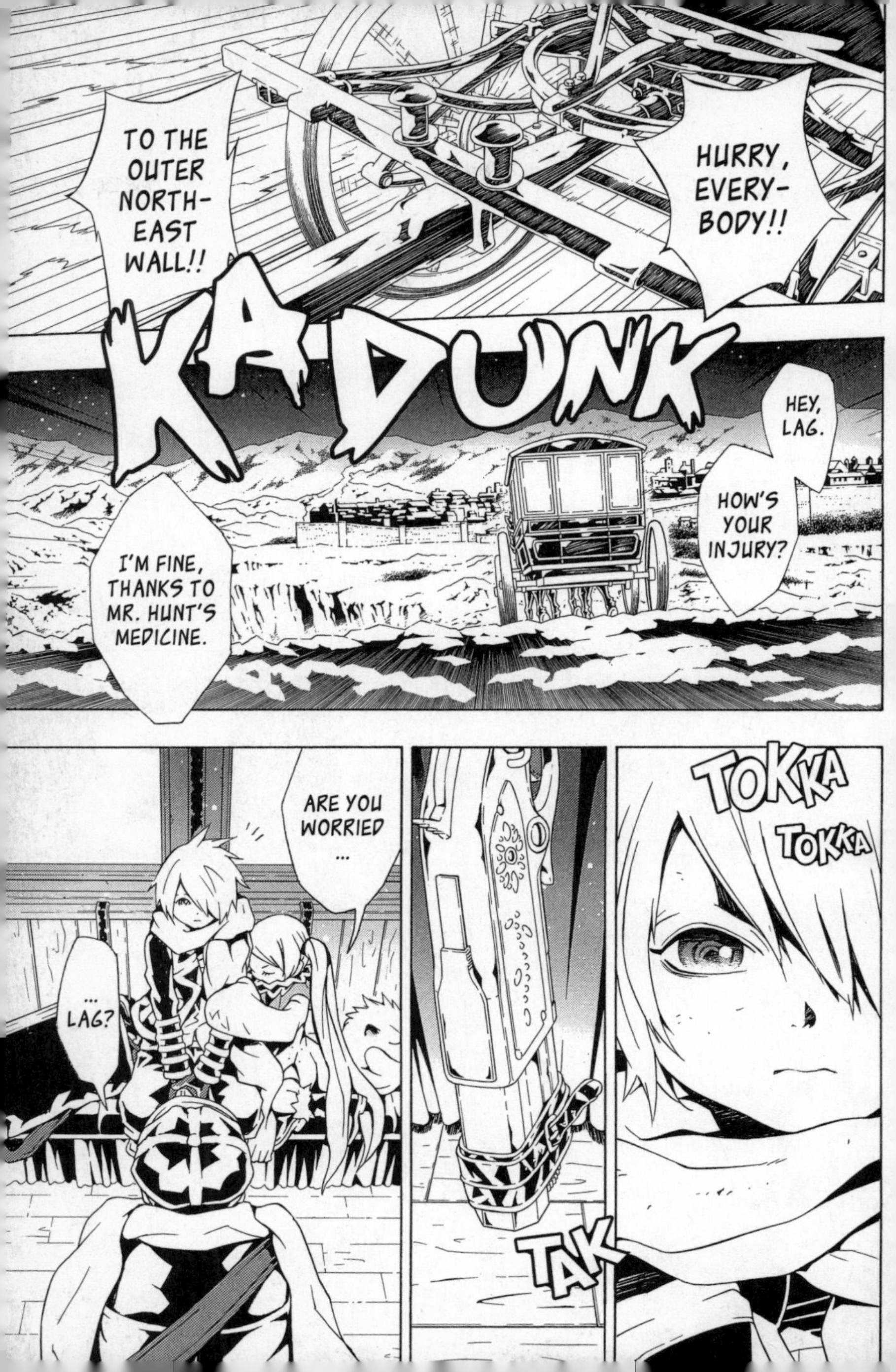
HURRY, EVERY-BODY!!
TO THE OUTER NORTH-EAST WALL!!
KA-DUNK
HEY, LAG.
HOW'S YOUR INJURY?
I'M FINE, THANKS TO MR. HUNT'S MEDICINE.
TOKKA
TOKKA
TAK
ARE YOU WORRIED ...
... LAG?

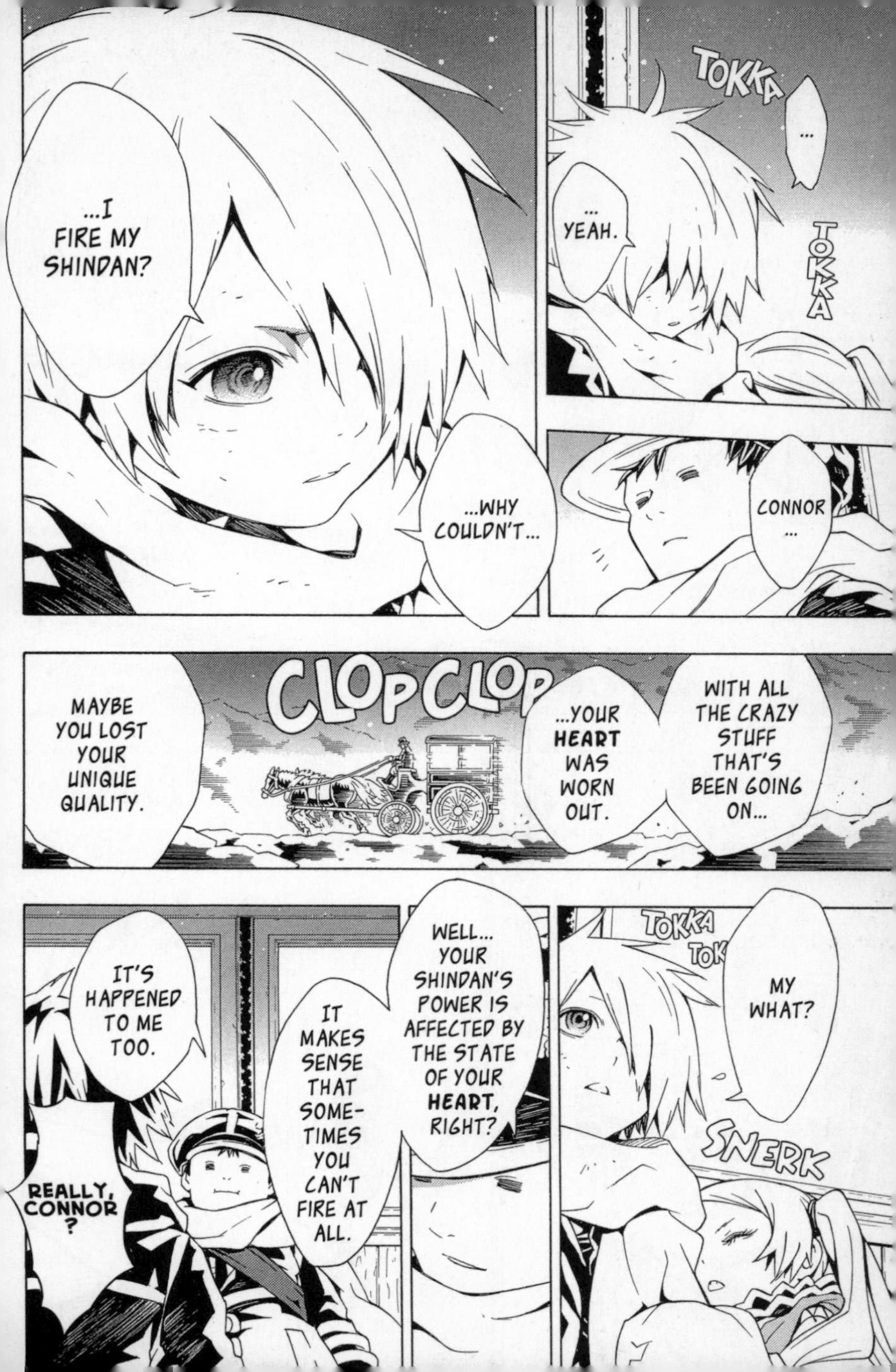
TOKKA
...
... YEAH.
TOKKA
TOKKA
CONNOR ...
...WHY COULDN'T...
...I FIRE MY SHINDAN?
WITH ALL THE CRAZY STUFF THAT'S BEEN GOING ON...
...YOUR **HEART** WAS WORN OUT.
CLOP CLOP
MAYBE YOU LOST YOUR UNIQUE QUALITY.
TOKKA
TOK
MY WHAT?
SNERK
WELL... YOUR SHINDAN'S POWER IS AFFECTED BY THE STATE OF YOUR **HEART**, RIGHT?
IT MAKES SENSE THAT SOME-TIMES YOU CAN'T FIRE AT ALL.
IT'S HAPPENED TO ME TOO.
REALLY, CONNOR?

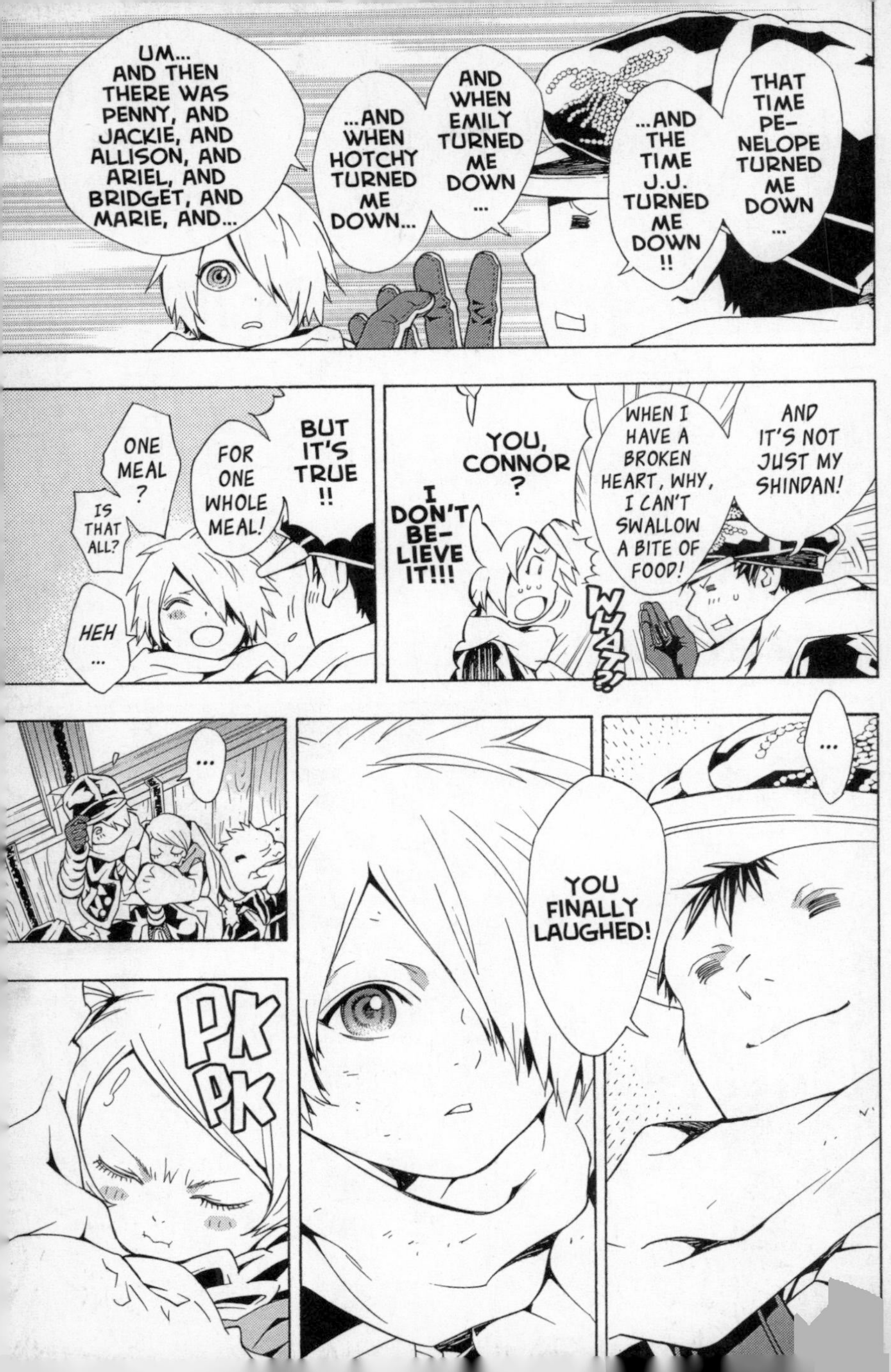
THAT TIME PE-NELOPE TURNED ME DOWN ...
...AND THE TIME J.J. TURNED ME DOWN !!
AND WHEN EMILY TURNED ME DOWN ...
...AND WHEN HOTCHY TURNED ME DOWN...
UM... AND THEN THERE WAS PENNY, AND JACKIE, AND ALLISON, AND ARIEL, AND BRIDGET, AND MARIE, AND...
AND IT'S NOT JUST MY SHINDAN!
WHEN I HAVE A BROKEN HEART, WHY, I CAN'T SWALLOW A BITE OF FOOD!
WHAT?!
YOU, CONNOR ?
I DON'T BE-LIEVE IT!!!
BUT IT'S TRUE !!
FOR ONE WHOLE MEAL!
ONE MEAL ?
IS THAT ALL?
HEH ...
...
YOU FINALLY LAUGHED!
...
PK PK

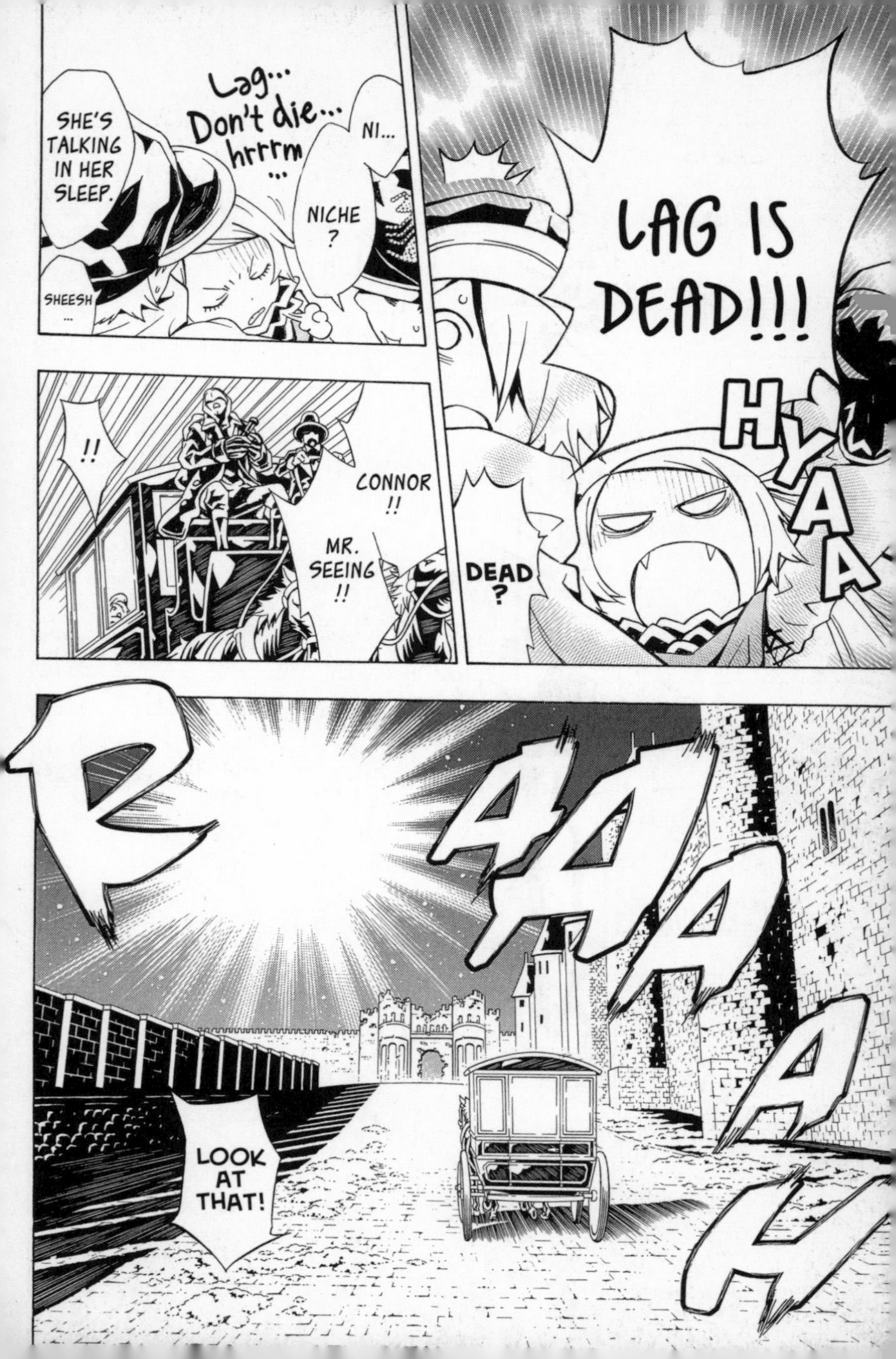
LAG IS DEAD!!!
HYAAA
DEAD?
NI...
NICHE?
Lag... Don't die... hrrrm ...
SHE'S TALKING IN HER SLEEP.
SHEESH ...
CONNOR !!
MR. SEEING !!
!!
RAAAAH
LOOK AT THAT!

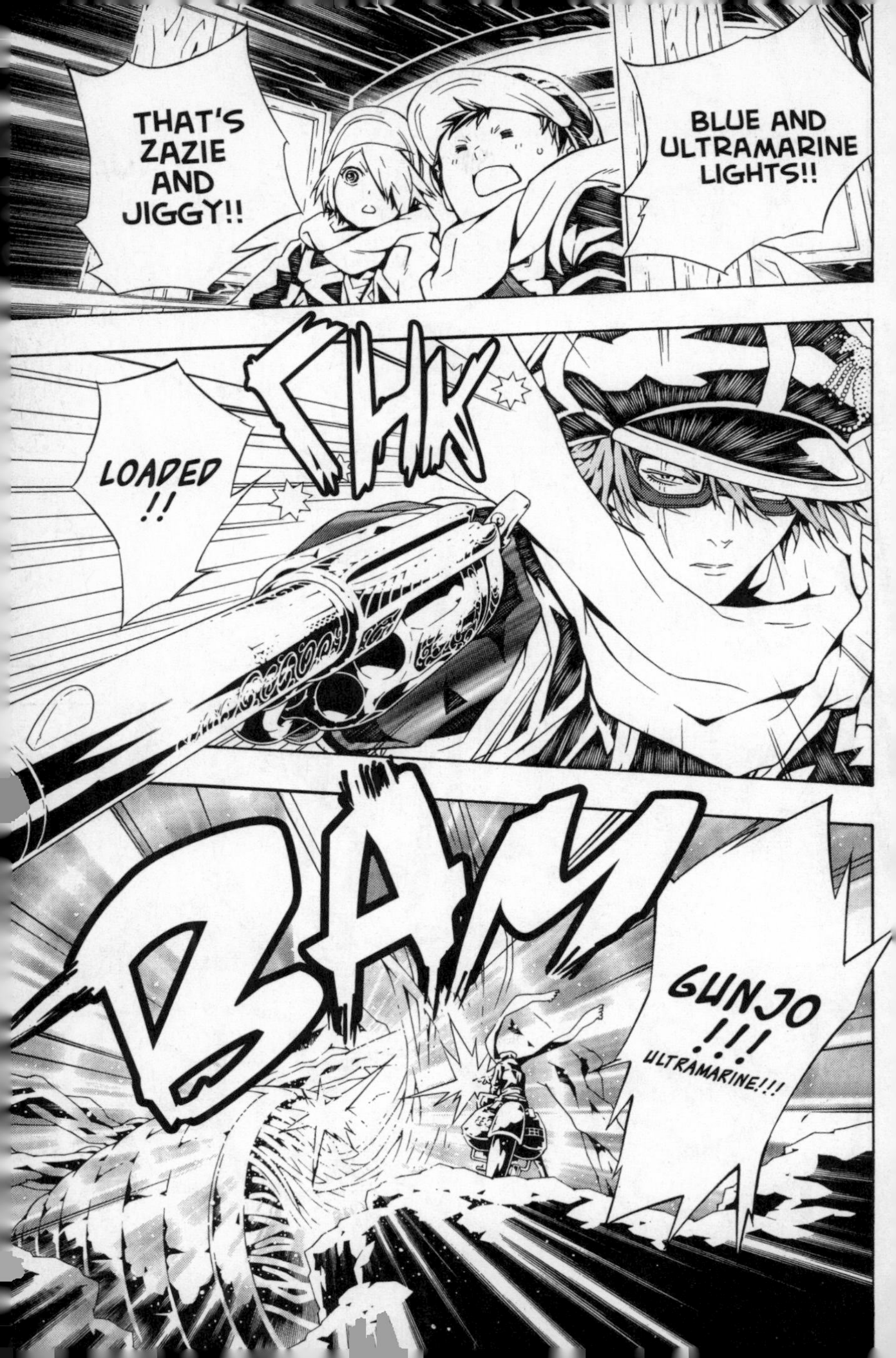
BLUE AND ULTRAMARINE LIGHTS!!
THAT'S ZAZIE AND JIGGY!!
CHK
LOADED!!
BAM
GUNJO!!!
ULTRAMARINE!!!

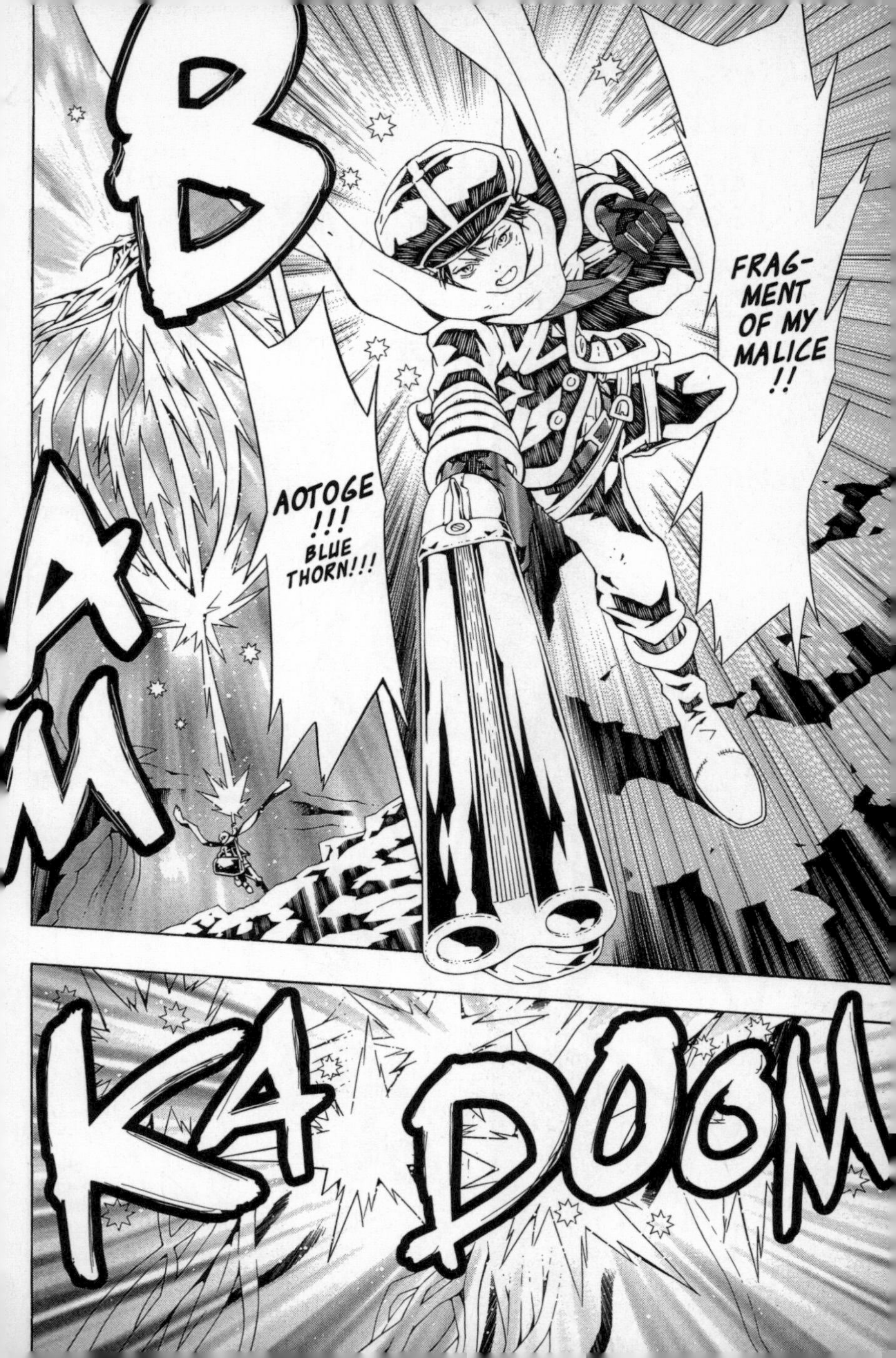
FRAG-MENT OF MY MALICE !!
AOTOGE !!! BLUE THORN!!!
BAM
KA DOOM

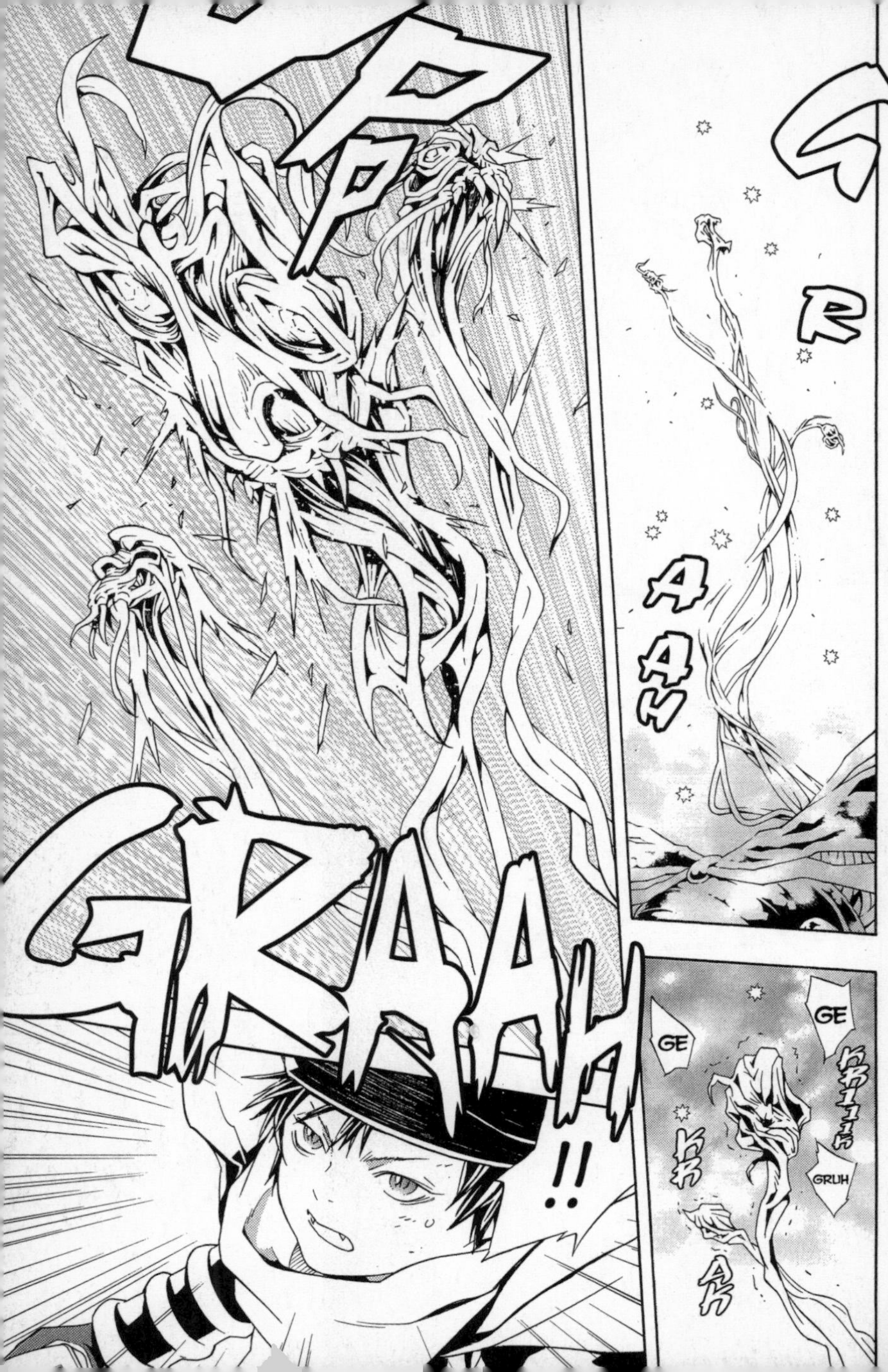
GRAAH
GE
KRIIIH
GRUH
GE
KK
AK
GRAAH!!

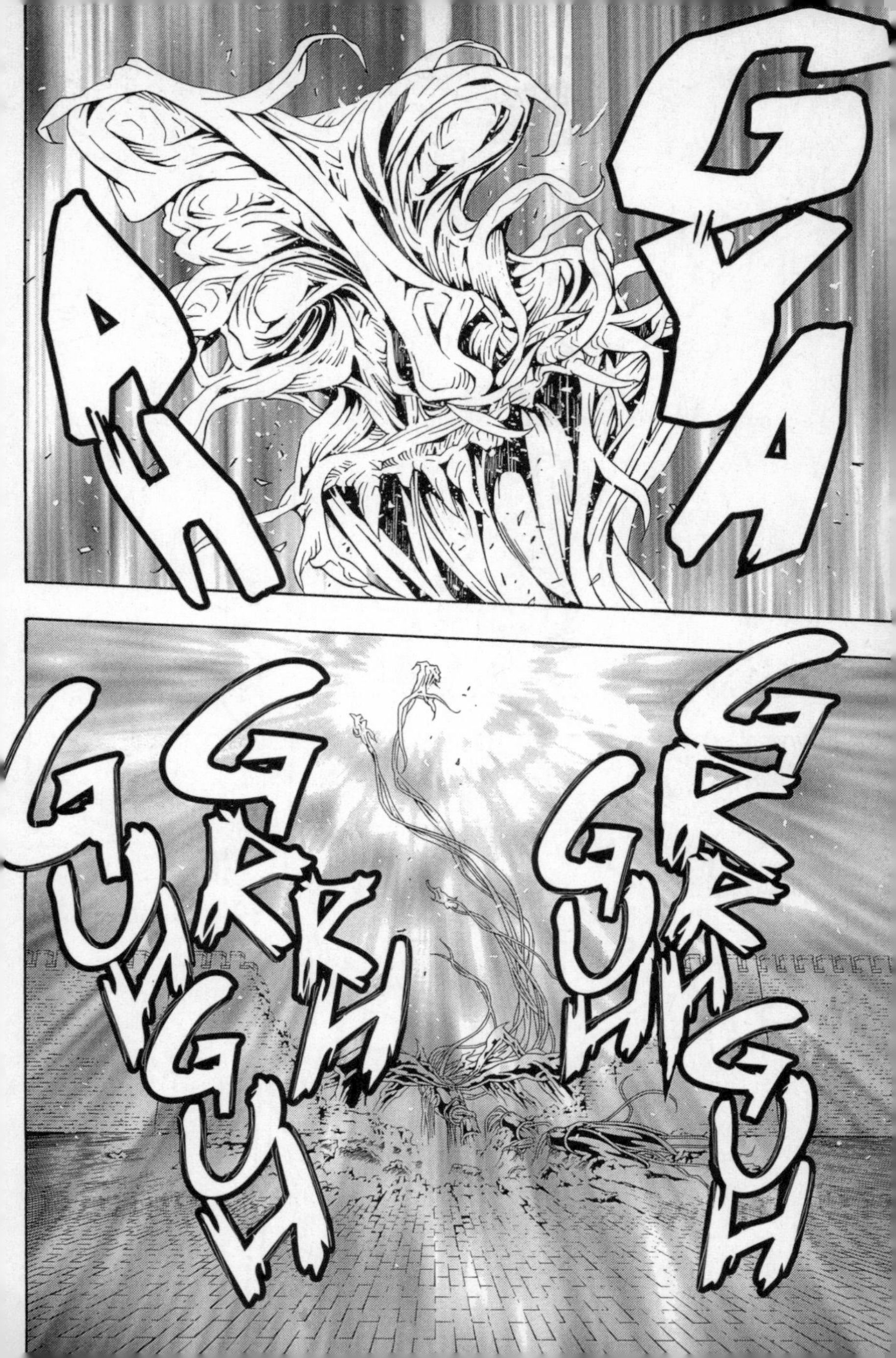

GAAAAH
GRRUUGH
GRRUUGH

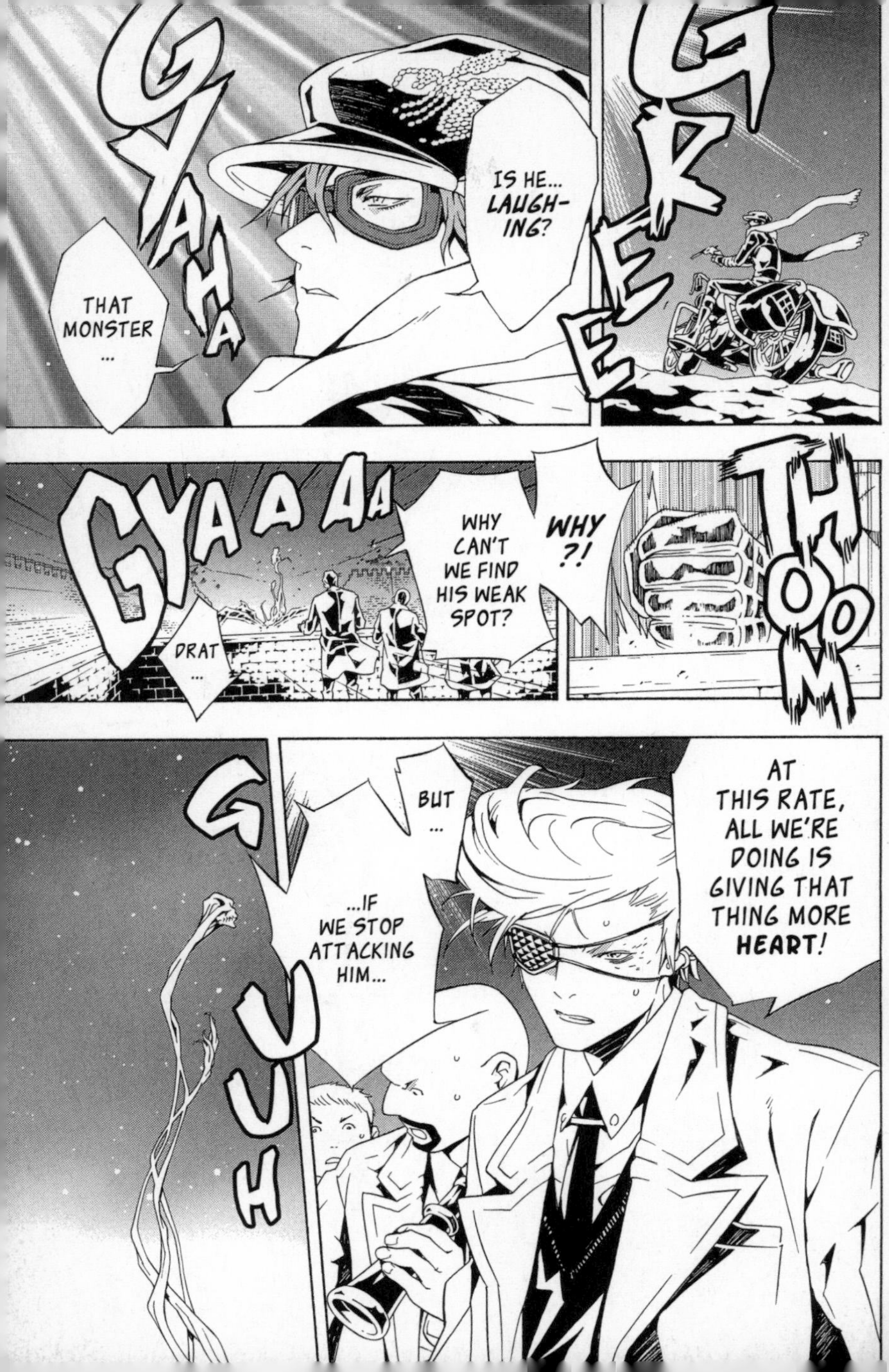
GREEE
IS HE... LAUGHING?
GYAHAHA
THAT MONSTER ...
THOOOM
WHY?!
WHY CAN'T WE FIND HIS WEAK SPOT?
GYAAAA
DRAT ...
AT THIS RATE, ALL WE'RE DOING IS GIVING THAT THING MORE HEART!
BUT ...
...IF WE STOP ATTACKING HIM...
GUUH

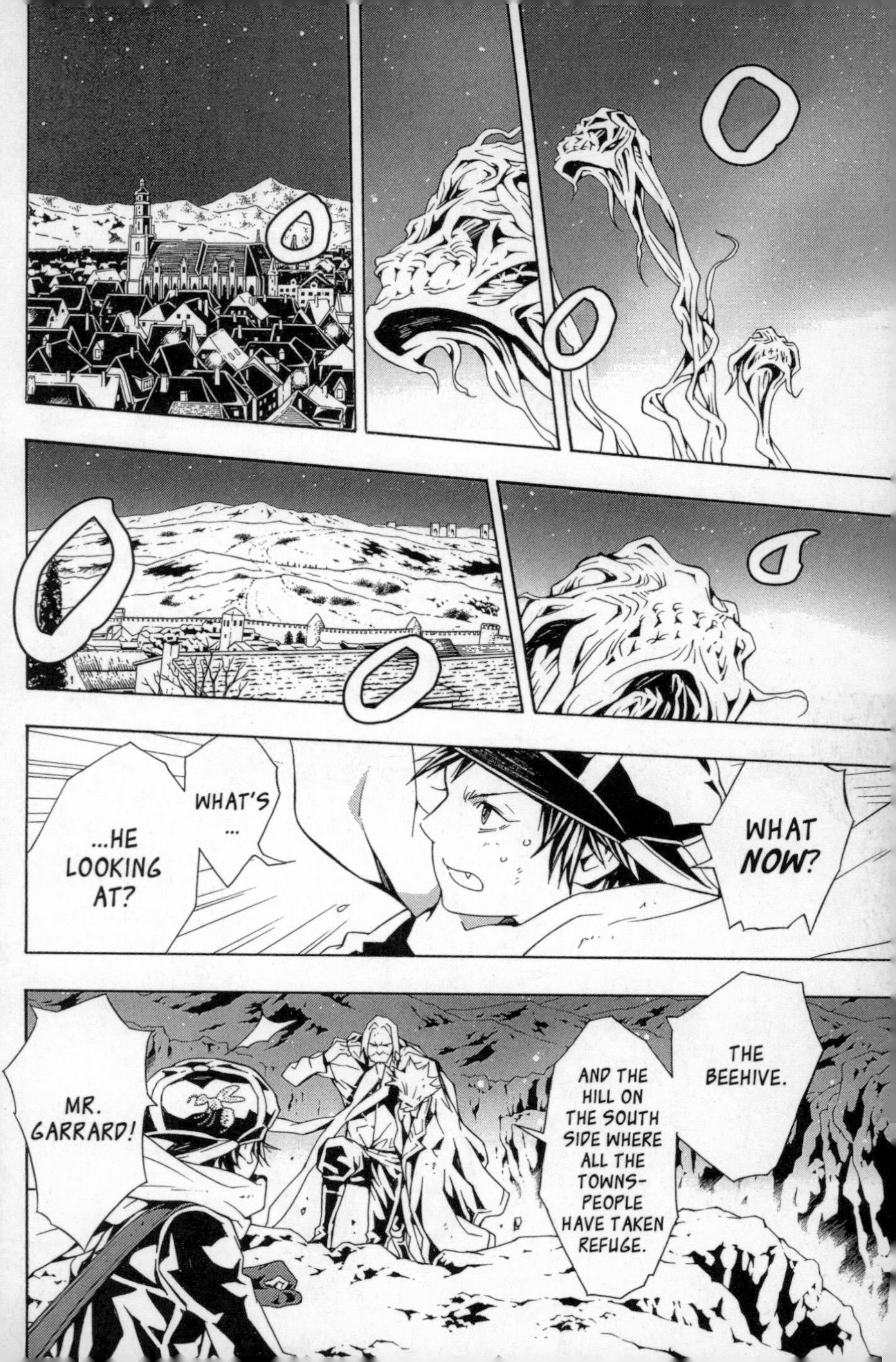
WHAT NOW?
WHAT'S ...
...HE LOOKING AT?
THE BEEHIVE.
AND THE HILL ON THE SOUTH SIDE WHERE ALL THE TOWNS-PEOPLE HAVE TAKEN REFUGE.
MR. GARRARD!

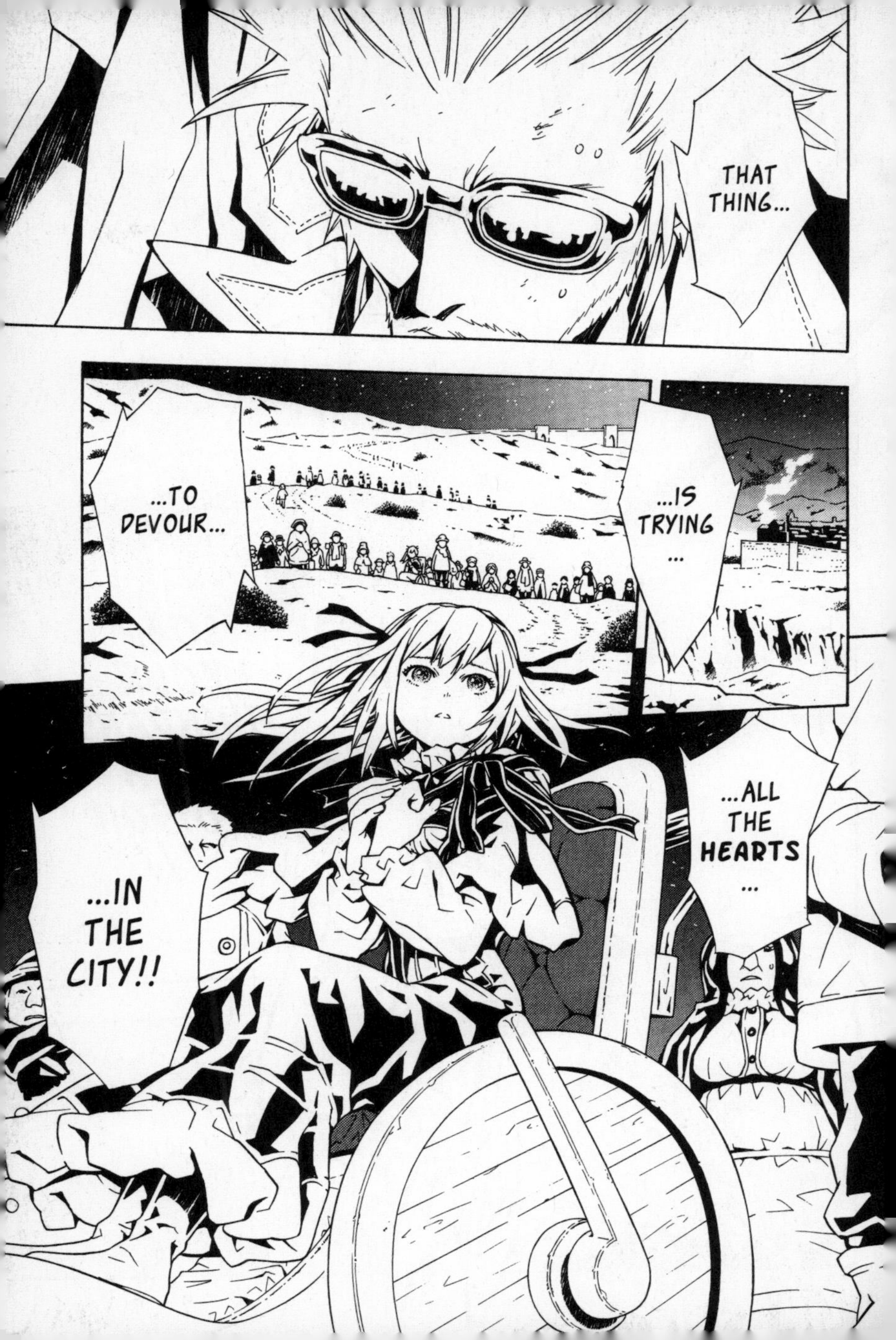
THAT THING...
...IS TRYING ...
...TO DEVOUR...
...ALL THE HEARTS ...
...IN THE CITY!!

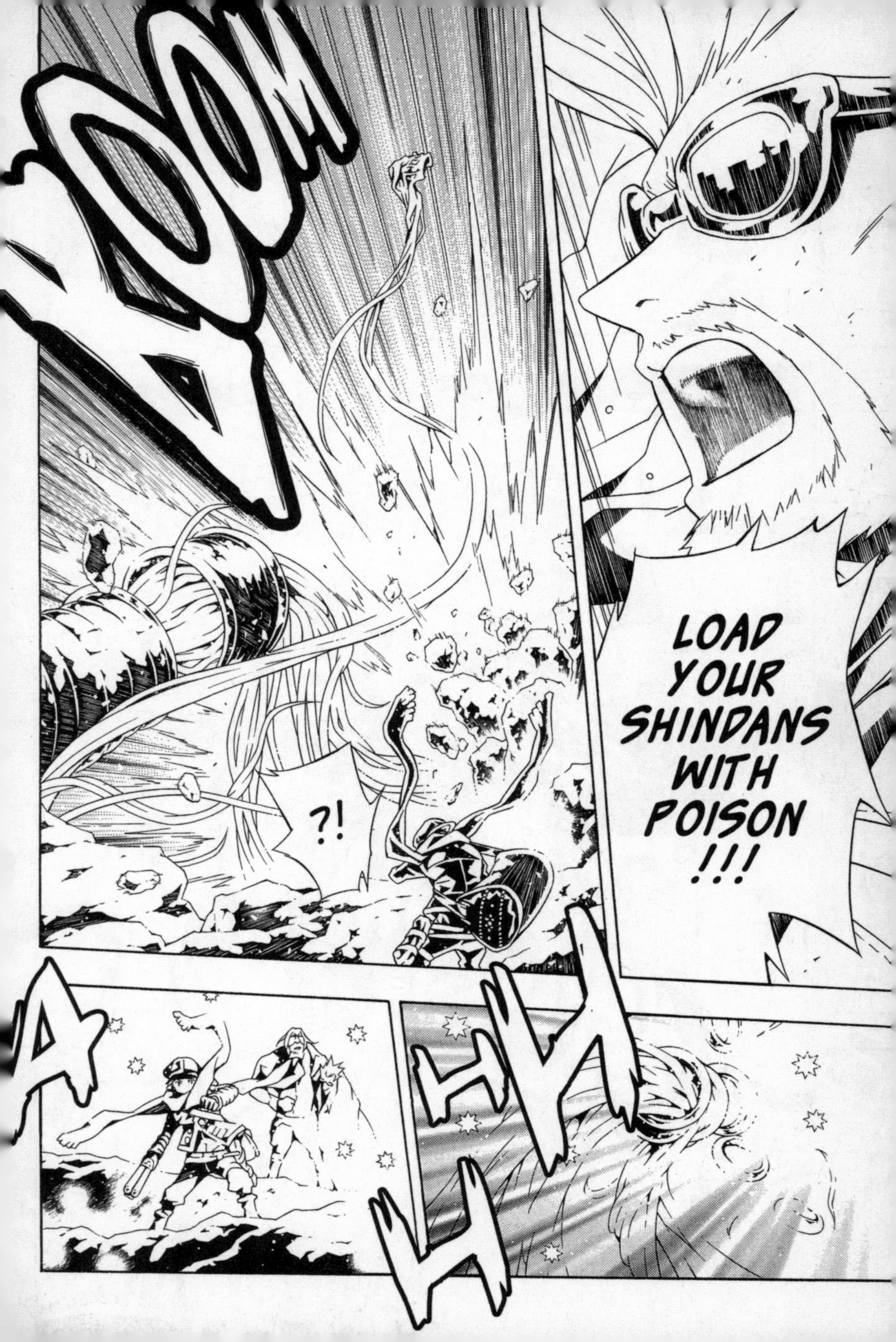
LOAD YOUR SHINDANS WITH POISON!!!
BOOM
?!

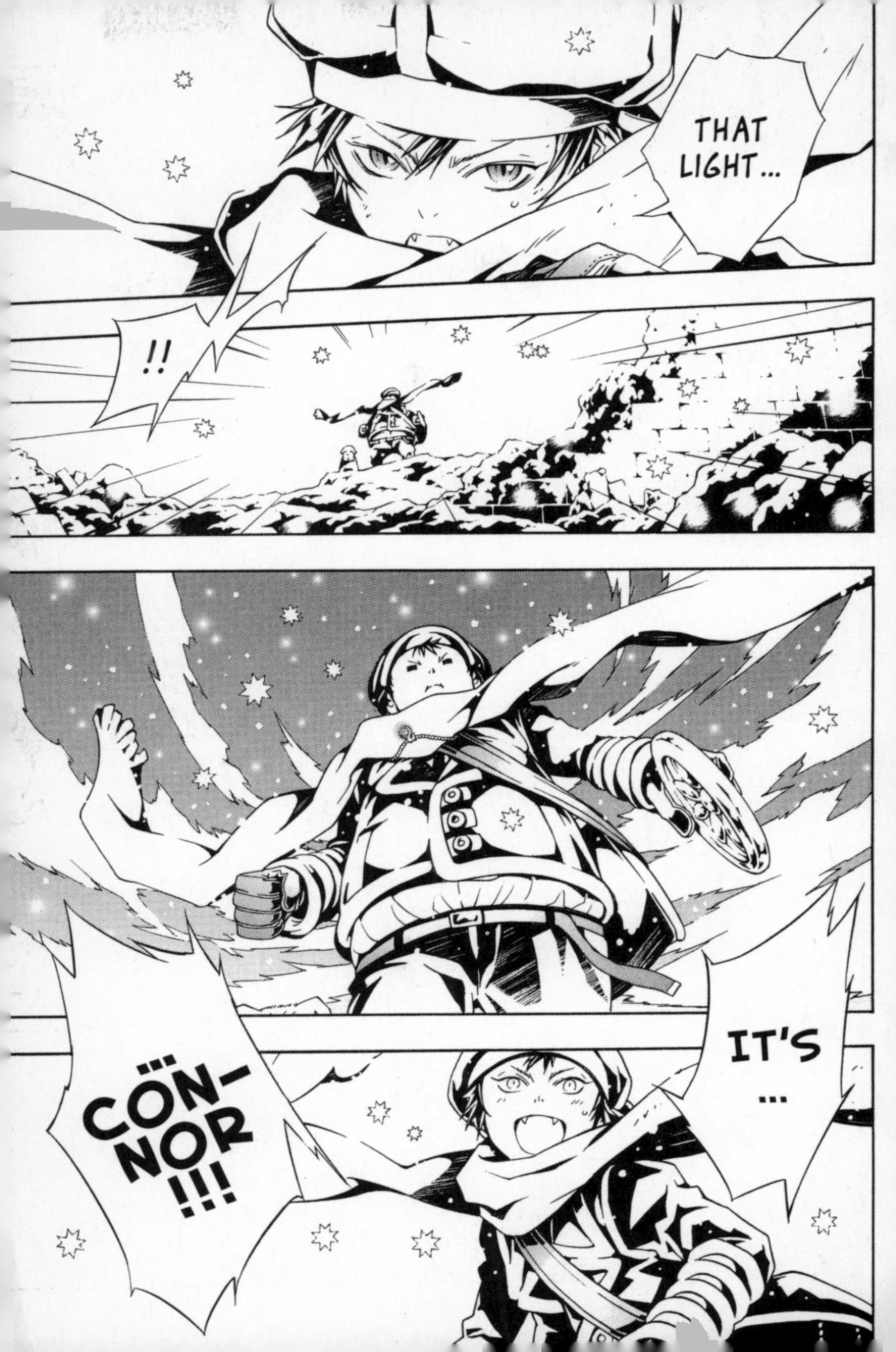
THAT LIGHT...
!!
IT'S ...
...CON-NOR!!!

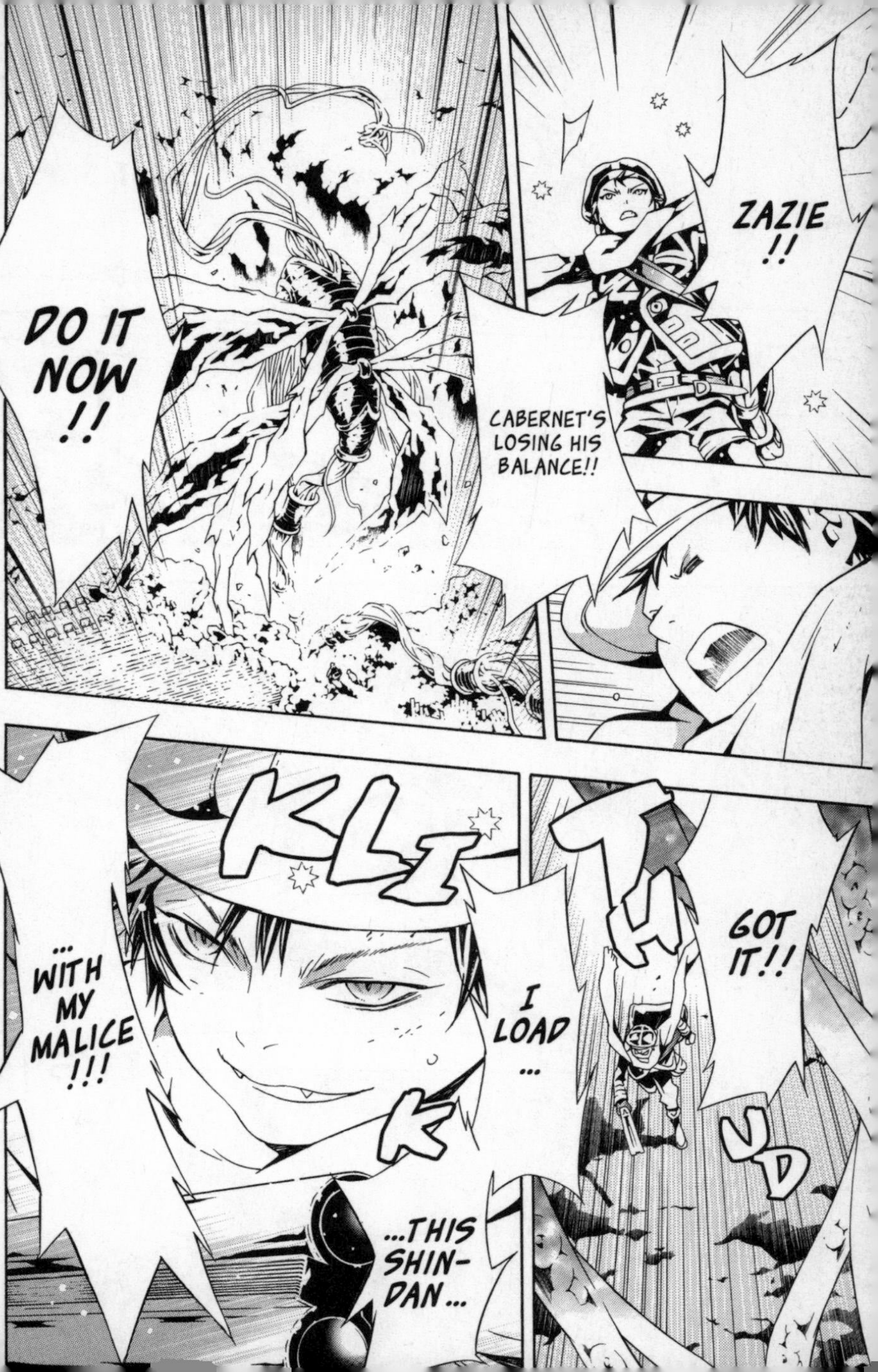
ZAZIE !!
CABERNET'S LOSING HIS BALANCE!!
DO IT NOW !!
GOT IT!!
THUD
KLIK
I LOAD ...
...THIS SHIN-DAN...
...WITH MY MALICE !!!

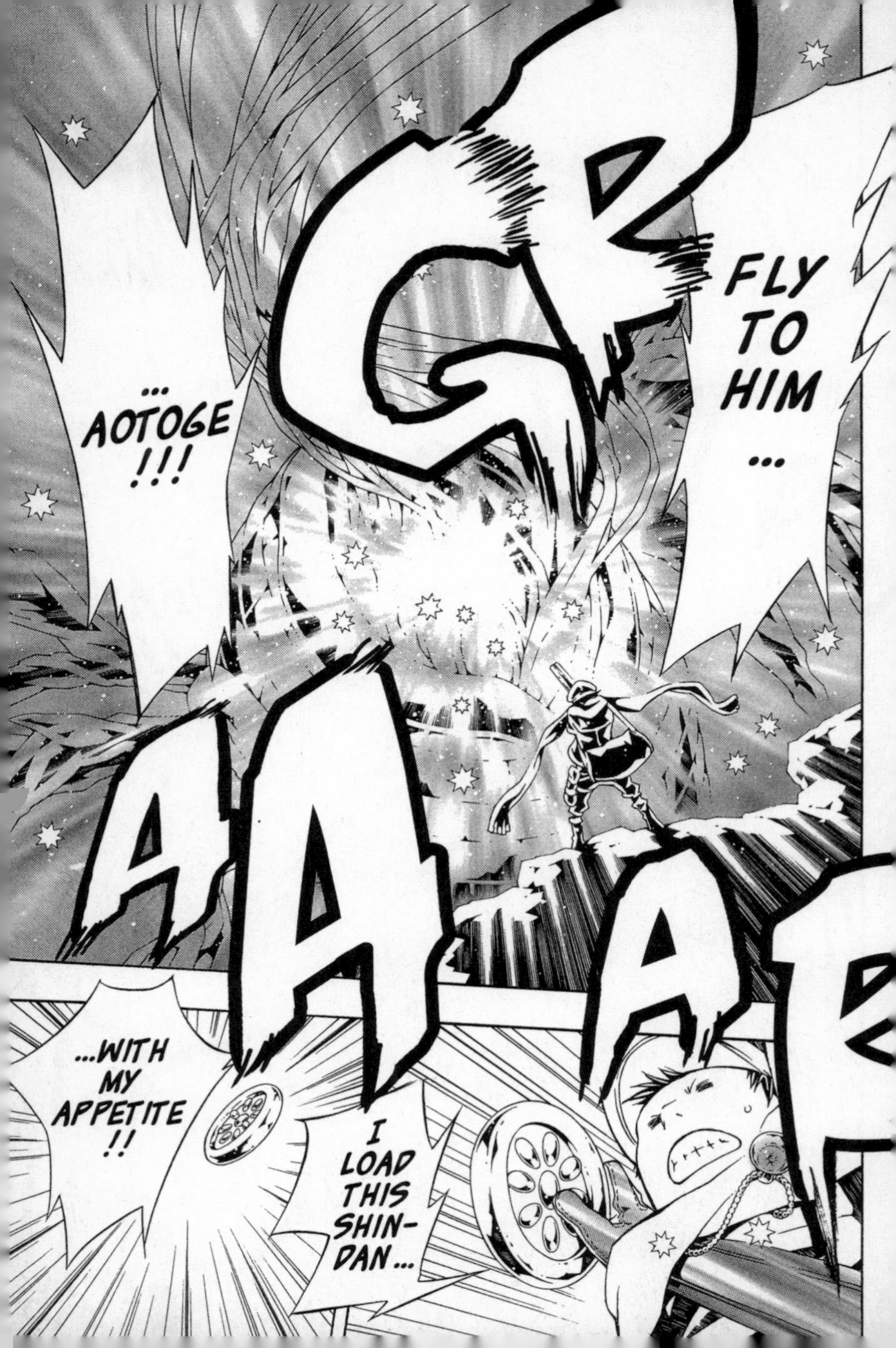
FLY TO HIM ...
... AOTOGE !!!
GAAA
I LOAD THIS SHIN-DAN...
...WITH MY APPETITE !!

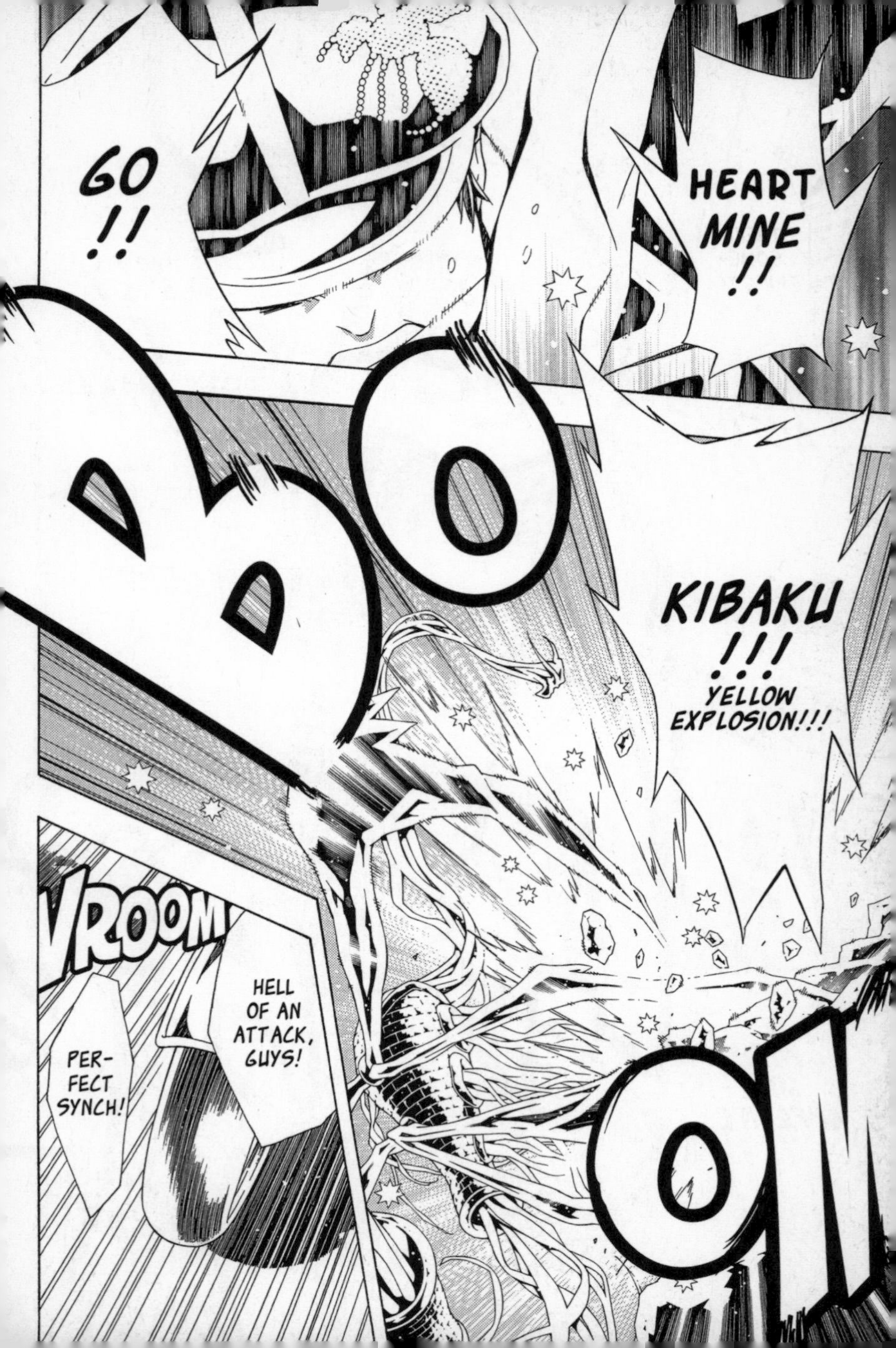
HEART MINE!!
GO!!
KIBAKU!!!
YELLOW EXPLOSION!!!
BOOOM
VROOM
HELL OF AN ATTACK, GUYS!
PER-FECT SYNCH!

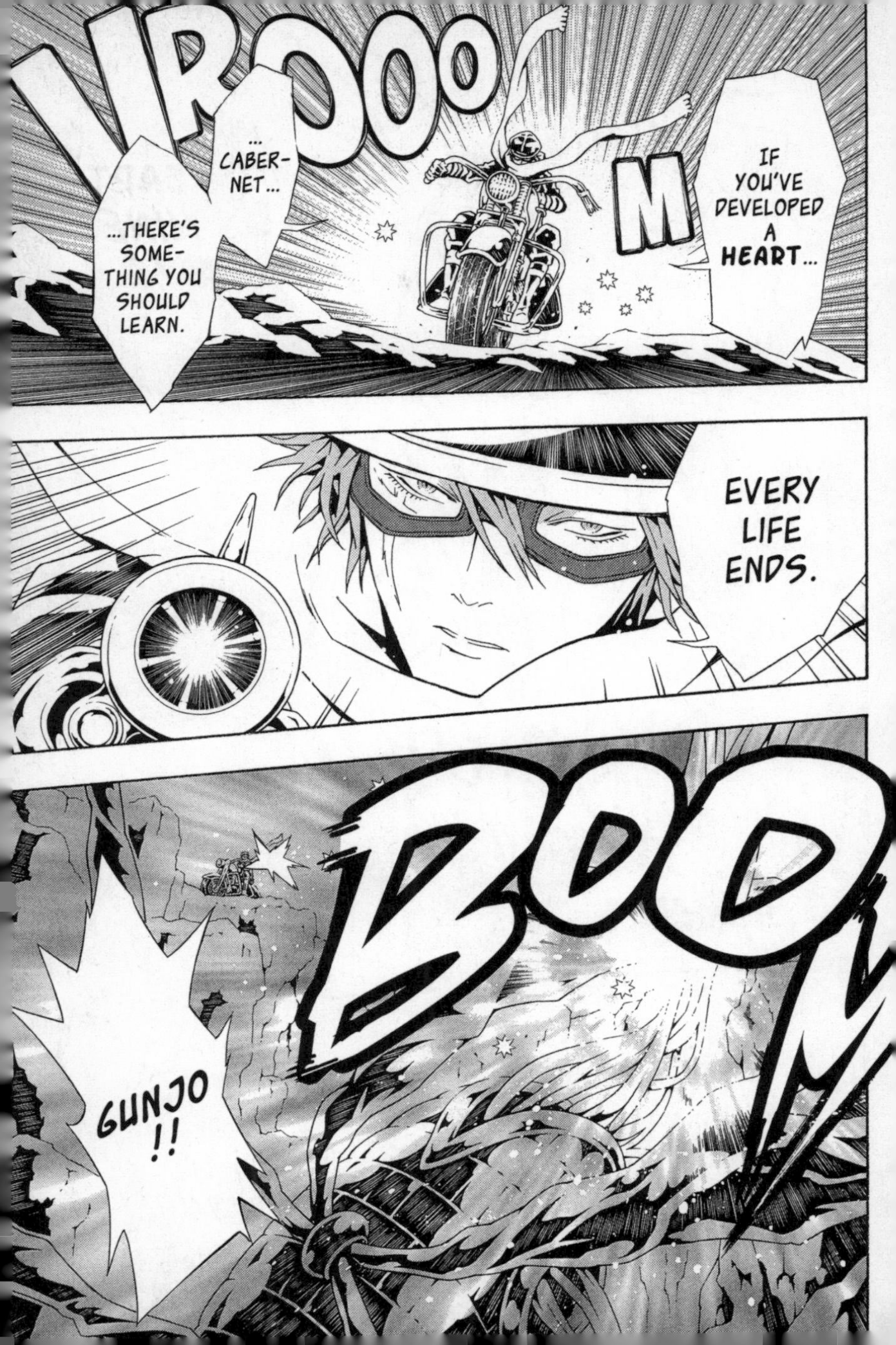
VROOOM
IF YOU'VE DEVELOPED A HEART...
...CABERNET...
...THERE'S SOMETHING YOU SHOULD LEARN.
EVERY LIFE ENDS.
BOOM
GUNJO!!

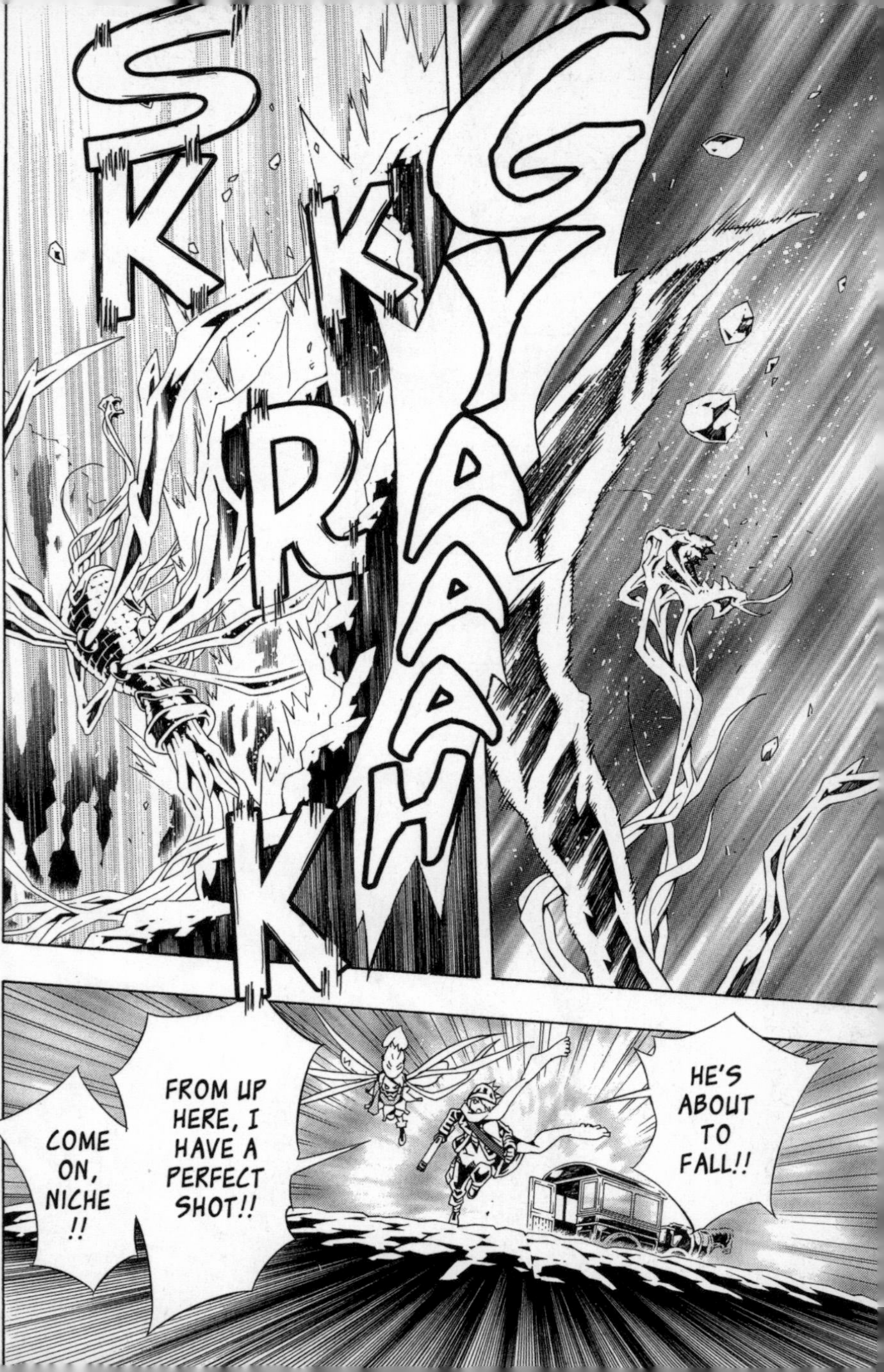
SKKRK
GYAAAH
HE'S ABOUT TO FALL!!
FROM UP HERE, I HAVE A PERFECT SHOT!!
COME ON, NICHE!!

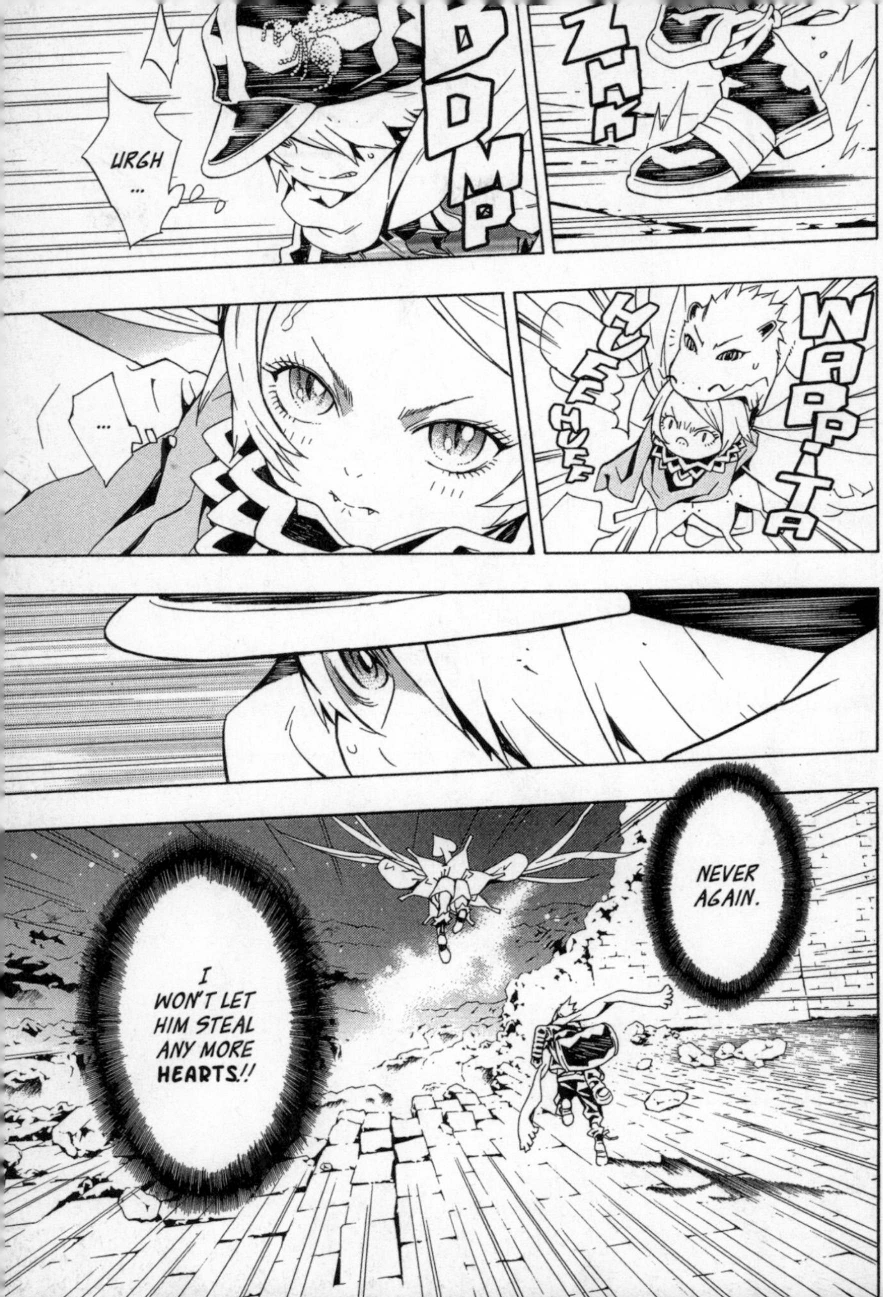
ZHAK
BDMP
URGH ...
WAPPITA
HUFF HUFF
...
NEVER AGAIN.
I WON'T LET HIM STEAL ANY MORE HEARTS!!

...MY
SHINDAN
!!!

TIME
TO
FIRE...

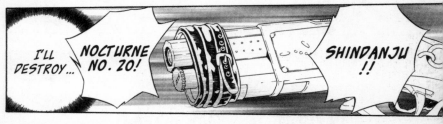

I'LL
DESTROY...

NOCTURNE
NO. 20!

SHINDANJU
!!

I
LOAD THIS
SHINDAN...

...WITH
MY
HEART!

...
CABERNET
!!

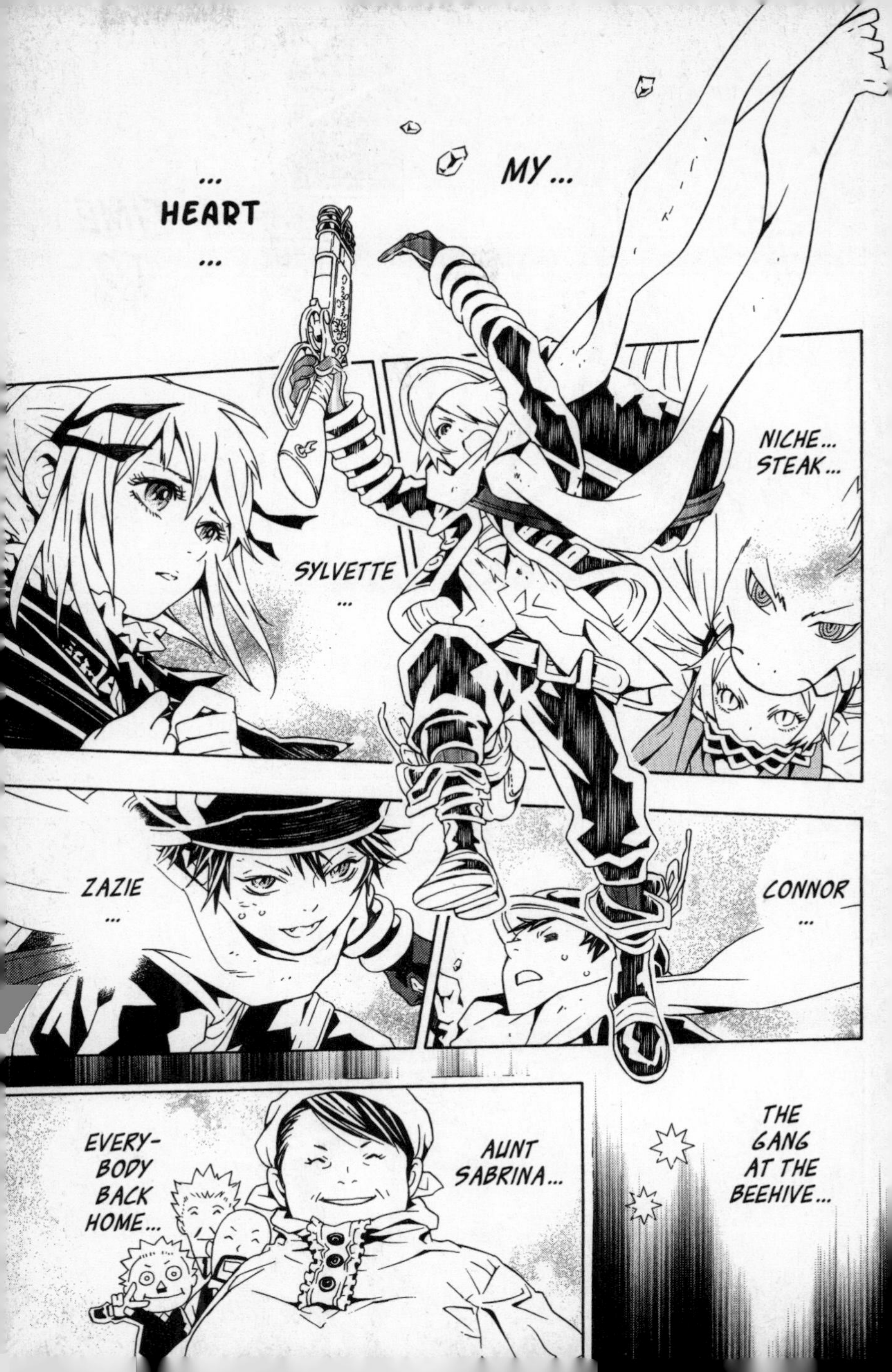
MY...
... HEART ...
NICHE... STEAK...
SYLVETTE ...
CONNOR ...
ZAZIE ...
THE GANG AT THE BEEHIVE...
AUNT SABRINA...
EVERY-BODY BACK HOME...

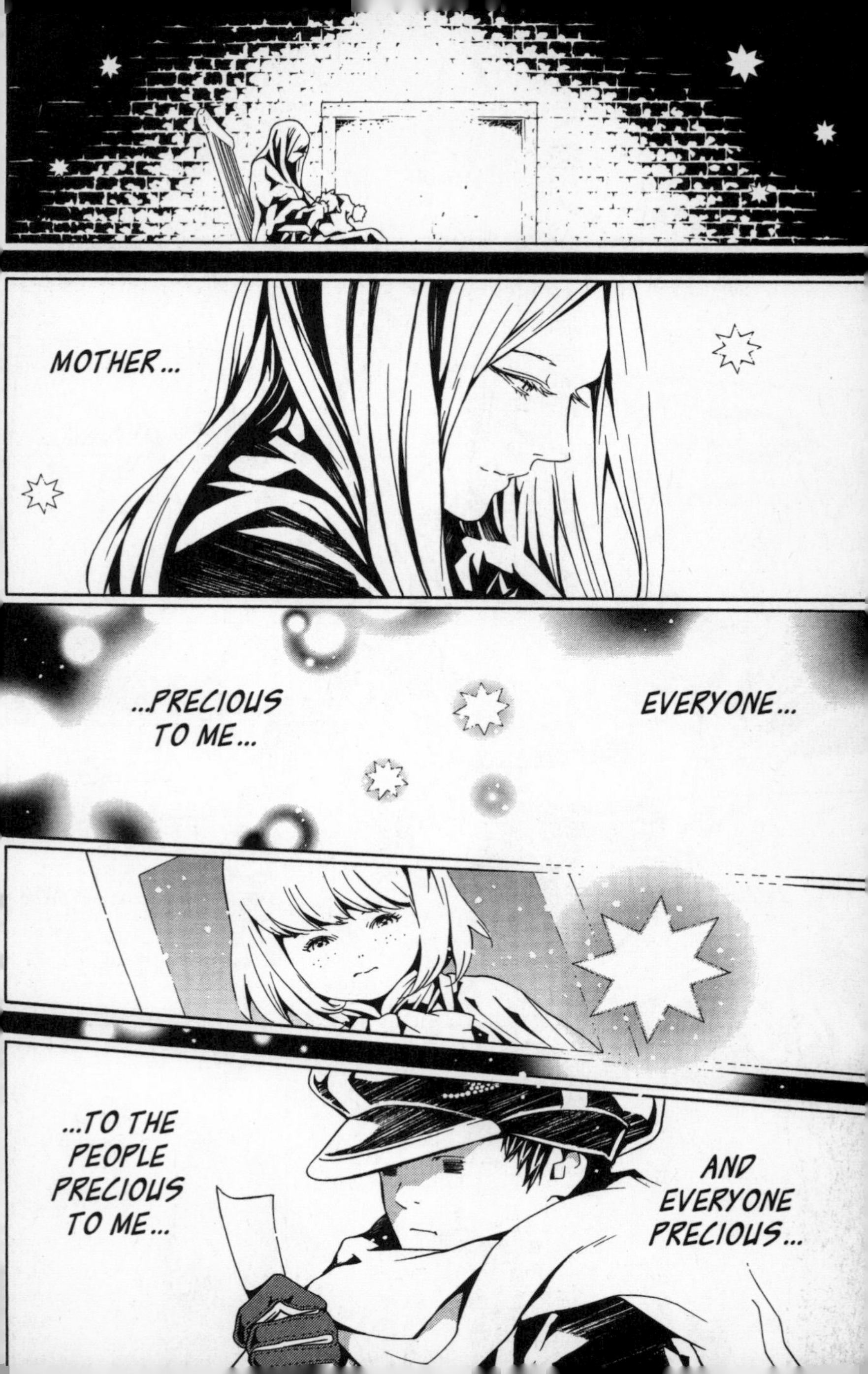
MOTHER...
EVERYONE...
...PRECIOUS TO ME...
AND EVERYONE PRECIOUS...
...TO THE PEOPLE PRECIOUS TO ME...

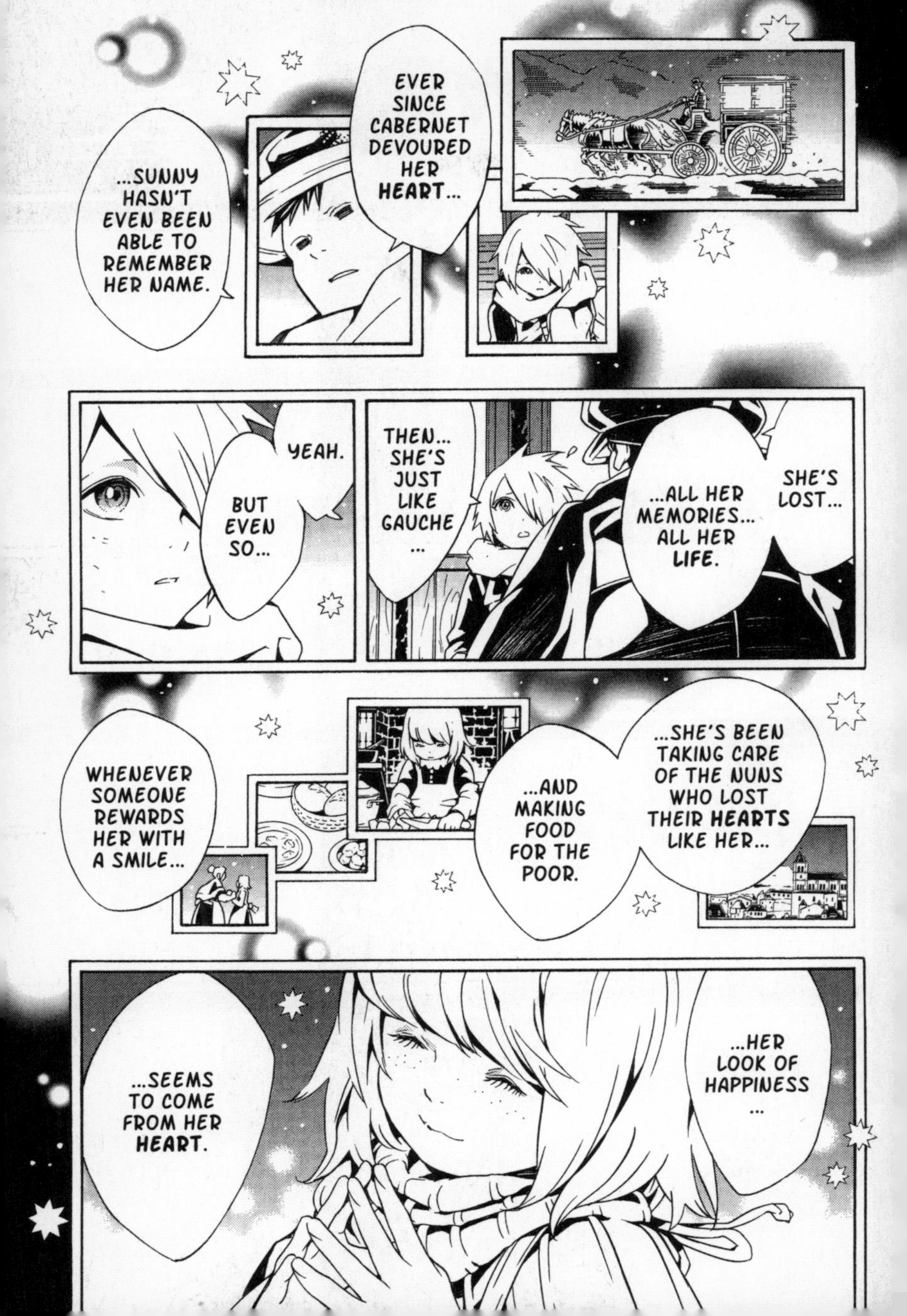
EVER SINCE CABERNET DEVOURED HER HEART...
...SUNNY HASN'T EVEN BEEN ABLE TO REMEMBER HER NAME.
SHE'S LOST...
...ALL HER MEMORIES... ALL HER LIFE.
THEN... SHE'S JUST LIKE GAUCHE...
YEAH.
BUT EVEN SO...
...SHE'S BEEN TAKING CARE OF THE NUNS WHO LOST THEIR HEARTS LIKE HER...
...AND MAKING FOOD FOR THE POOR.
WHENEVER SOMEONE REWARDS HER WITH A SMILE...
...HER LOOK OF HAPPINESS...
...SEEMS TO COME FROM HER HEART.

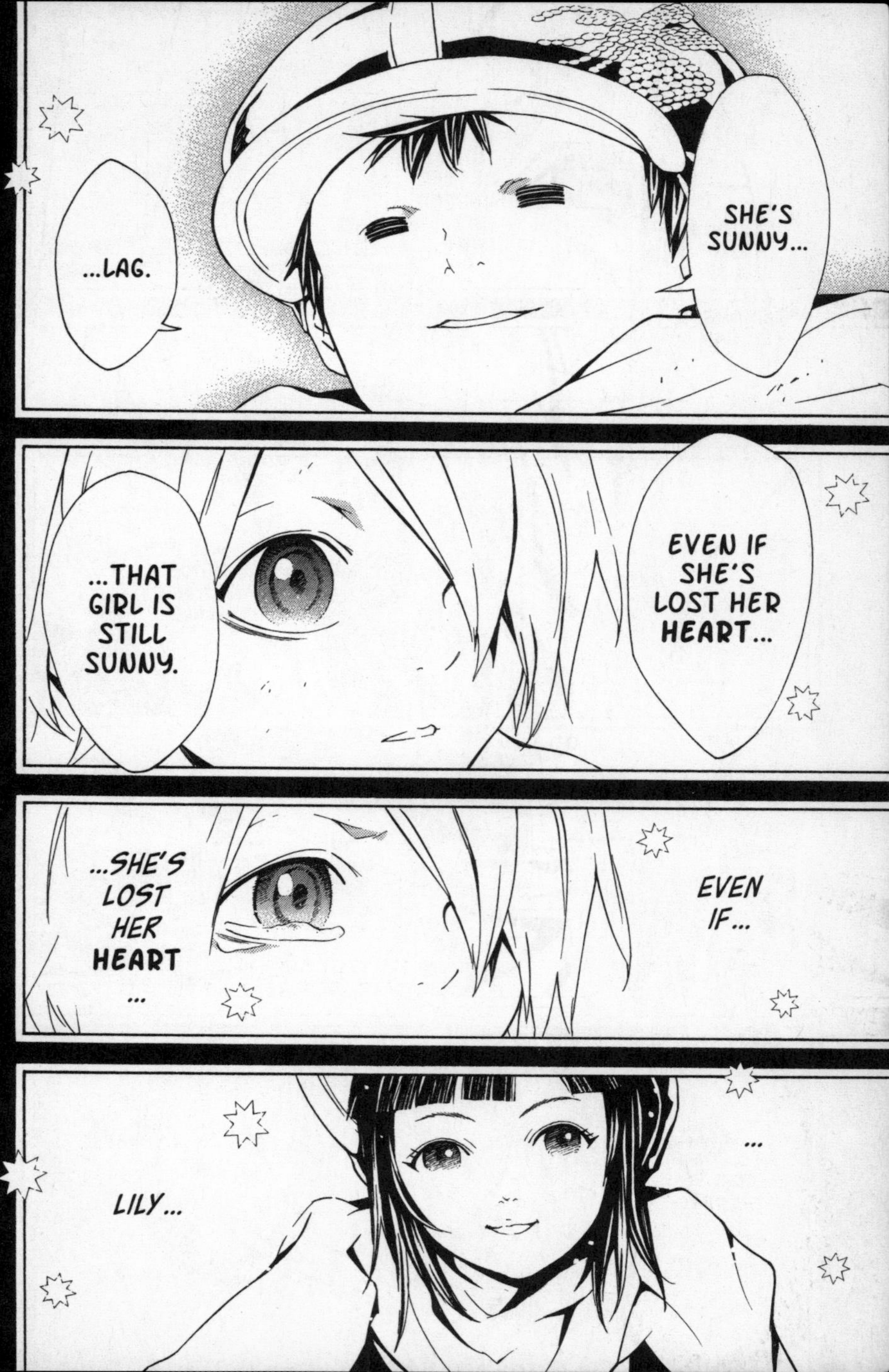
SHE'S SUNNY...
...LAG.
EVEN IF SHE'S LOST HER HEART...
...THAT GIRL IS STILL SUNNY.
EVEN IF...
...SHE'S LOST HER HEART ...
...
LILY...

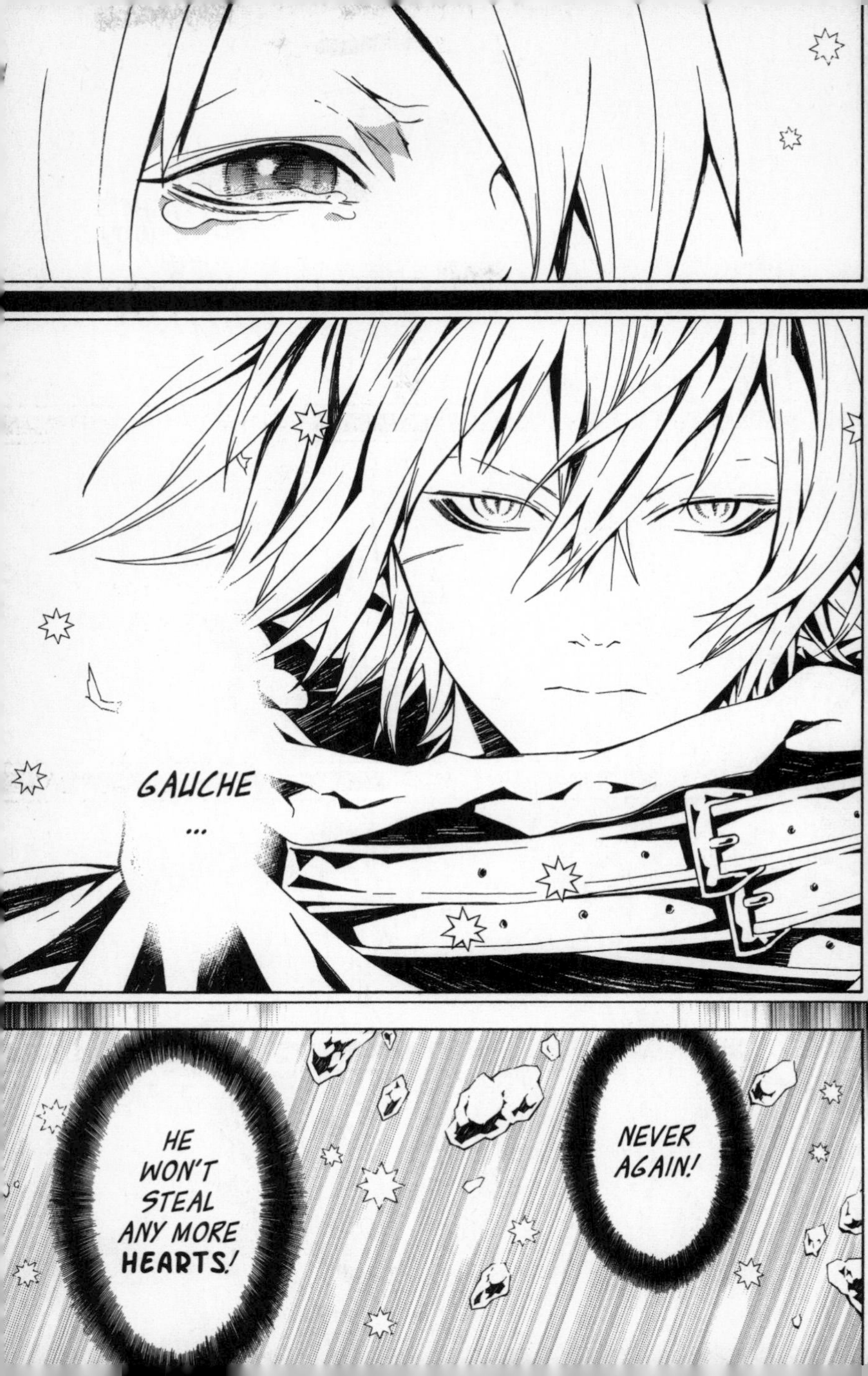
GAUCHE ...
NEVER AGAIN!
HE WON'T STEAL ANY MORE HEARTS!

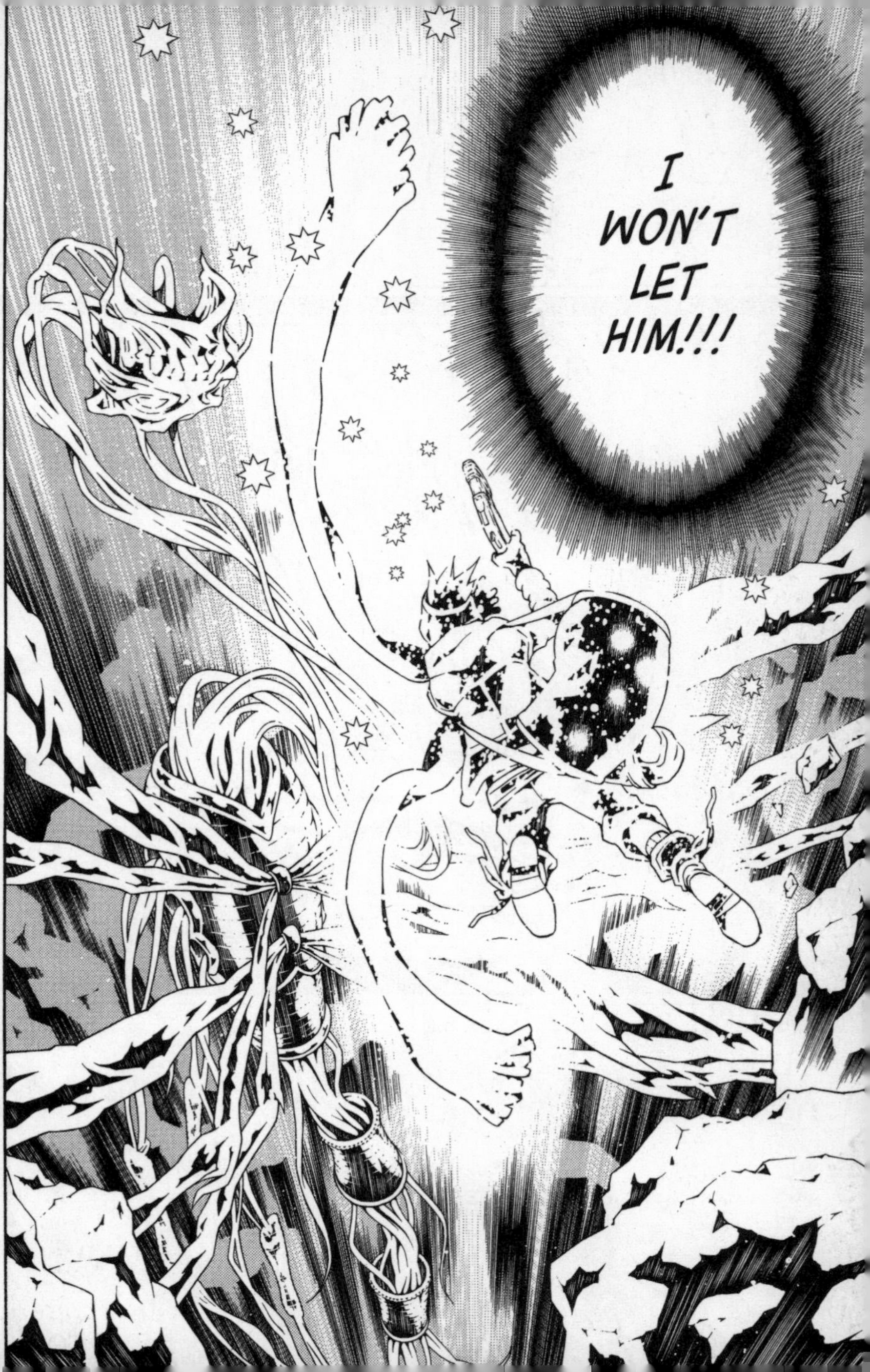
I WON'T LET HIM!!!

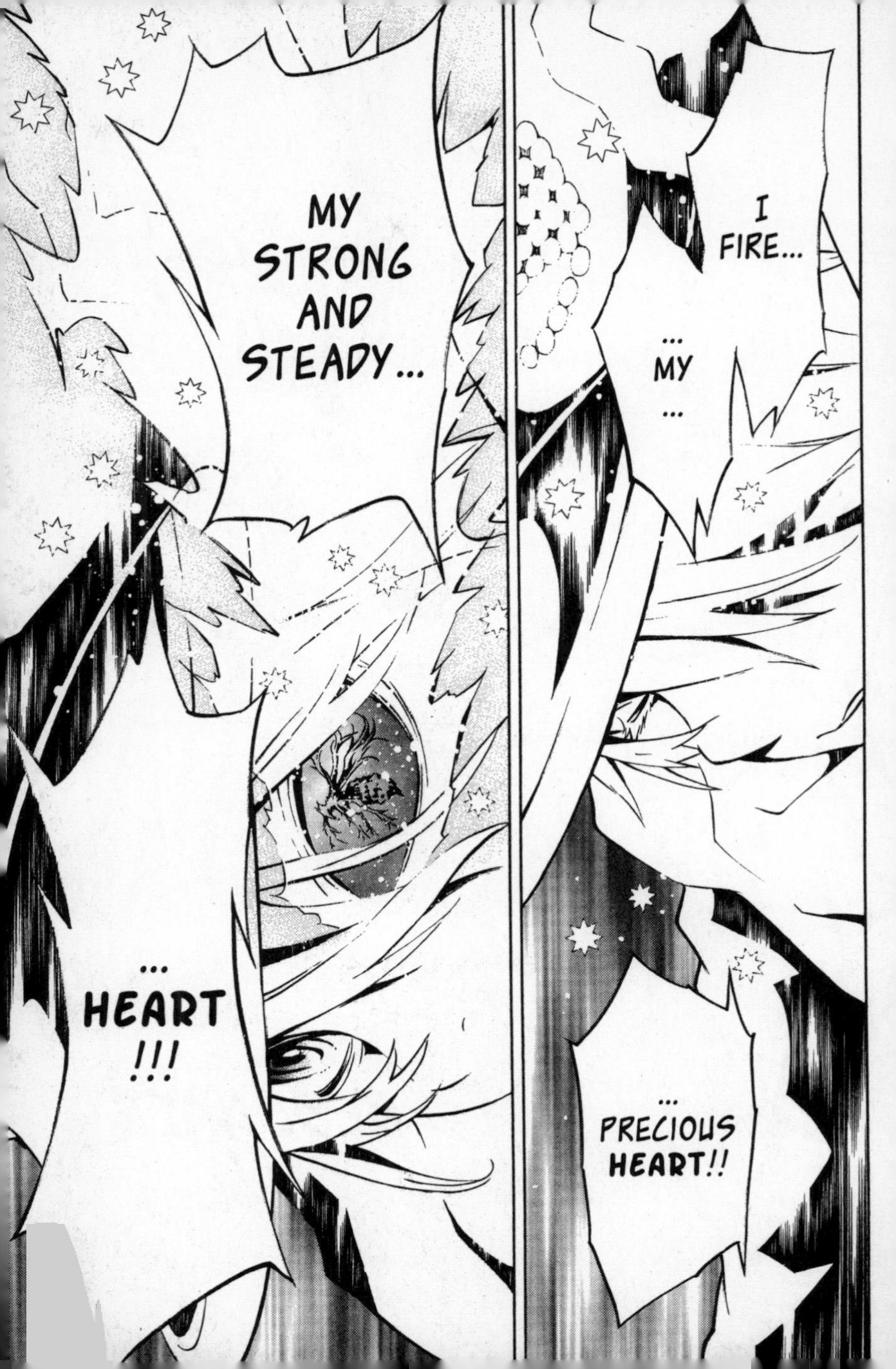
I FIRE...
... MY ...
... PRECIOUS HEART!!
MY STRONG AND STEADY...
... HEART!!!

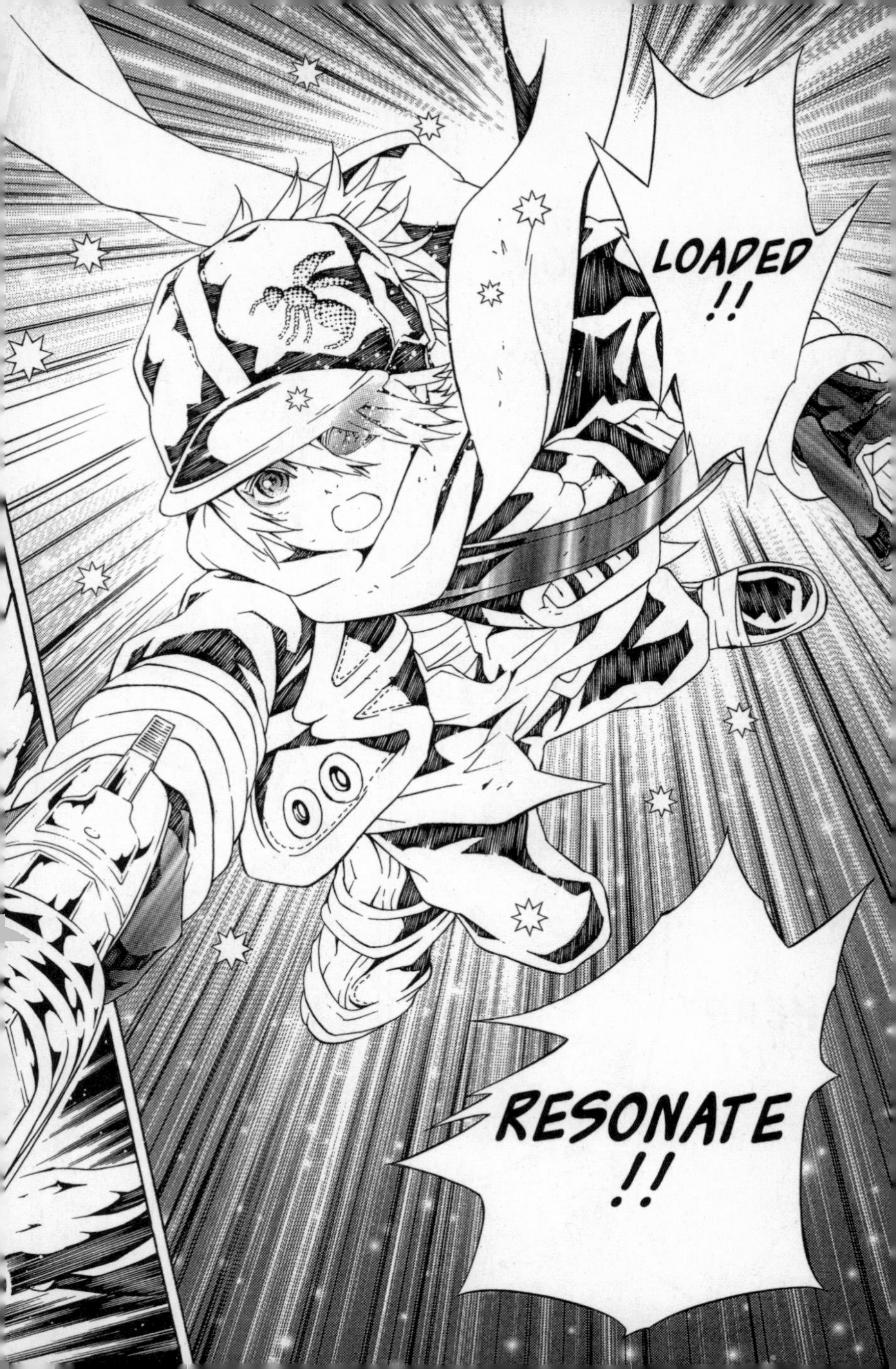
LOADED !!
RESONATE !!

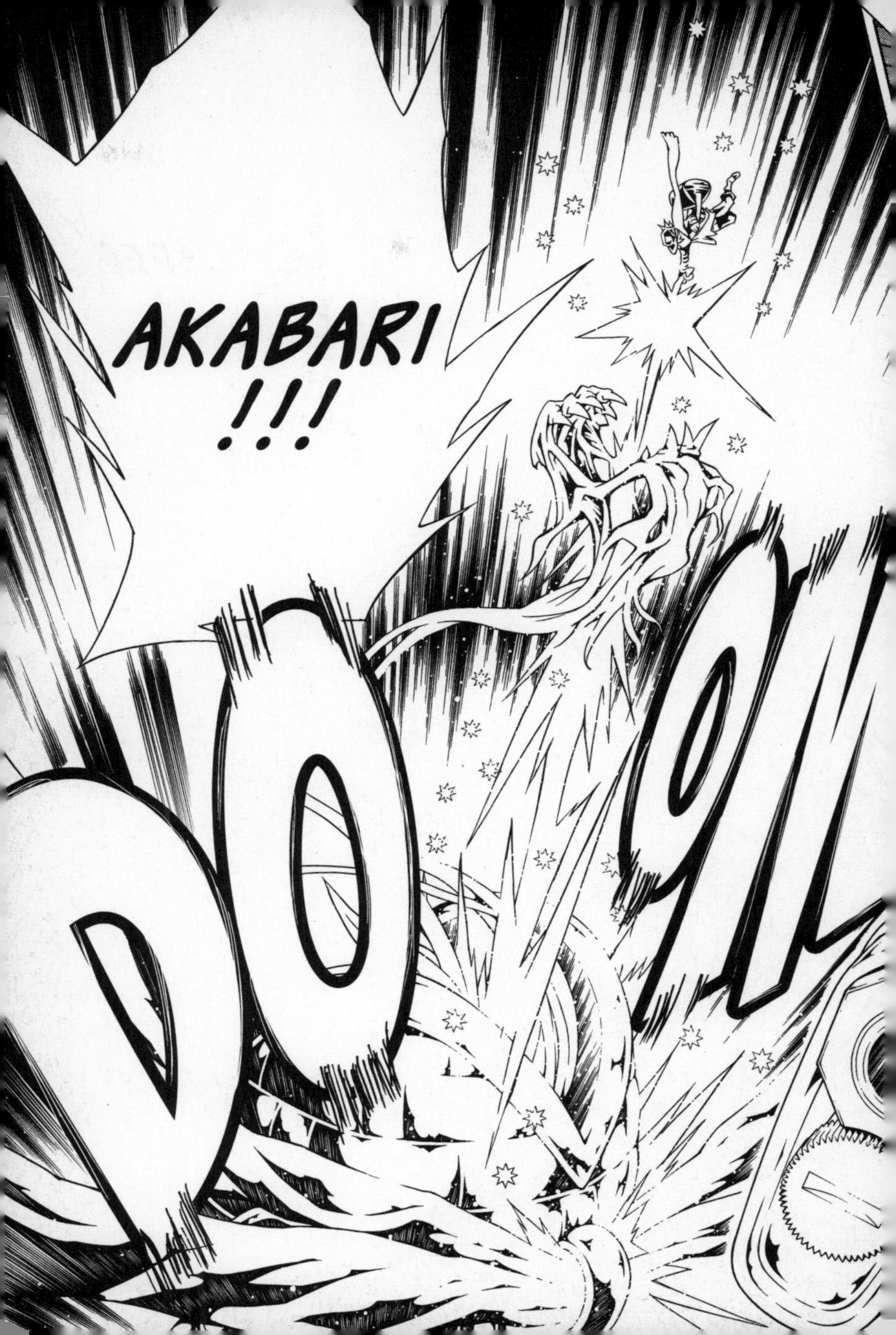
AKABARI
!!!
DOOM

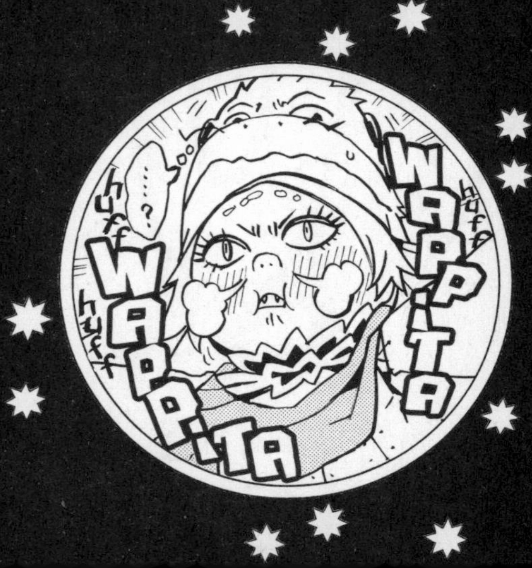
WAPPITA
huff
WAPPITA
huff
huff
...?

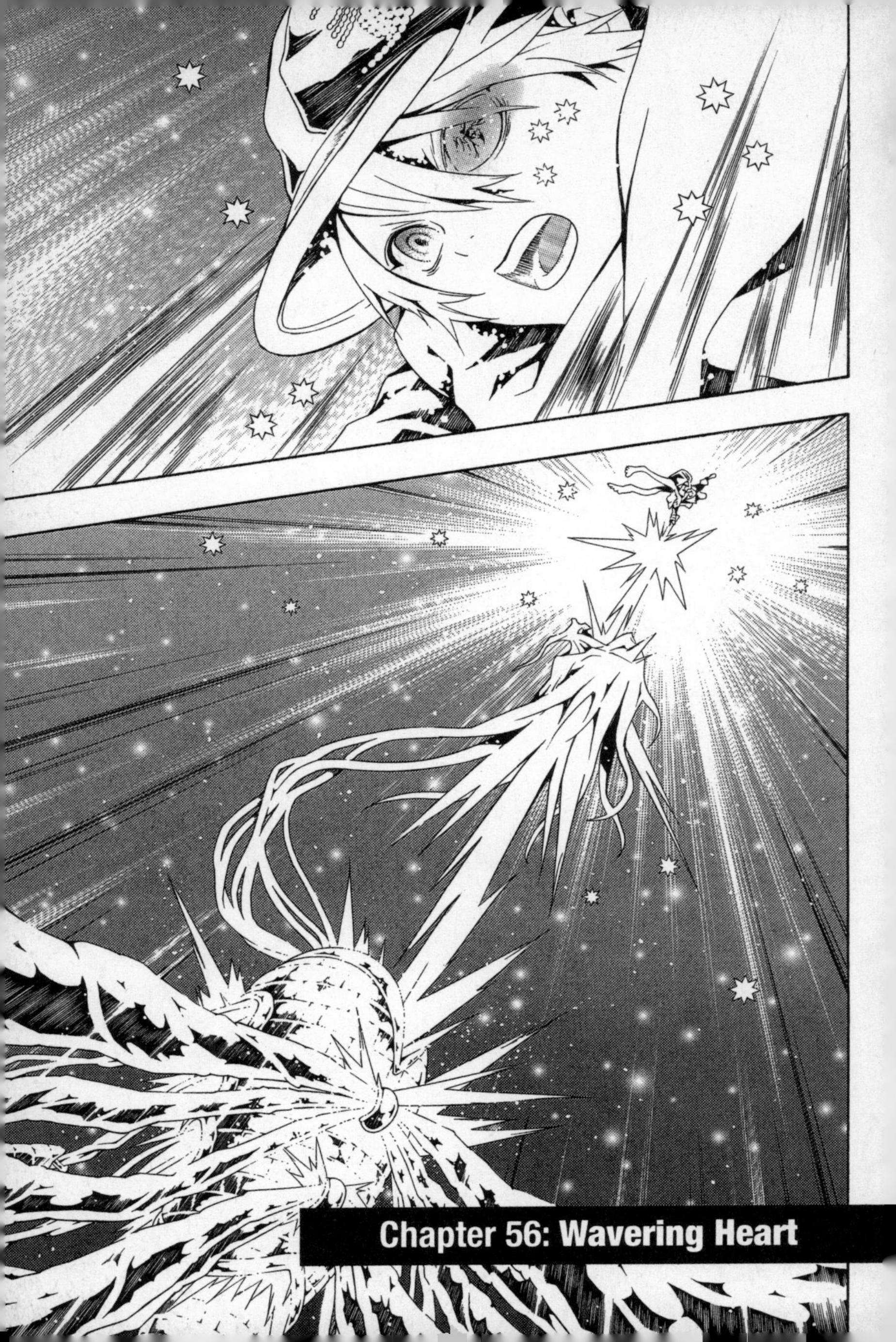
Chapter 56: Wavering Heart

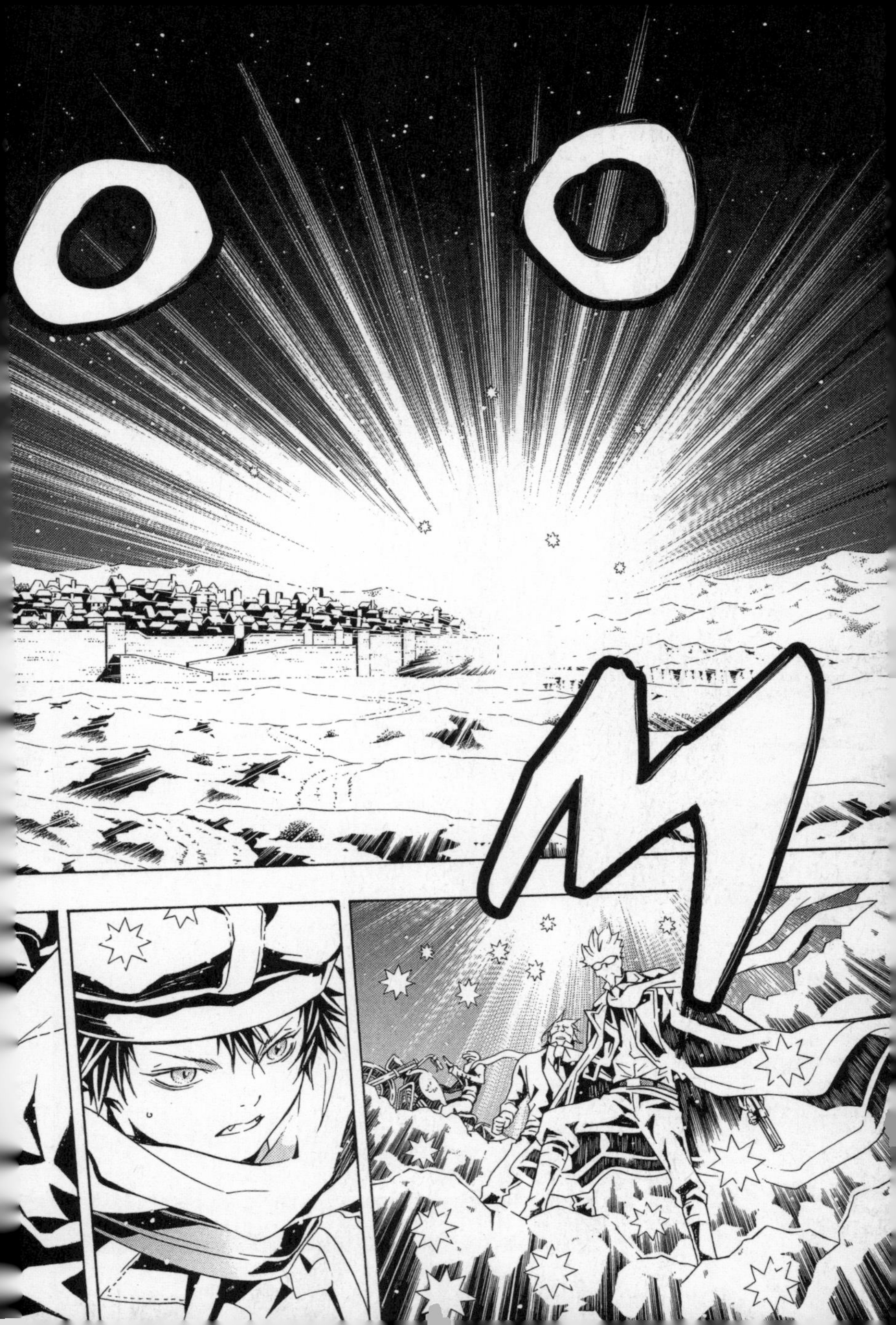
OOM!

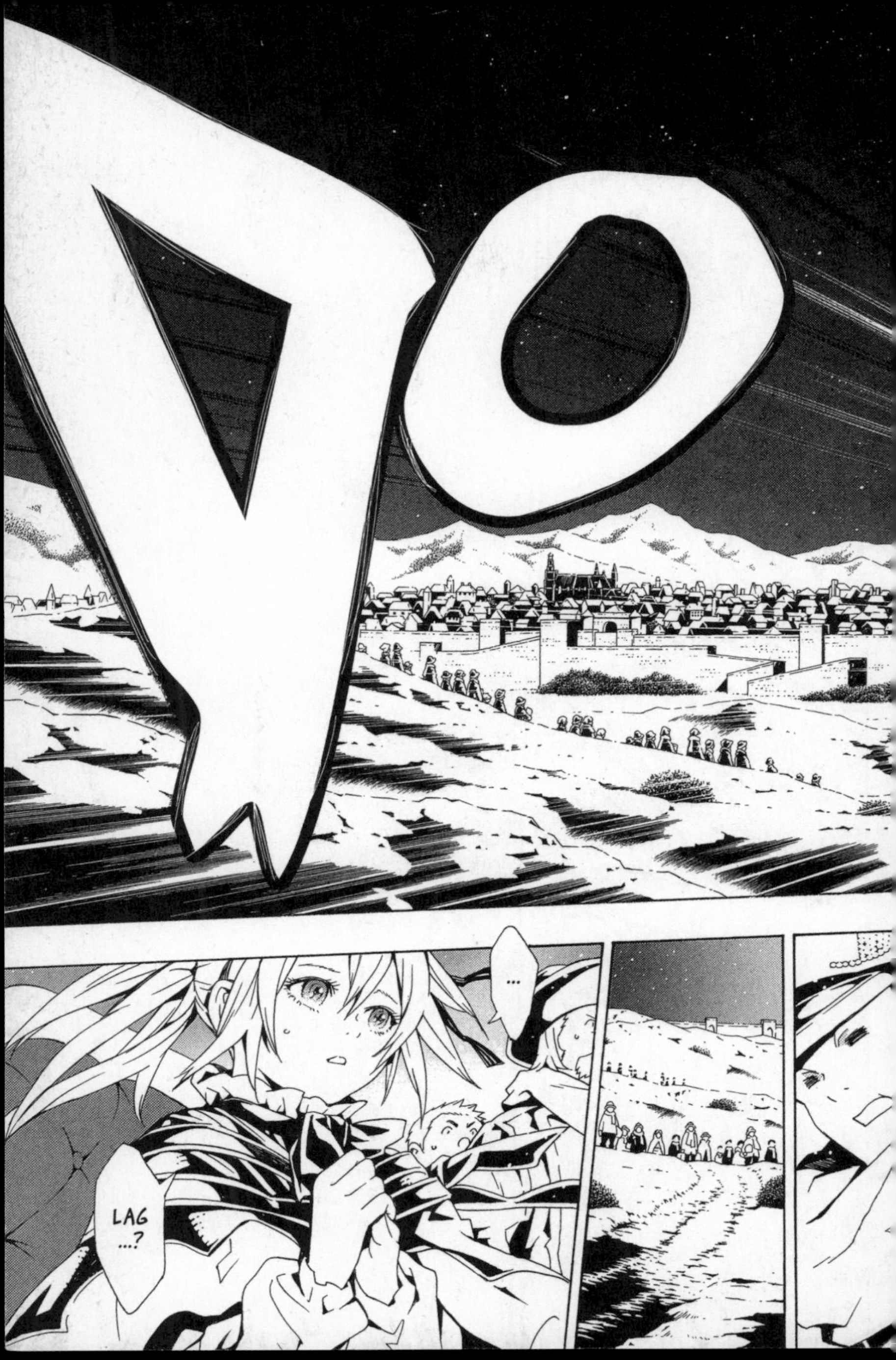
...
LAG ...?

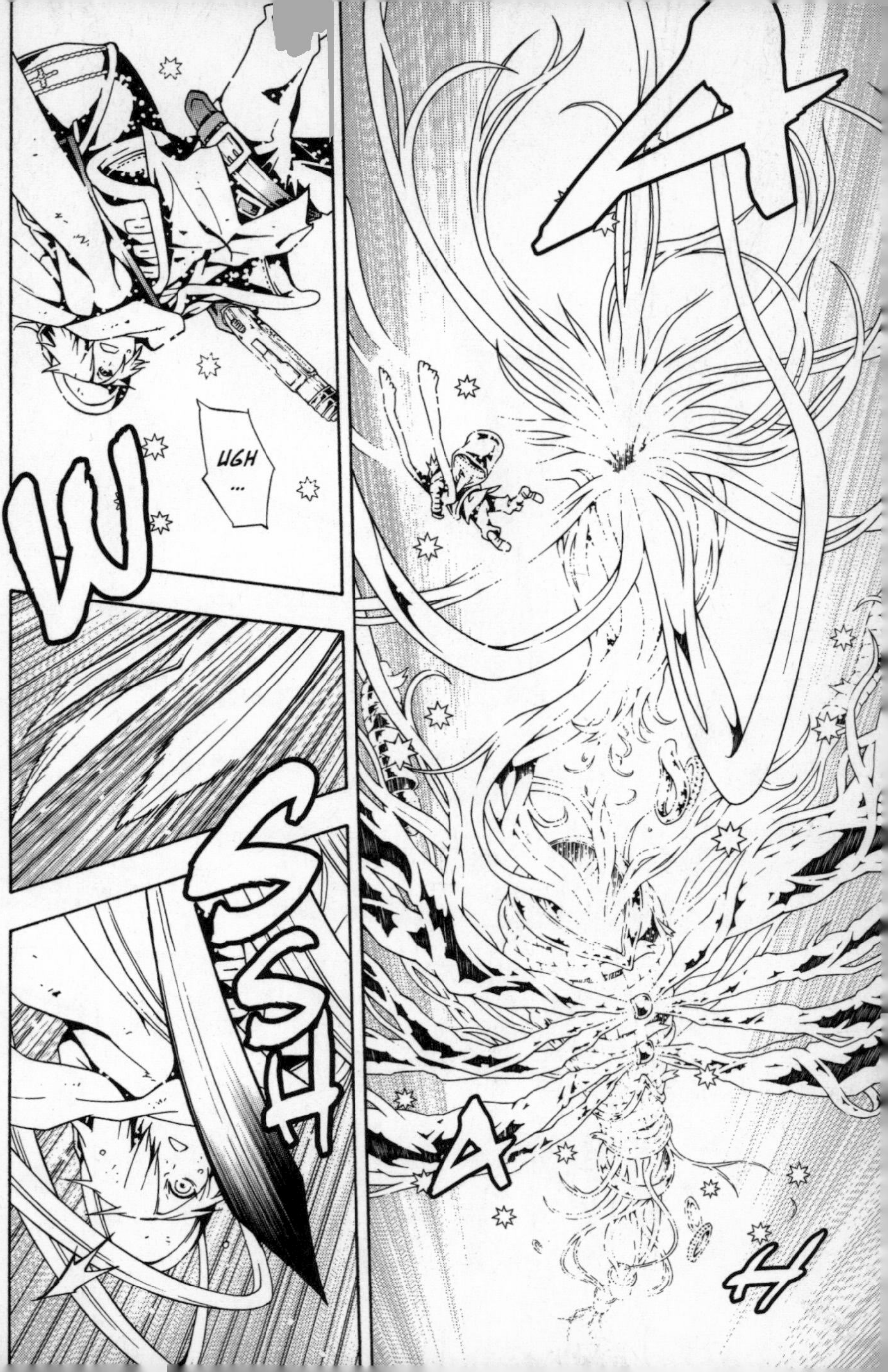
UGH ...

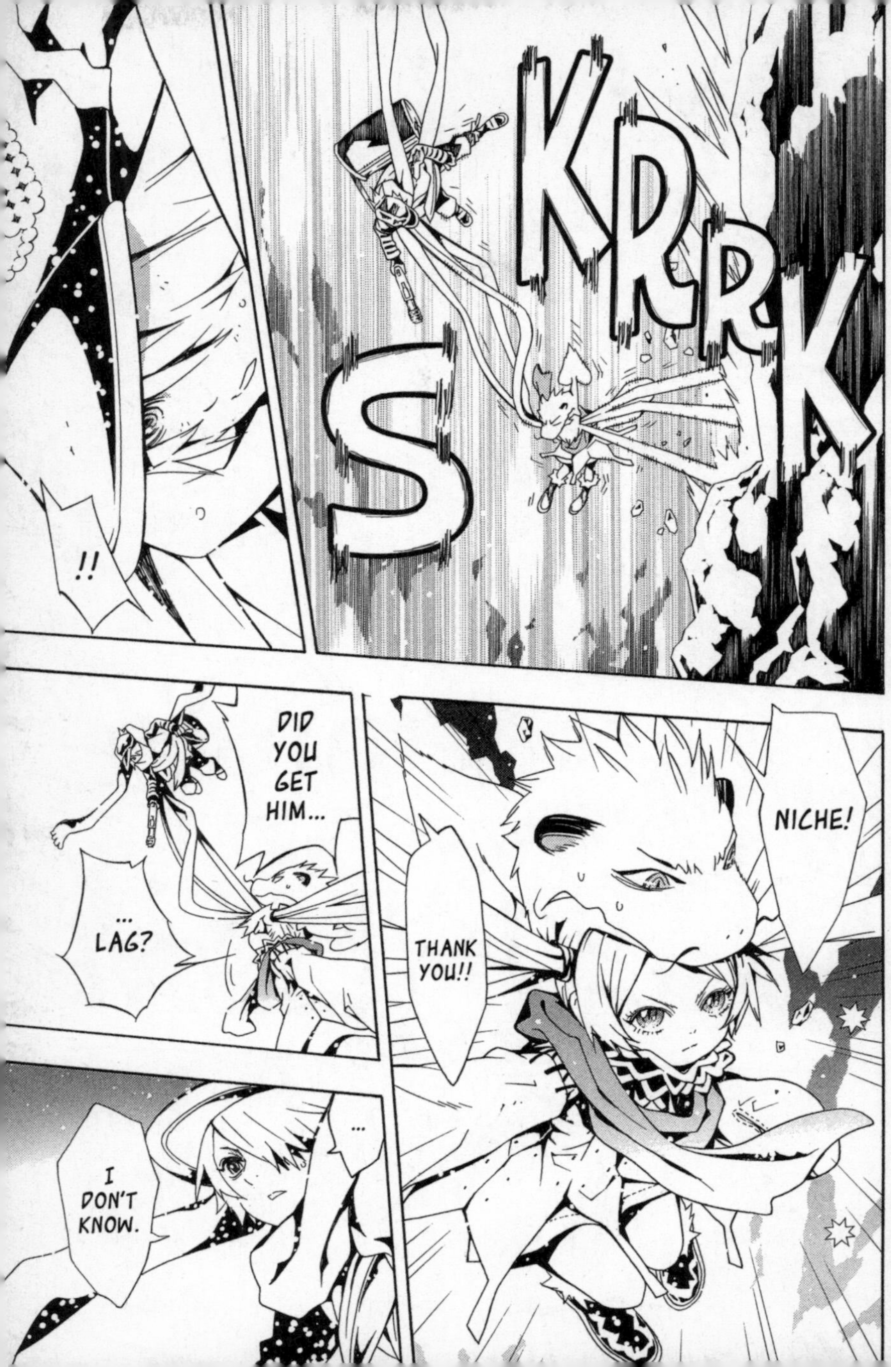
KRRK
S
!!
NICHE!
THANK YOU!!
DID YOU GET HIM...
...LAG?
...
I DON'T KNOW.

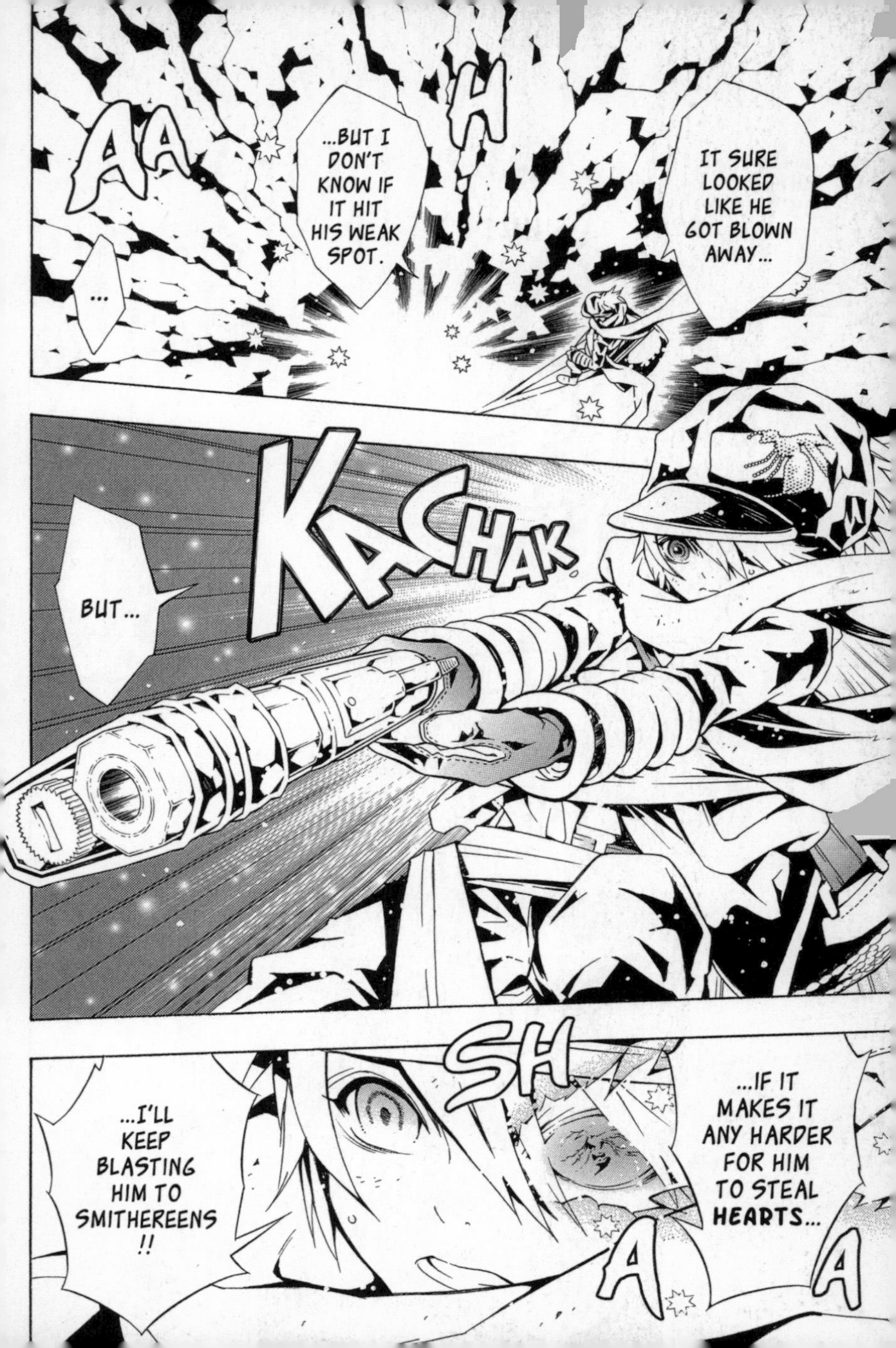

IT SURE LOOKED LIKE HE GOT BLOWN AWAY...
...BUT I DON'T KNOW IF IT HIT HIS WEAK SPOT.
AAH
...
KACHAK
BUT...
SH
...IF IT MAKES IT ANY HARDER FOR HIM TO STEAL **HEARTS**...
A A
...I'LL KEEP BLASTING HIM TO SMITHEREENS!!

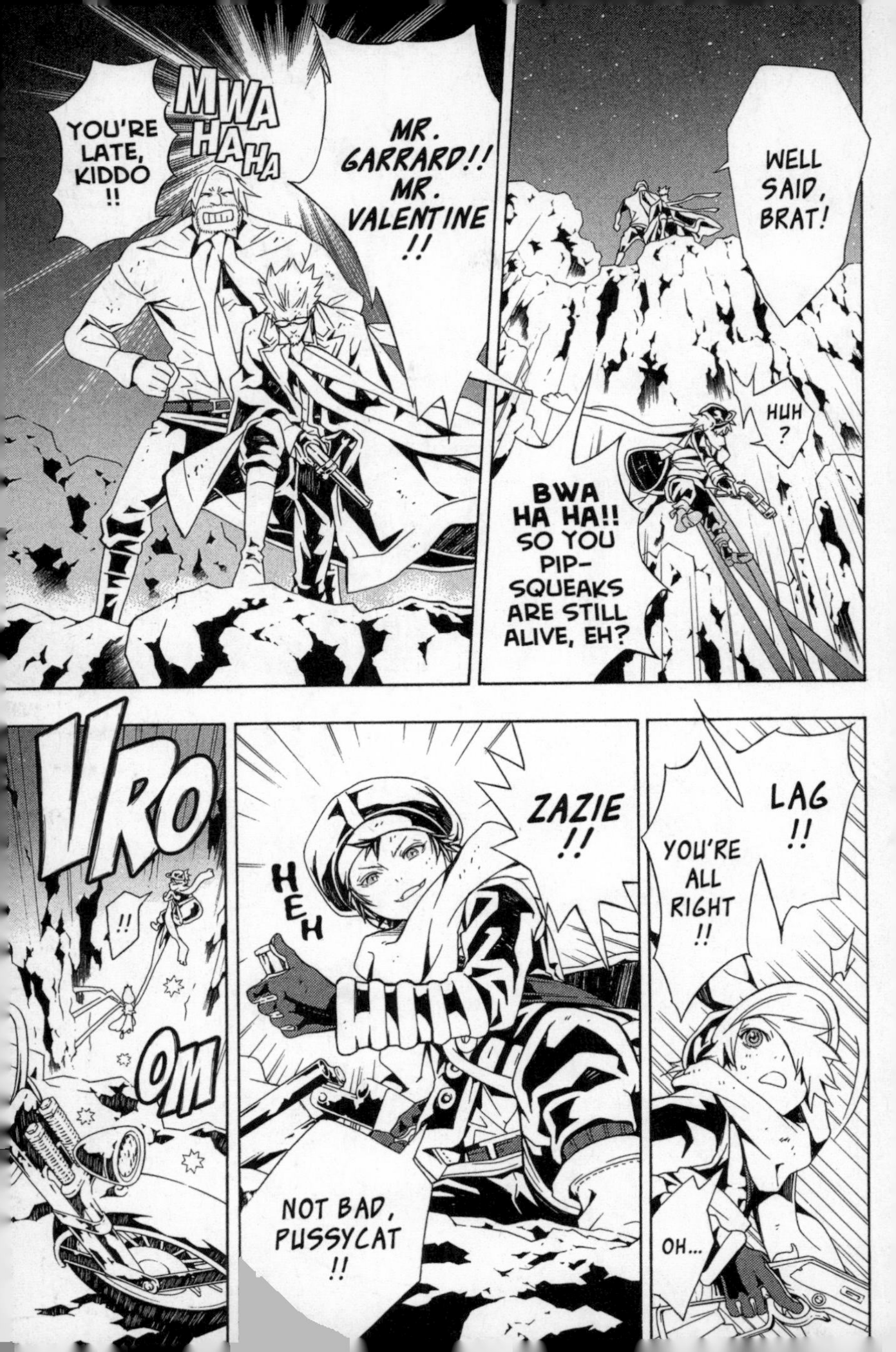
WELL SAID, BRAT!
HUH?
BWA HA HA!! SO YOU PIP-SQUEAKS ARE STILL ALIVE, EH?
MR. GARRARD!! MR. VALENTINE!!
MWA HAHAHA
YOU'RE LATE, KIDDO!!
LAG!!
YOU'RE ALL RIGHT!!
OH...
ZAZIE!!
HEH
NOT BAD, PUSSYCAT!!
VROOM
!!

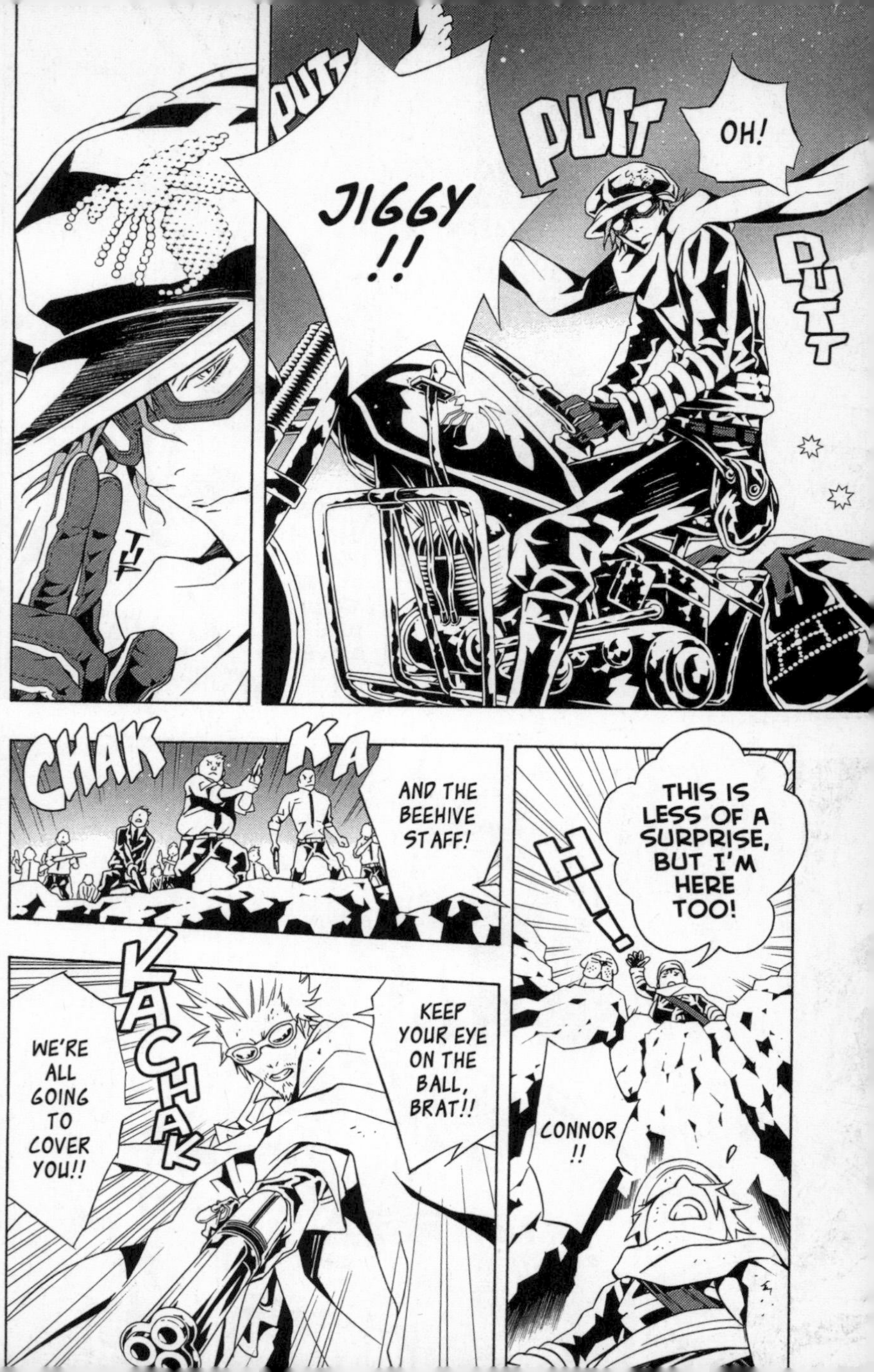
OH!
PUTT
PUTT
PUTT
JIGGY !!
THIS IS LESS OF A SURPRISE, BUT I'M HERE TOO!
HI!
AND THE BEEHIVE STAFF!
KA
CHAK
CONNOR !!
KEEP YOUR EYE ON THE BALL, BRAT!!
KACHAK
WE'RE ALL GOING TO COVER YOU!!

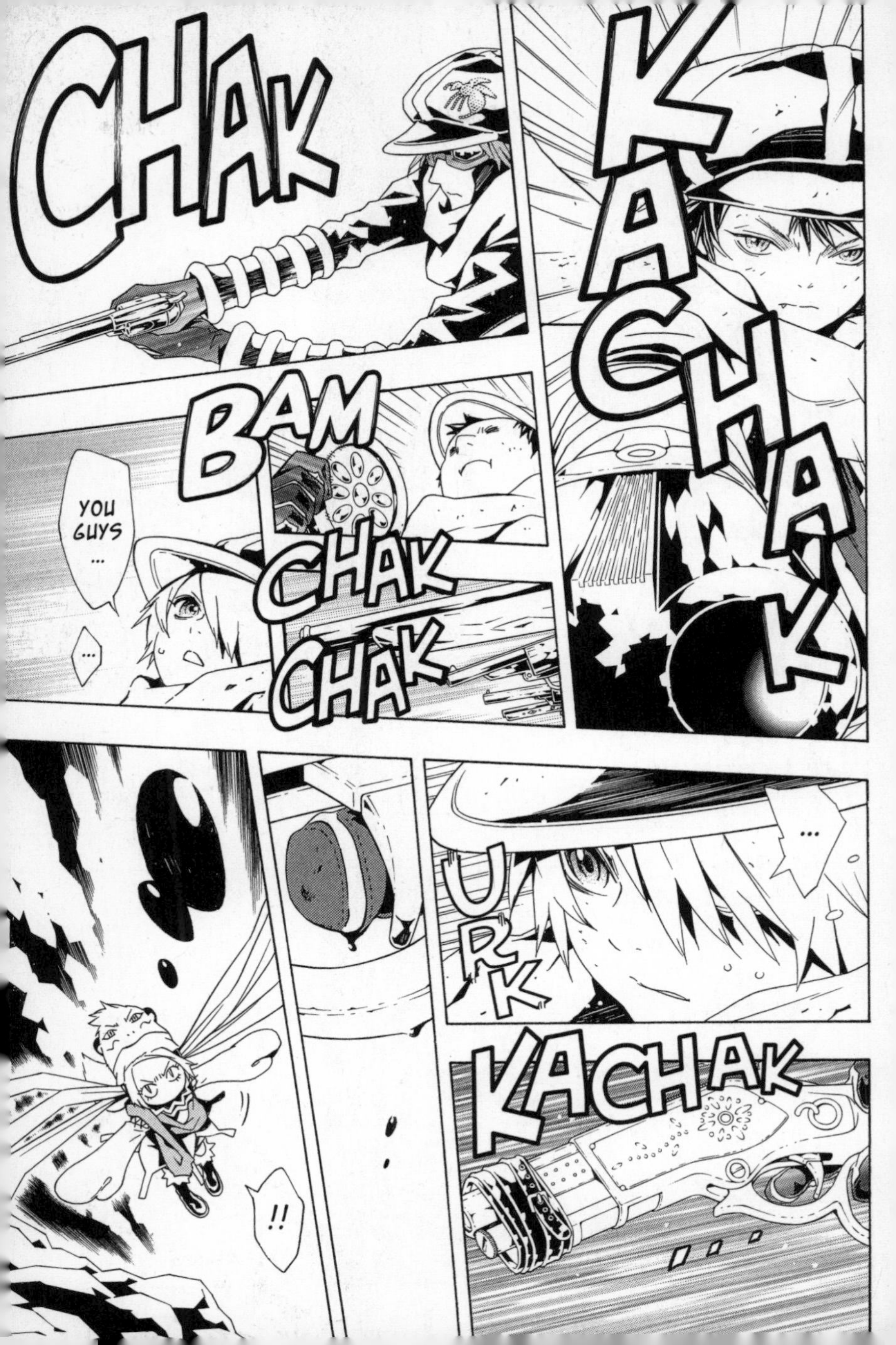
KACHAK
CHAK
BAM
CHAK
CHAK
YOU GUYS ...
...
...
URK
KACHAK
!!

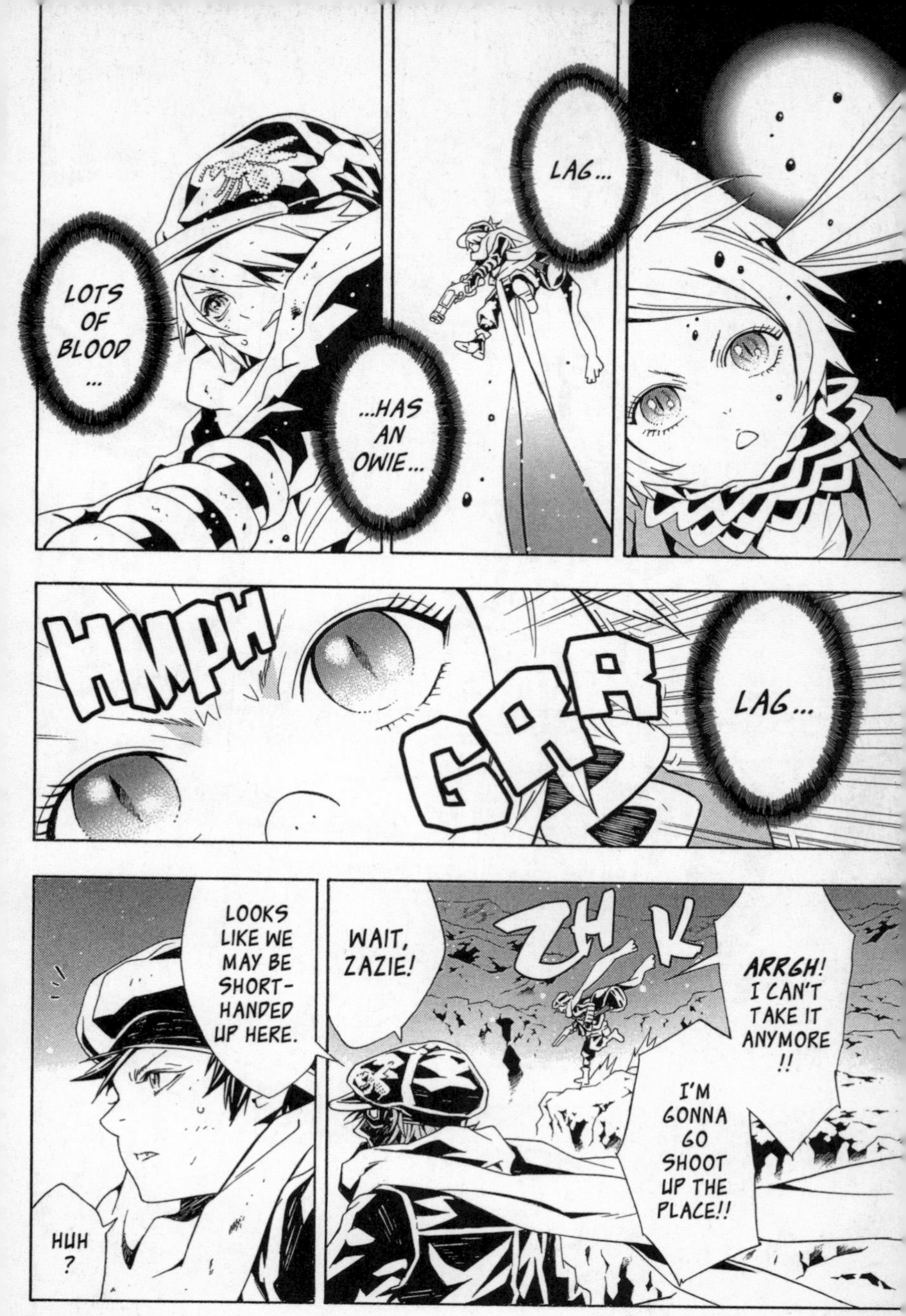

LAG...
...HAS AN OWIE...
LOTS OF BLOOD ...
LAG...
GAR
HMPH
ZH K
ARRGH! I CAN'T TAKE IT ANYMORE !!
I'M GONNA GO SHOOT UP THE PLACE!!
WAIT, ZAZIE!
LOOKS LIKE WE MAY BE SHORT-HANDED UP HERE.
HUH ?

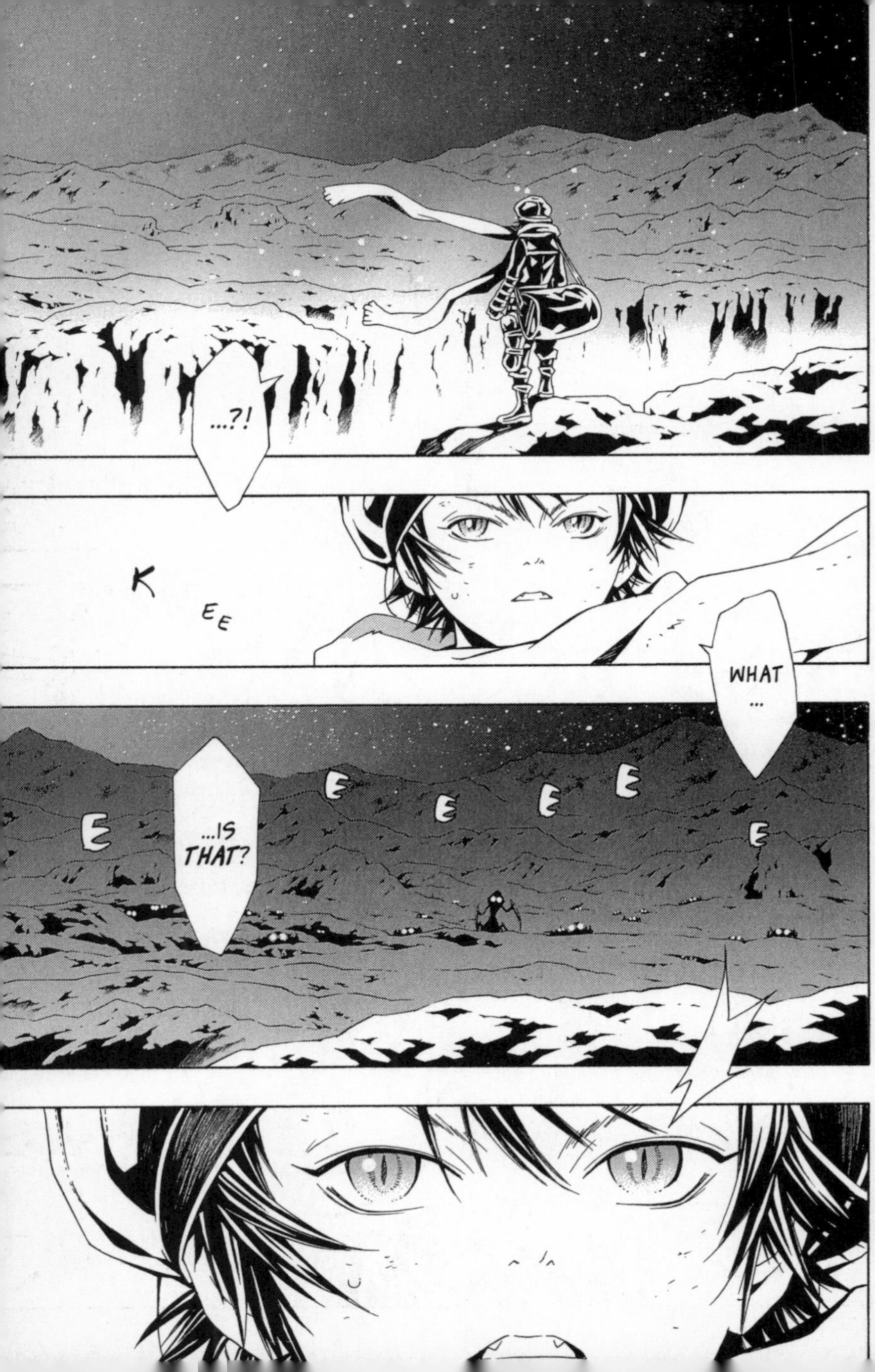
...?!
K
EE
WHAT ...
E E E E E E
...IS THAT?

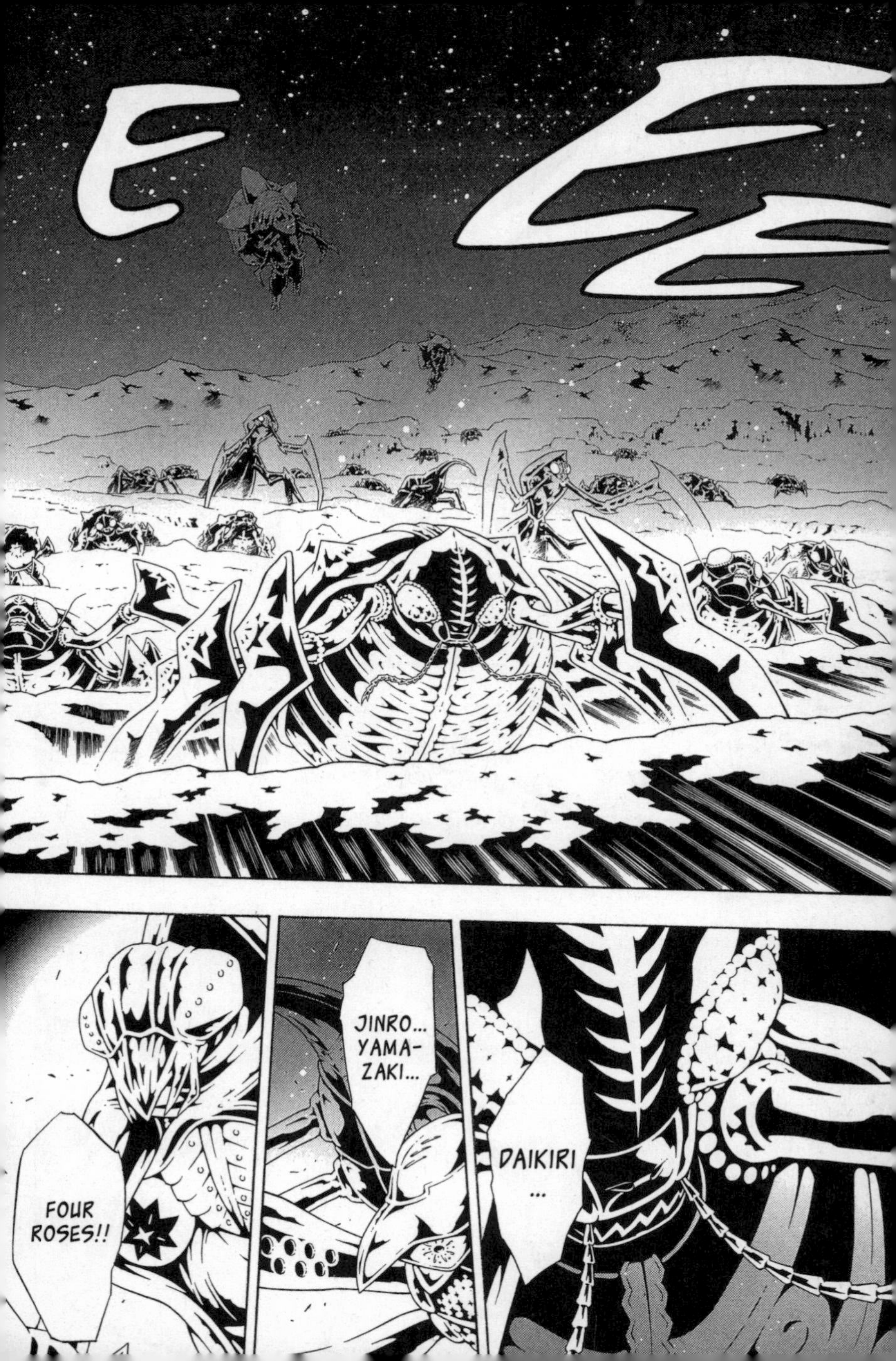
DAIKIRI ...
JINRO... YAMA-ZAKI...
FOUR ROSES!!

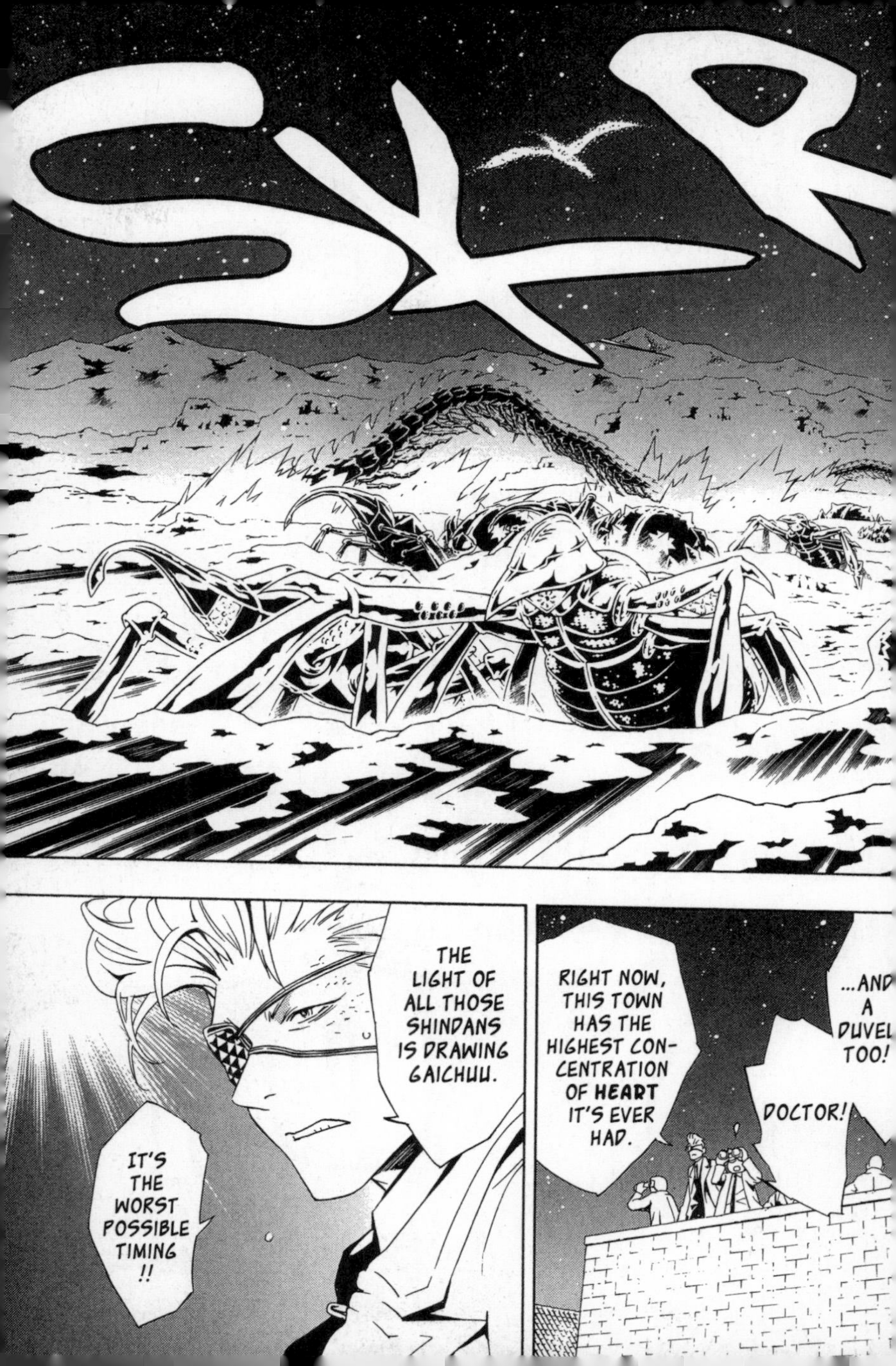
...AND A DUVEL TOO!
DOCTOR!
RIGHT NOW, THIS TOWN HAS THE HIGHEST CON-CENTRATION OF HEART IT'S EVER HAD.
THE LIGHT OF ALL THOSE SHINDANS IS DRAWING GAICHUU.
IT'S THE WORST POSSIBLE TIMING!!

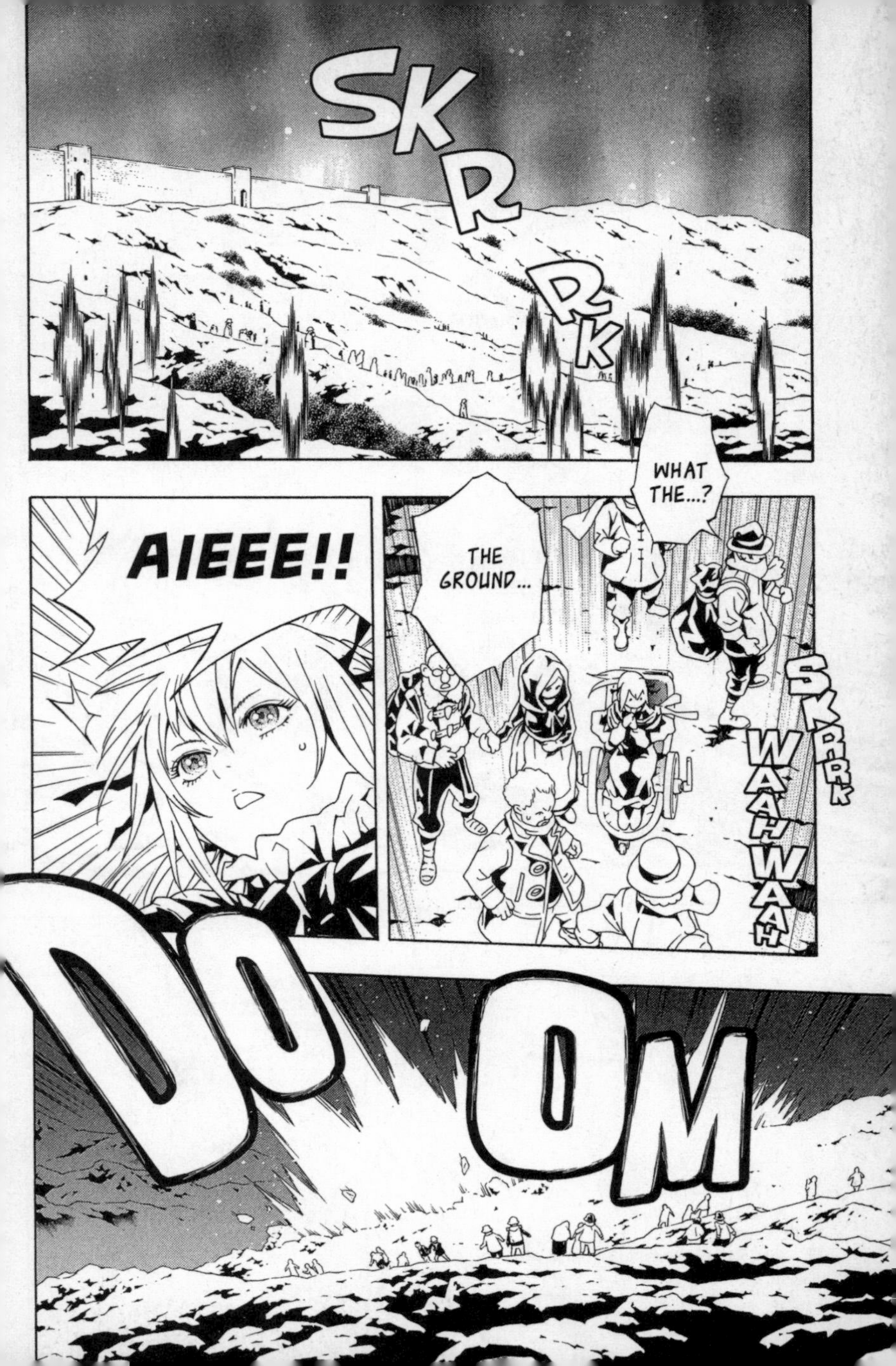
SKRRK
WHAT THE...?
THE GROUND...
SKRRK
WAAHWAAH
AIEEE!!
DOOM

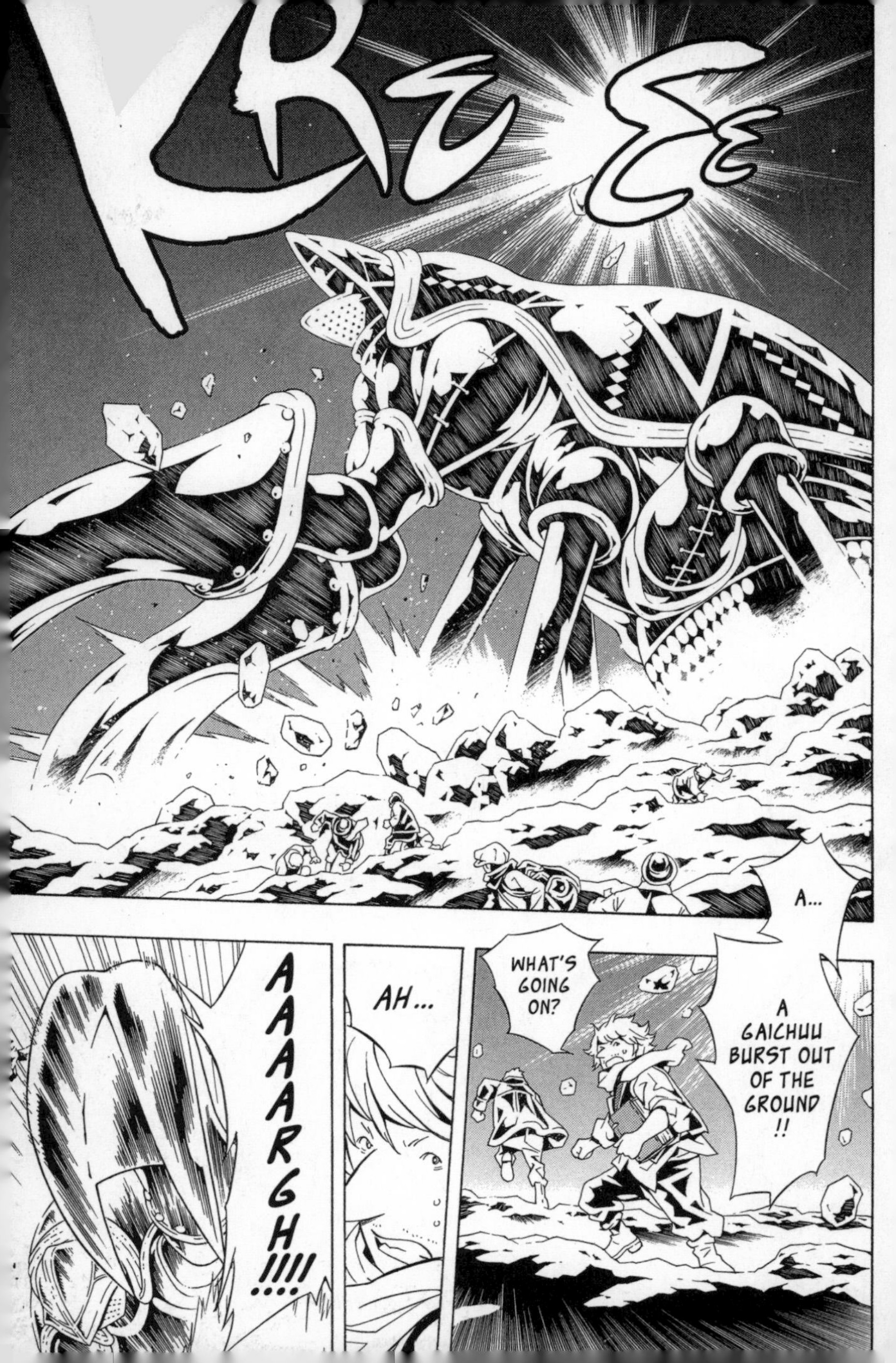
KREEE
A...
WHAT'S GOING ON?
A GAICHUU BURST OUT OF THE GROUND!!
AH...
AAAAARGH!!!!!

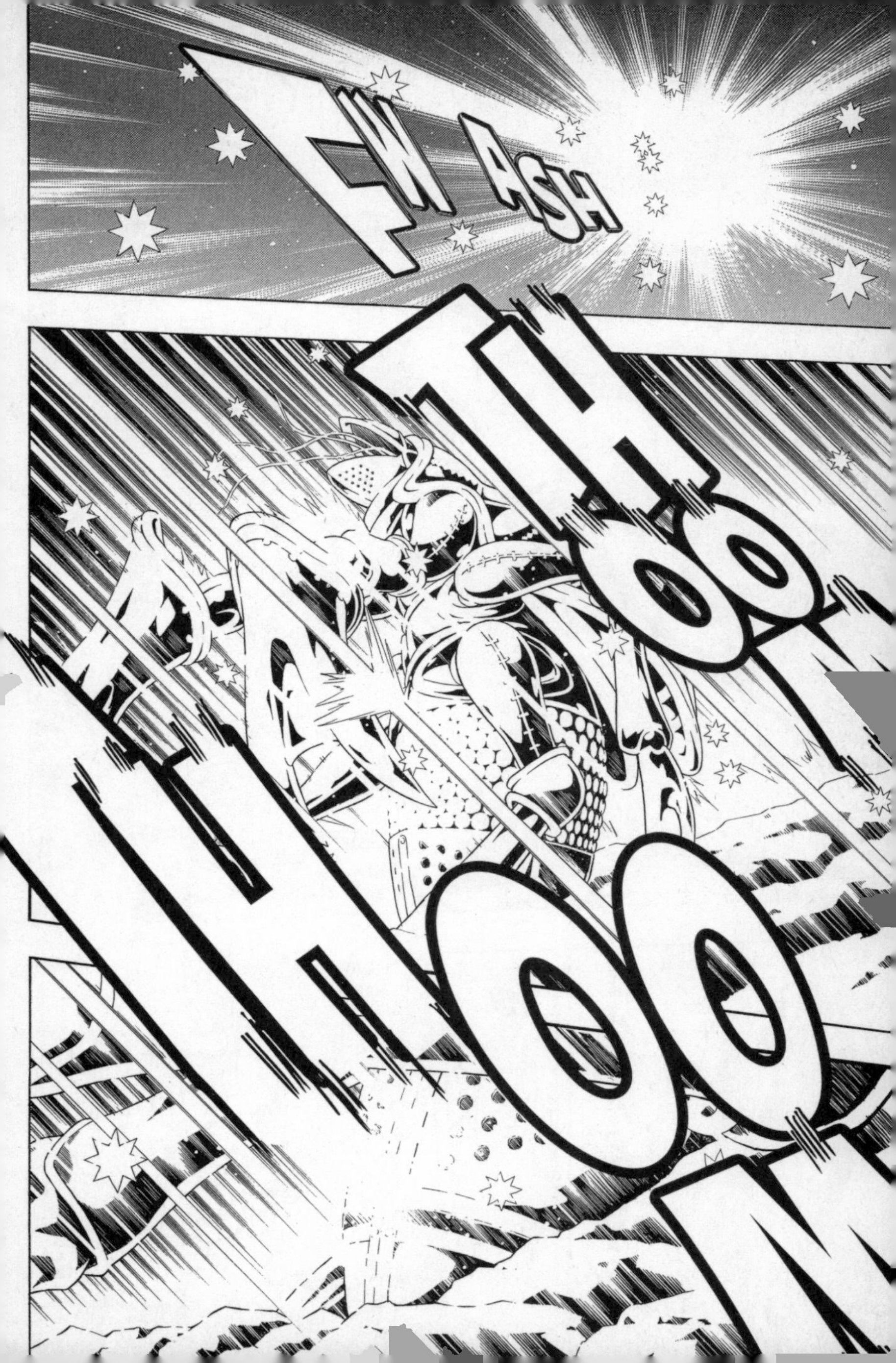
FWASH

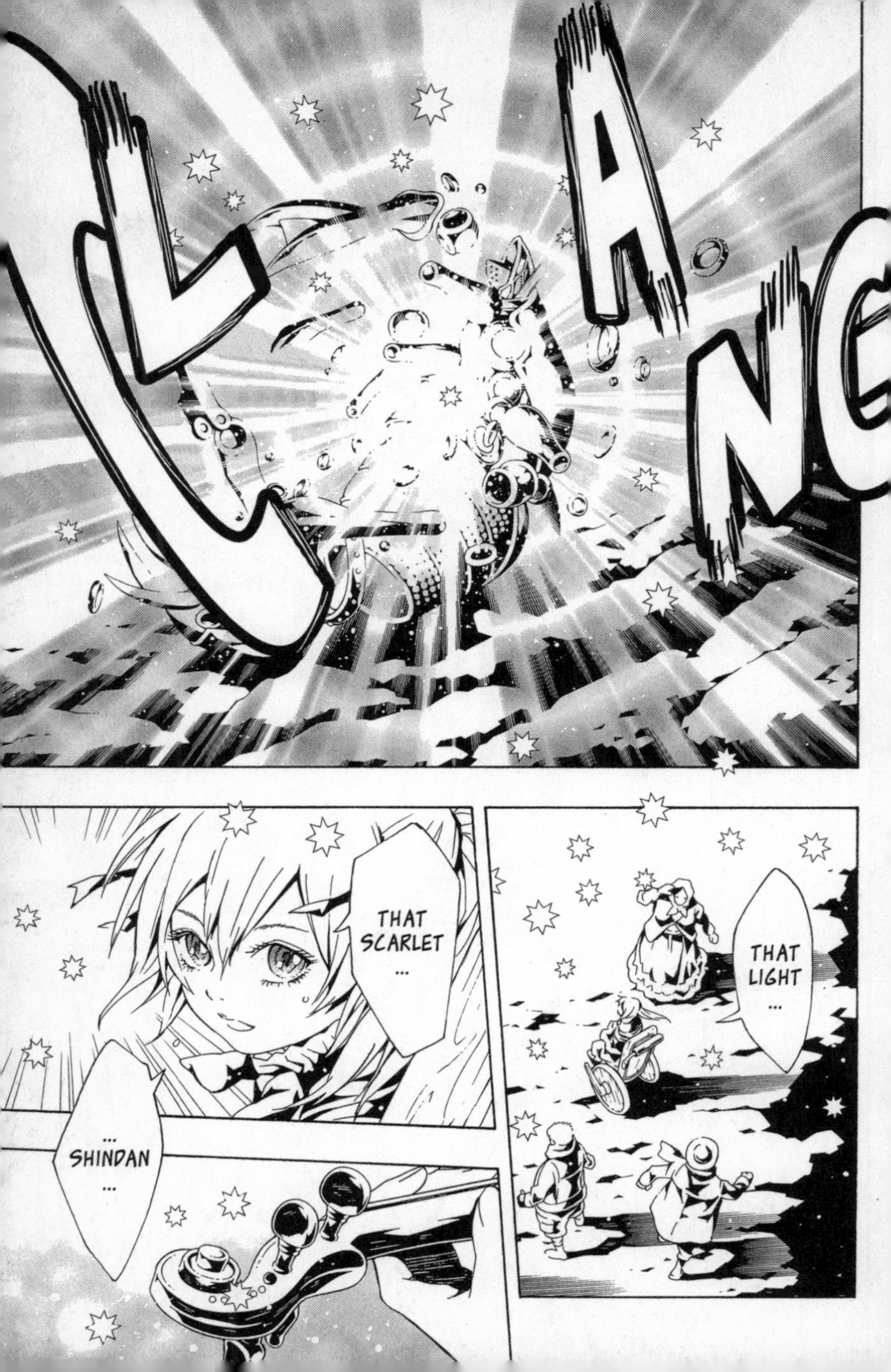
CLANG
THAT LIGHT ...
THAT SCARLET ...
... SHINDAN ...

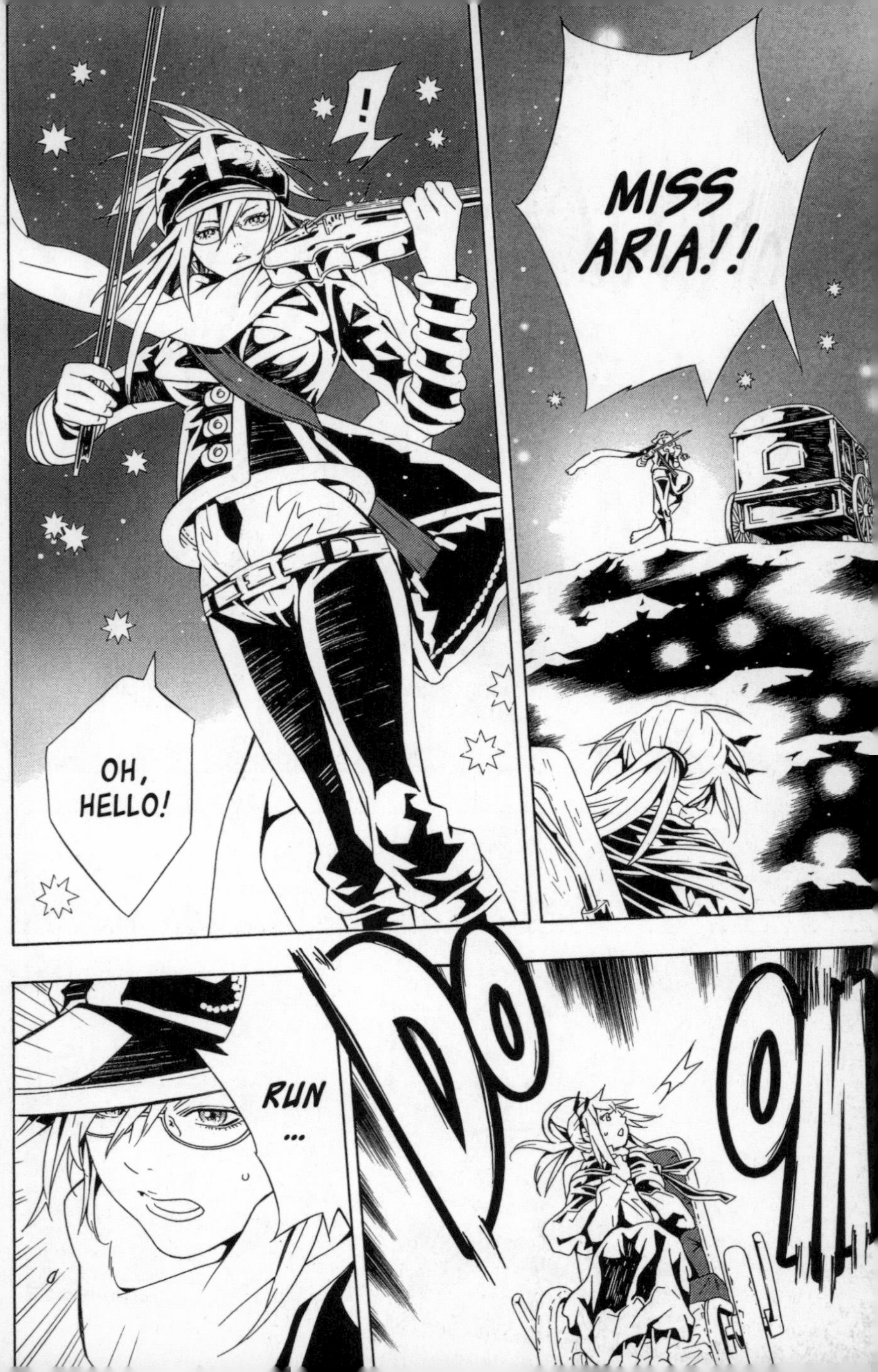
MISS ARIA!!
!
OH, HELLO!
RUN ...

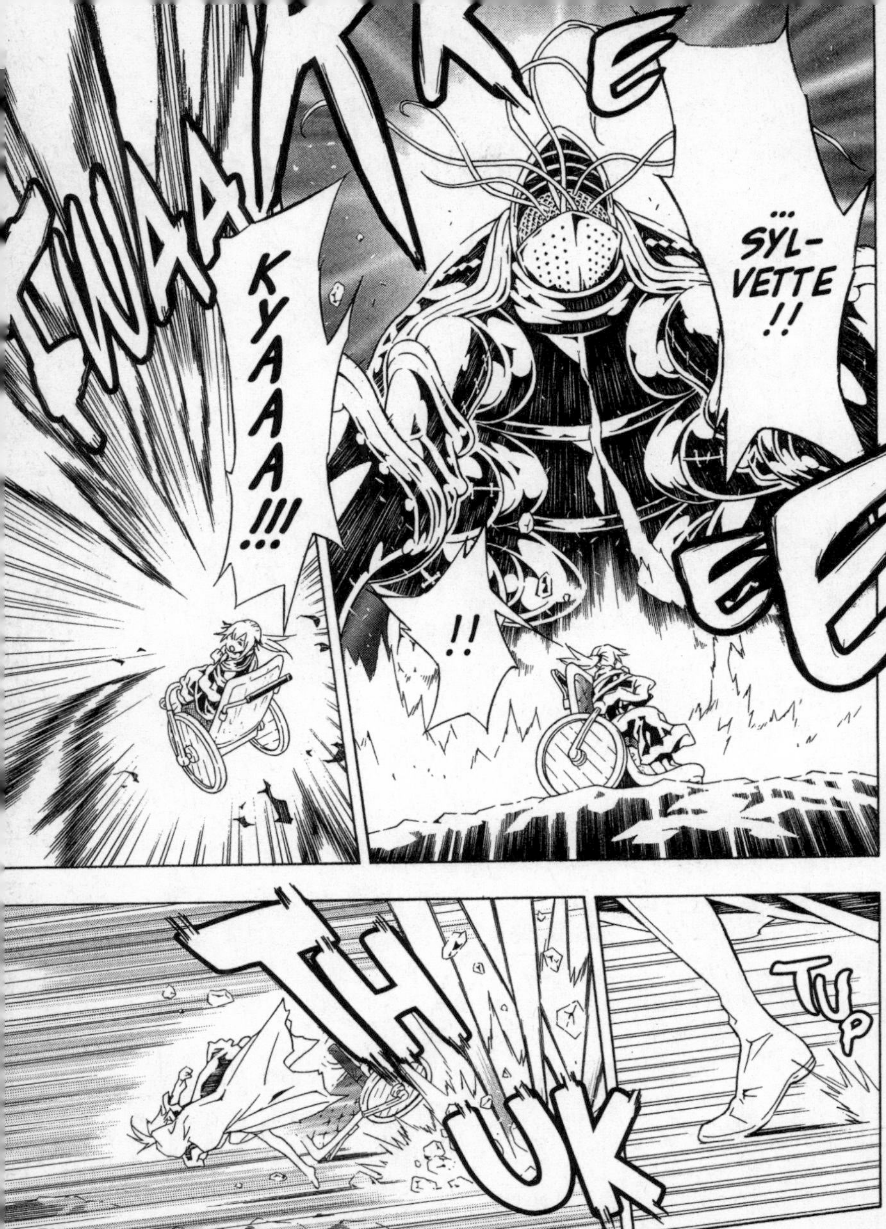
...SYL-
VETTE
!!
!!
KYAAAA!!!
TUP
THUK

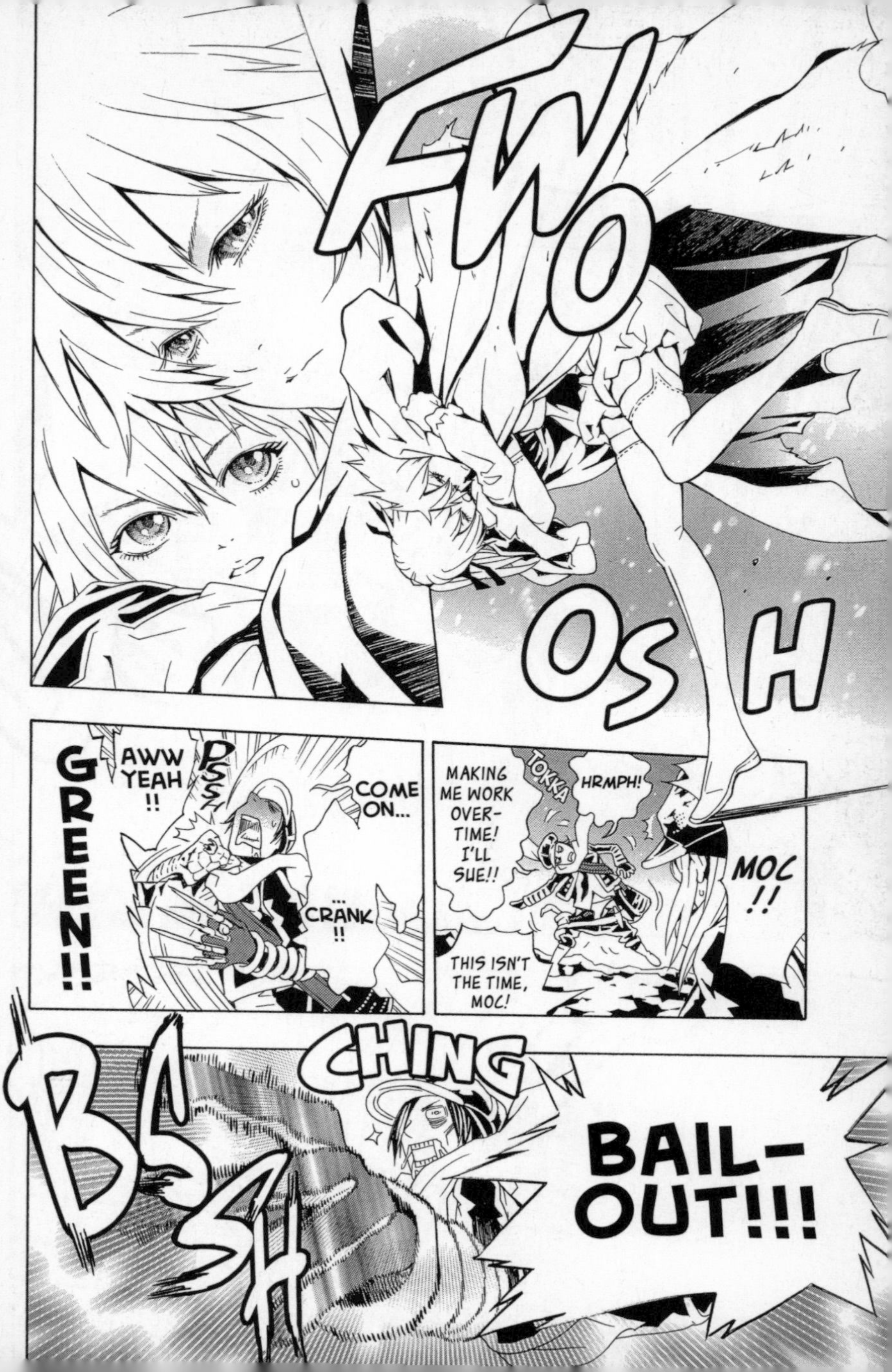
FWO
OSH
HRMPH!
TOKKA
MAKING ME WORK OVER-TIME! I'LL SUE!!
MOC!!
THIS ISN'T THE TIME, MOC!
COME ON...
PSSH
AWW YEAH!!
GREEN!!
...CRANK!!
BAIL-OUT!!!
CHING
BASH

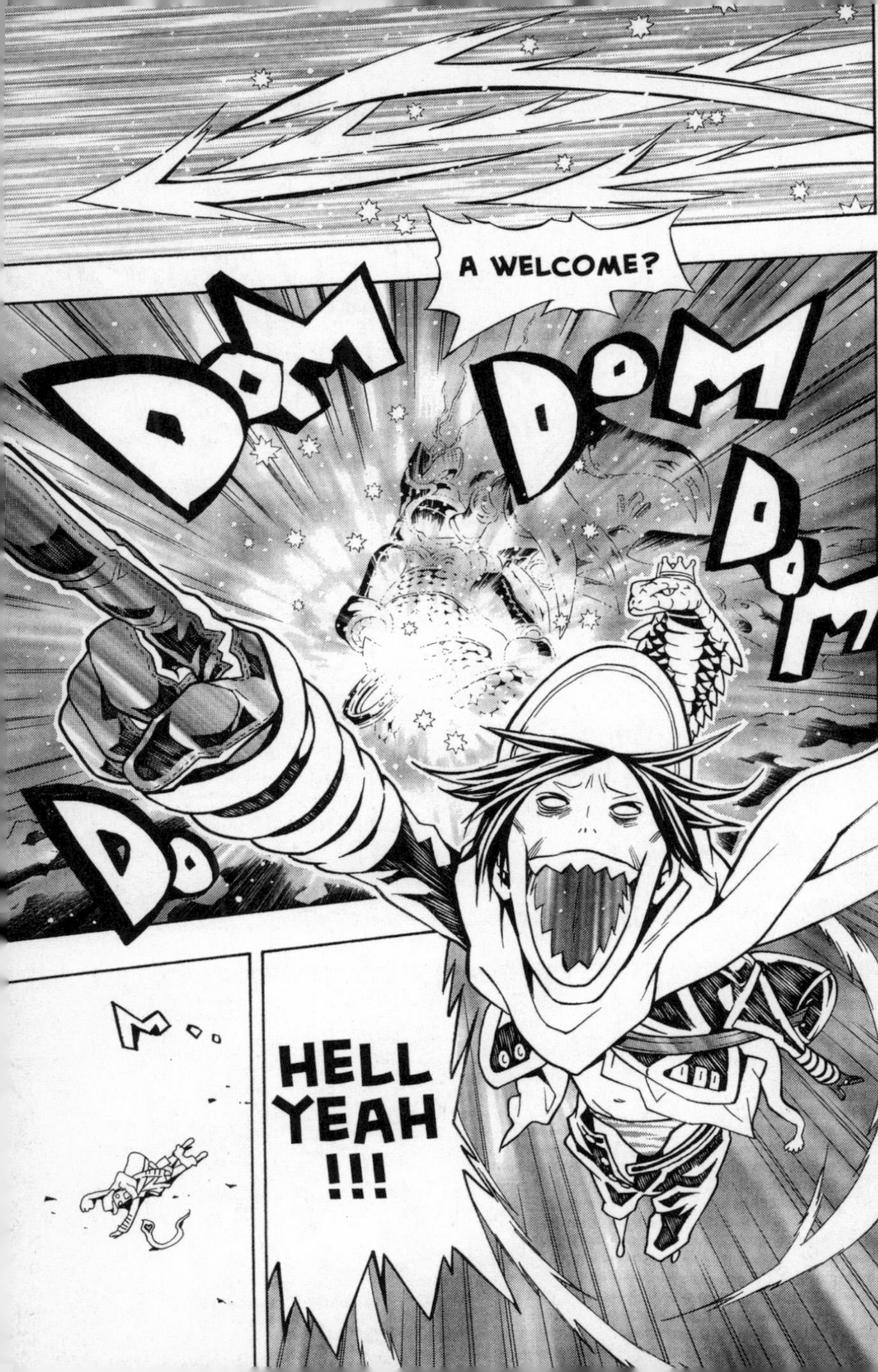
A WELCOME?
DOM
DOM
DOM
DOM
DO
HELL YEAH !!!
M..

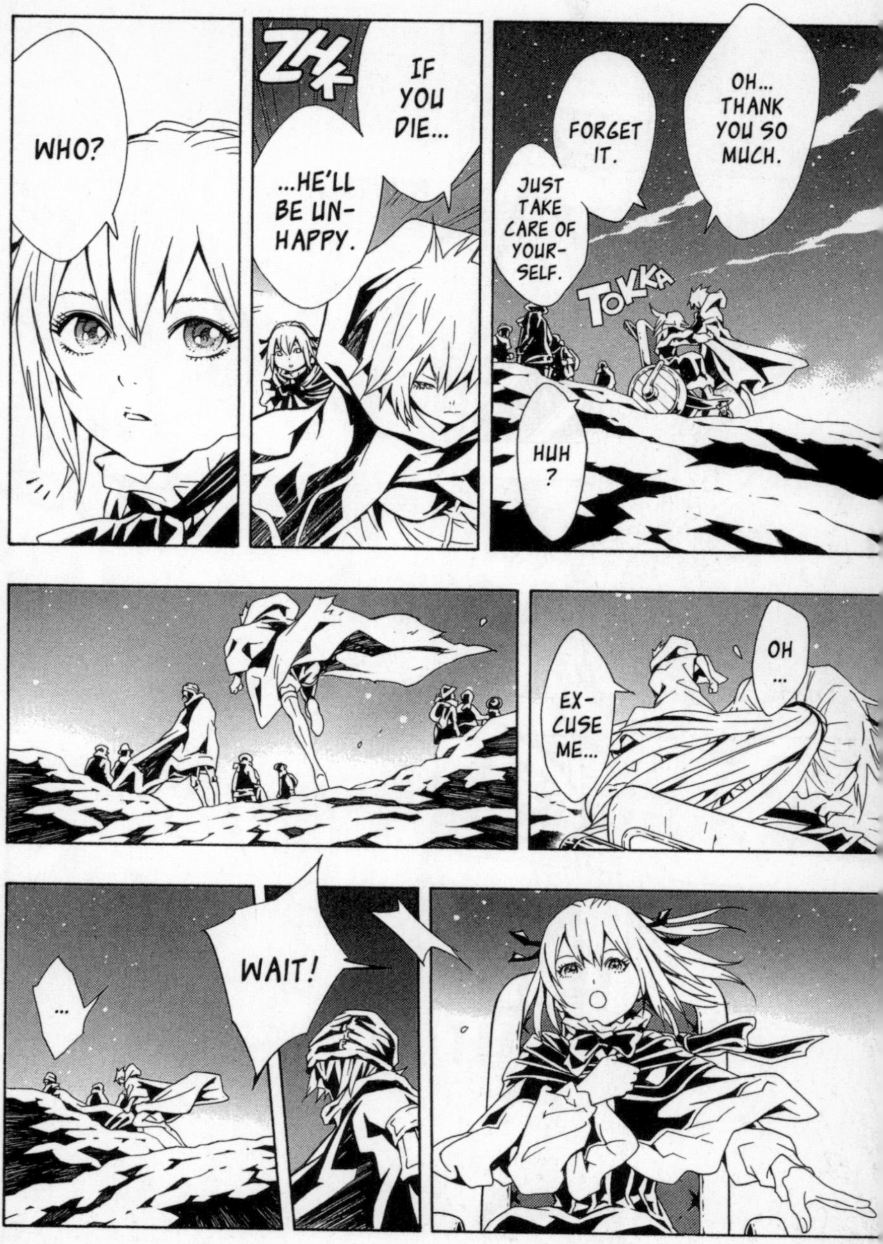
OH... THANK YOU SO MUCH.
FORGET IT.
JUST TAKE CARE OF YOUR-SELF.
TOKKA
HUH?
ZHK
IF YOU DIE...
...HE'LL BE UN-HAPPY.
WHO?
OH ...
EX-CUSE ME...
WAIT!
...

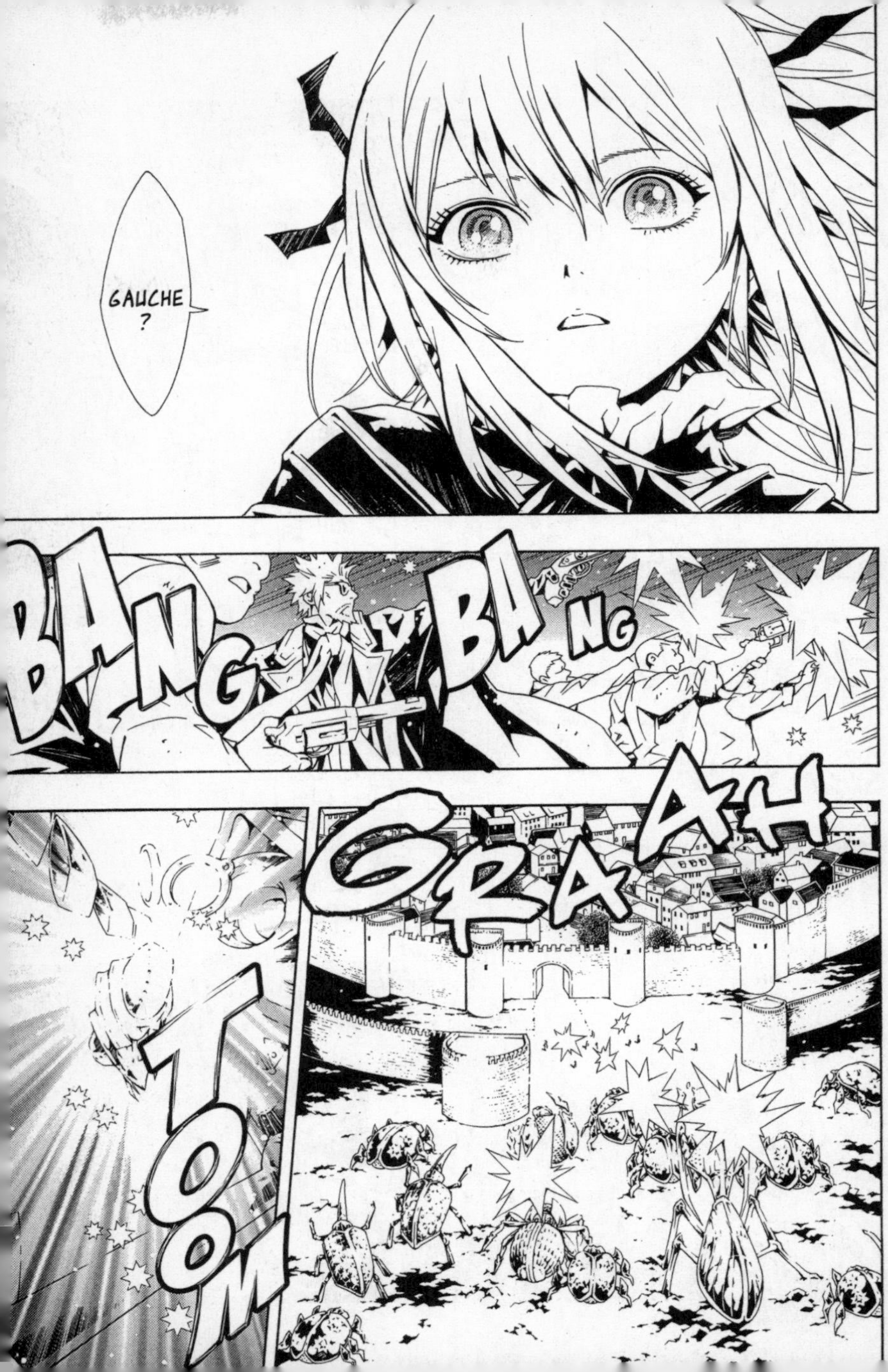
GAUCHE
?
BANG
BANG
GRAAH
TOOOM

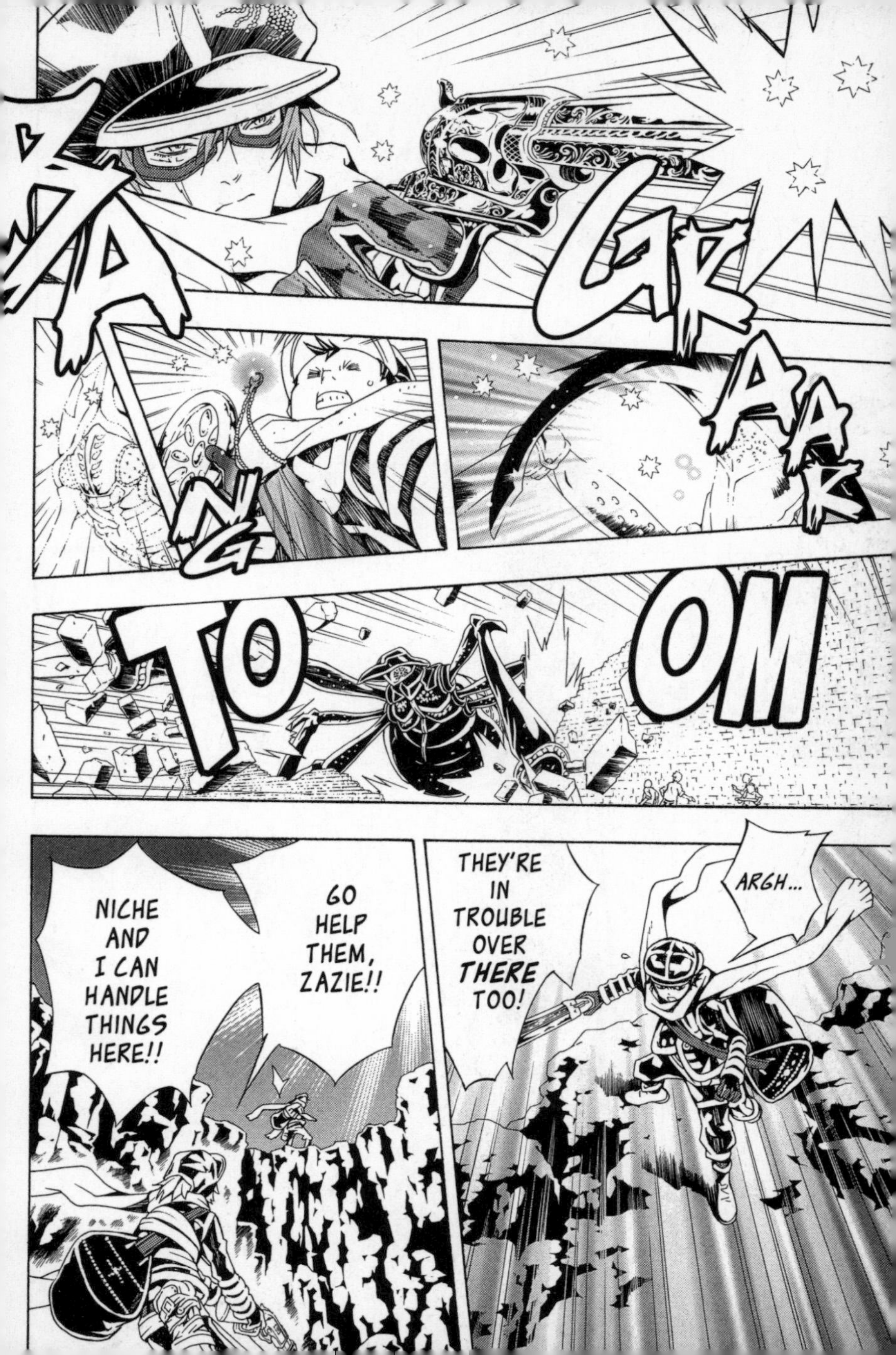
TOOM
ARGH...
THEY'RE IN TROUBLE OVER THERE TOO!
GO HELP THEM, ZAZIE!!
NICHE AND I CAN HANDLE THINGS HERE!!

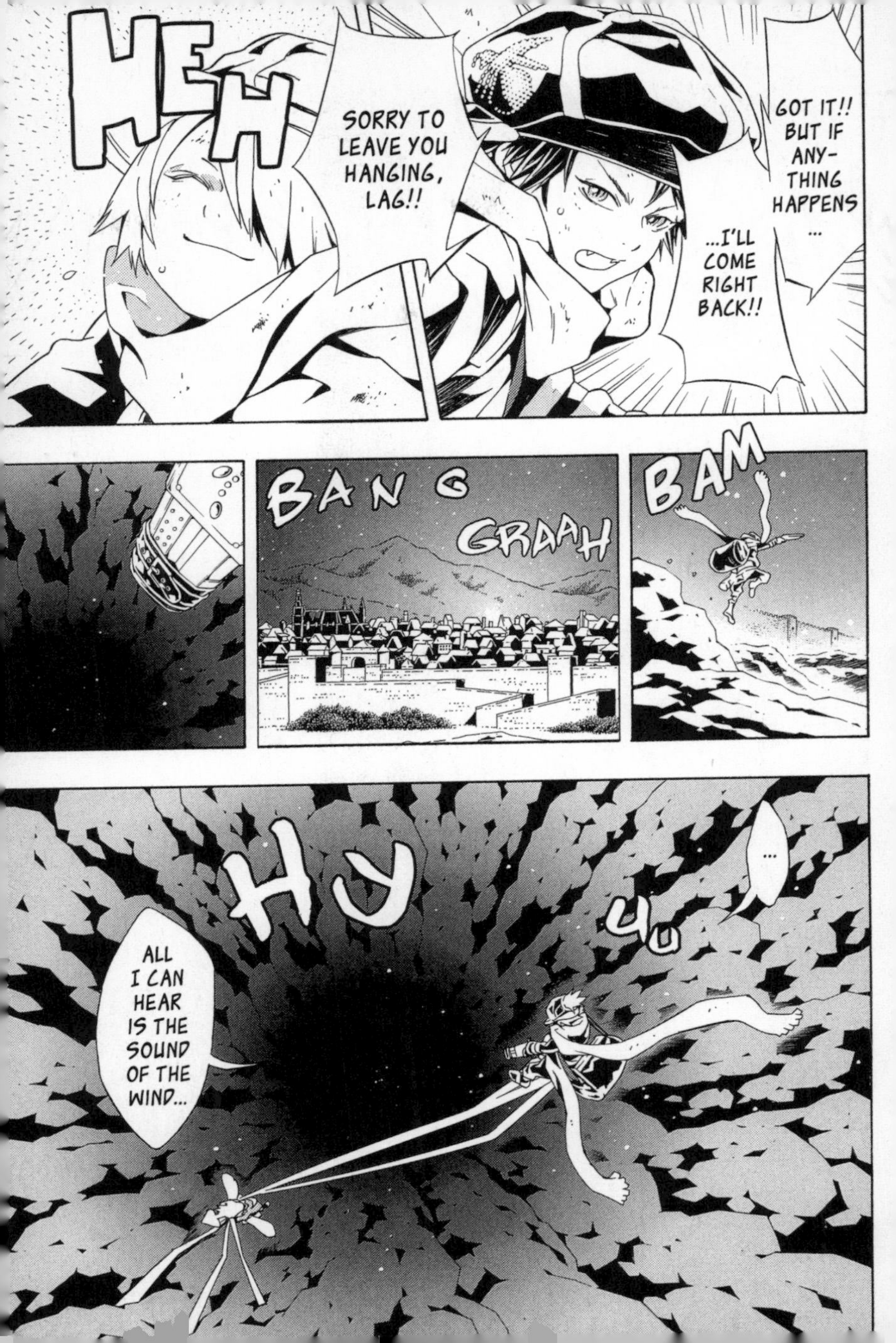
GOT IT!! BUT IF ANY-THING HAPPENS ...
...I'LL COME RIGHT BACK!!
SORRY TO LEAVE YOU HANGING, LAG!!
HEH
BAM
BANG
GRAAH
...
HYUU
ALL I CAN HEAR IS THE SOUND OF THE WIND...

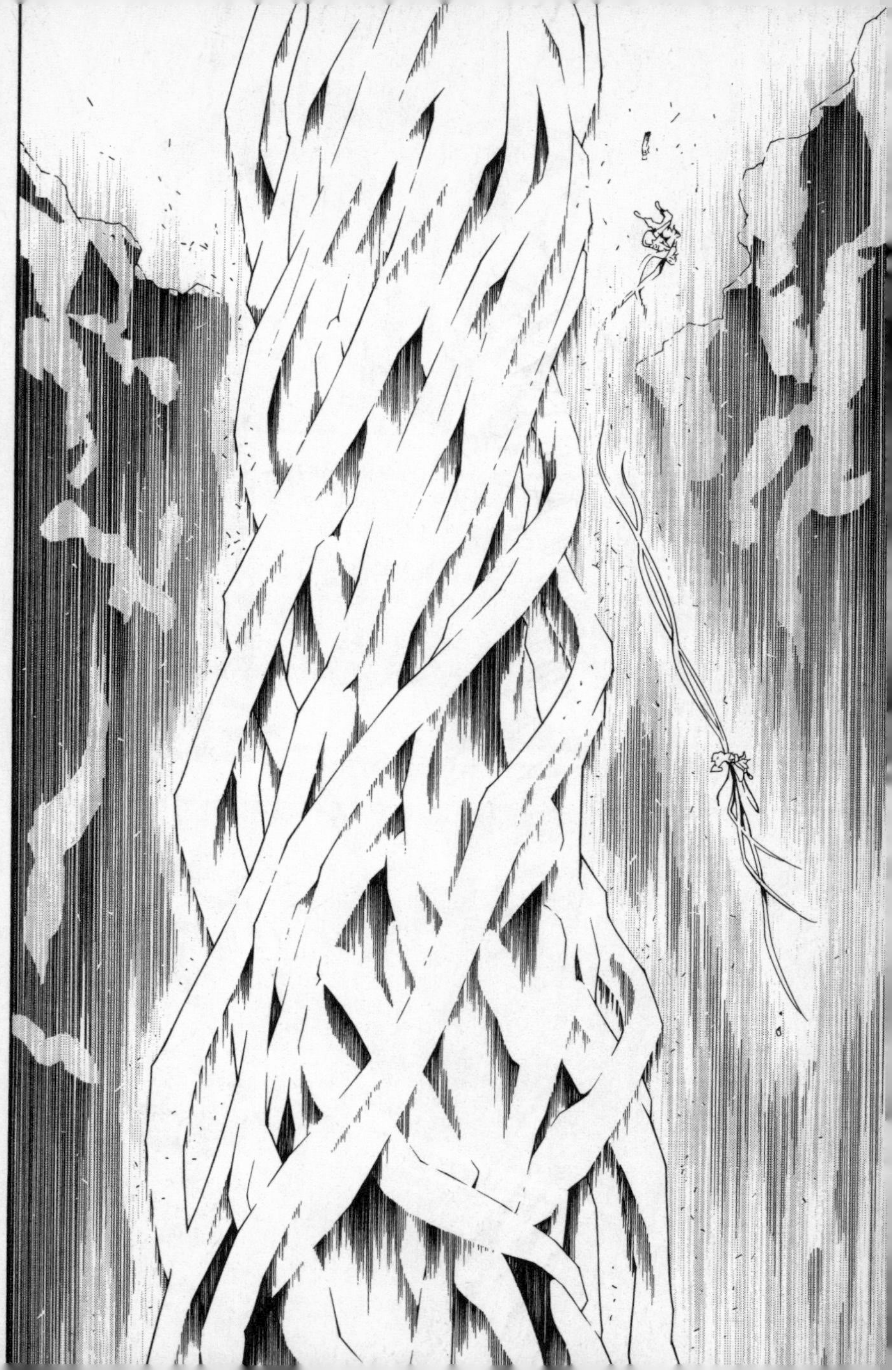

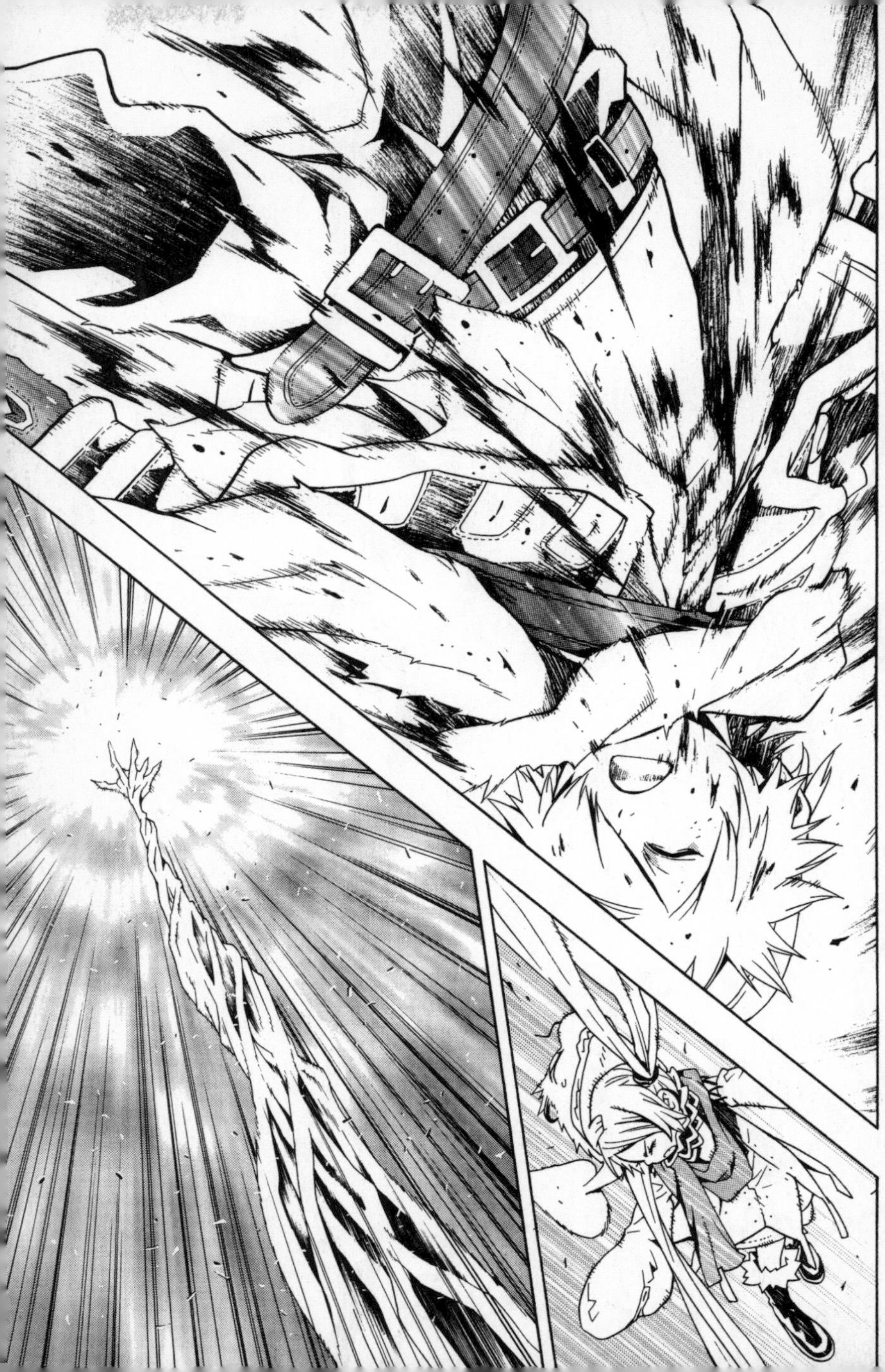

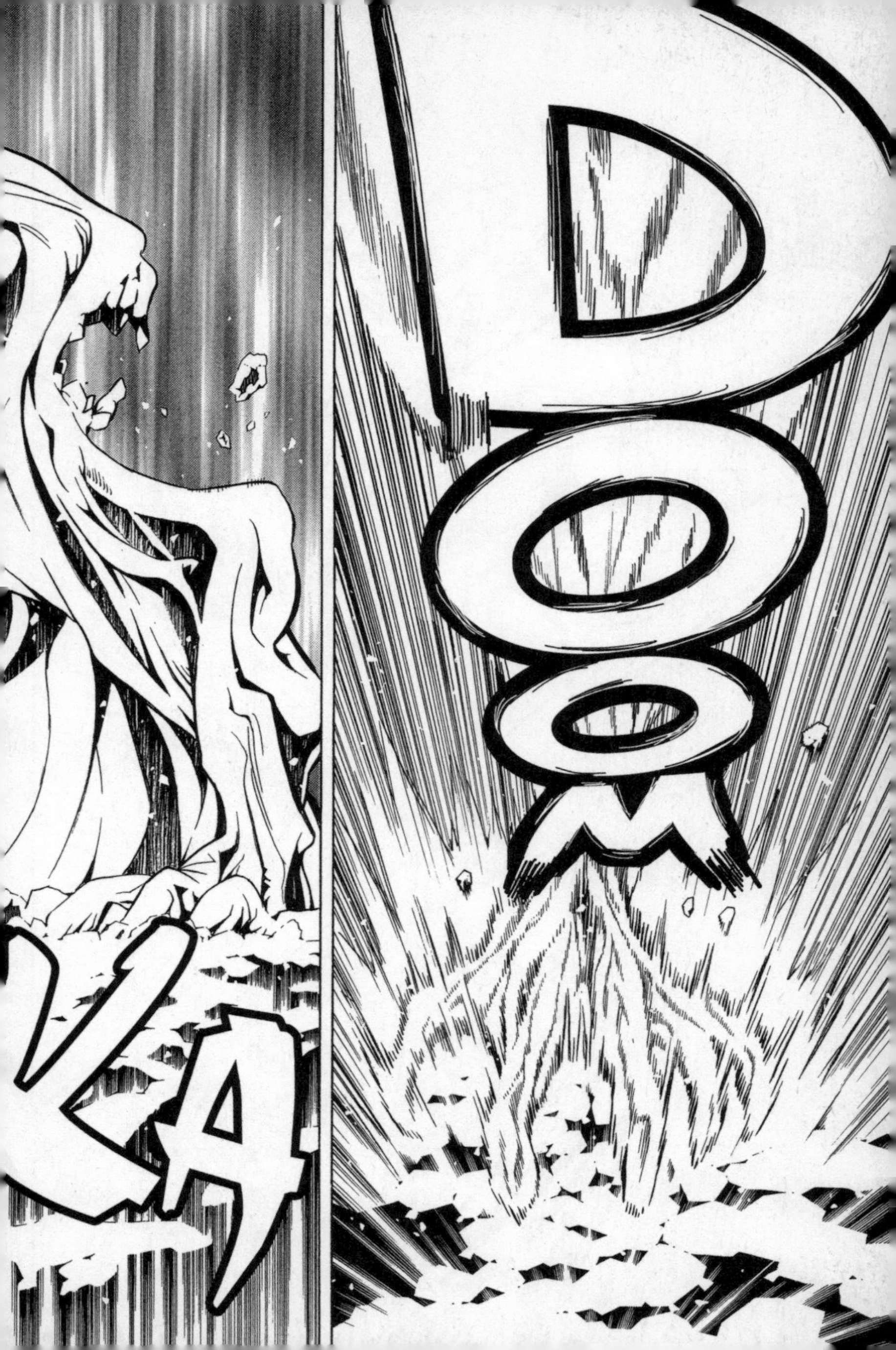
DOOM

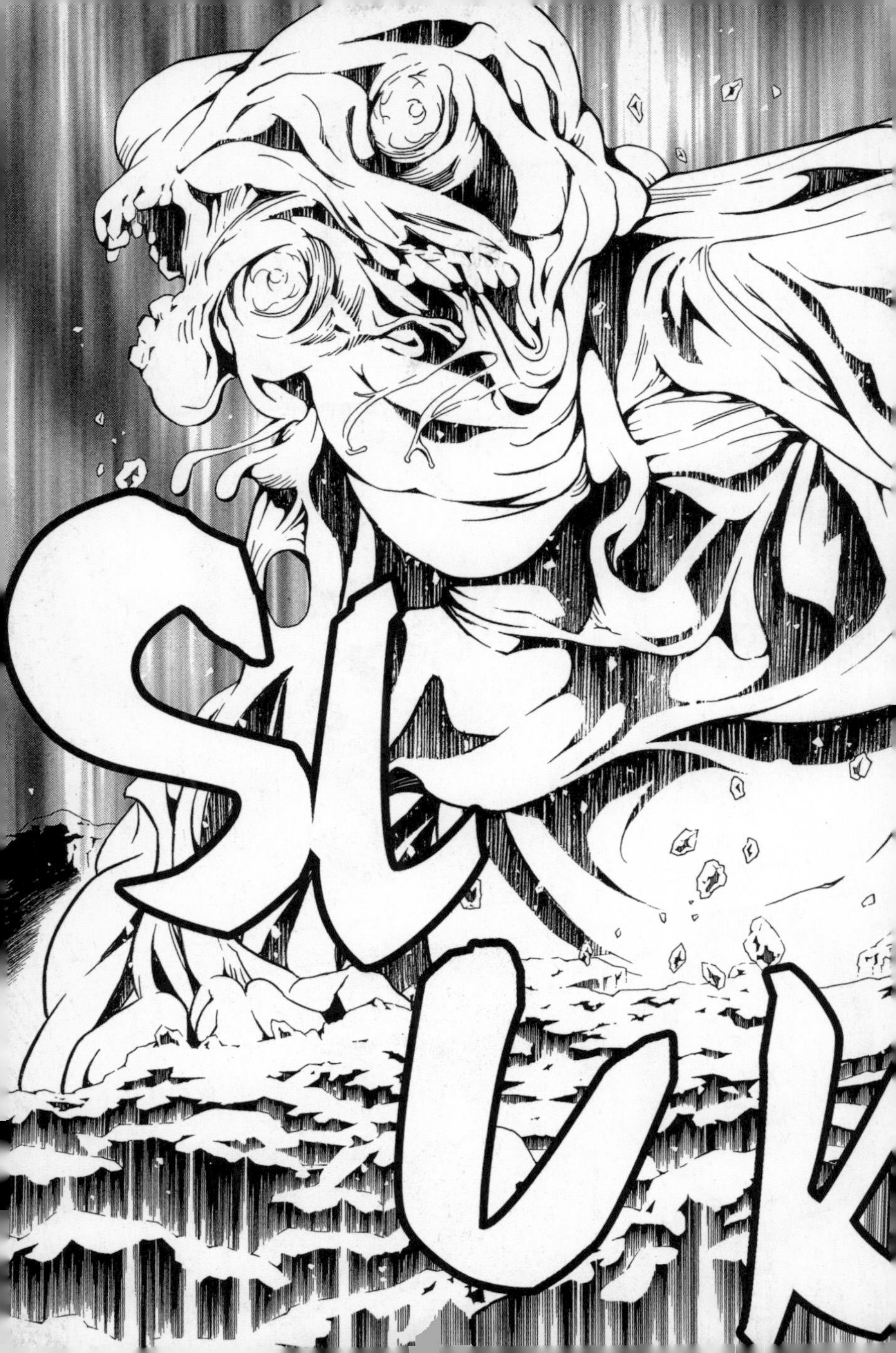
SLUK

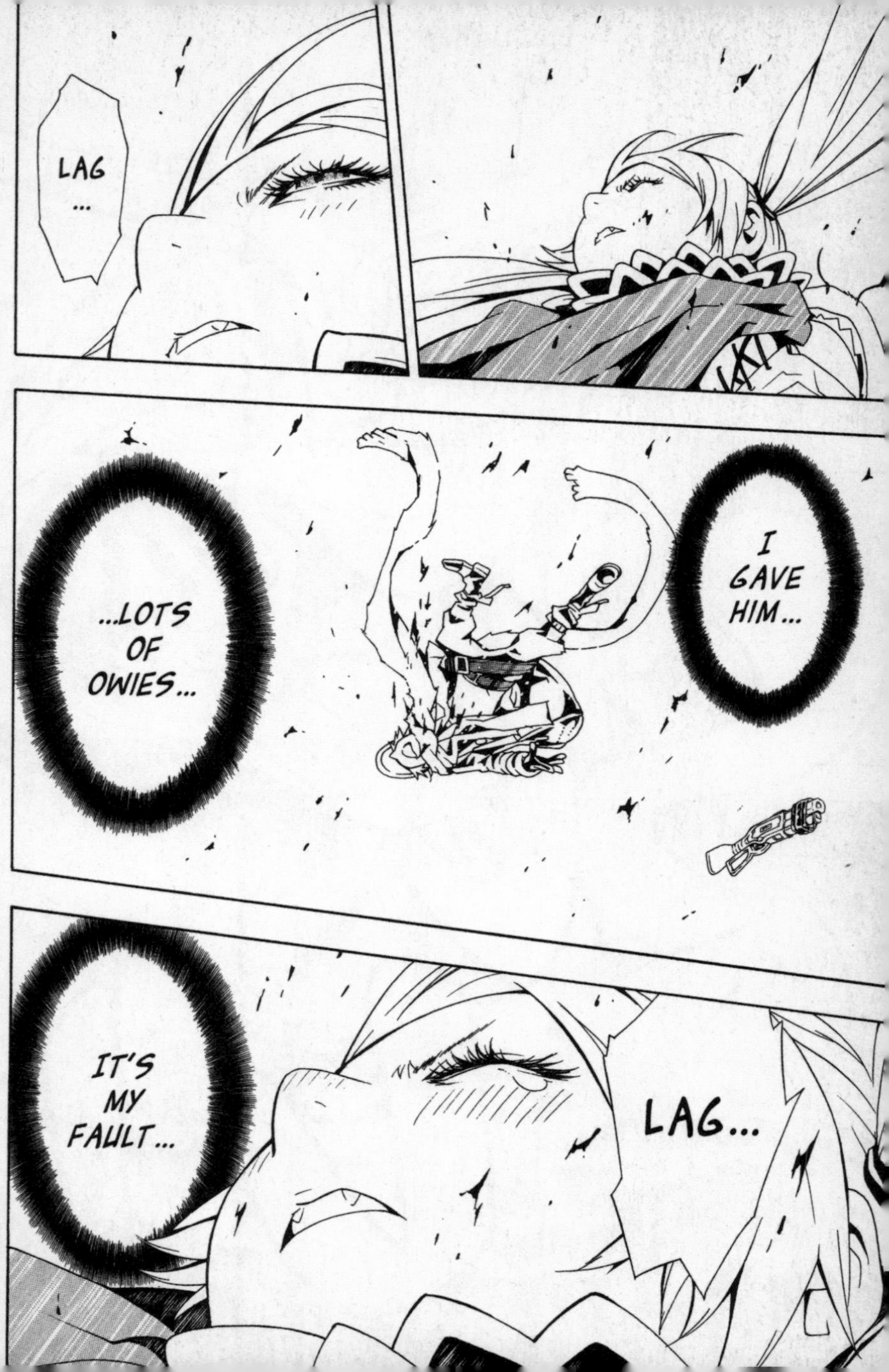
LAG ...
I GAVE HIM...
...LOTS OF OWIES...
LAG...
IT'S MY FAULT...

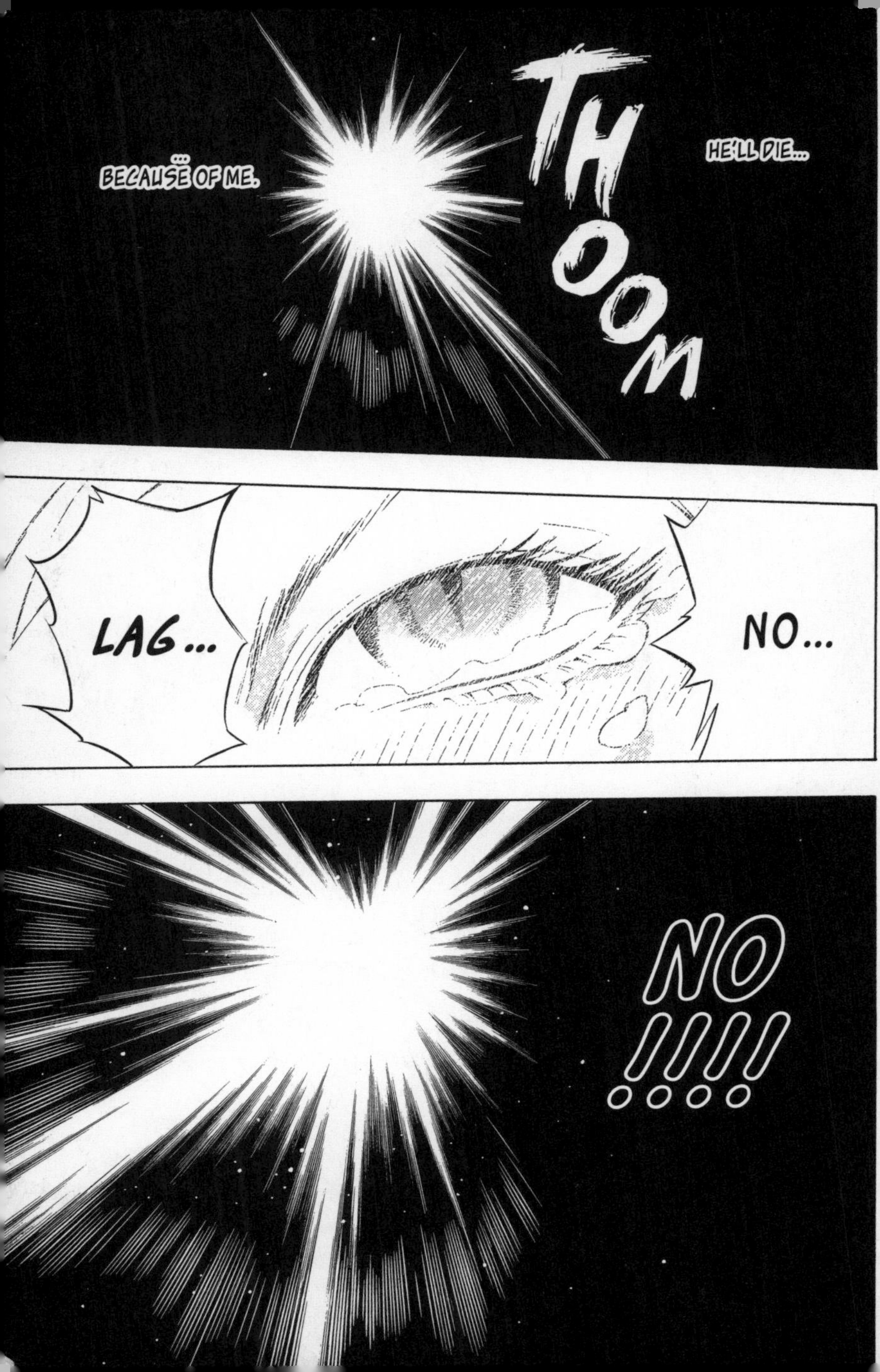
HE'LL DIE...
THOOM
...BECAUSE OF ME.
NO...
LAG...
NO!!!!

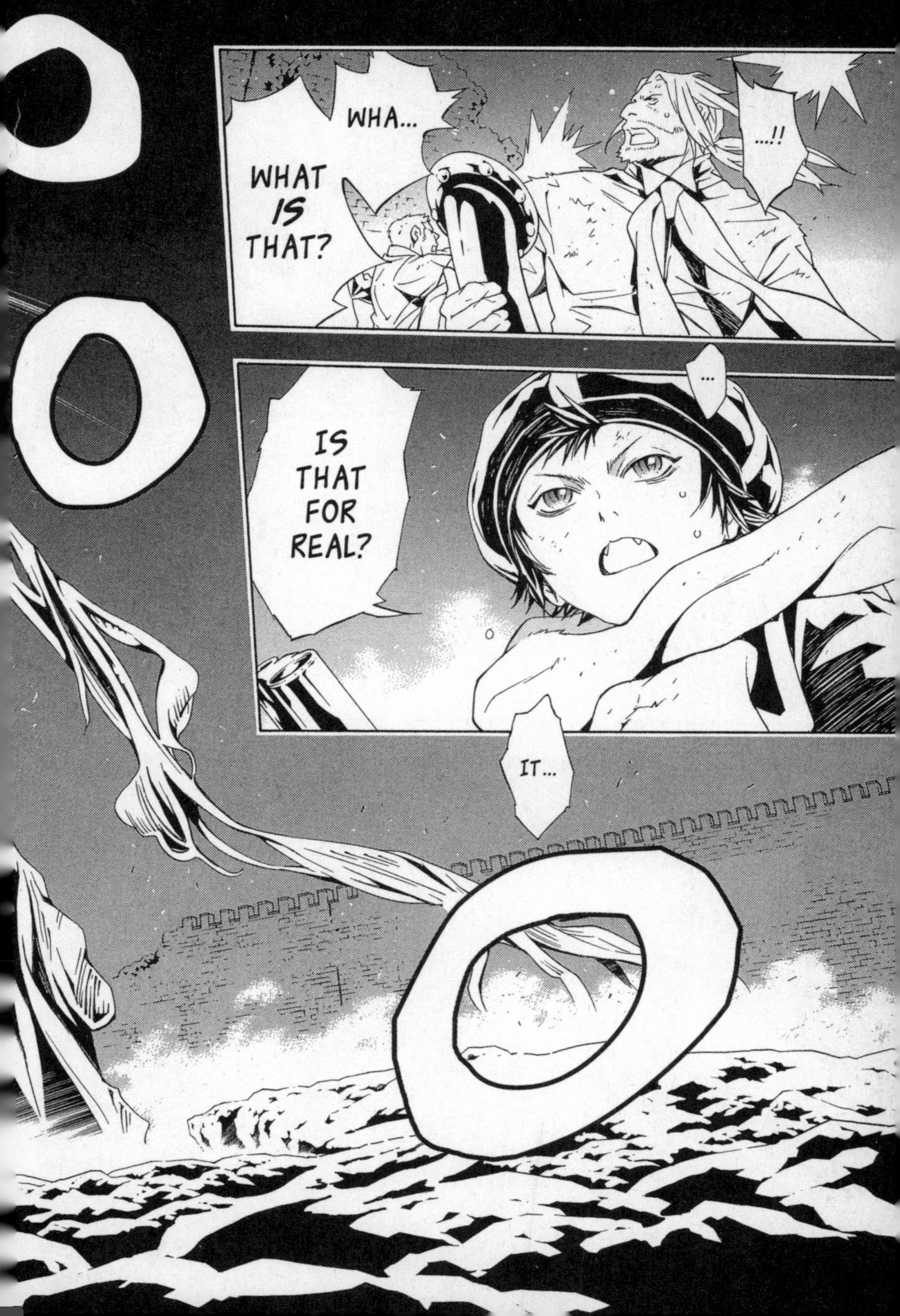
...!!
WHA...
WHAT *IS* THAT?
...
IS THAT FOR REAL?
IT...

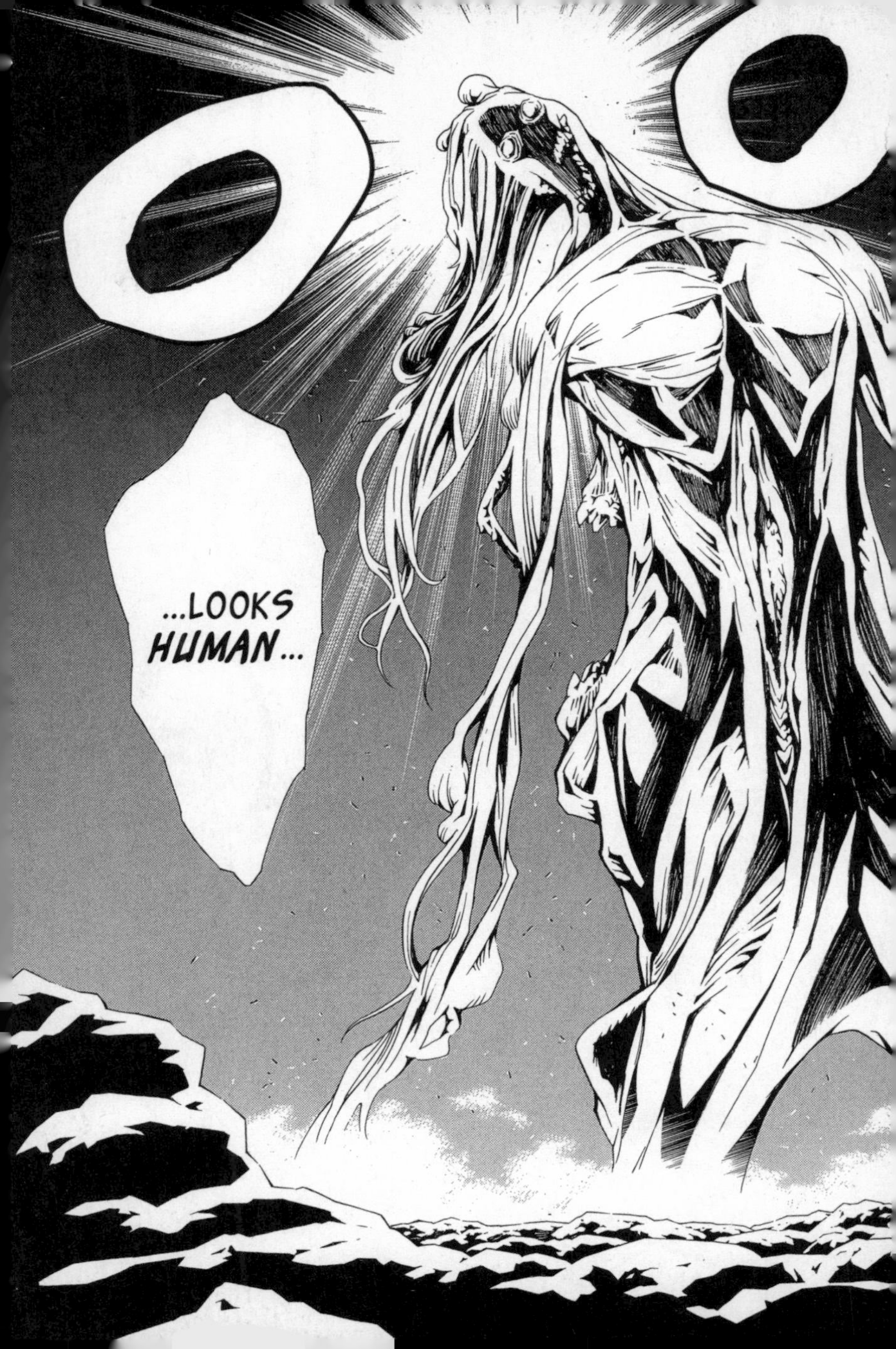
...LOOKS HUMAN...

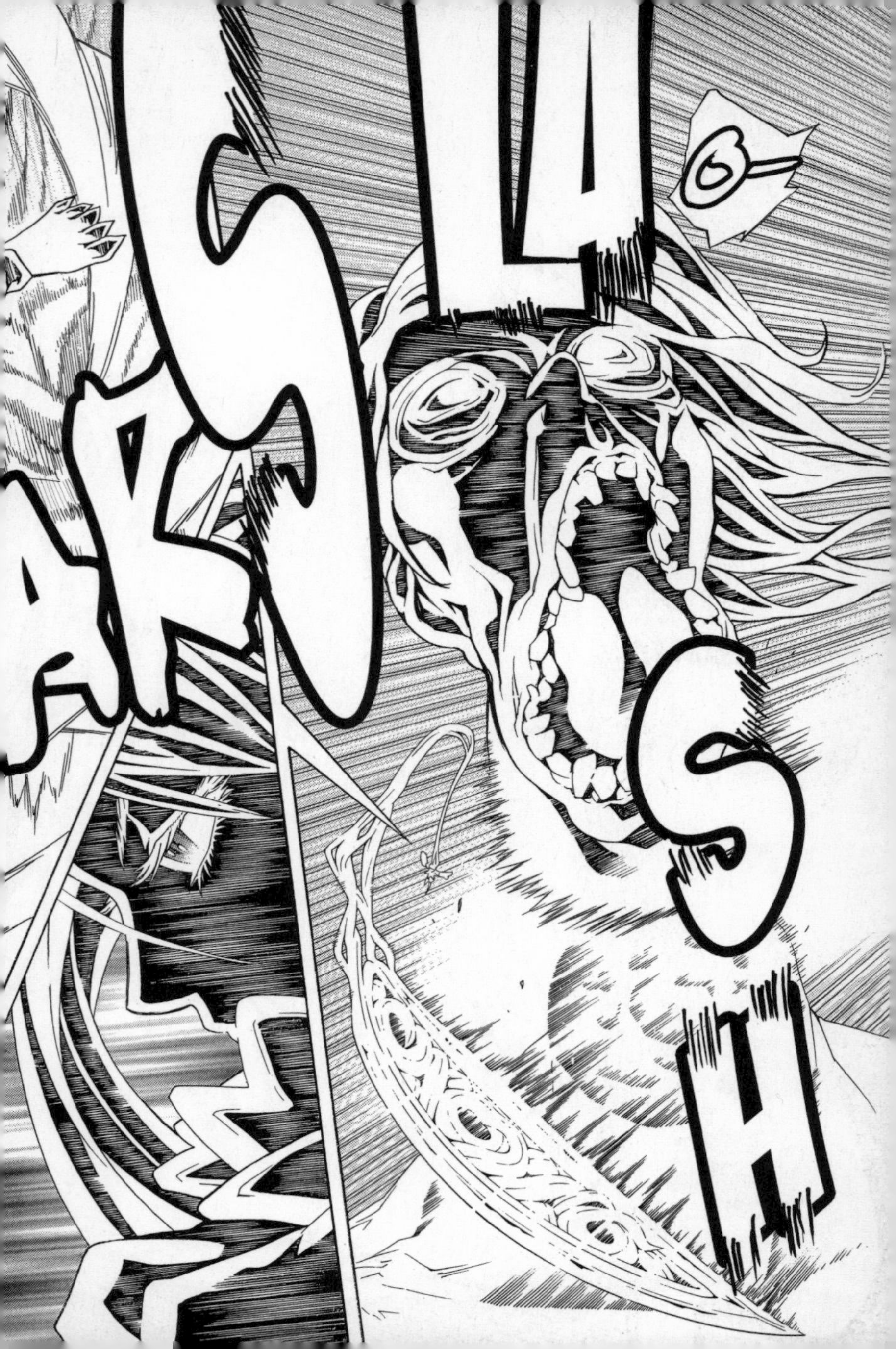
SLASH

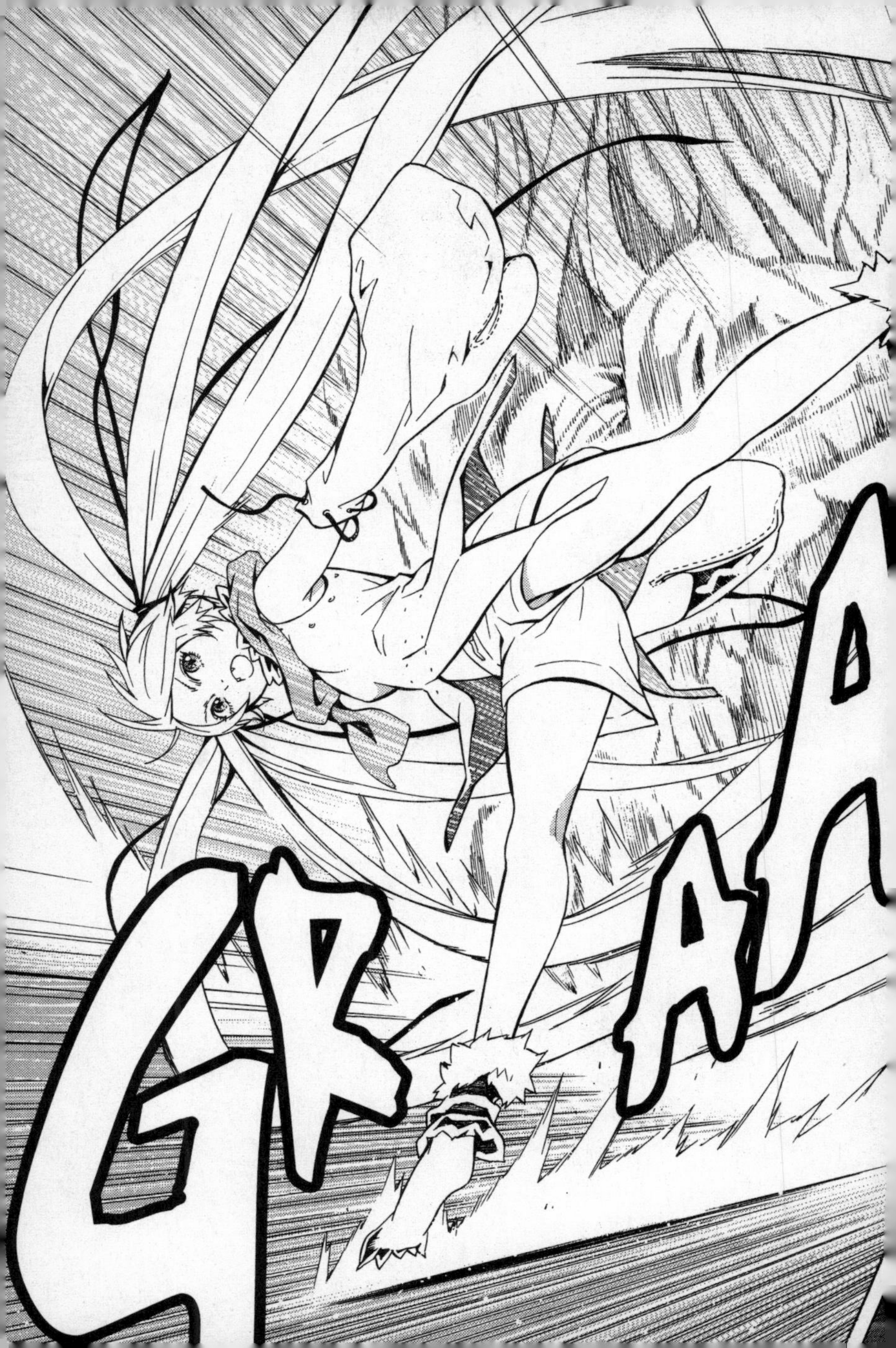
GRAA

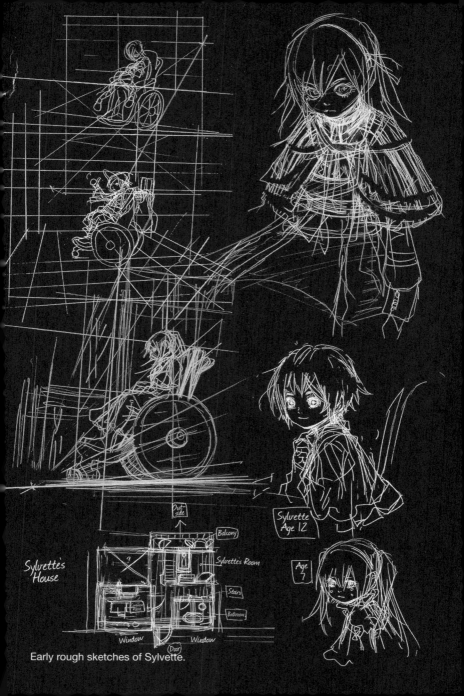

Out side

Balcony

Sylvette's Room

Stairs

Bathroom

Sylvette's
House

Window

Door

Window

Sylvette
Age 12

Age
7

Early rough sketches of Sylvette.

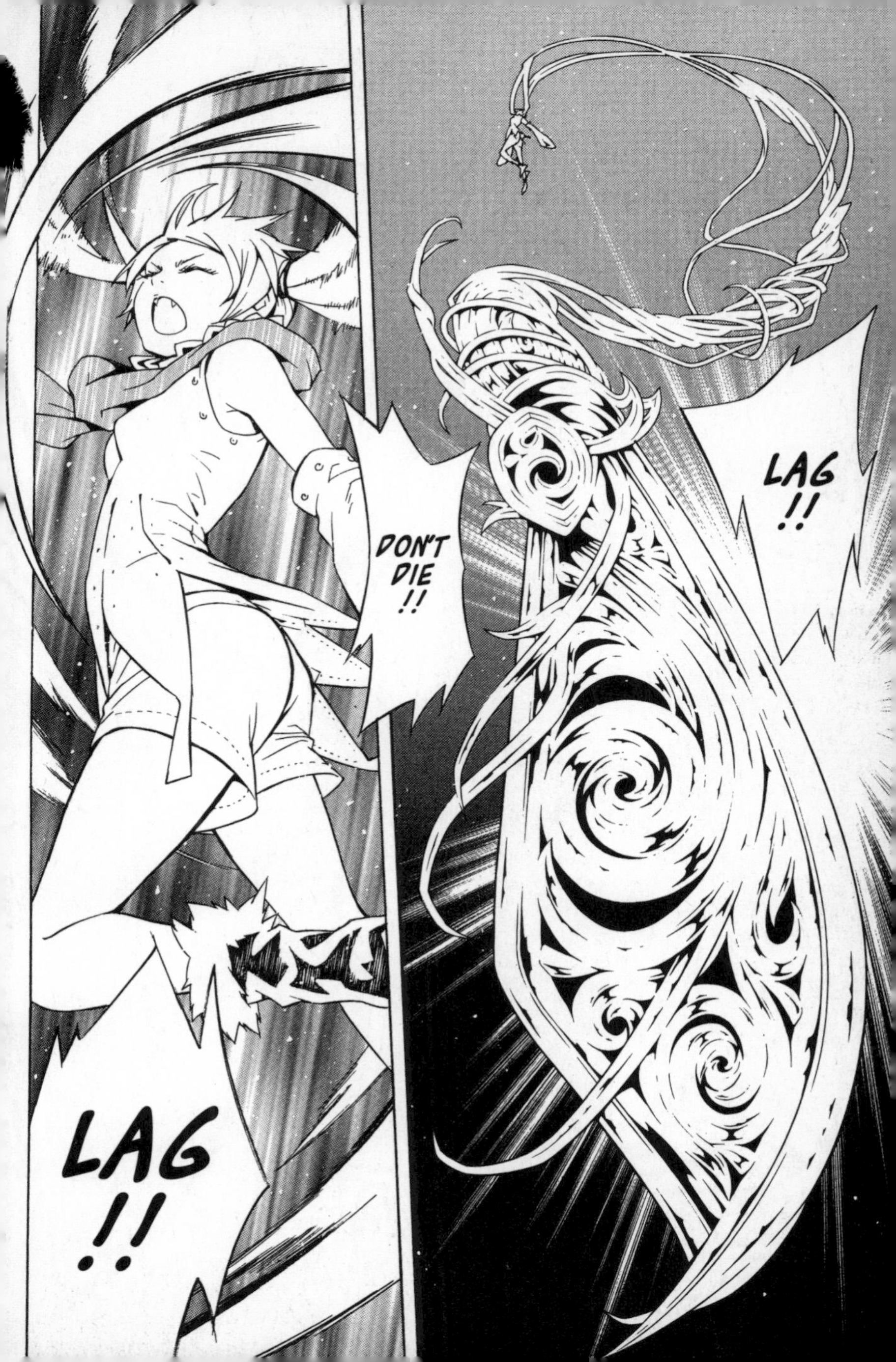
LAG !!
DON'T DIE !!
LAG !!

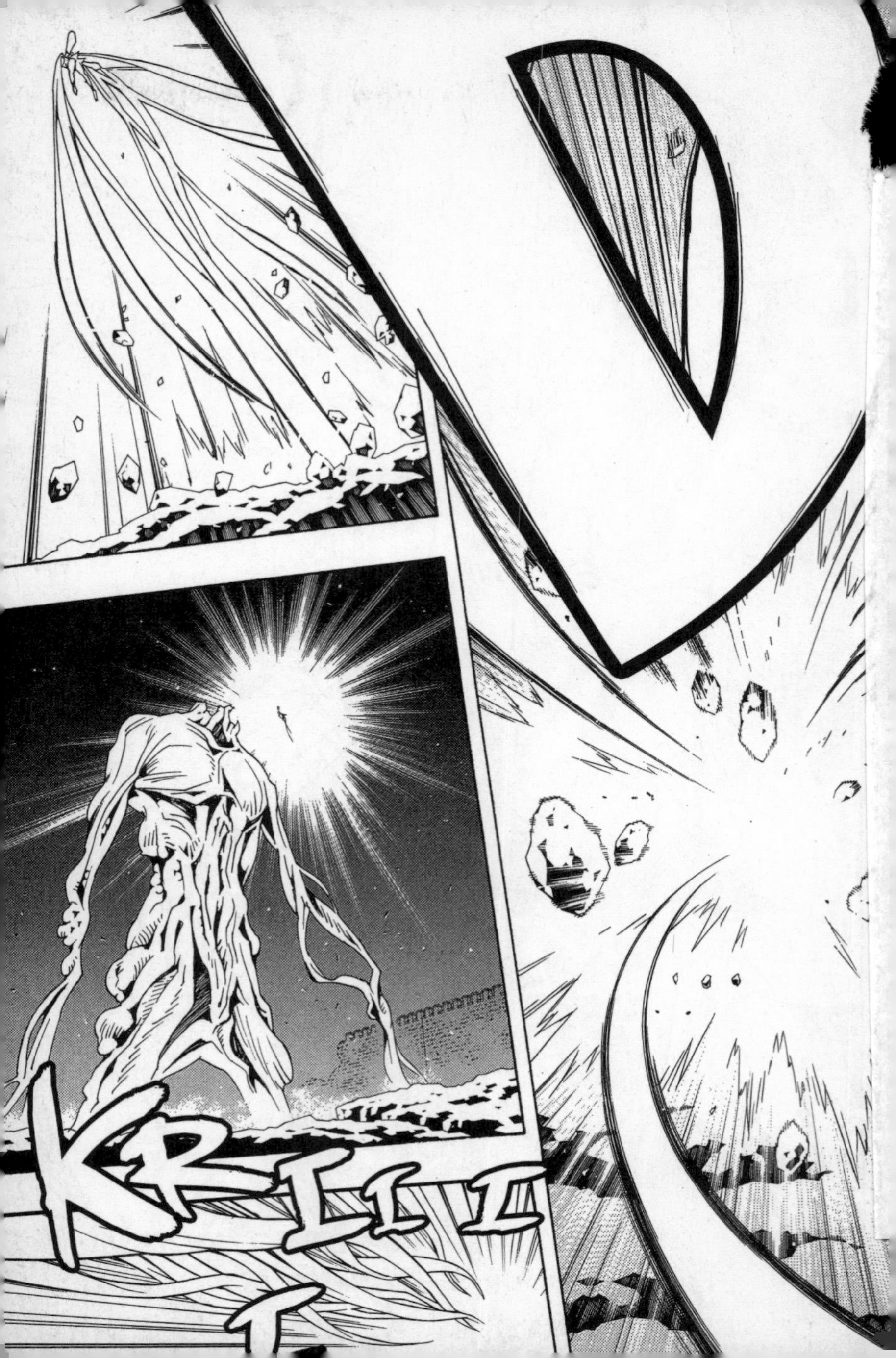
KRIII

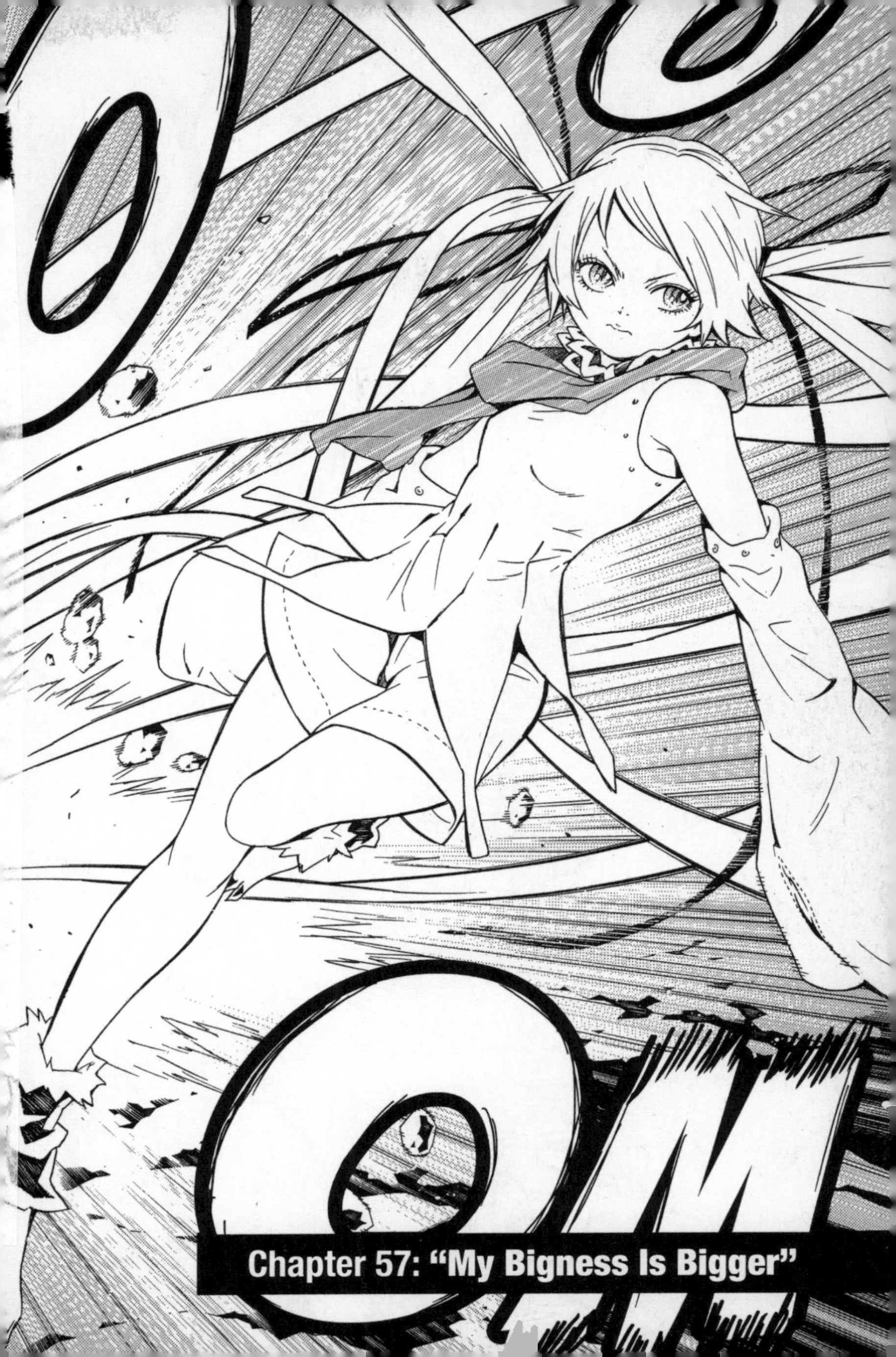

Chapter 57: "My Bigness Is Bigger"

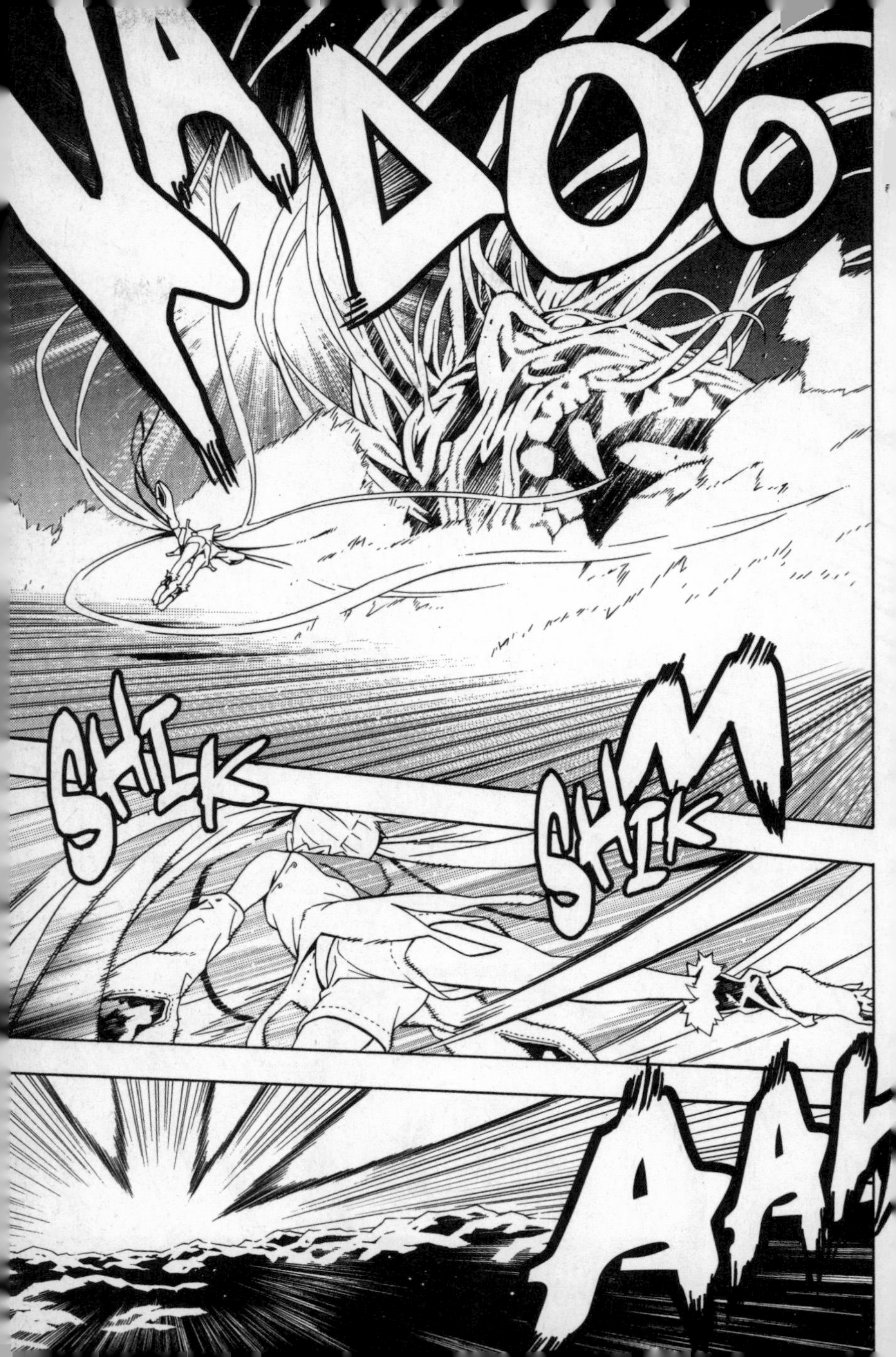
SHIK
SHIK

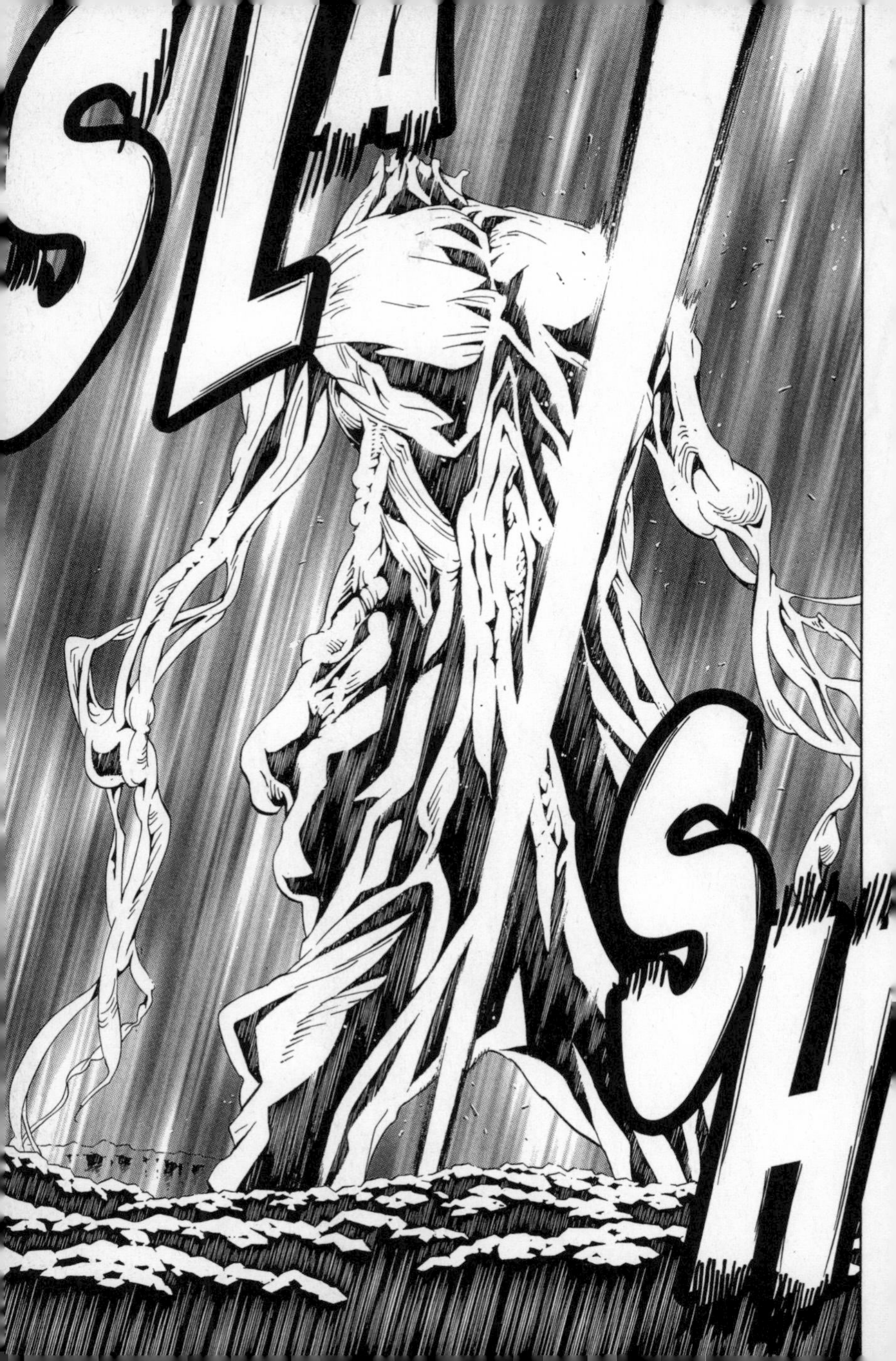
SLASH

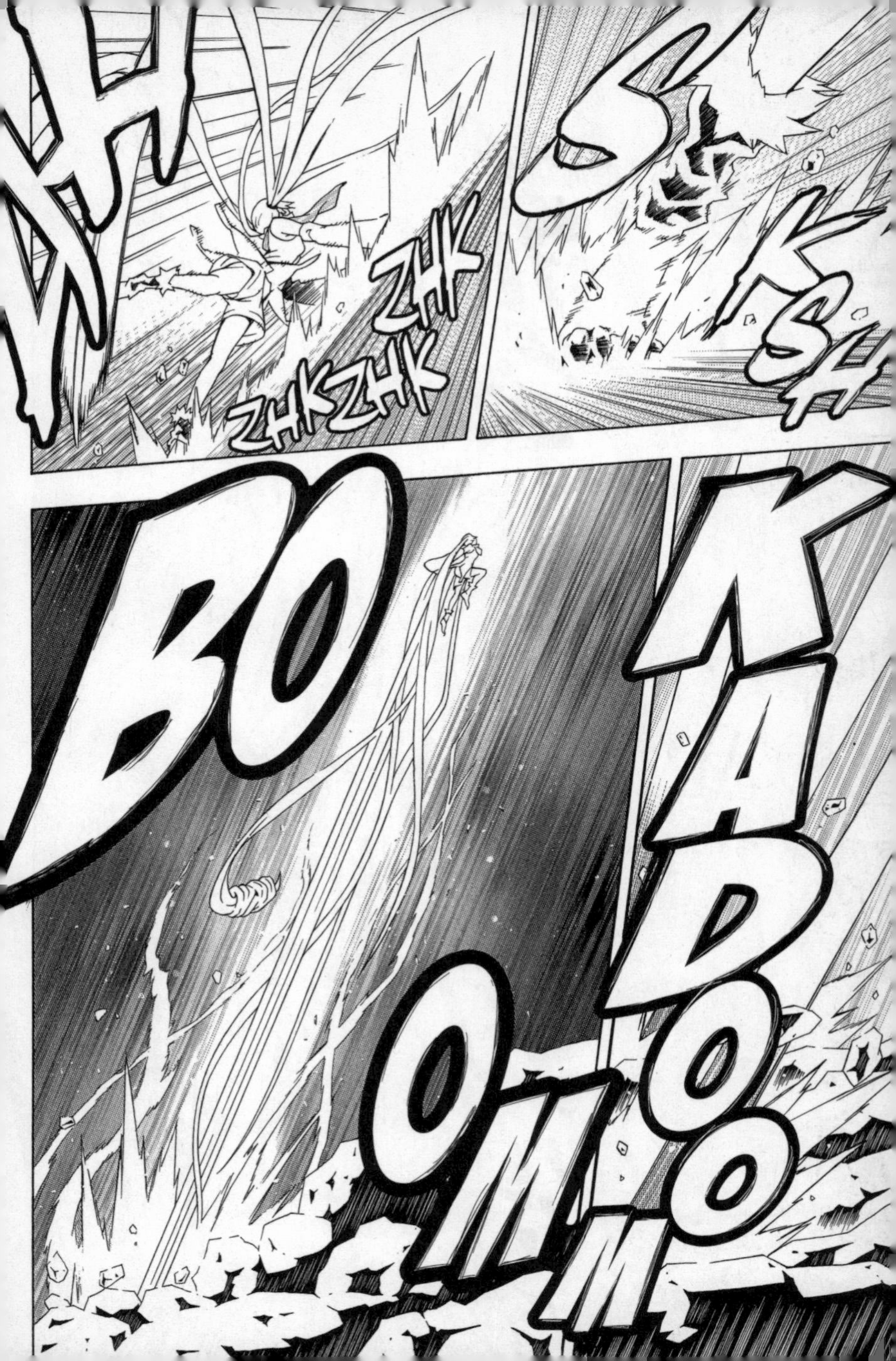
KSH
ZHK
ZHKZHK
KADOOM
BOOM

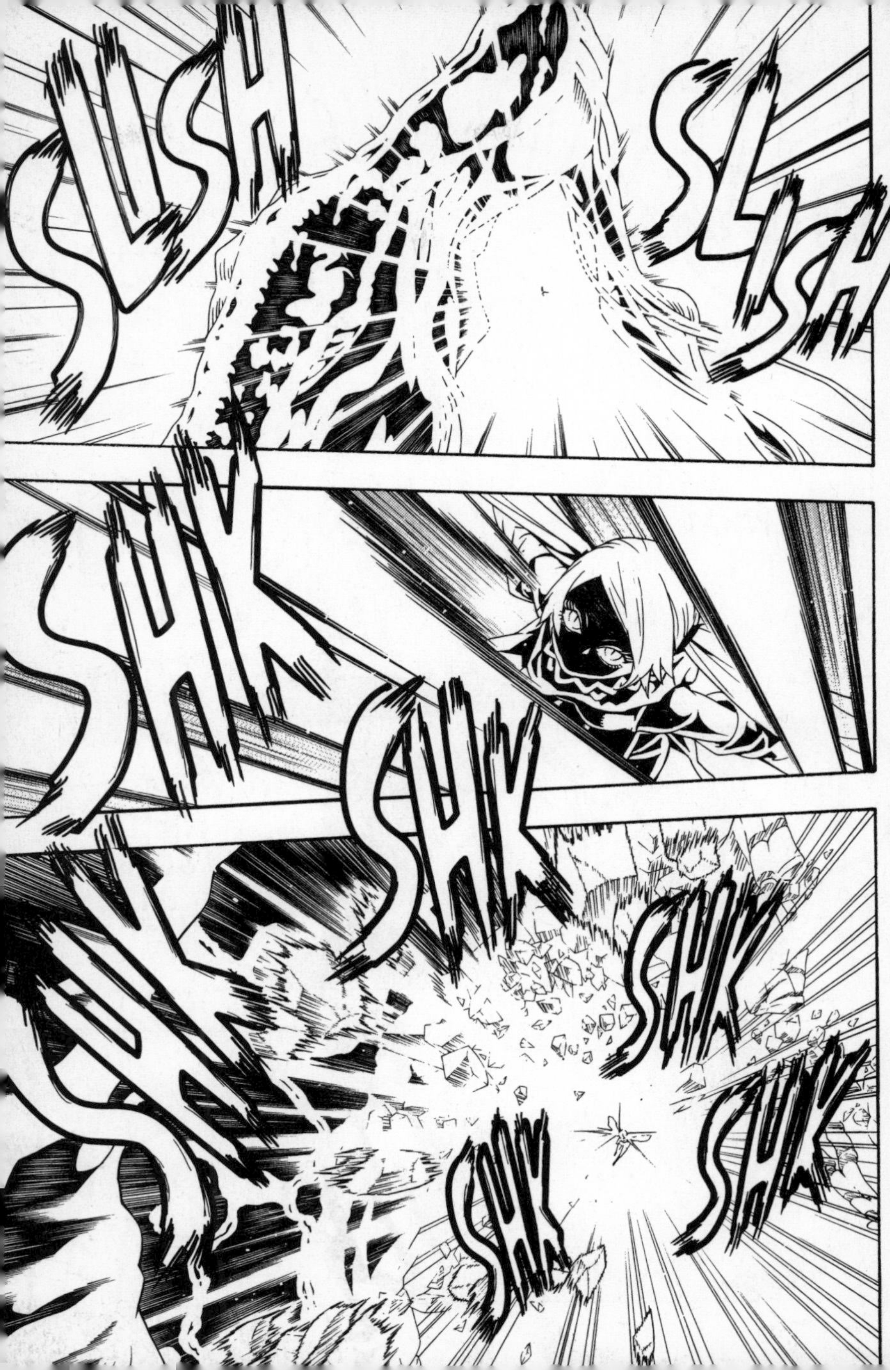
SLISH
SLISH
SHK
SHK
SHK
SHK
SHK
SHK

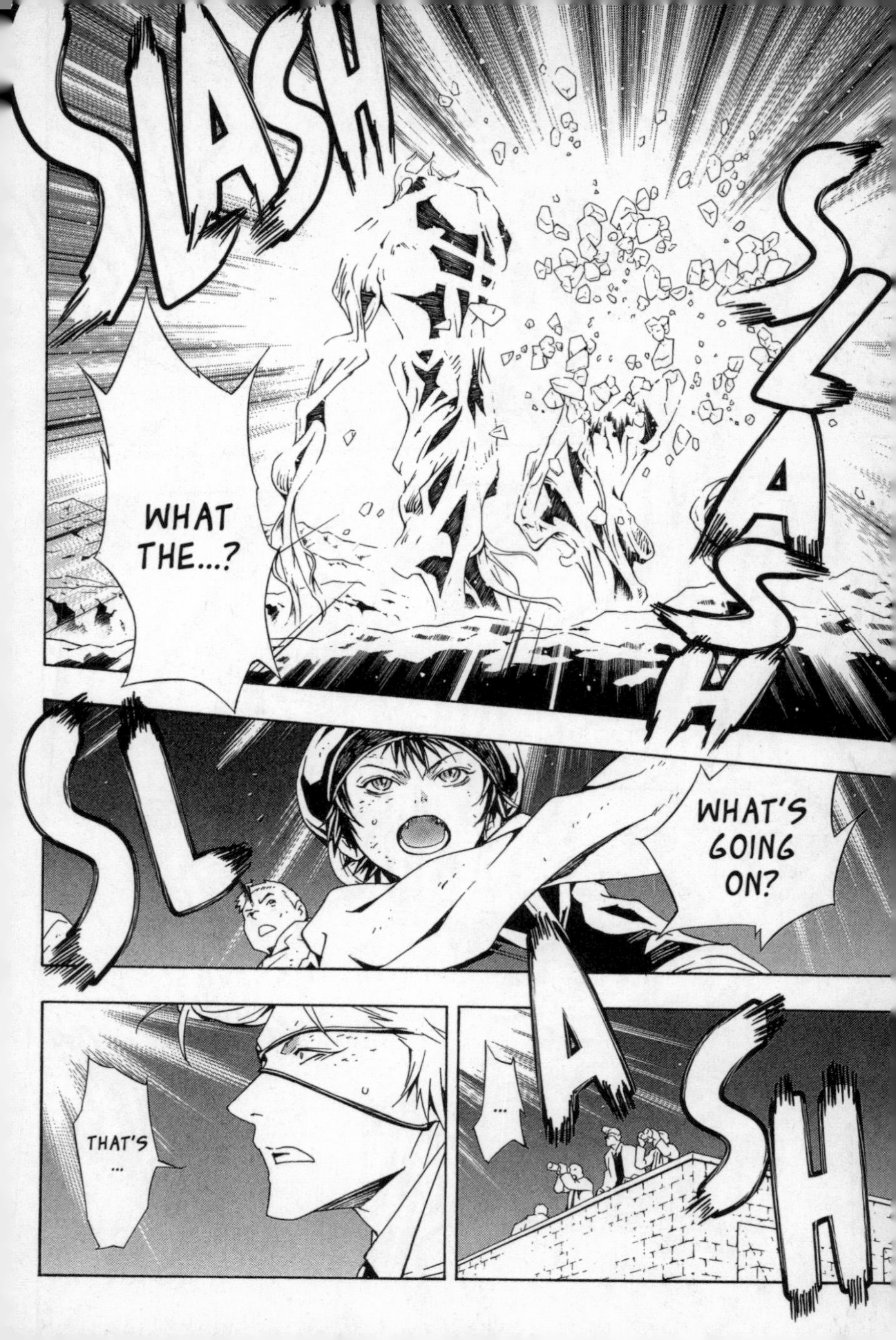
SLASH
SLASH
WHAT THE...?
WHAT'S GOING ON?
SLASH
...
THAT'S ...

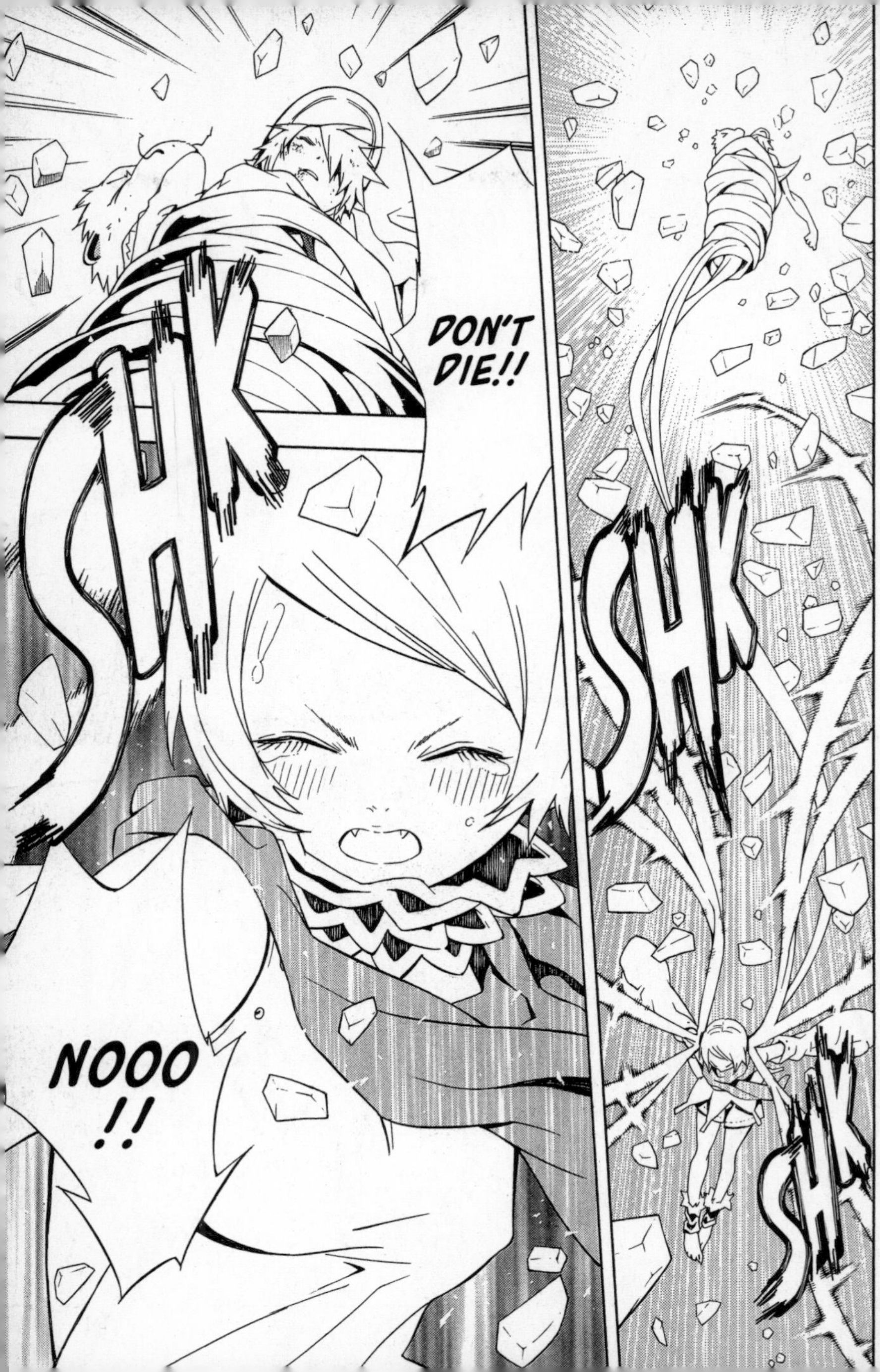
SHK
SHK
DON'T DIE!!
SHK
NOOO !!

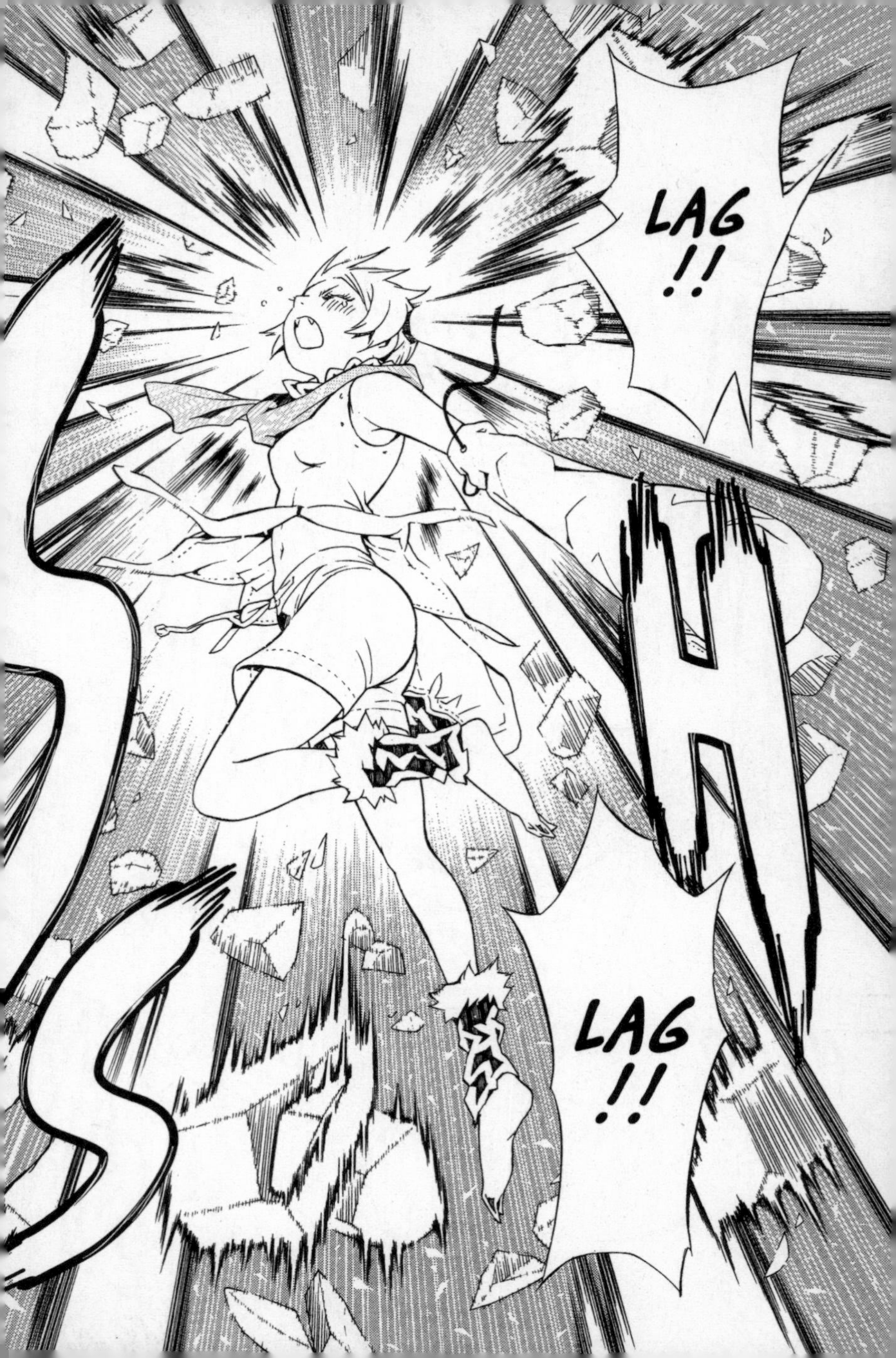
LAG !!
LAG !!

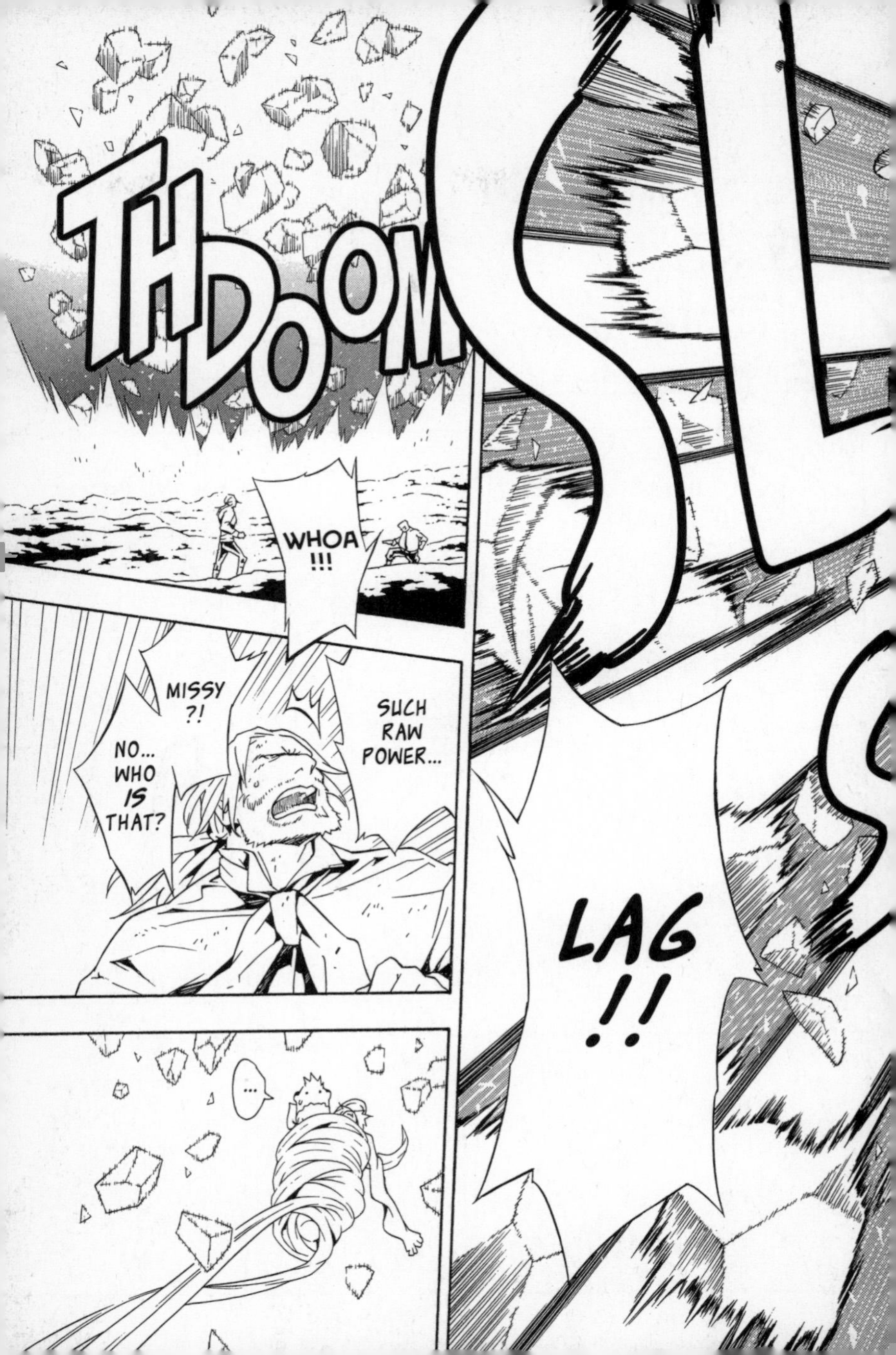
SL
S
LAG!!
THDOOM
WHOA!!!
SUCH RAW POWER...
MISSY?!
NO... WHO *IS* THAT?
...

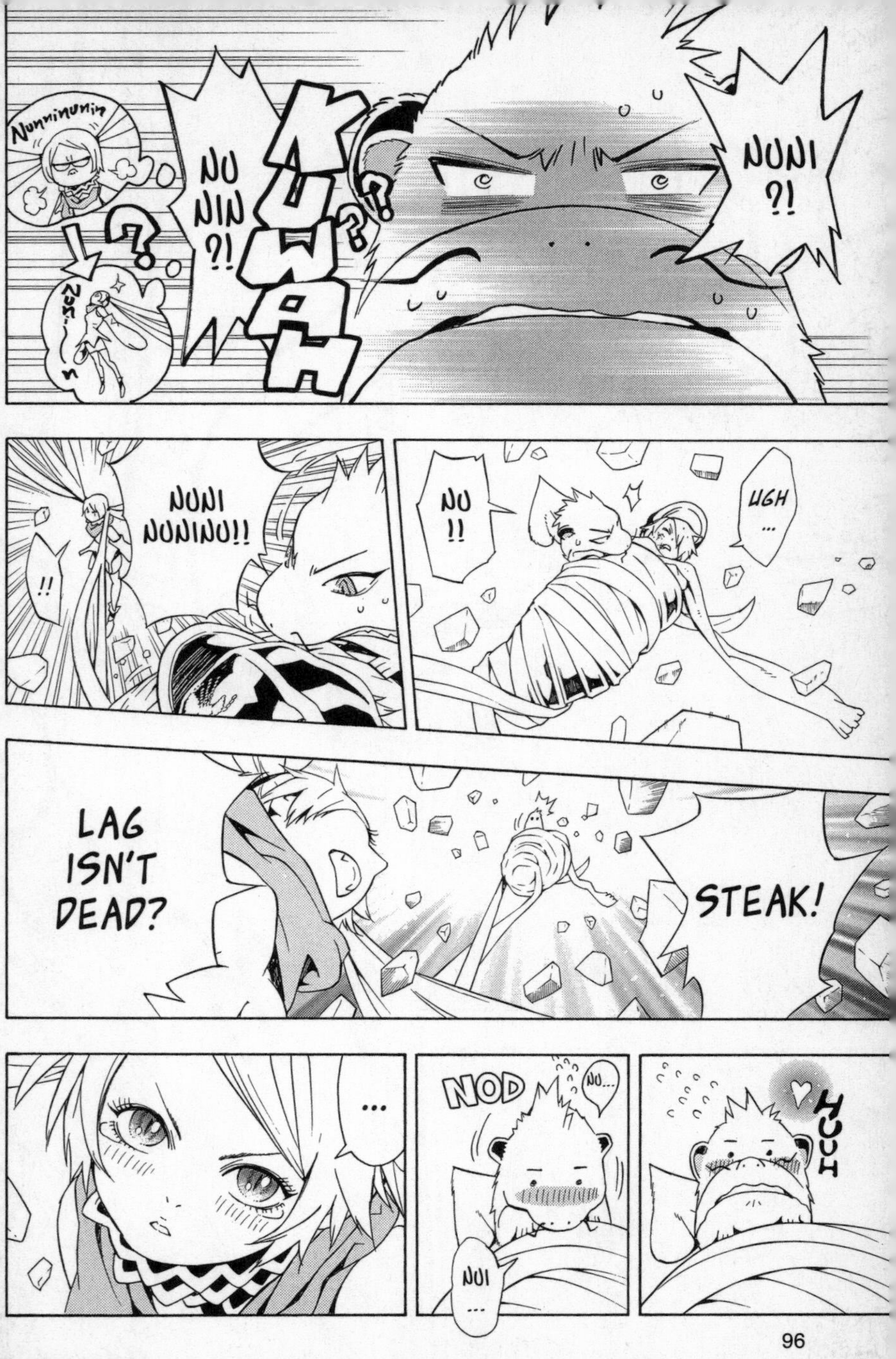
NUNI ?!
KUWAH
NU NIN ?!
Nunninunin
Nuni...~n
UGH ...
NU !!
NUNI NUNINU!!
!!
STEAK!
LAG ISN'T DEAD?
HUUH
NOD
NU...
NUI ...
...

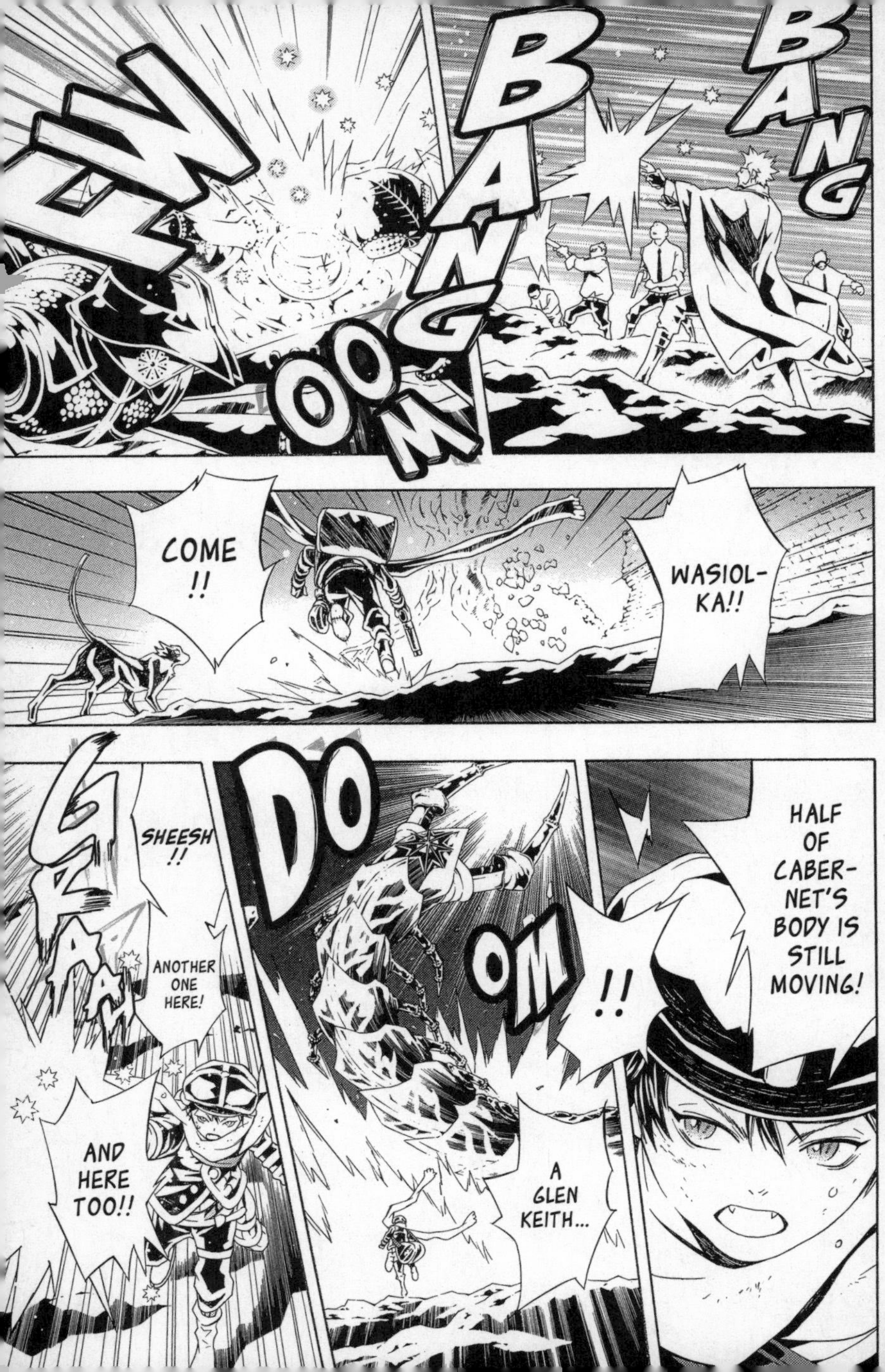
BANG
BANG
WOOM
WASIOL-KA!!
COME !!
HALF OF CABER-NET'S BODY IS STILL MOVING!
!!
DOOM
A GLEN KEITH...
SHEESH !!
ANOTHER ONE HERE!
AND HERE TOO!!

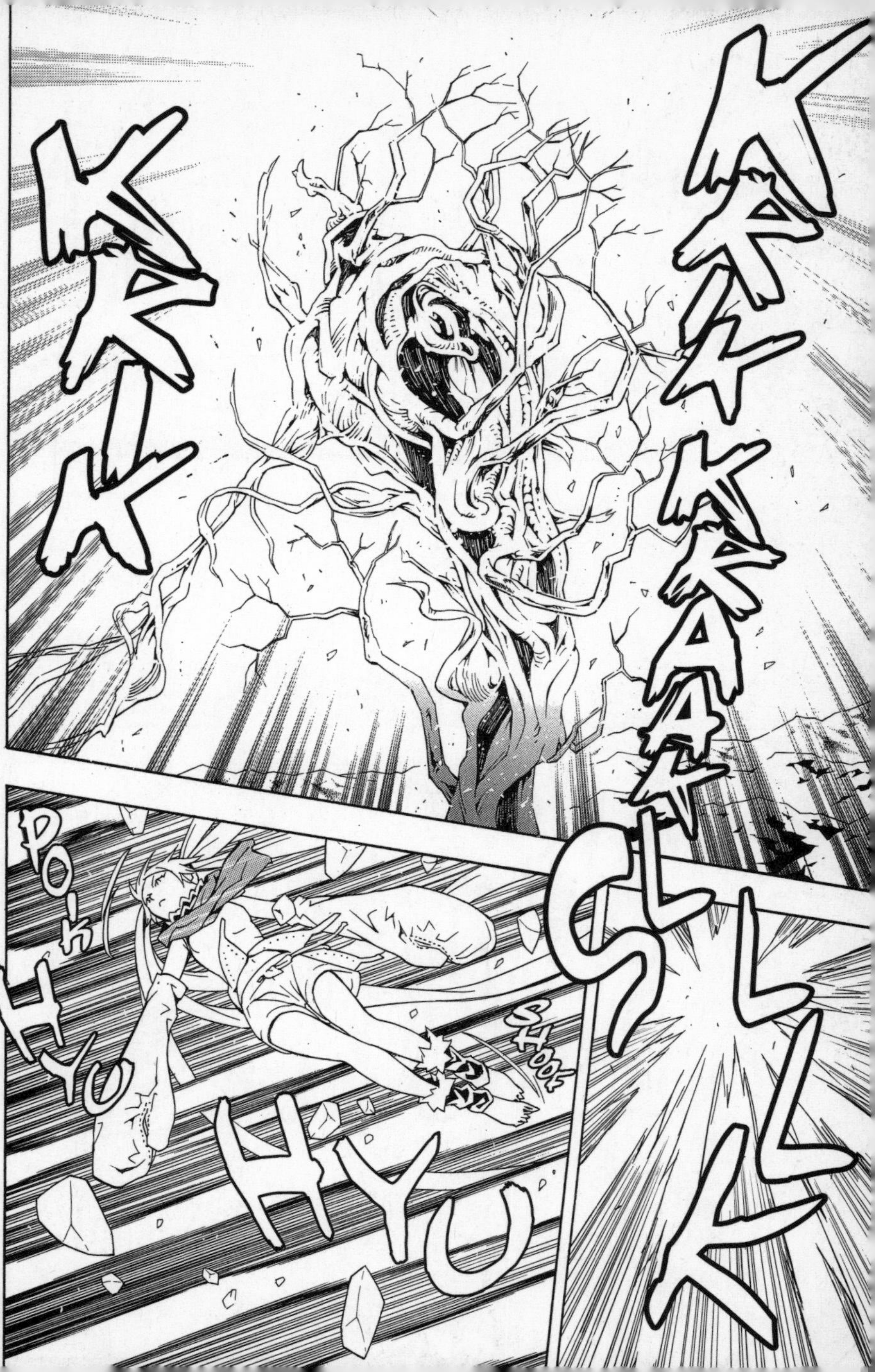
KRKKRAAK
KRK
SLLLK
SHOOK
HYU
HYU
POiK

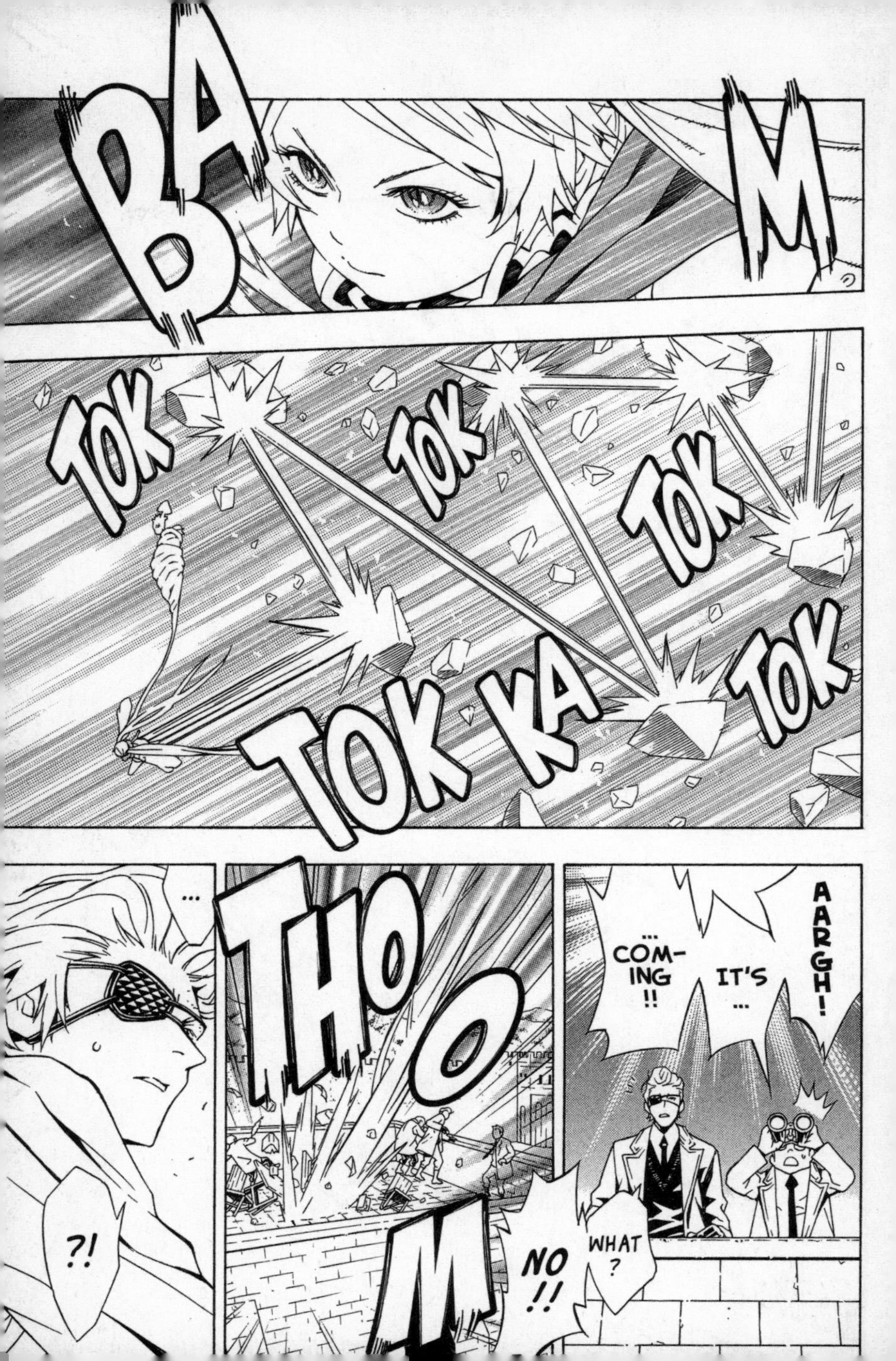
BAM
TOK
TOK
TOK
TOK
KA
TOK
AARGH!
IT'S ...
... COMING !!
WHAT ?
NO !!
THOOM
...
?!

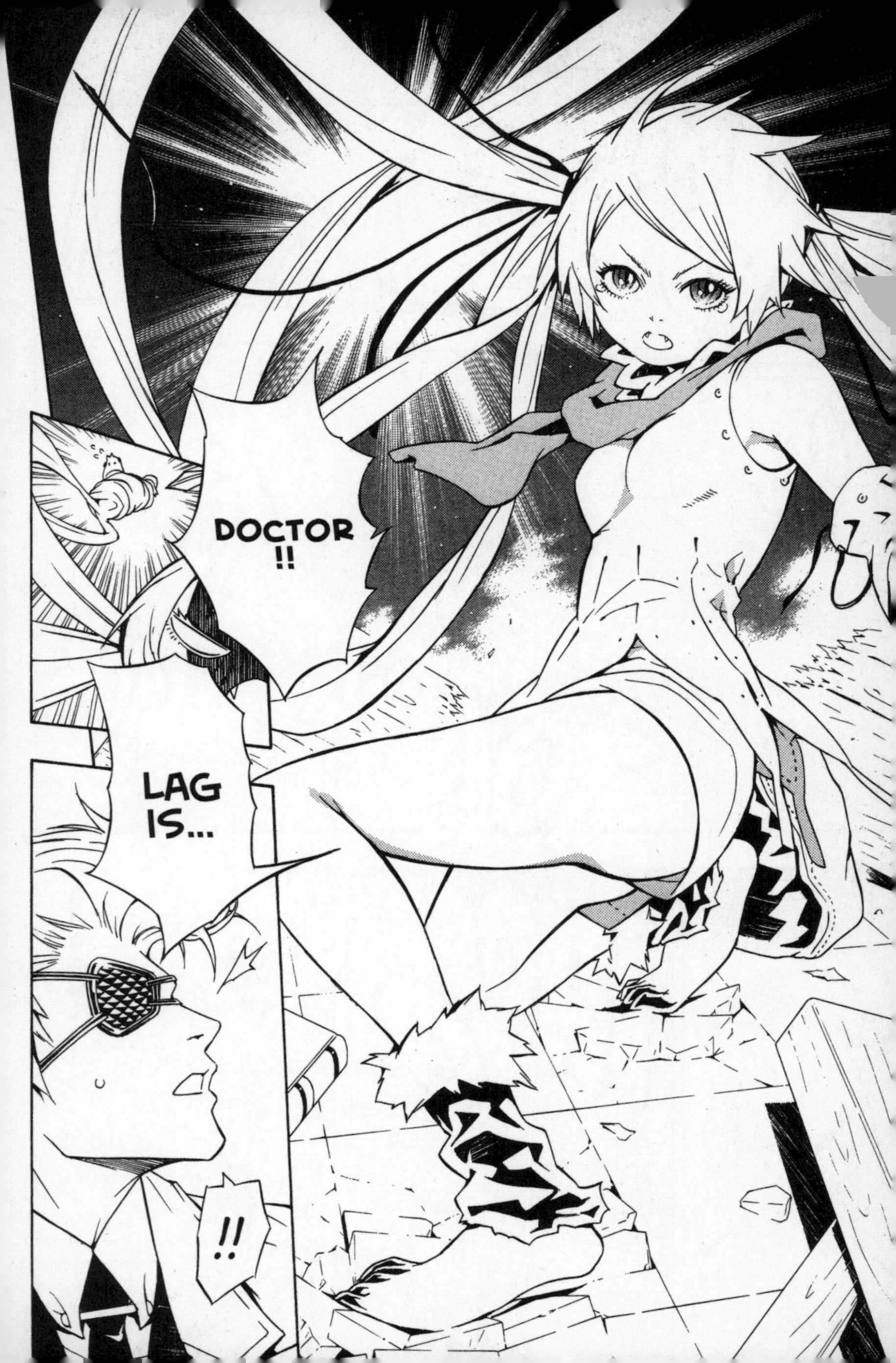
DOCTOR !!
LAG IS...
!!

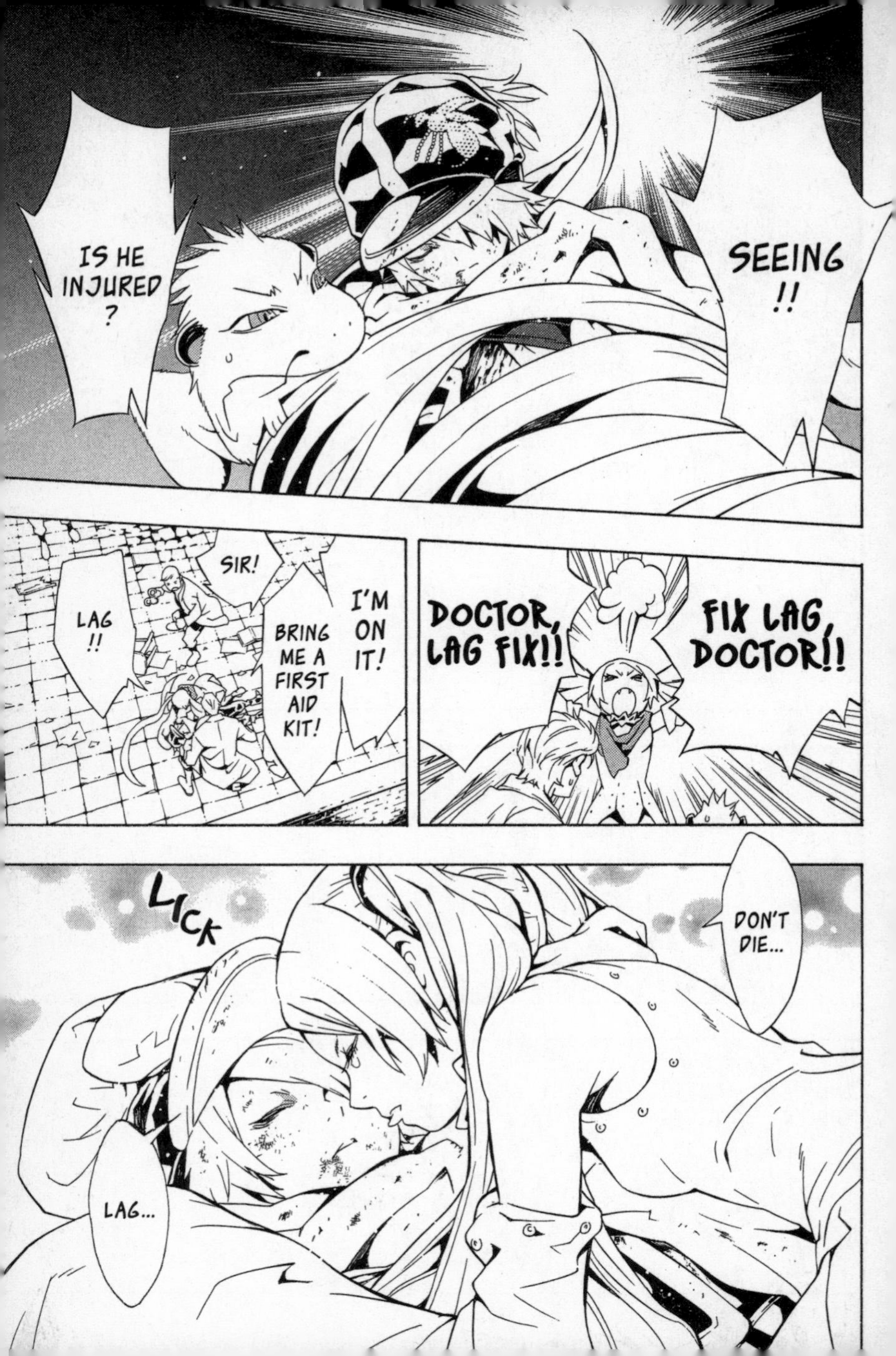
SEEING !!
IS HE INJURED ?
FIX LAG, DOCTOR!!
DOCTOR, LAG FIX!!
SIR!
I'M ON IT!
BRING ME A FIRST AID KIT!
LAG !!
DON'T DIE...
LICK
LAG...

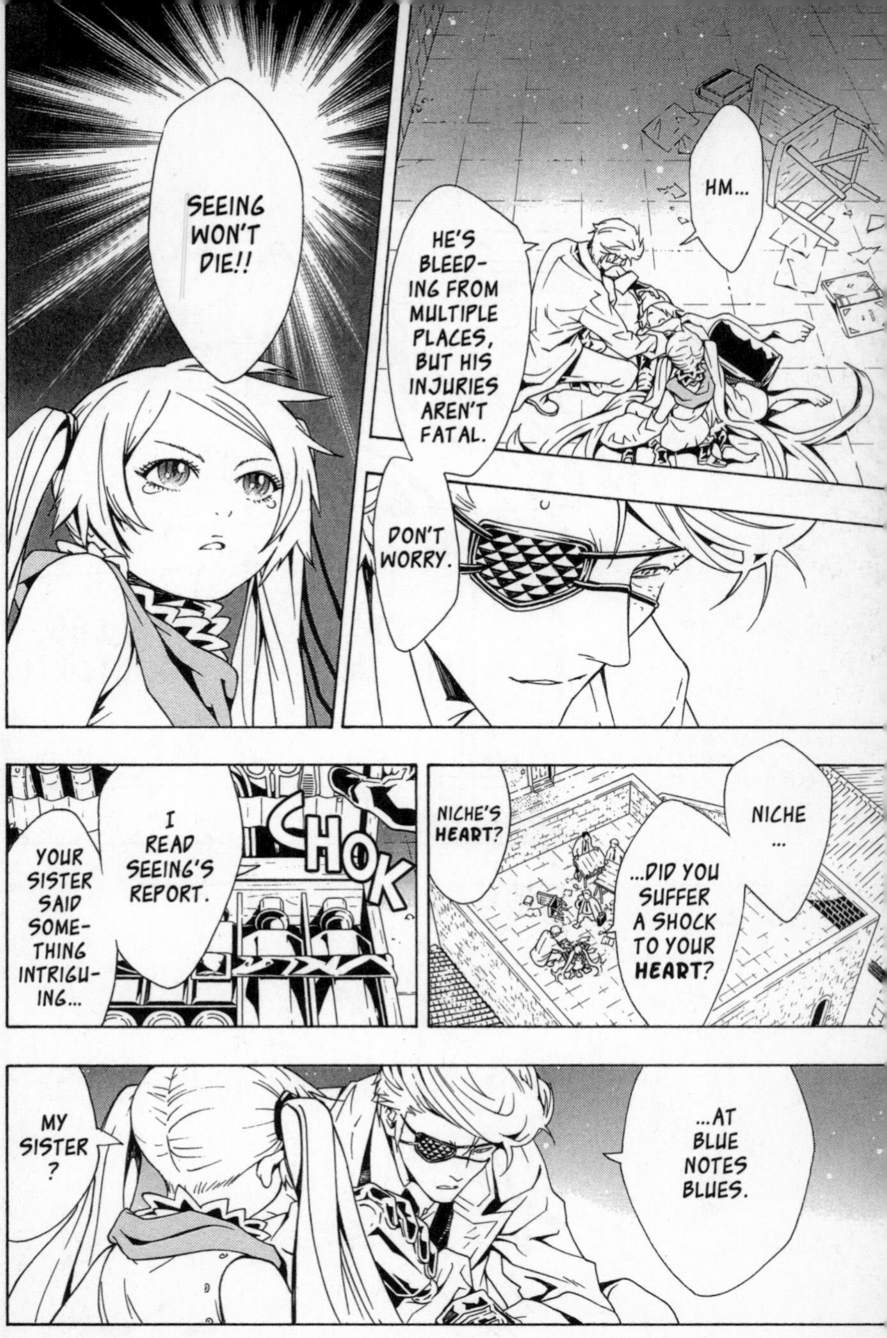
HM...
HE'S BLEEDING FROM MULTIPLE PLACES, BUT HIS INJURIES AREN'T FATAL.
DON'T WORRY.
SEEING WON'T DIE!!
NICHE ...
...DID YOU SUFFER A SHOCK TO YOUR HEART?
NICHE'S HEART?
I READ SEEING'S REPORT.
CHOK
YOUR SISTER SAID SOMETHING INTRIGUING...
...AT BLUE NOTES BLUES.
MY SISTER?

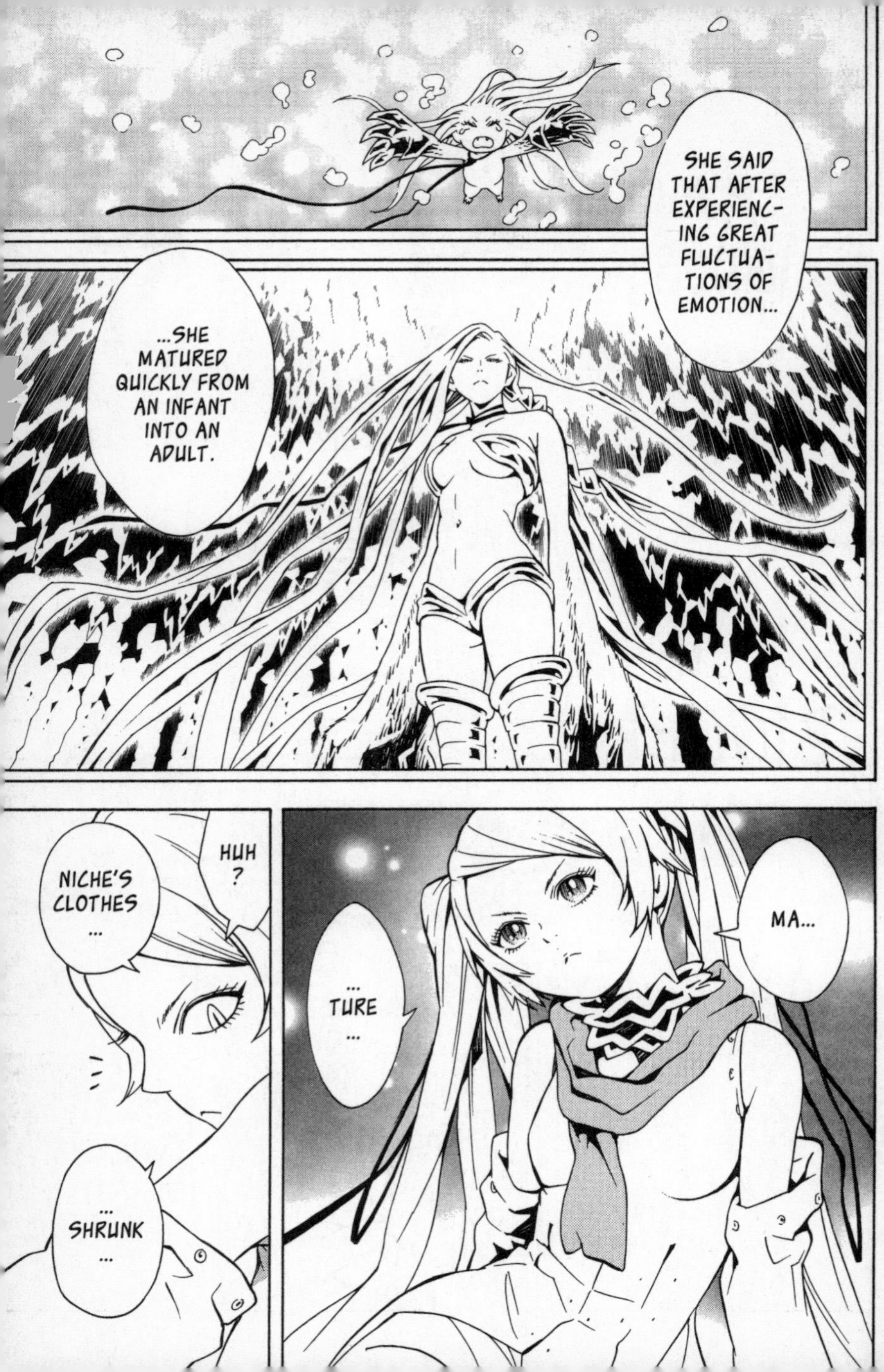
SHE SAID THAT AFTER EXPERIENCING GREAT FLUCTUATIONS OF EMOTION...
...SHE MATURED QUICKLY FROM AN INFANT INTO AN ADULT.
MA...
...TURE...
HUH?
NICHE'S CLOTHES...
...SHRUNK...

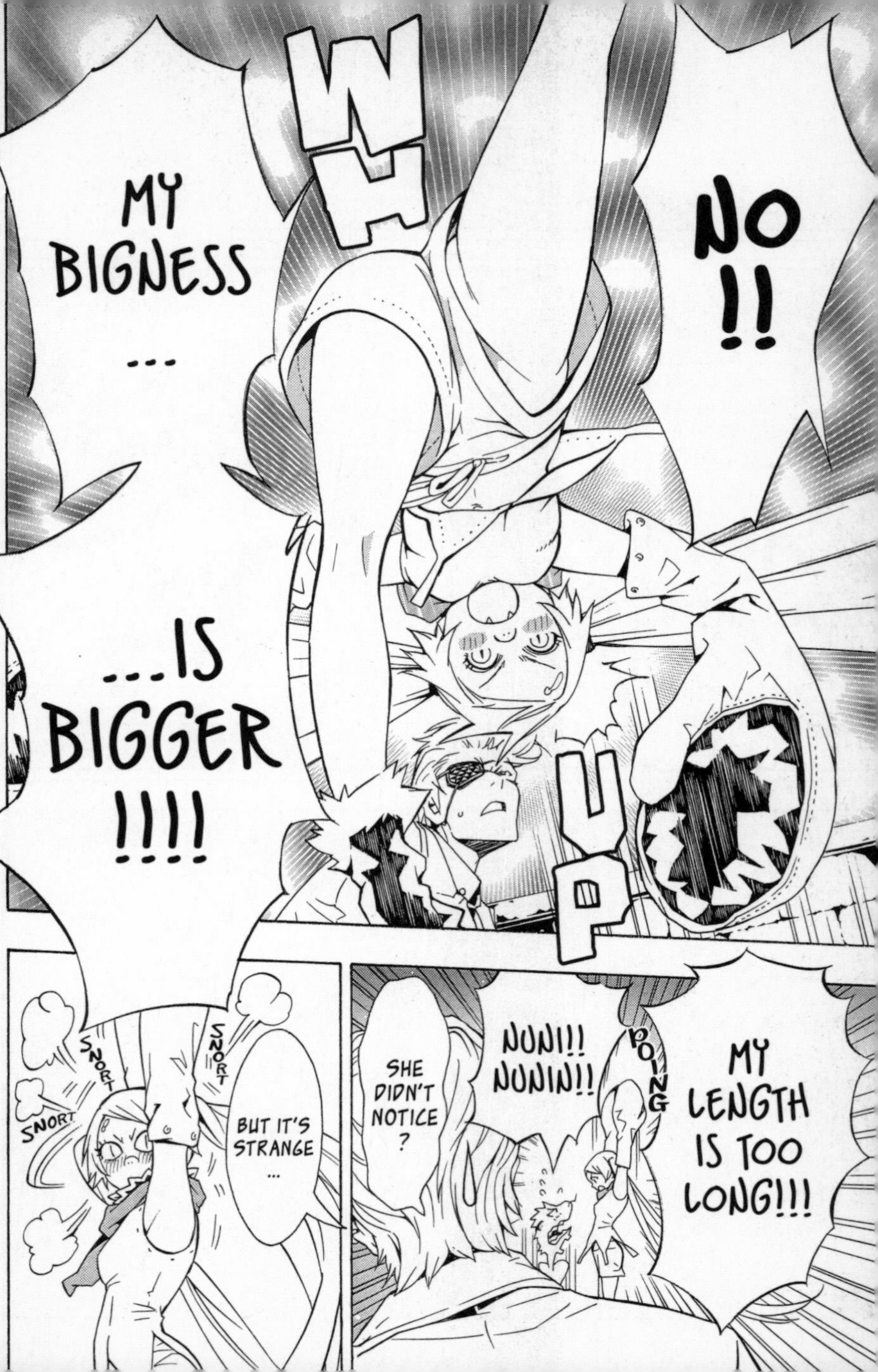
NO !!
WH
MY BIGNESS ...
...IS BIGGER !!!!
UP
MY LENGTH IS TOO LONG!!!
DOING
NUNI!!! NUNIN!!
SHE DIDN'T NOTICE ?
BUT IT'S STRANGE ...
SNORT
SNORT
SNORT

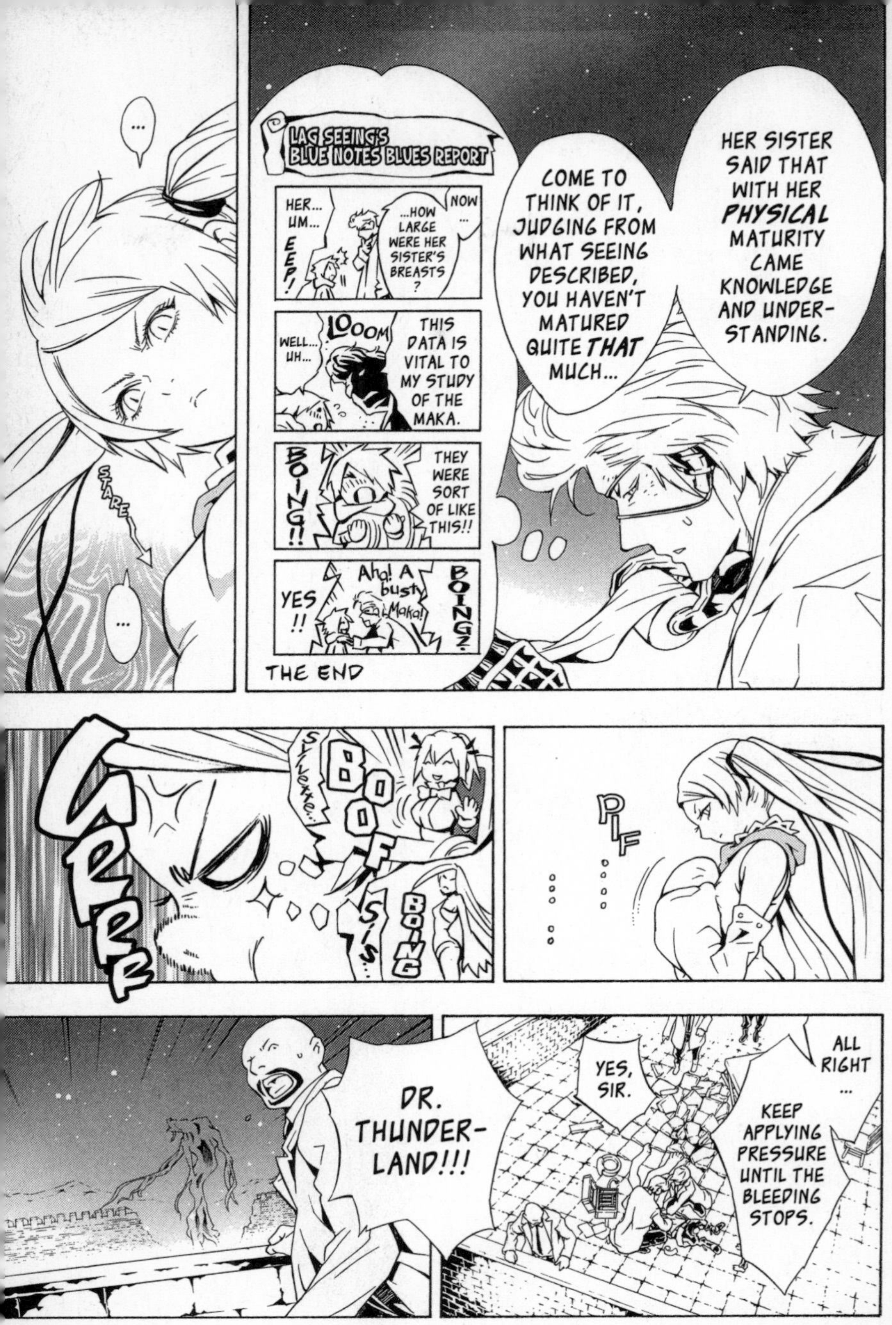
HER SISTER SAID THAT WITH HER *PHYSICAL* MATURITY CAME KNOWLEDGE AND UNDERSTANDING.
COME TO THINK OF IT, JUDGING FROM WHAT SEEING DESCRIBED, YOU HAVEN'T MATURED QUITE *THAT* MUCH...
LAG SEEING'S BLUE NOTES BLUES REPORT
NOW ...
...HOW LARGE WERE HER SISTER'S BREASTS?
HER... UM...
EEP!
THIS DATA IS VITAL TO MY STUDY OF THE MAKA.
LOOOM
WELL... UH...
THEY WERE SORT OF LIKE THIS!!
BOING!!
BOING?
Aha! A busty Maka!
YES!!
THE END
...
STARE
...
PIF
......
Sylvette...
BOOF
Sis...
BOING
ALL RIGHT ...
KEEP APPLYING PRESSURE UNTIL THE BLEEDING STOPS.
YES, SIR.
DR. THUNDERLAND!!!

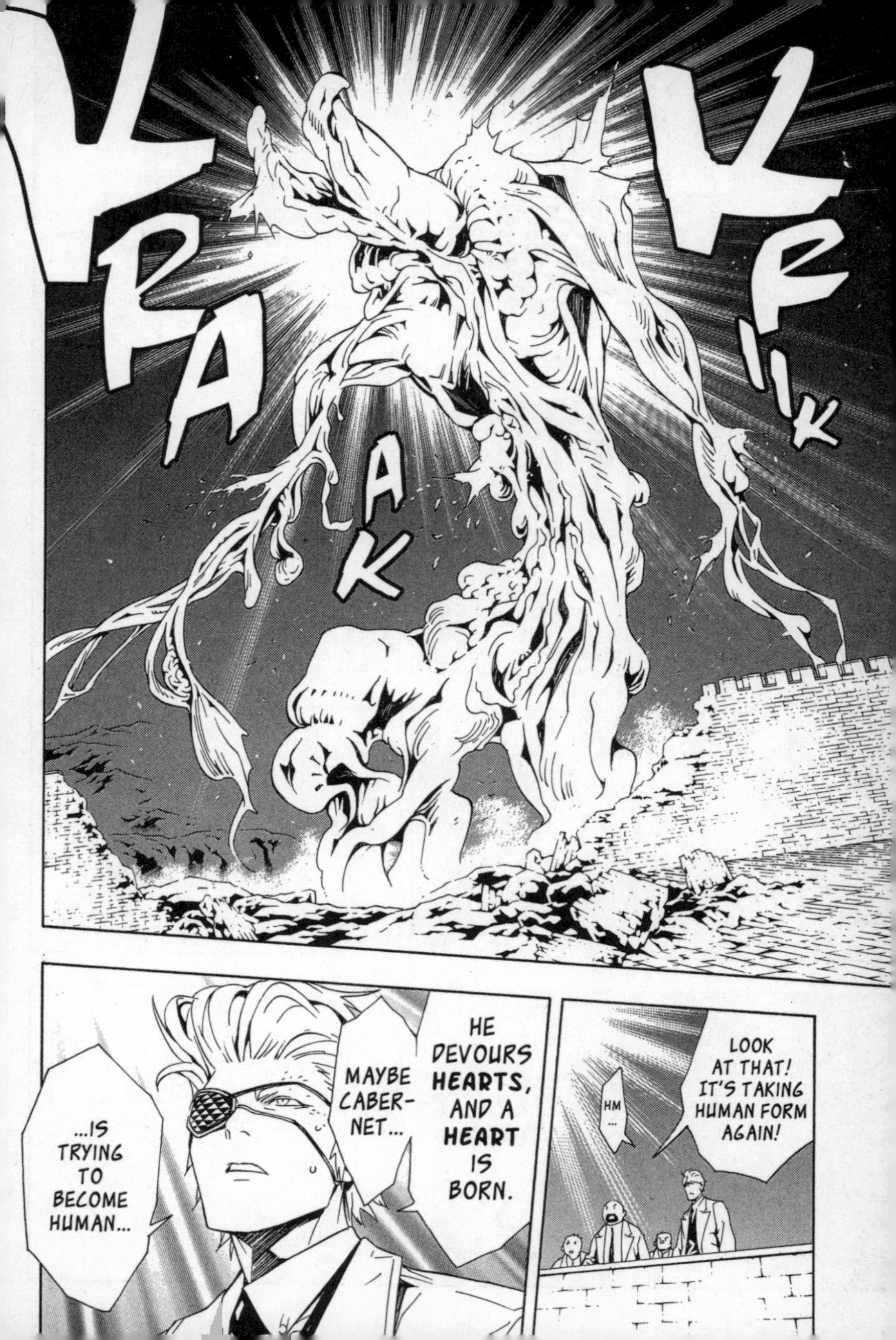
KRIIIK
KRAAK
LOOK AT THAT! IT'S TAKING HUMAN FORM AGAIN!
HM...
HE DEVOURS HEARTS, AND A HEART IS BORN.
MAYBE CABER-NET...
...IS TRYING TO BECOME HUMAN...

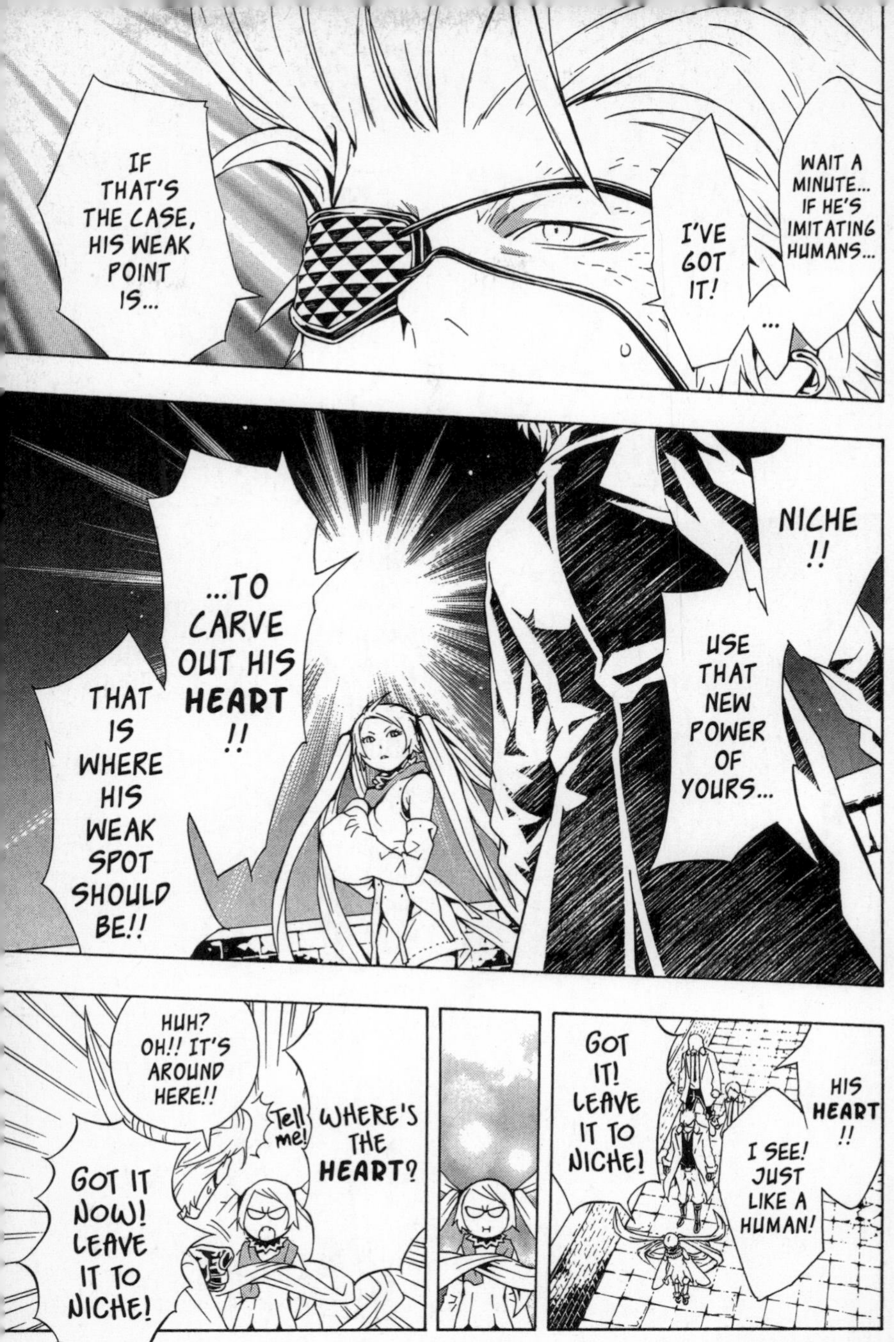
WAIT A MINUTE... IF HE'S IMITATING HUMANS...
I'VE GOT IT!
...
IF THAT'S THE CASE, HIS WEAK POINT IS...
NICHE!!
USE THAT NEW POWER OF YOURS...
...TO CARVE OUT HIS HEART!!
THAT IS WHERE HIS WEAK SPOT SHOULD BE!!
HIS HEART!!
I SEE! JUST LIKE A HUMAN!
GOT IT! LEAVE IT TO NICHE!
WHERE'S THE HEART?
Tell me!
HUH? OH!! IT'S AROUND HERE!!
GOT IT NOW! LEAVE IT TO NICHE!

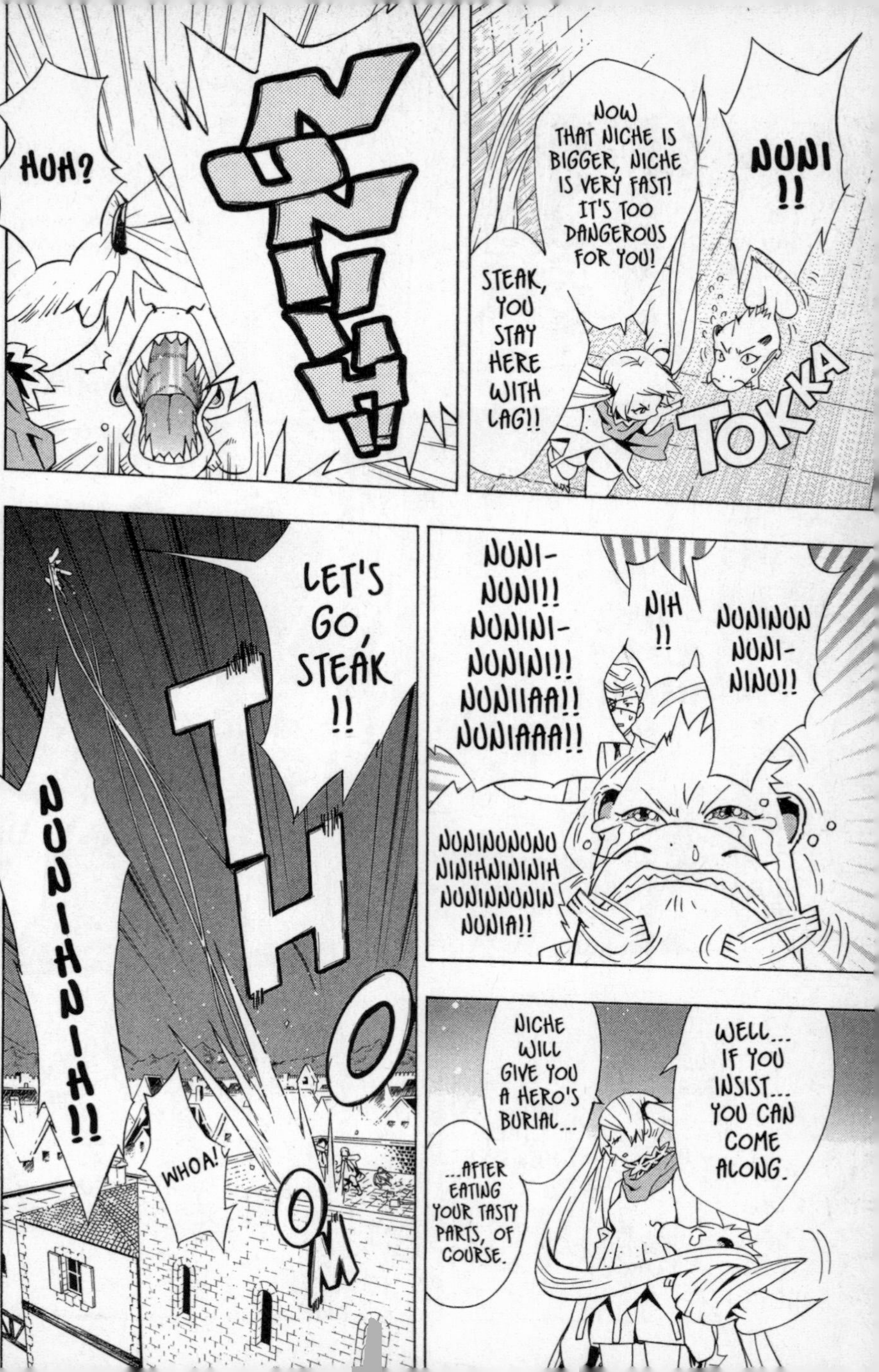
NUNI !!
NOW THAT NICHE IS BIGGER, NICHE IS VERY FAST! IT'S TOO DANGEROUS FOR YOU!
STEAK, YOU STAY HERE WITH LAG!!
TOKKA
NUNIH!!
HUH?
NUNINUN NUNI-NINU!!
NIH !!
NUNI-NUNI!! NUNINI-NUNINI!! NUNIIAA!! NUNIAAA!!
NUNINONUNU NINIHNININIH NUNINNONIN NUNIA!!
WELL... IF YOU INSIST... YOU CAN COME ALONG.
NICHE WILL GIVE YOU A HERO'S BURIAL...
...AFTER EATING YOUR TASTY PARTS, OF COURSE.
LET'S GO, STEAK !!
THOOOM
NUNIHANIH!!
WHOA!

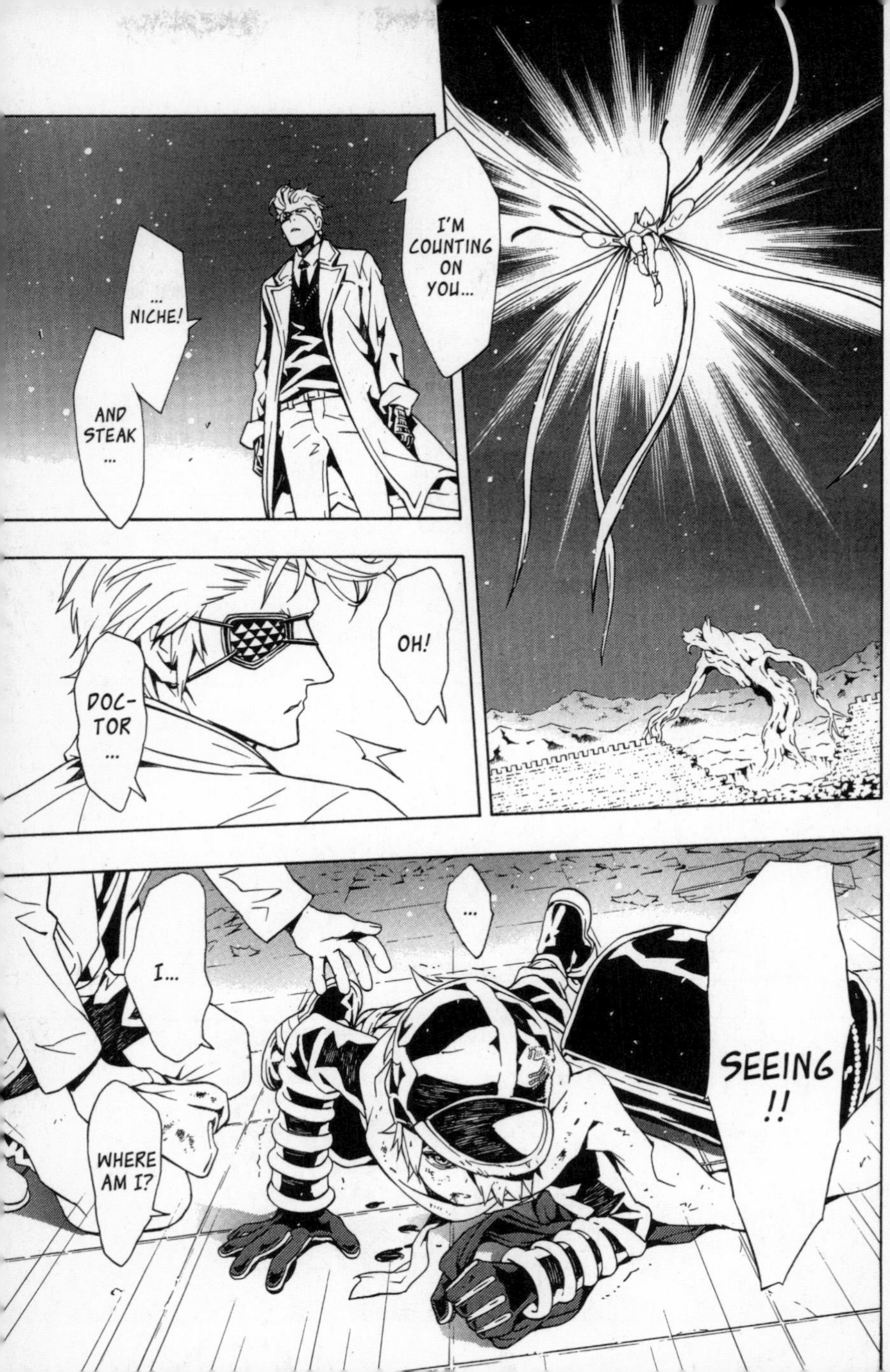
I'M COUNTING ON YOU...
... NICHE!
AND STEAK ...
OH!
DOCTOR ...
SEEING !!
...
I...
WHERE AM I?

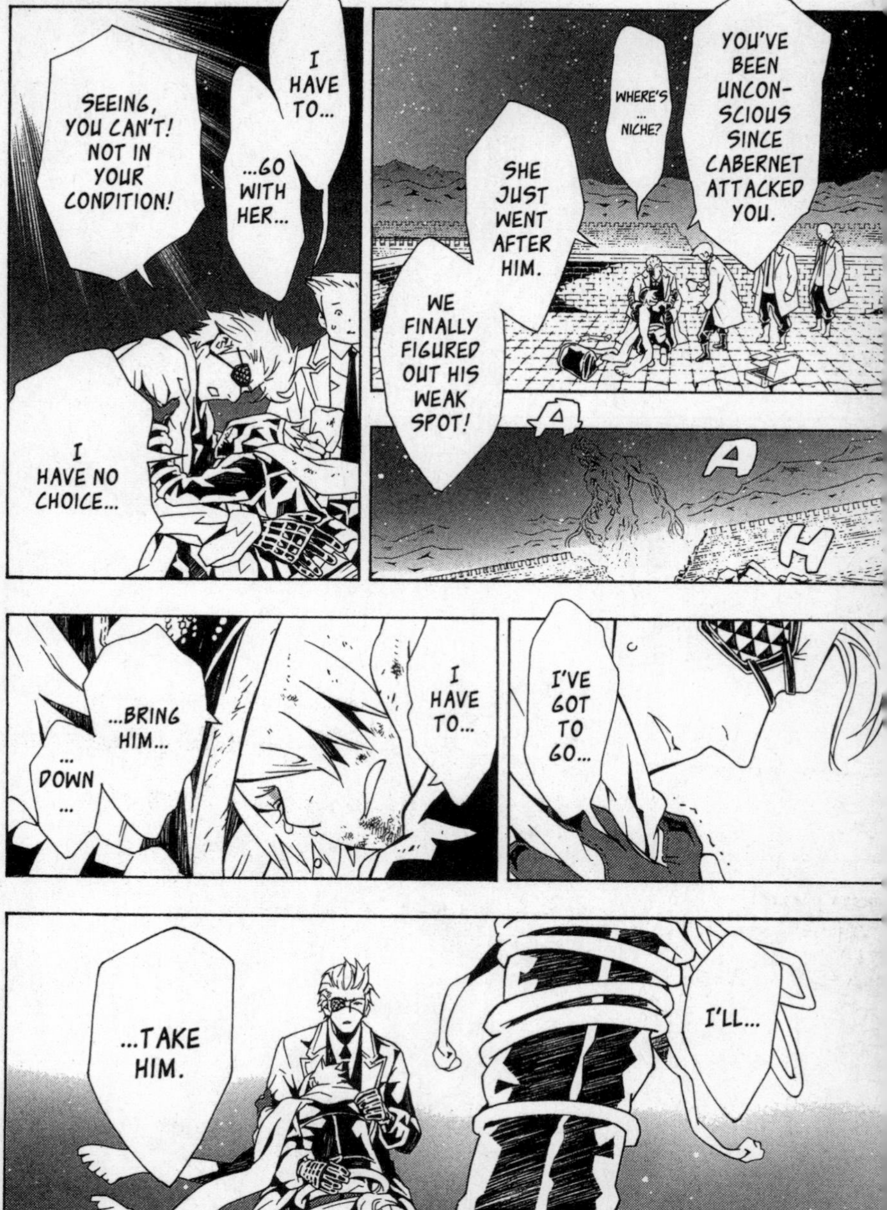
YOU'VE BEEN UNCON-SCIOUS SINCE CABERNET ATTACKED YOU.
WHERE'S ... NICHE?
SHE JUST WENT AFTER HIM.
WE FINALLY FIGURED OUT HIS WEAK SPOT!
AAH
I HAVE TO...
...GO WITH HER...
SEEING, YOU CAN'T! NOT IN YOUR CONDITION!
I HAVE NO CHOICE...
I'VE GOT TO GO...
I HAVE TO...
...BRING HIM...
... DOWN ...
I'LL...
...TAKE HIM.

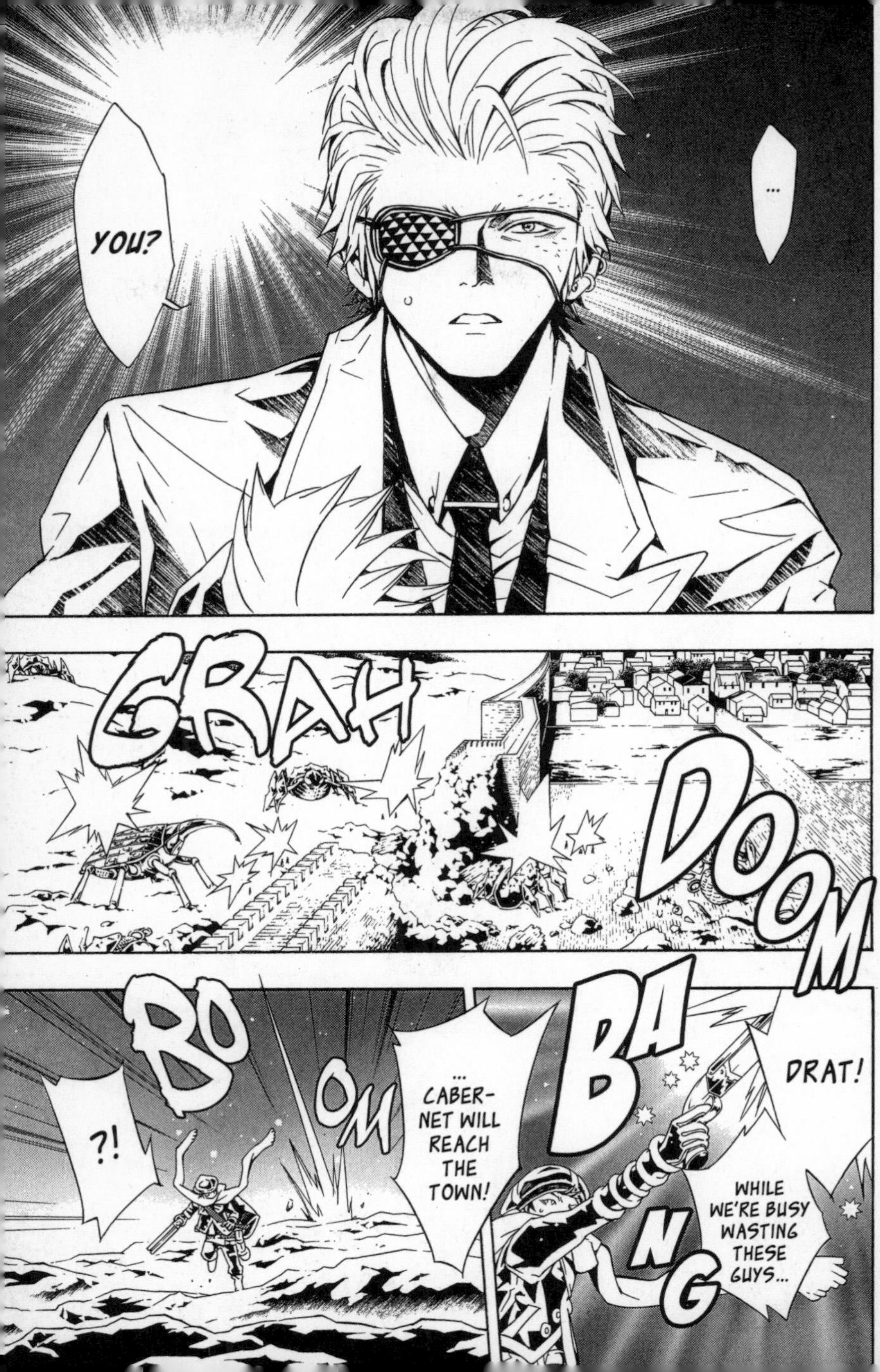
...
YOU?
DOOM
GRAH
DRAT!
BANG
WHILE WE'RE BUSY WASTING THESE GUYS...
... CABER-NET WILL REACH THE TOWN!
BOOM
?!

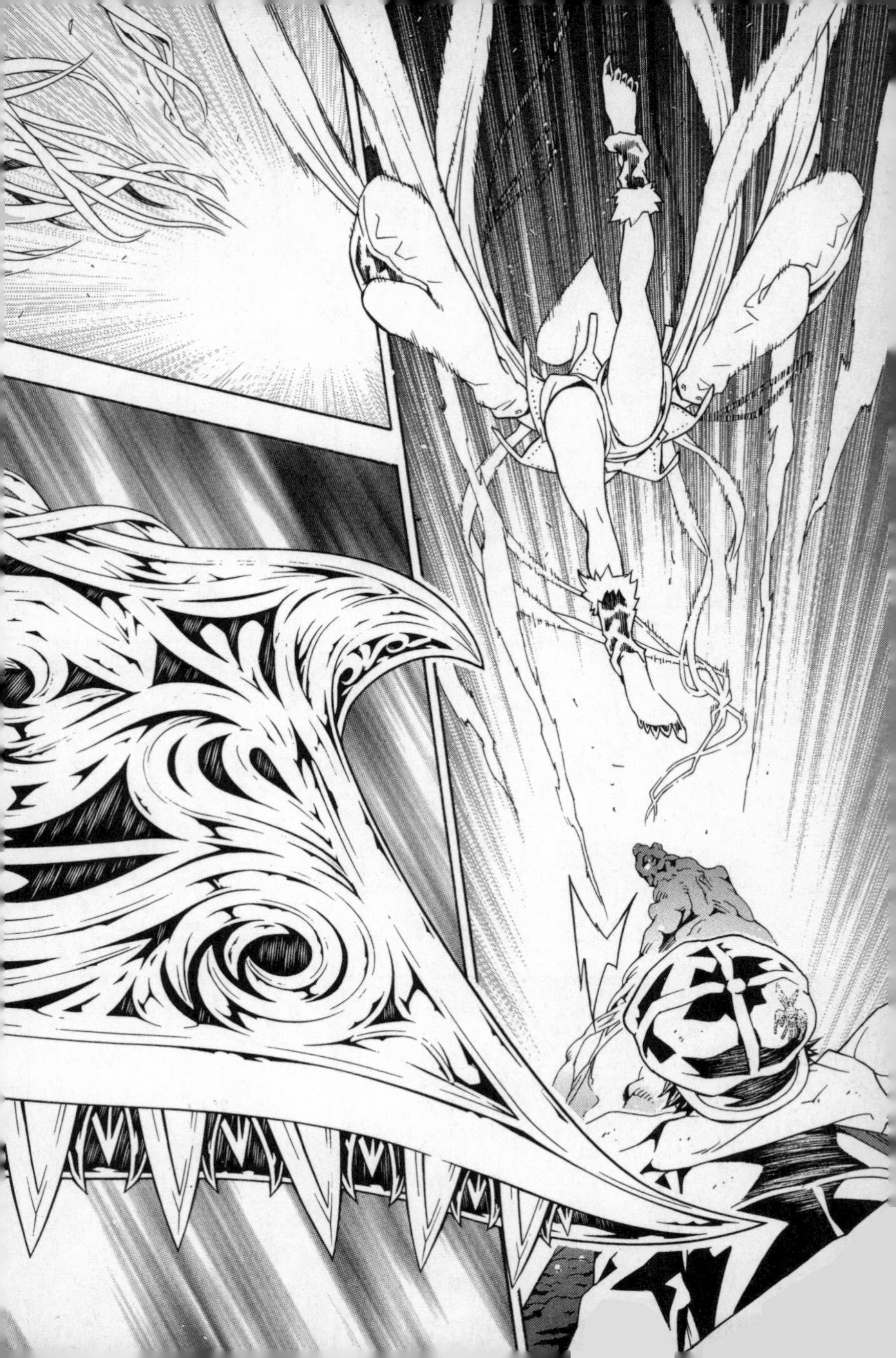

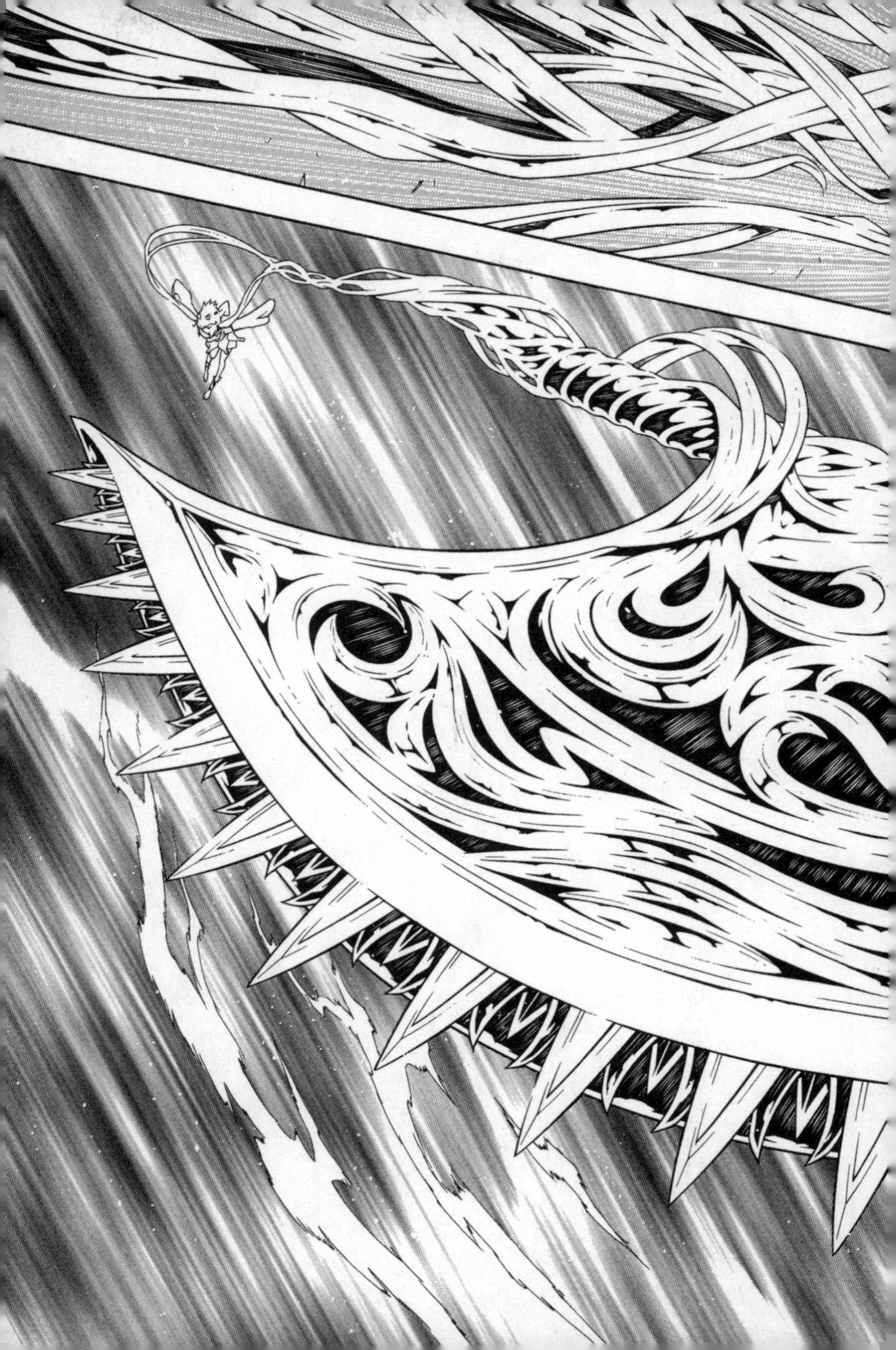

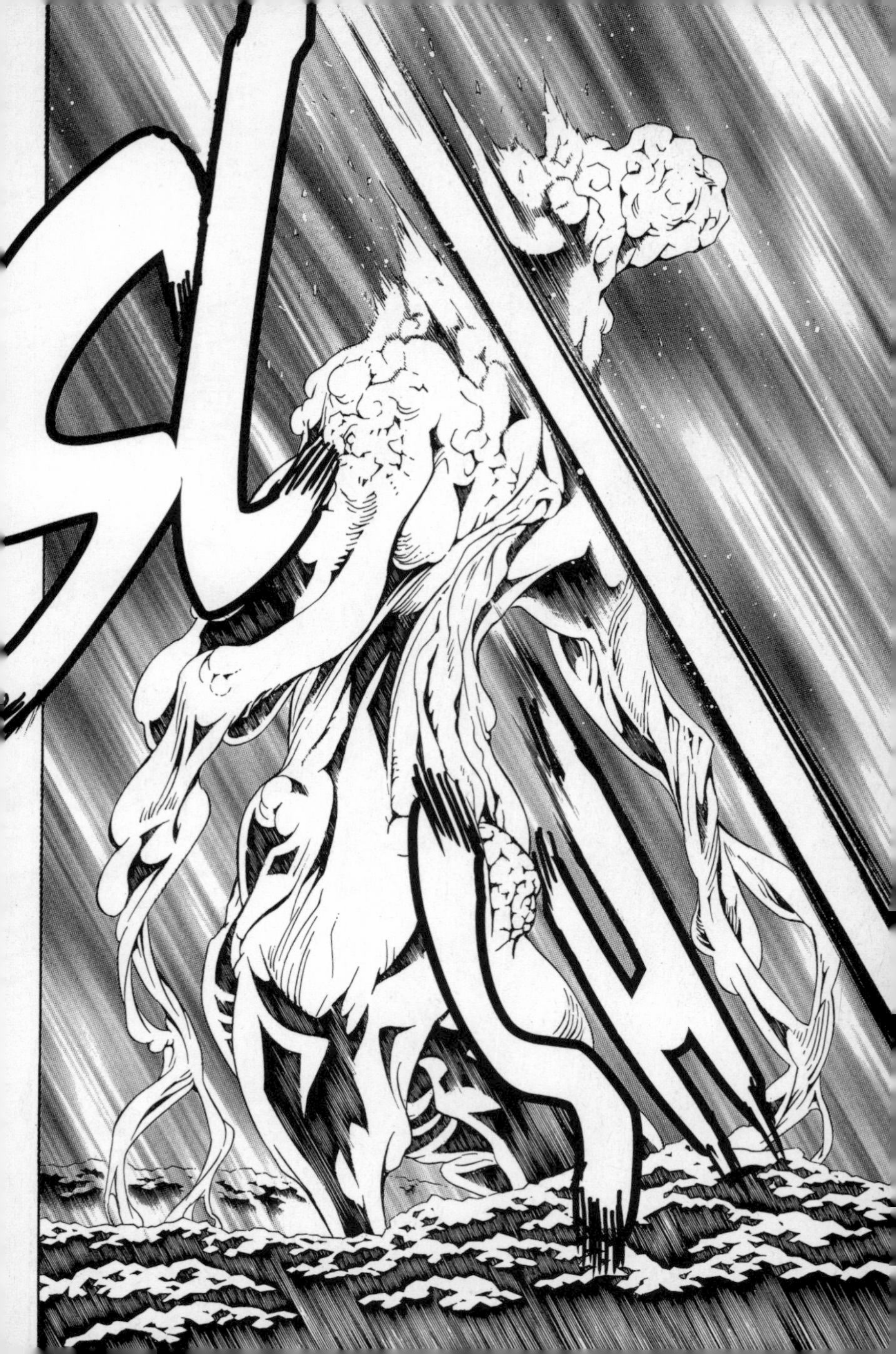

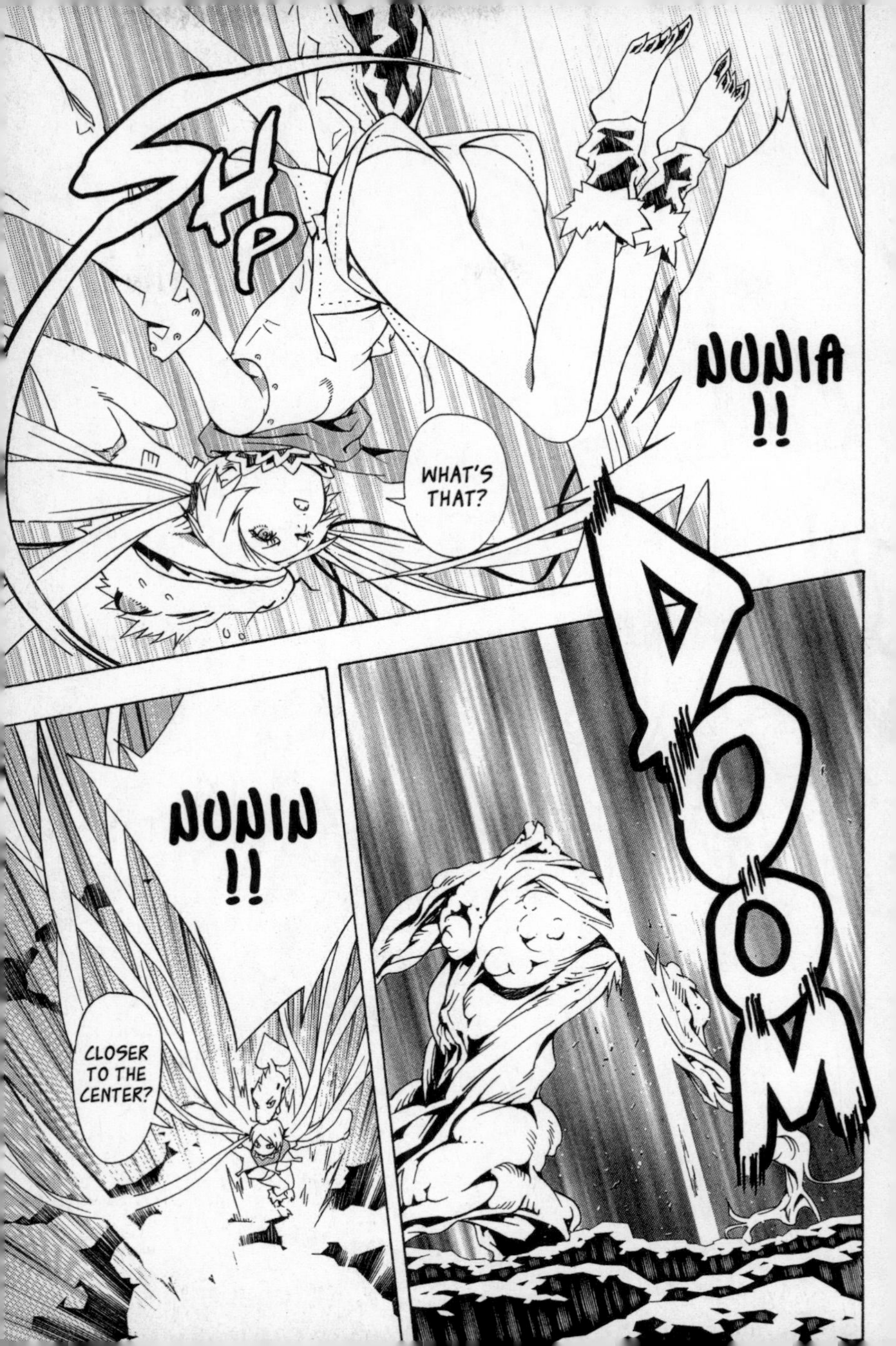
NUNIA!!
SHP
WHAT'S THAT?
DOOM
NUNIN!!
CLOSER TO THE CENTER?

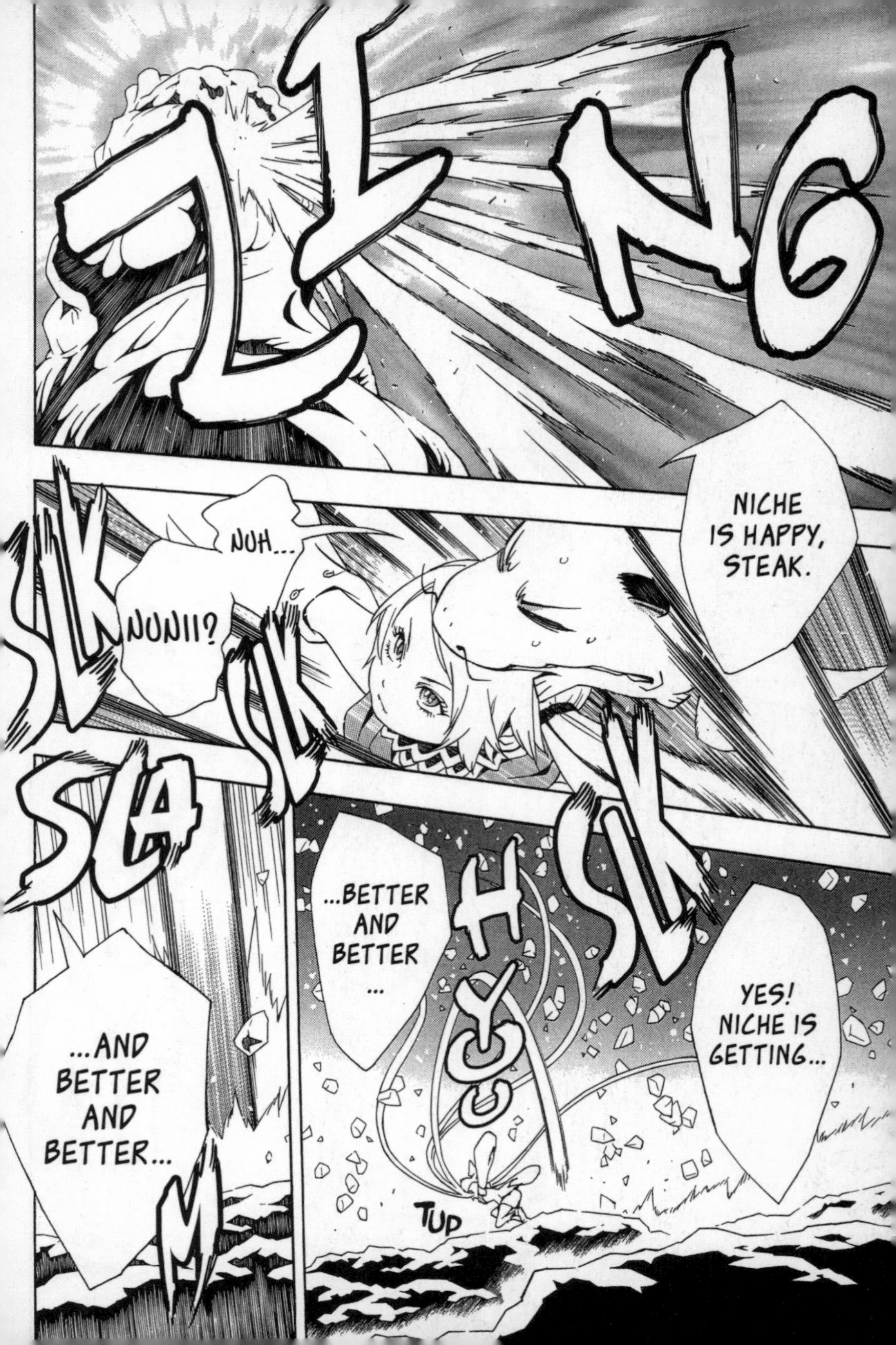
ZING
NICHE IS HAPPY, STEAK.
NUH...
NUNII?
YES! NICHE IS GETTING...
...BETTER AND BETTER ...
TUP
...AND BETTER AND BETTER...

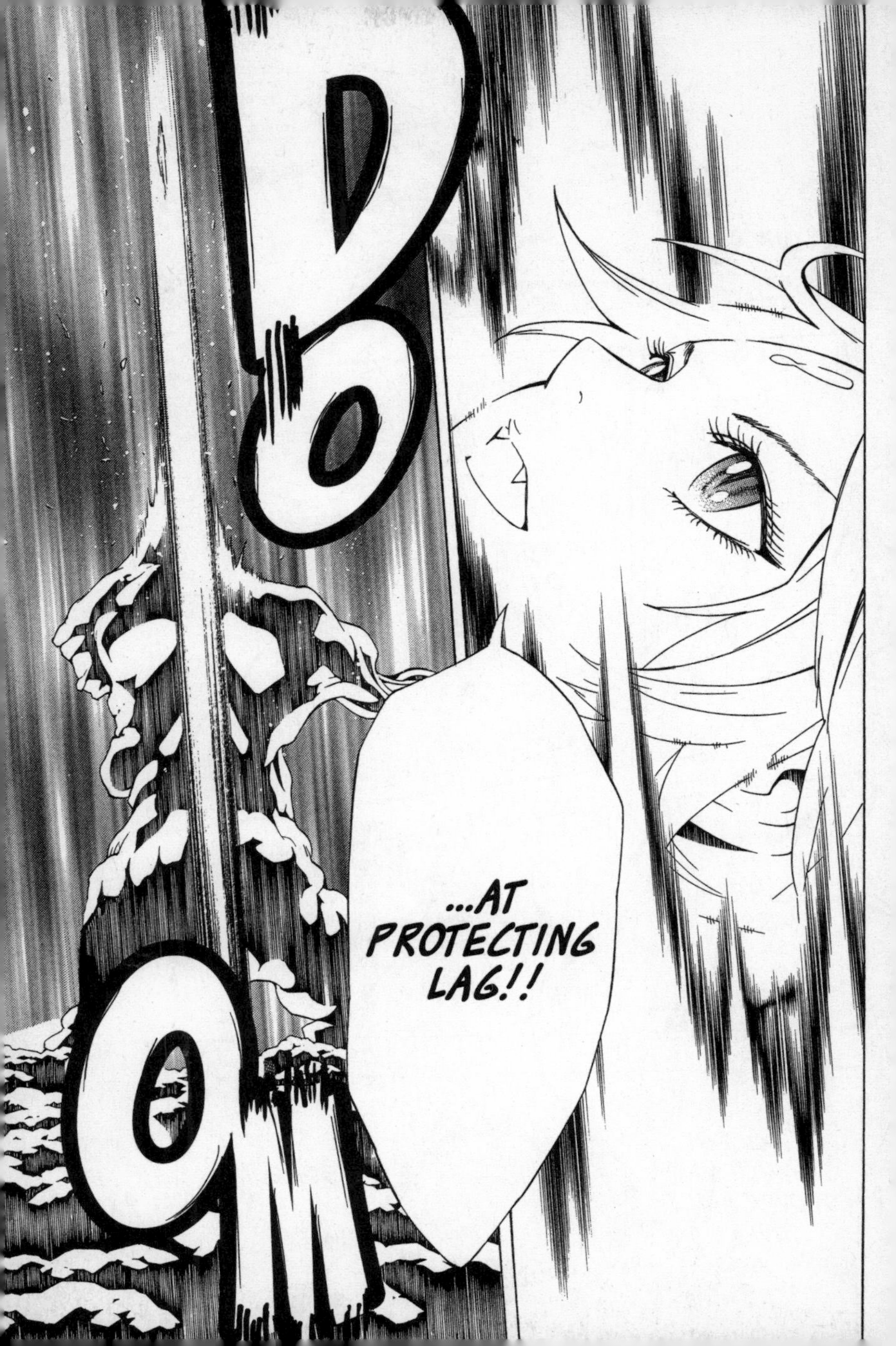
...AT PROTECTING LAG!!
DOOM

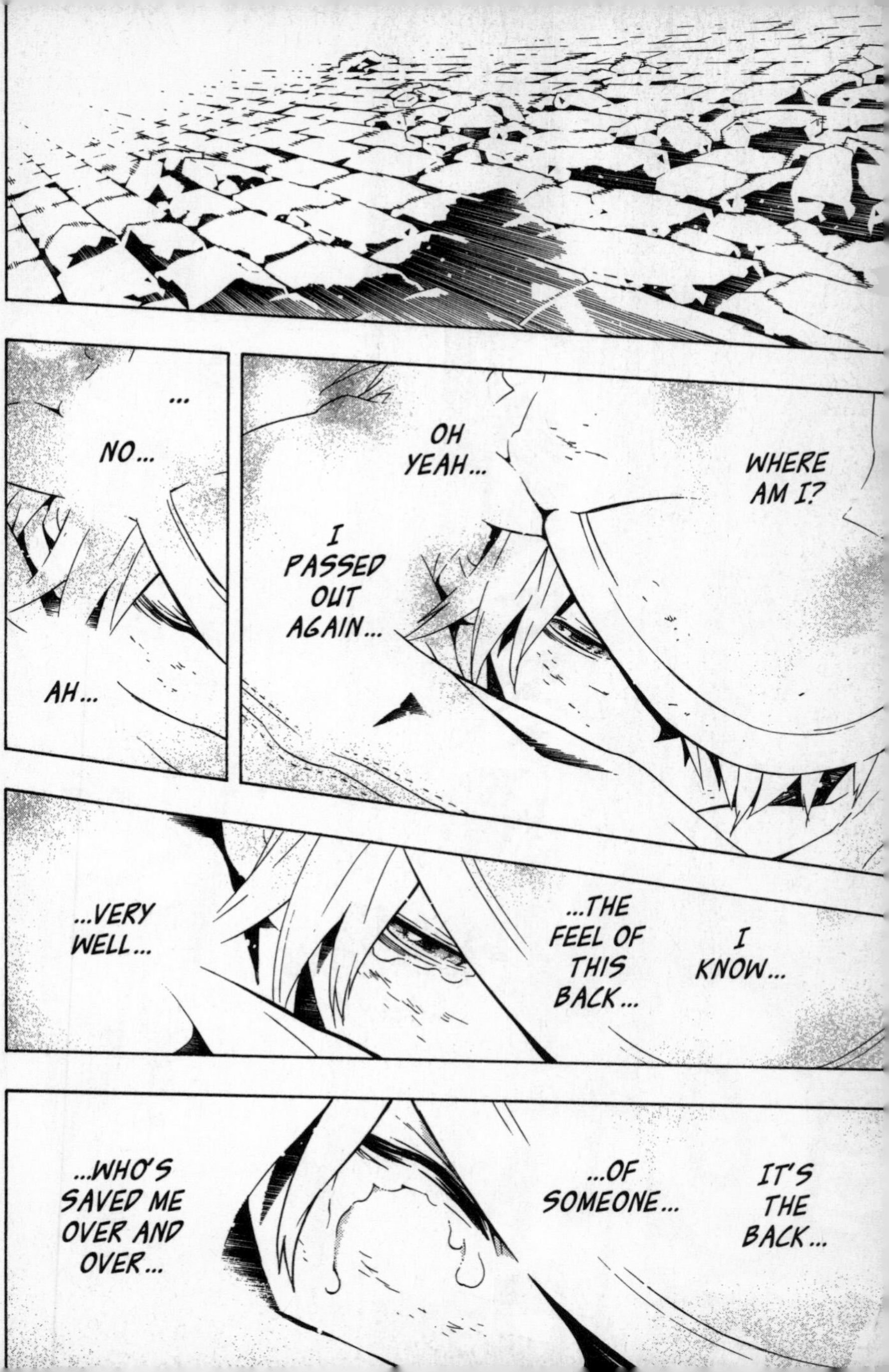
WHERE AM I?
OH YEAH...
I PASSED OUT AGAIN...
...
NO...
AH...
I KNOW...
...THE FEEL OF THIS BACK...
...VERY WELL...
IT'S THE BACK...
...OF SOMEONE...
...WHO'S SAVED ME OVER AND OVER...

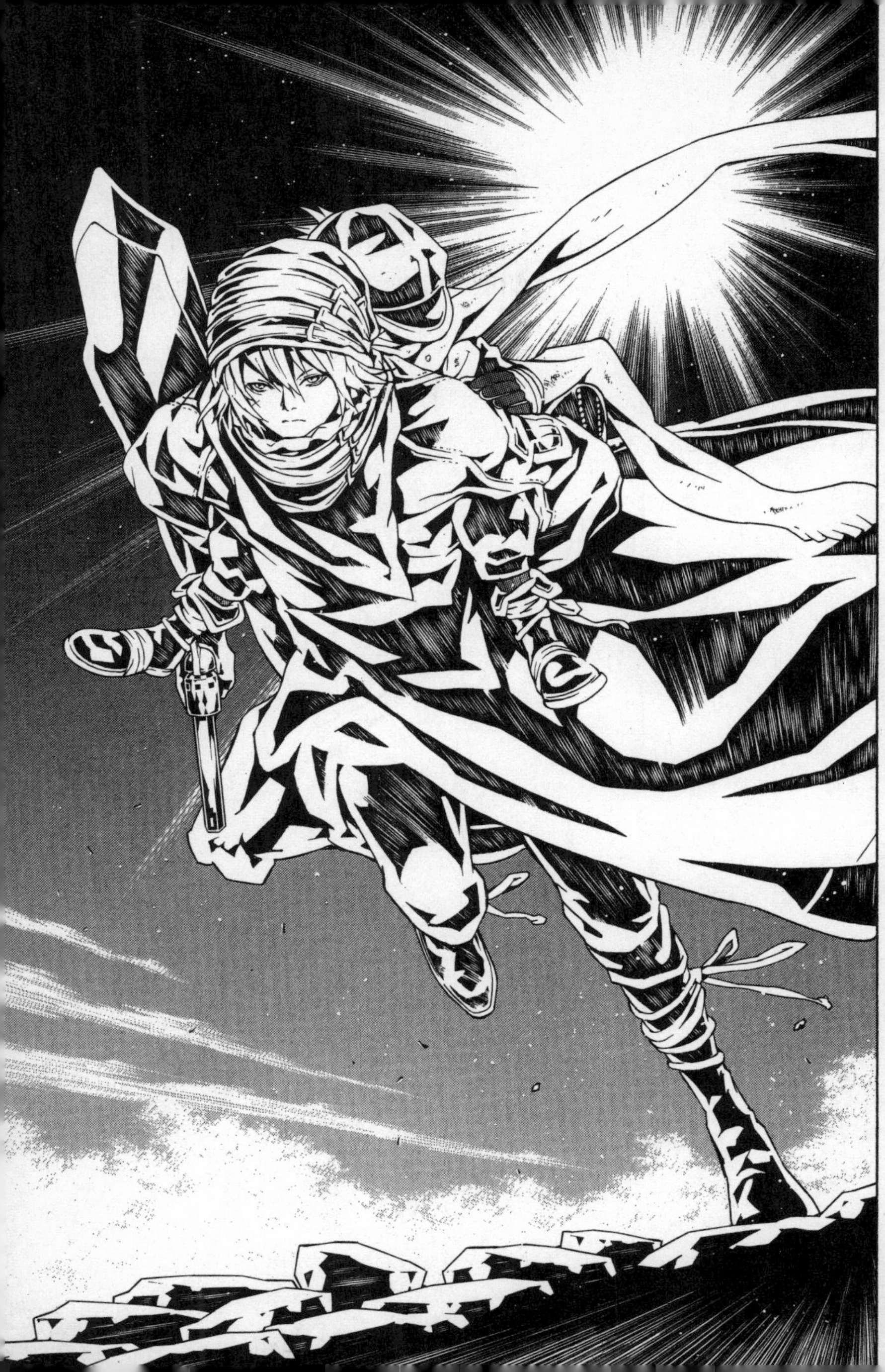

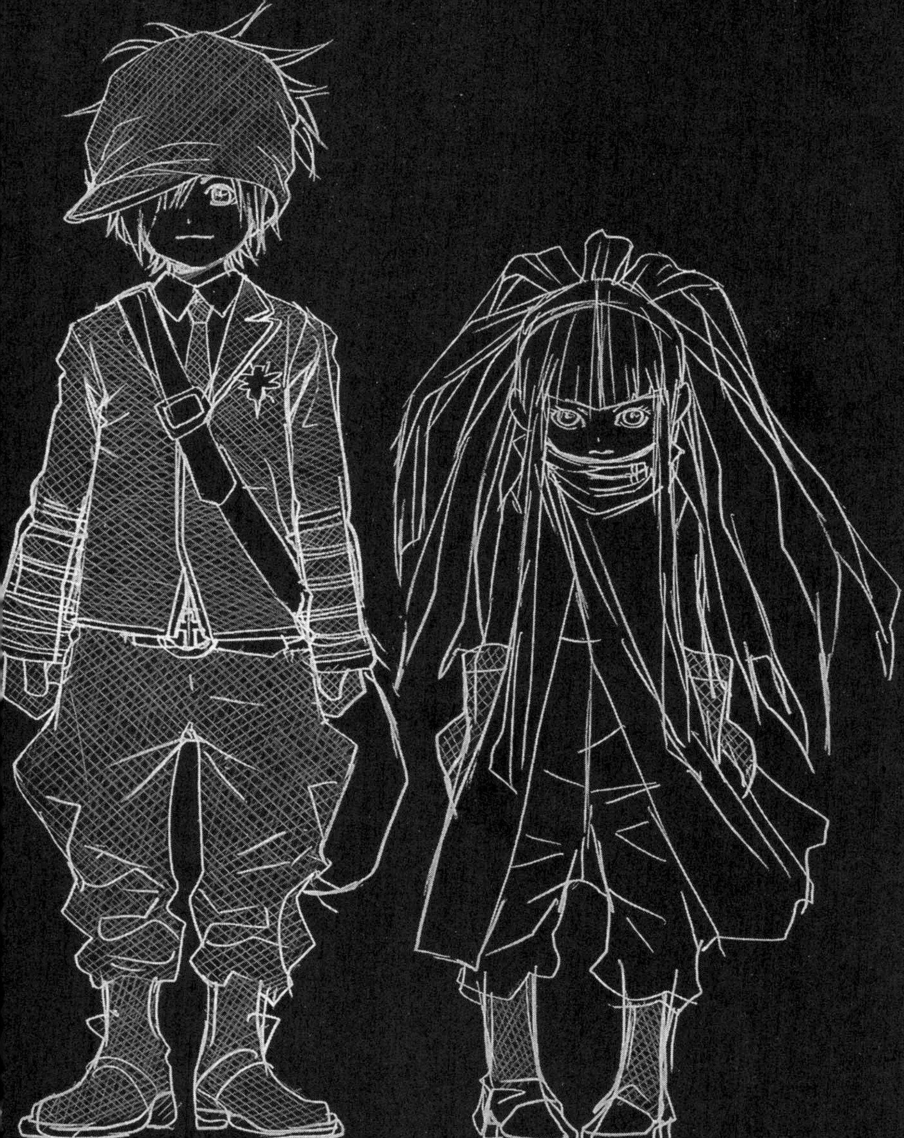

Early rough sketch of Lag and Niche before this manga launched.

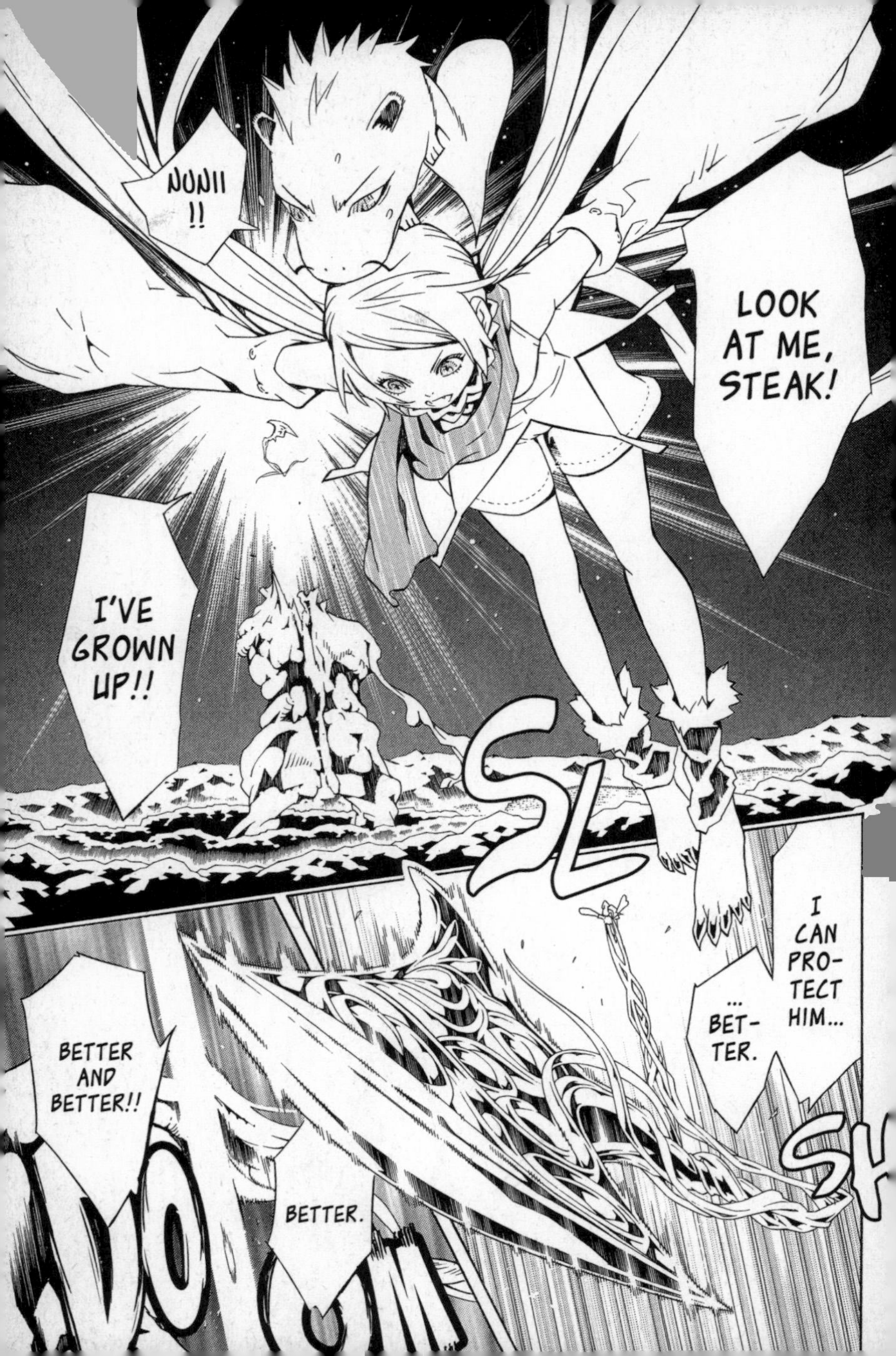
LOOK AT ME, STEAK!
NUNII !!
I'VE GROWN UP!!
SL
I CAN PROTECT HIM...
... BET- TER.
BETTER AND BETTER!!
BETTER.
SH

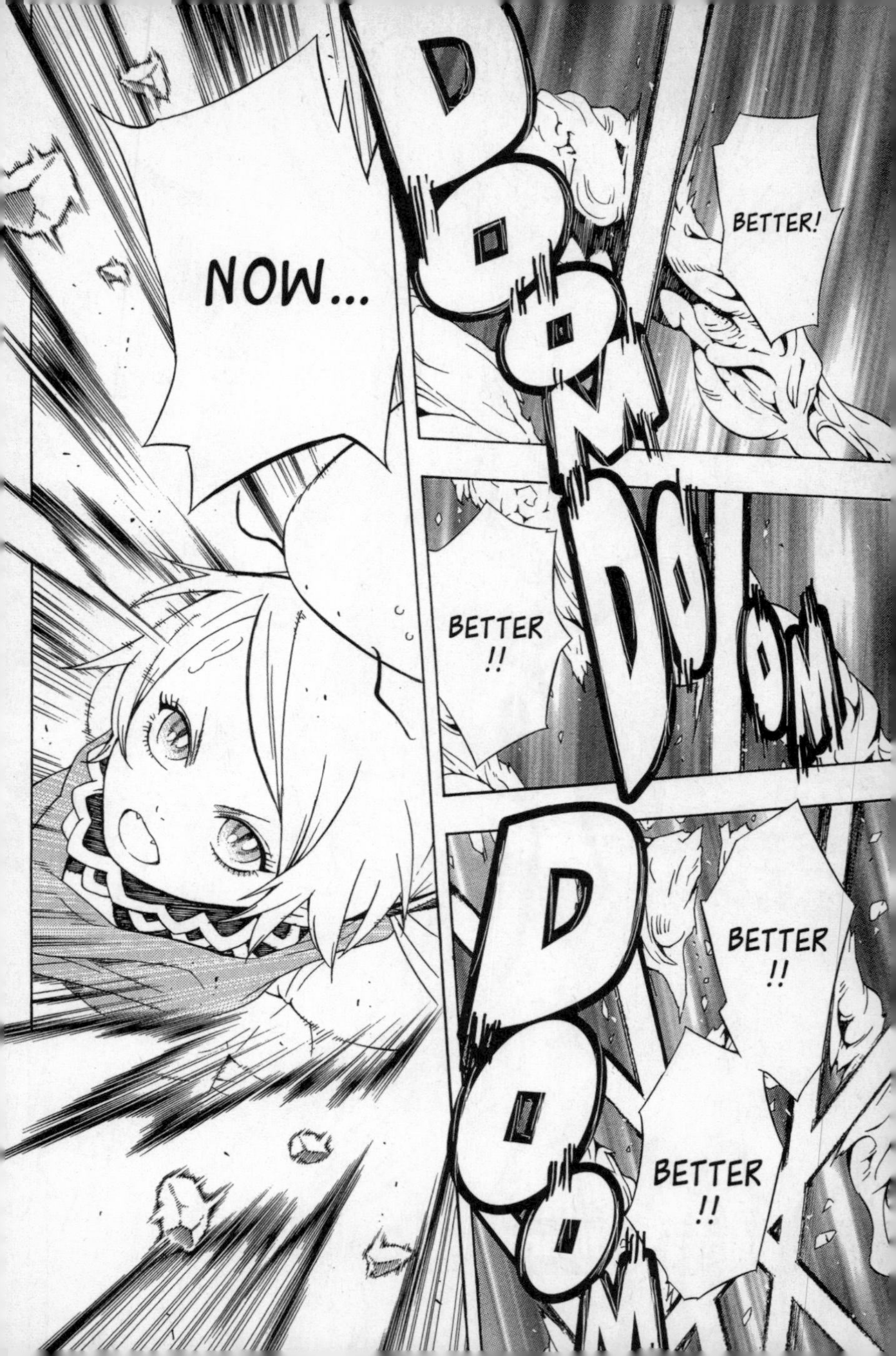
BETTER!
DOOM
BETTER !!
DOOM
BETTER !!
BETTER !!
DOOM
NOW...

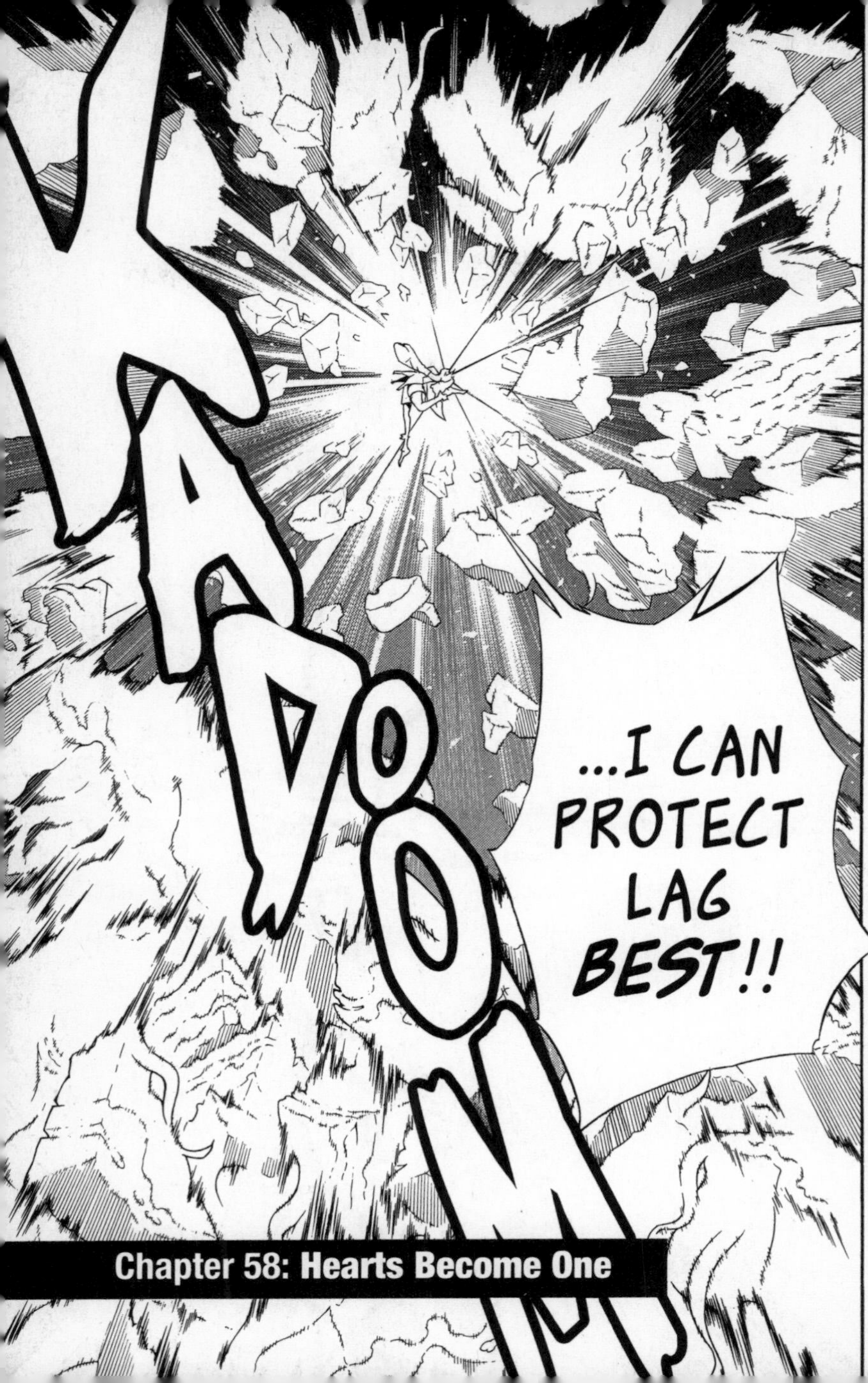
...I CAN PROTECT LAG BEST!!

Chapter 58: Hearts Become One

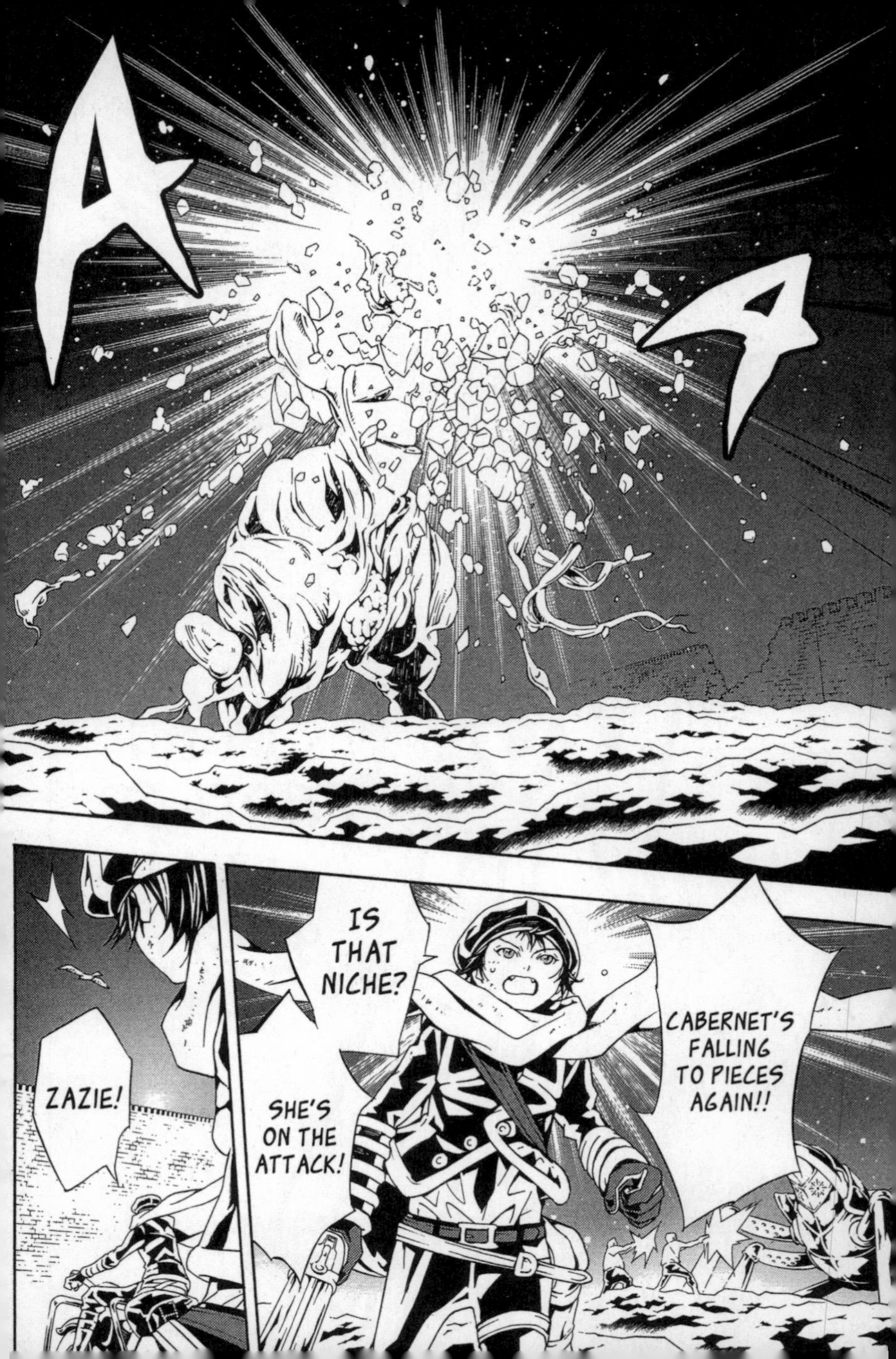
A
A
CABERNET'S FALLING TO PIECES AGAIN!!
IS THAT NICHE?
SHE'S ON THE ATTACK!
ZAZIE!

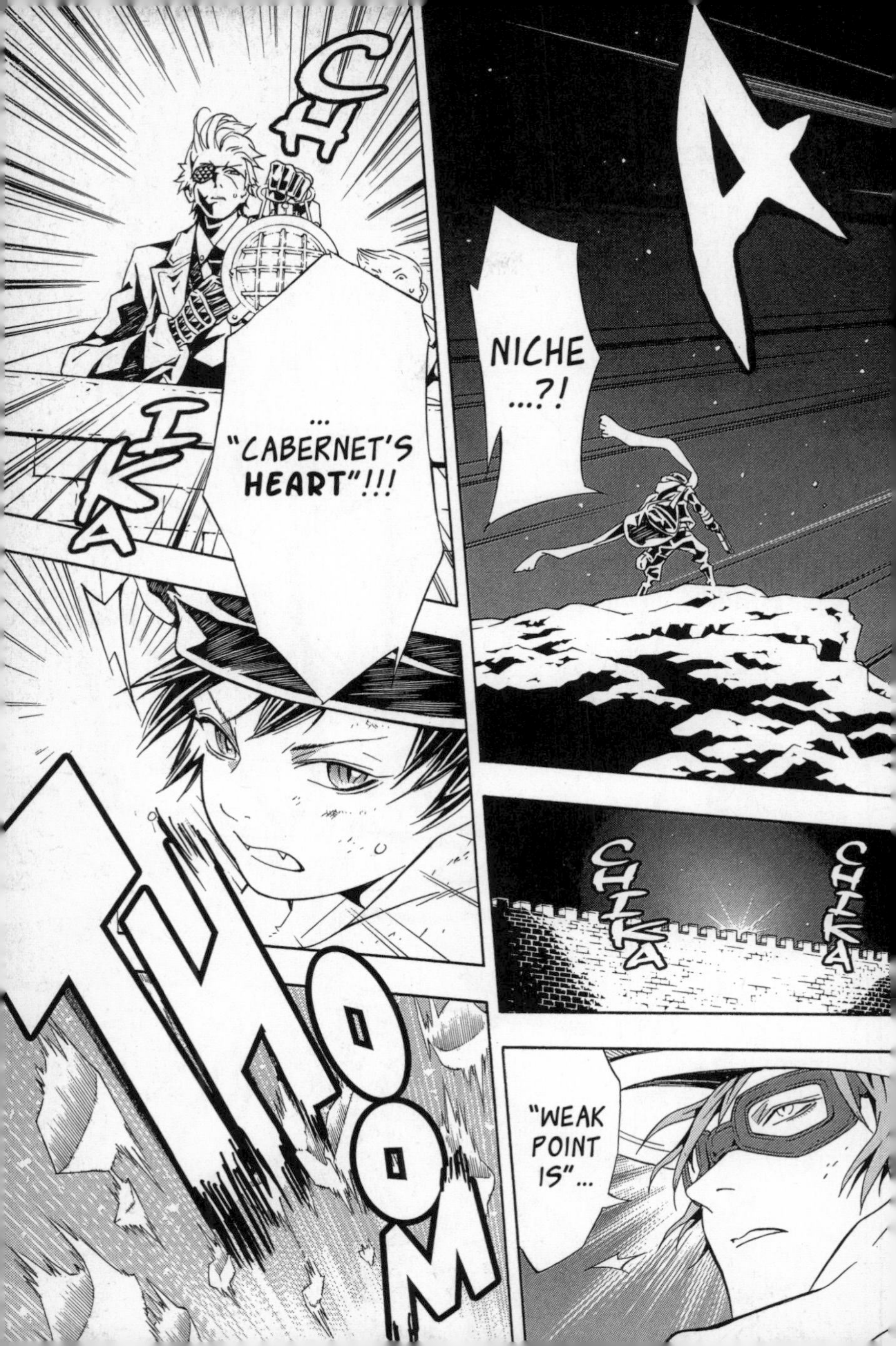
A
NICHE ...?!
CHIKA
CHIKA
"WEAK POINT IS"...
CH
IKA
... "CABERNET'S HEART"!!!
WHOOM

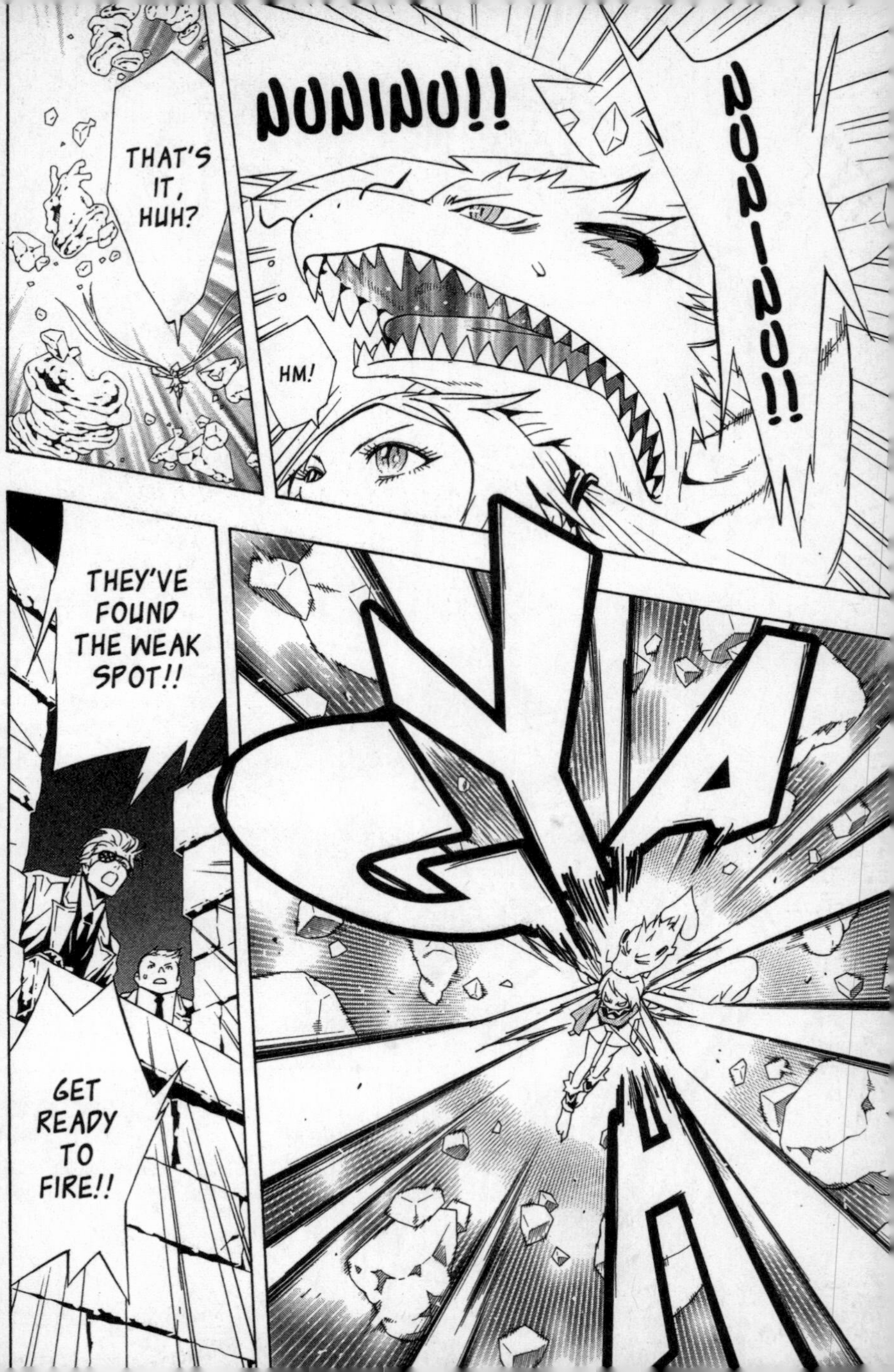
NUNINU!!
NUNINU!!
HM!
THAT'S IT, HUH?
THEY'VE FOUND THE WEAK SPOT!!
GET READY TO FIRE!!

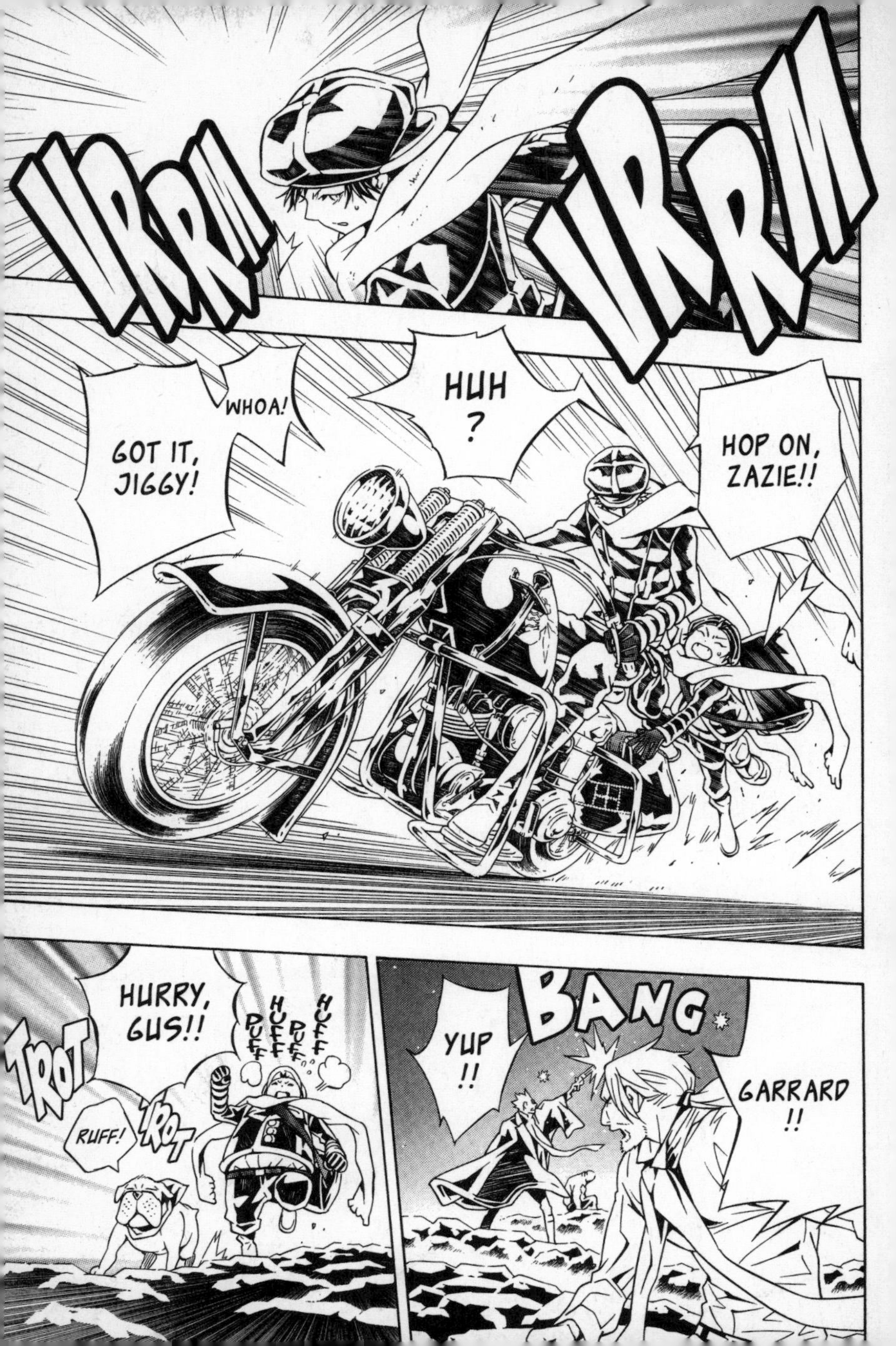
VRRM
VRRM
HOP ON, ZAZIE!!
HUH?
WHOA!
GOT IT, JIGGY!
GARRARD!!
BANG
YUP!!
HUFF PUFF
HUFF PUFF
HURRY, GUS!!
TROT
TROT
RUFF!

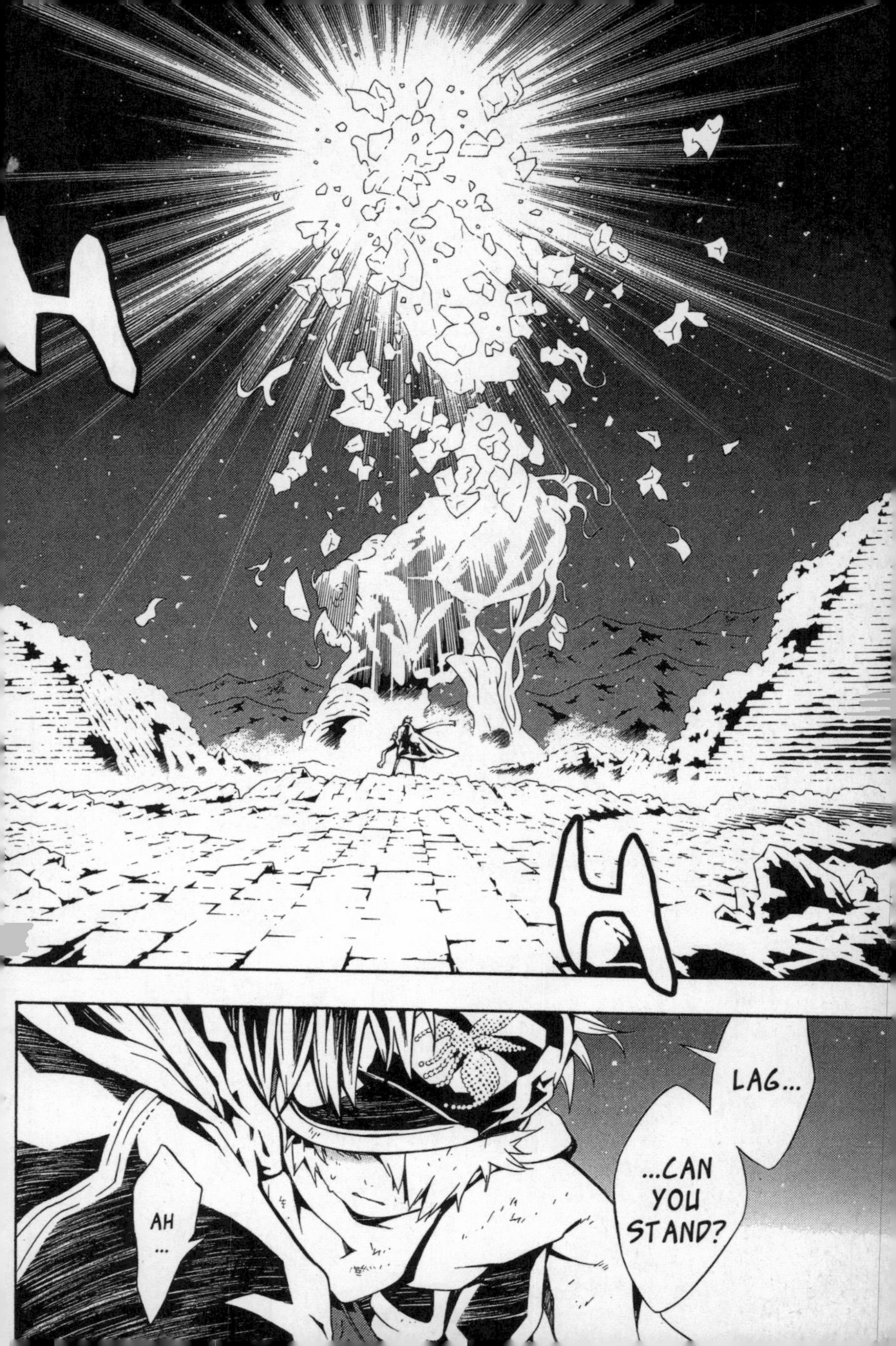
H
H
LAG...
...CAN YOU STAND?
AH ...

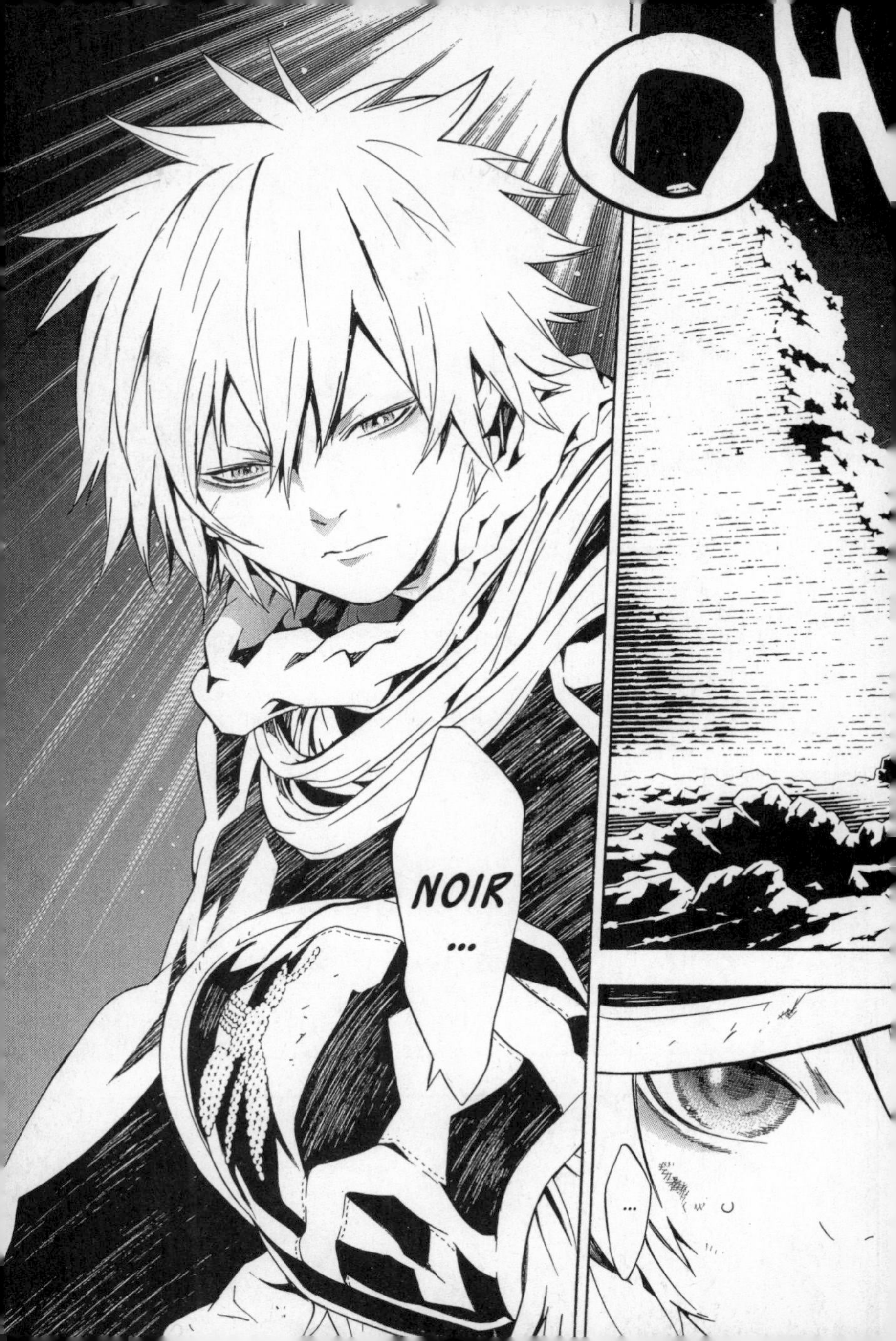
OH
NOIR
...
...

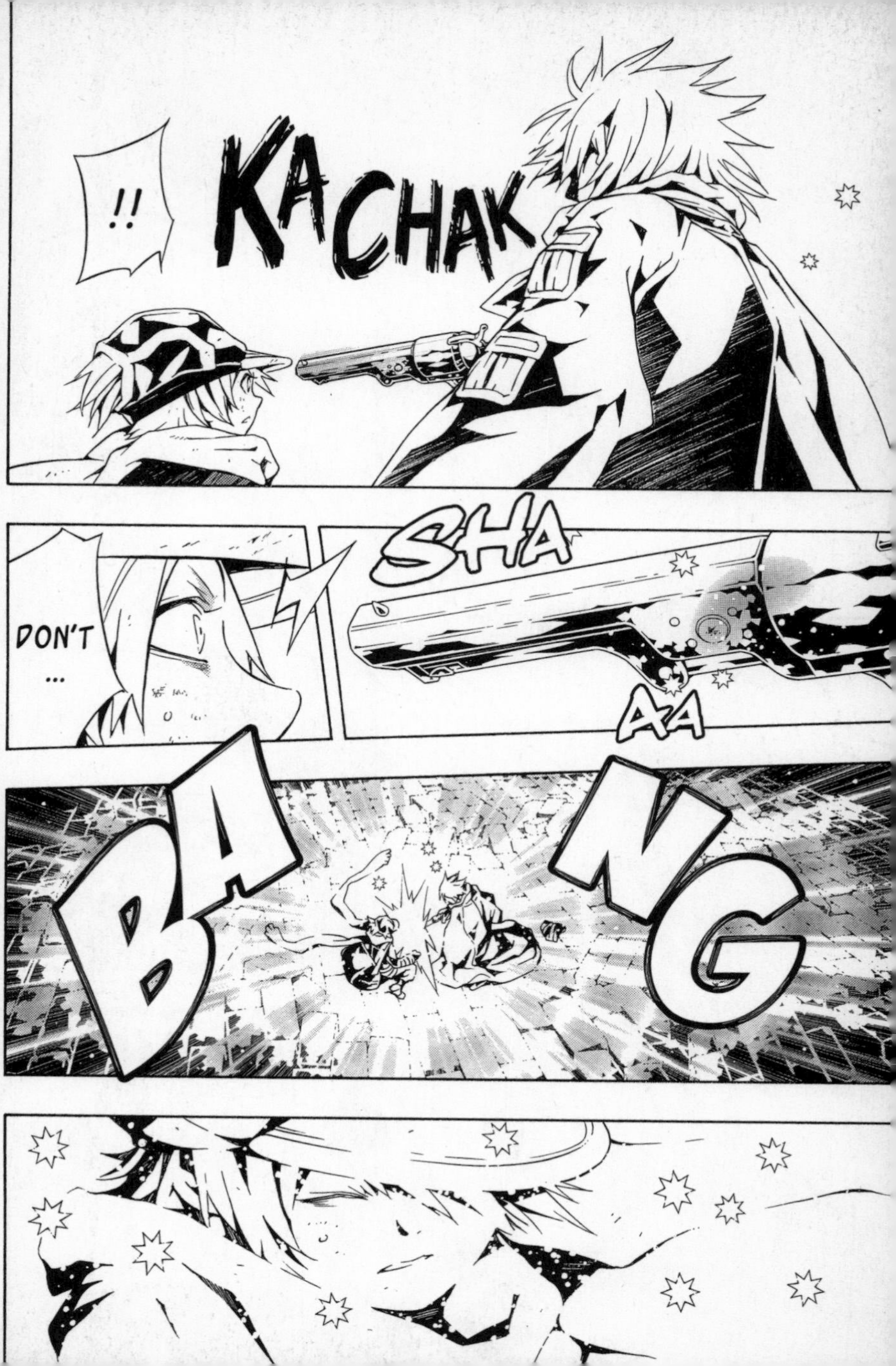
KACHAK
!!
SHA
AA
DON'T
...
BANG

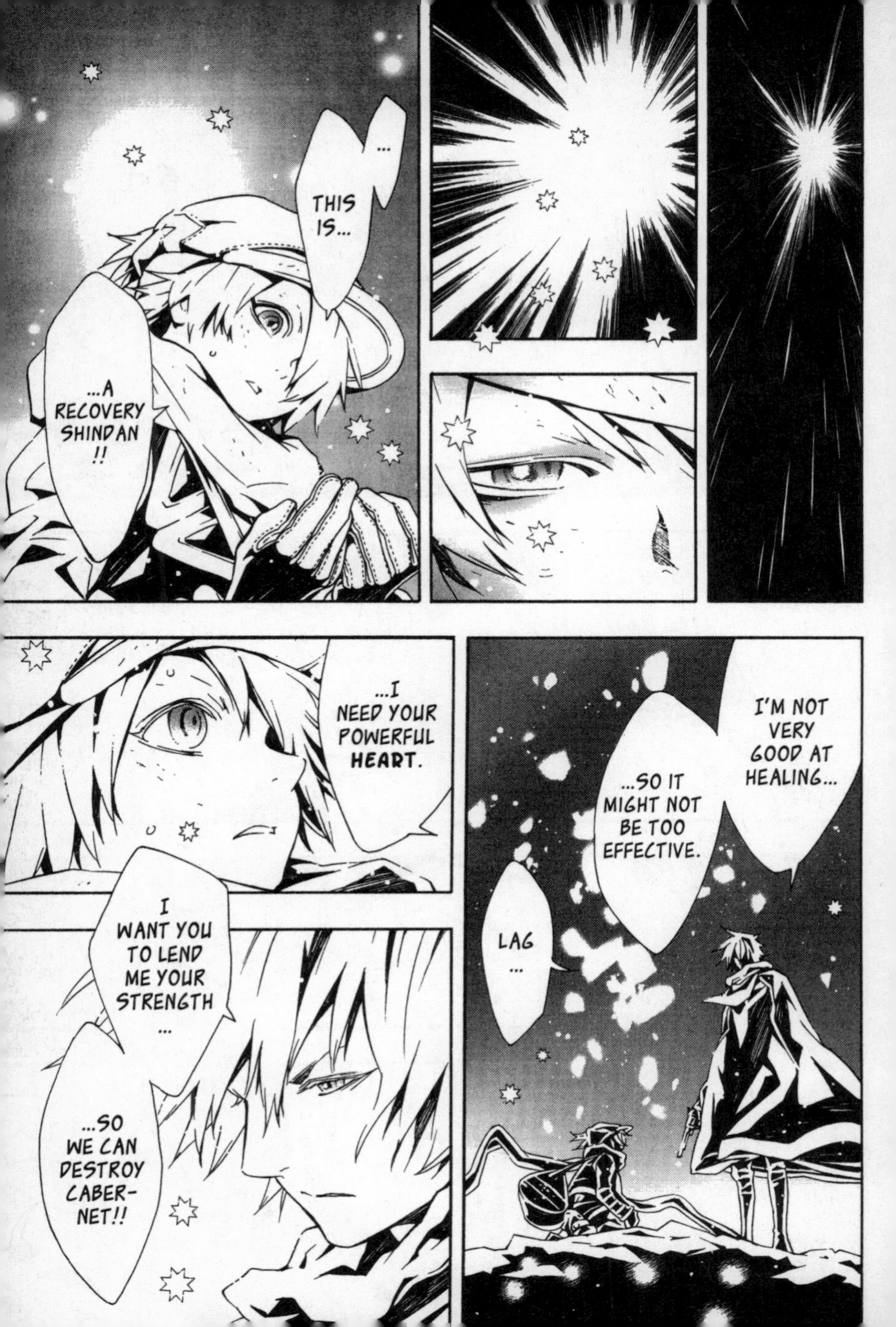
...
THIS IS...
...A RECOVERY SHINDAN!!
I'M NOT VERY GOOD AT HEALING...
...SO IT MIGHT NOT BE TOO EFFECTIVE.
LAG...
...I NEED YOUR POWERFUL HEART.
I WANT YOU TO LEND ME YOUR STRENGTH...
...SO WE CAN DESTROY CABER-NET!!

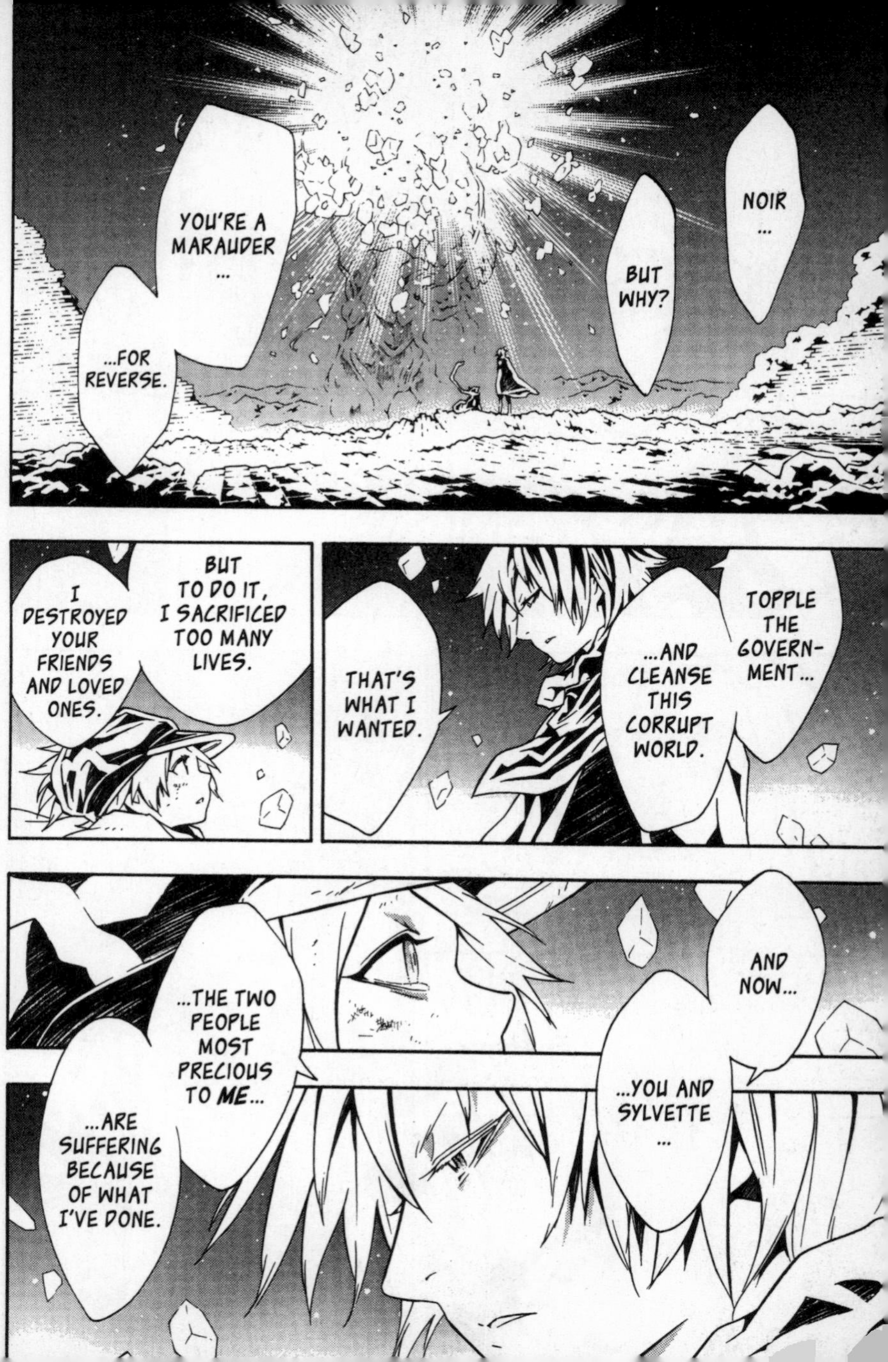
NOIR ...
BUT WHY?
YOU'RE A MARAUDER ...
...FOR REVERSE.
TOPPLE THE GOVERN-MENT...
...AND CLEANSE THIS CORRUPT WORLD.
THAT'S WHAT I WANTED.
BUT TO DO IT, I SACRIFICED TOO MANY LIVES.
I DESTROYED YOUR FRIENDS AND LOVED ONES.
AND NOW...
...YOU AND SYLVETTE ...
...THE TWO PEOPLE MOST PRECIOUS TO *ME*...
...ARE SUFFERING BECAUSE OF WHAT I'VE DONE.

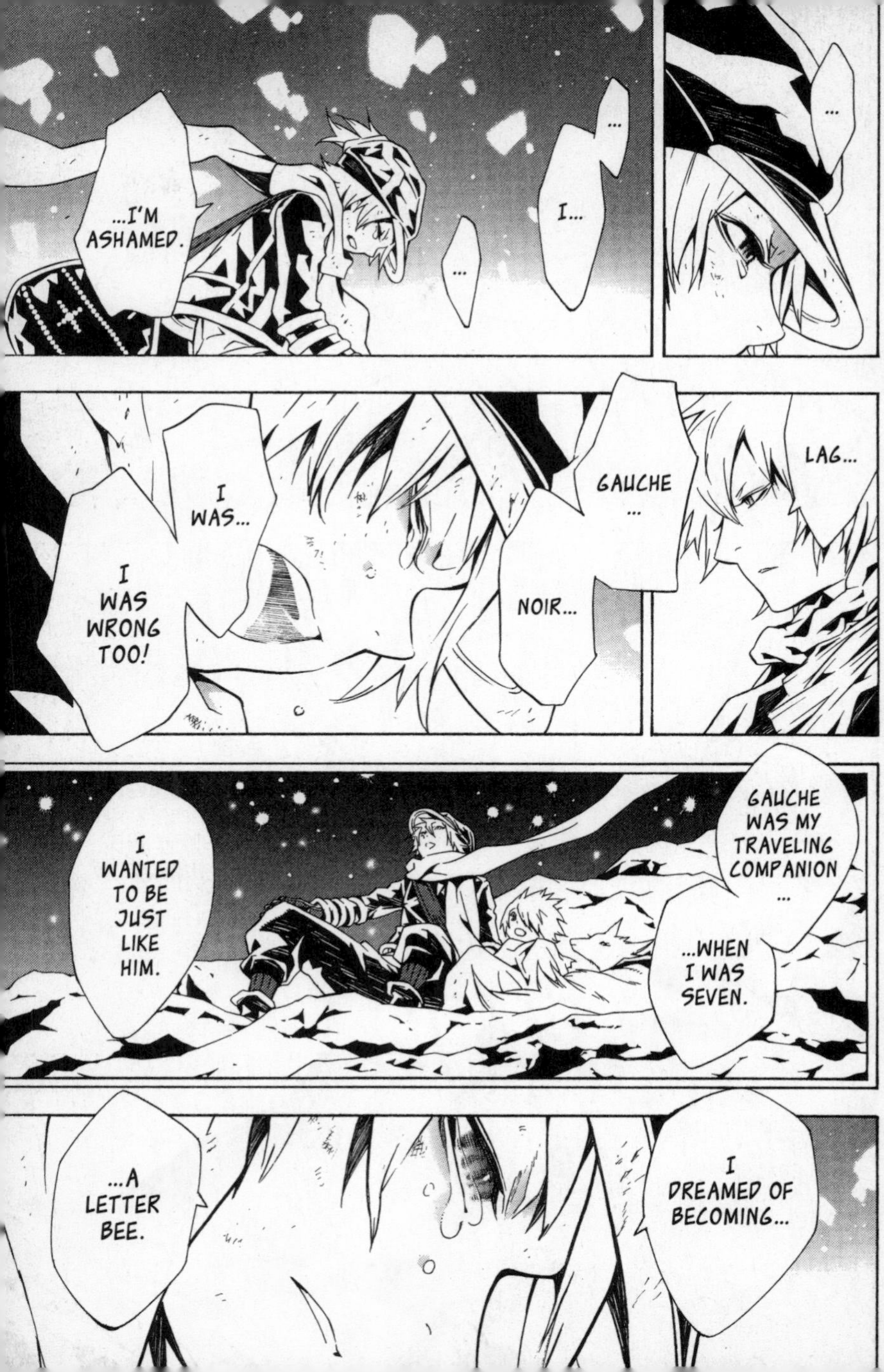
...
...
I...
...
...I'M ASHAMED.
LAG...
GAUCHE ...
NOIR...
I WAS...
I WAS WRONG TOO!
GAUCHE WAS MY TRAVELING COMPANION ...
...WHEN I WAS SEVEN.
I WANTED TO BE JUST LIKE HIM.
I DREAMED OF BECOMING...
...A LETTER BEE.

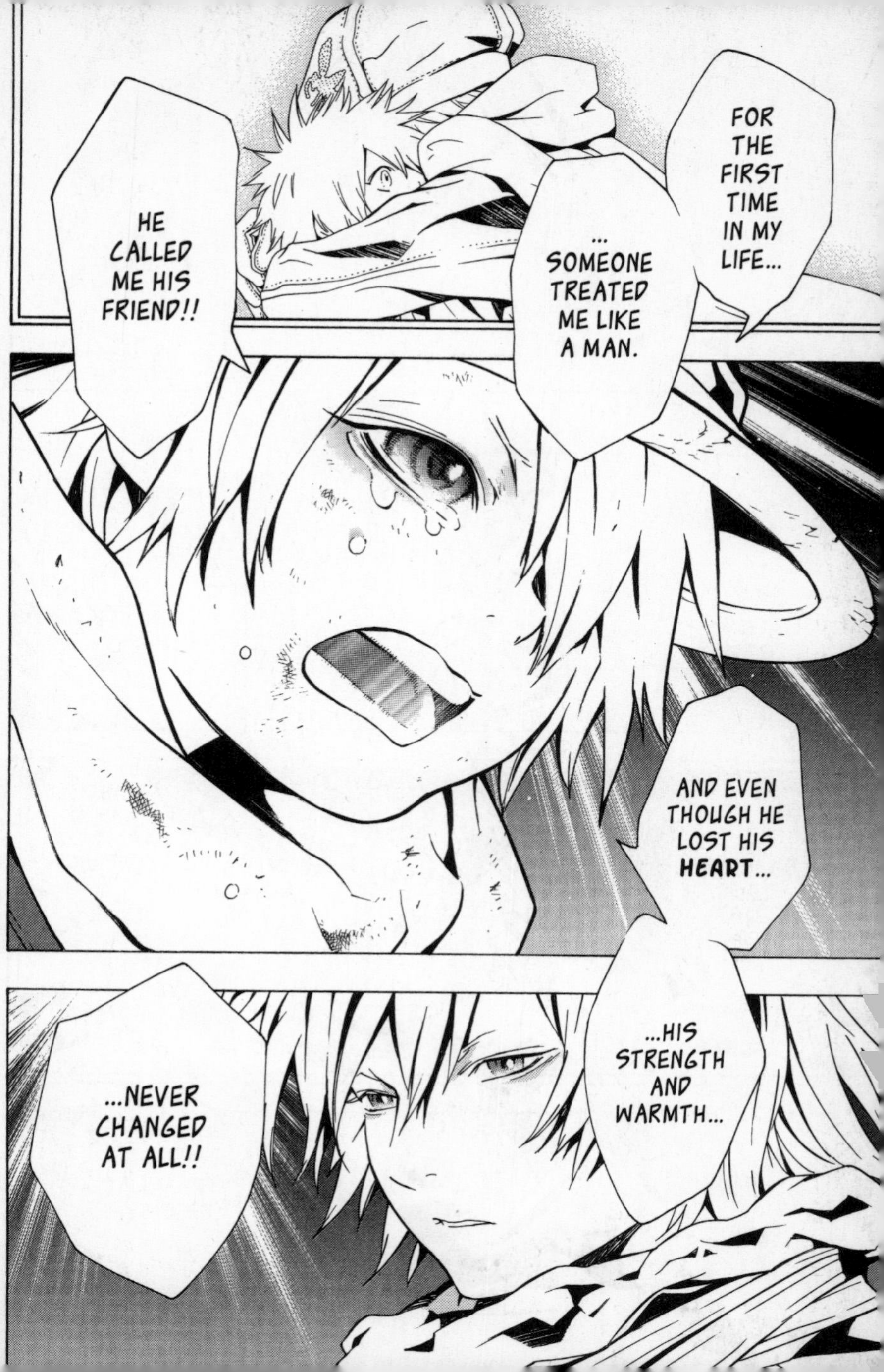
FOR THE FIRST TIME IN MY LIFE...
...SOMEONE TREATED ME LIKE A MAN.
HE CALLED ME HIS FRIEND!!
AND EVEN THOUGH HE LOST HIS **HEART**...
...HIS STRENGTH AND WARMTH...
...NEVER CHANGED AT ALL!!

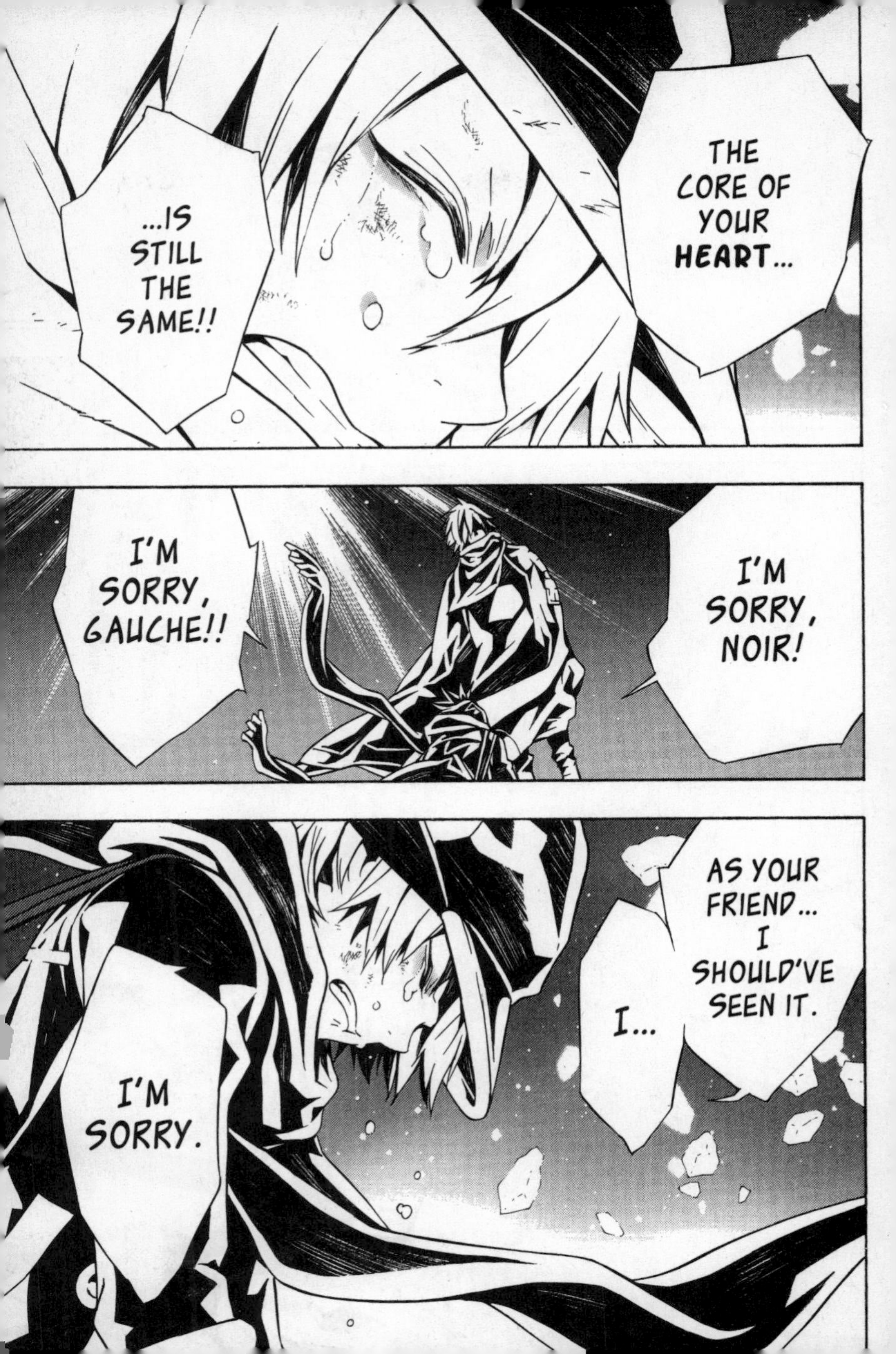
THE CORE OF YOUR HEART...
...IS STILL THE SAME!!
I'M SORRY, NOIR!
I'M SORRY, GAUCHE!!
AS YOUR FRIEND... I SHOULD'VE SEEN IT.
I...
I'M SORRY.

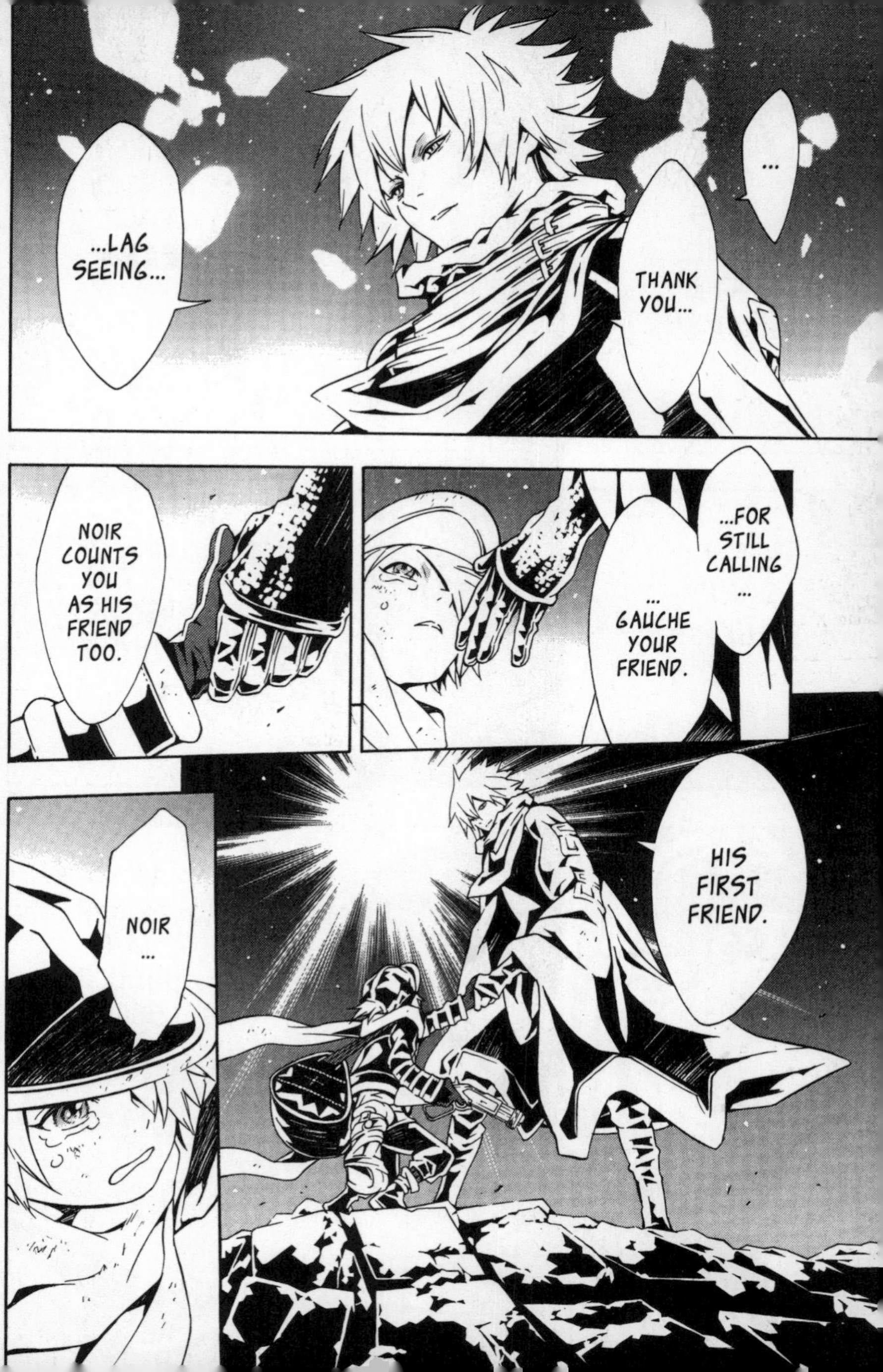
...
THANK YOU...
...LAG SEEING...
...FOR STILL CALLING ...
... GAUCHE YOUR FRIEND.
NOIR COUNTS YOU AS HIS FRIEND TOO.
HIS FIRST FRIEND.
NOIR ...

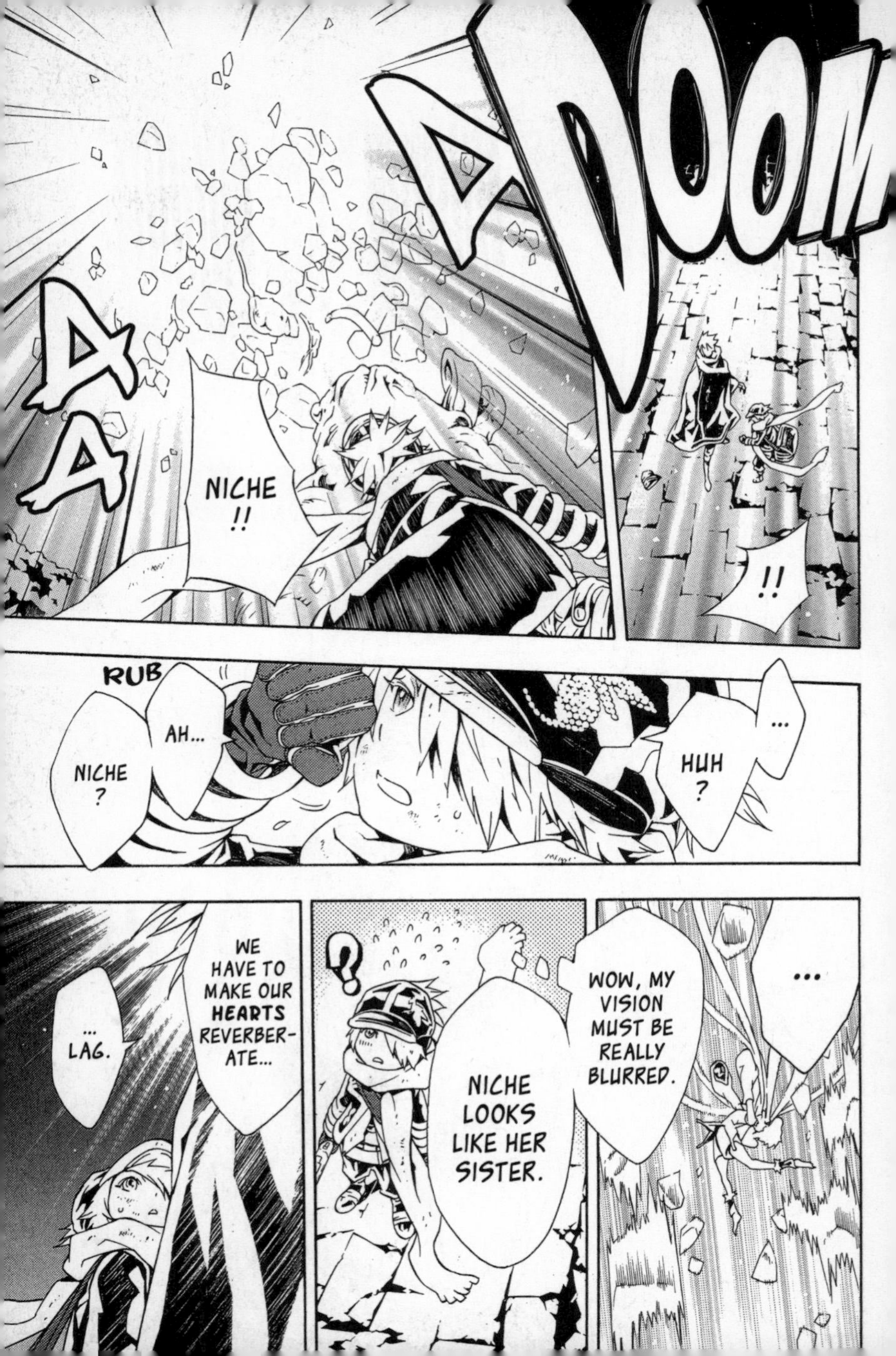
!!
DOOM
AA
NICHE!!
...
HUH?
AH...
NICHE?
RUB
...
WOW, MY VISION MUST BE REALLY BLURRED.
NICHE LOOKS LIKE HER SISTER.
WE HAVE TO MAKE OUR HEARTS REVERBER-ATE...
...LAG.

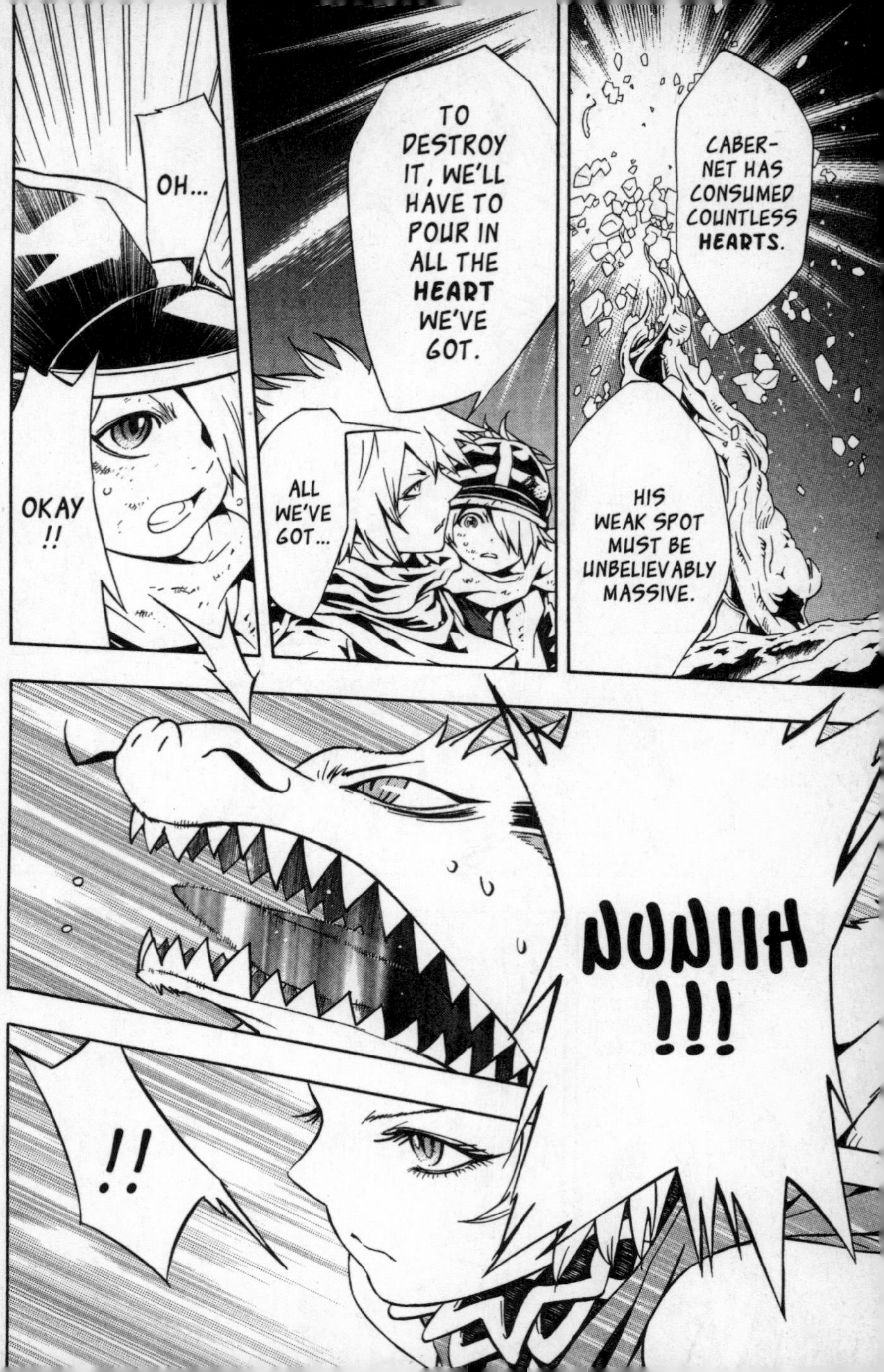
CABERNET HAS CONSUMED COUNTLESS HEARTS.
HIS WEAK SPOT MUST BE UNBELIEVABLY MASSIVE.
TO DESTROY IT, WE'LL HAVE TO POUR IN ALL THE HEART WE'VE GOT.
ALL WE'VE GOT...
OH...
OKAY !!
NUNIIH !!!
!!

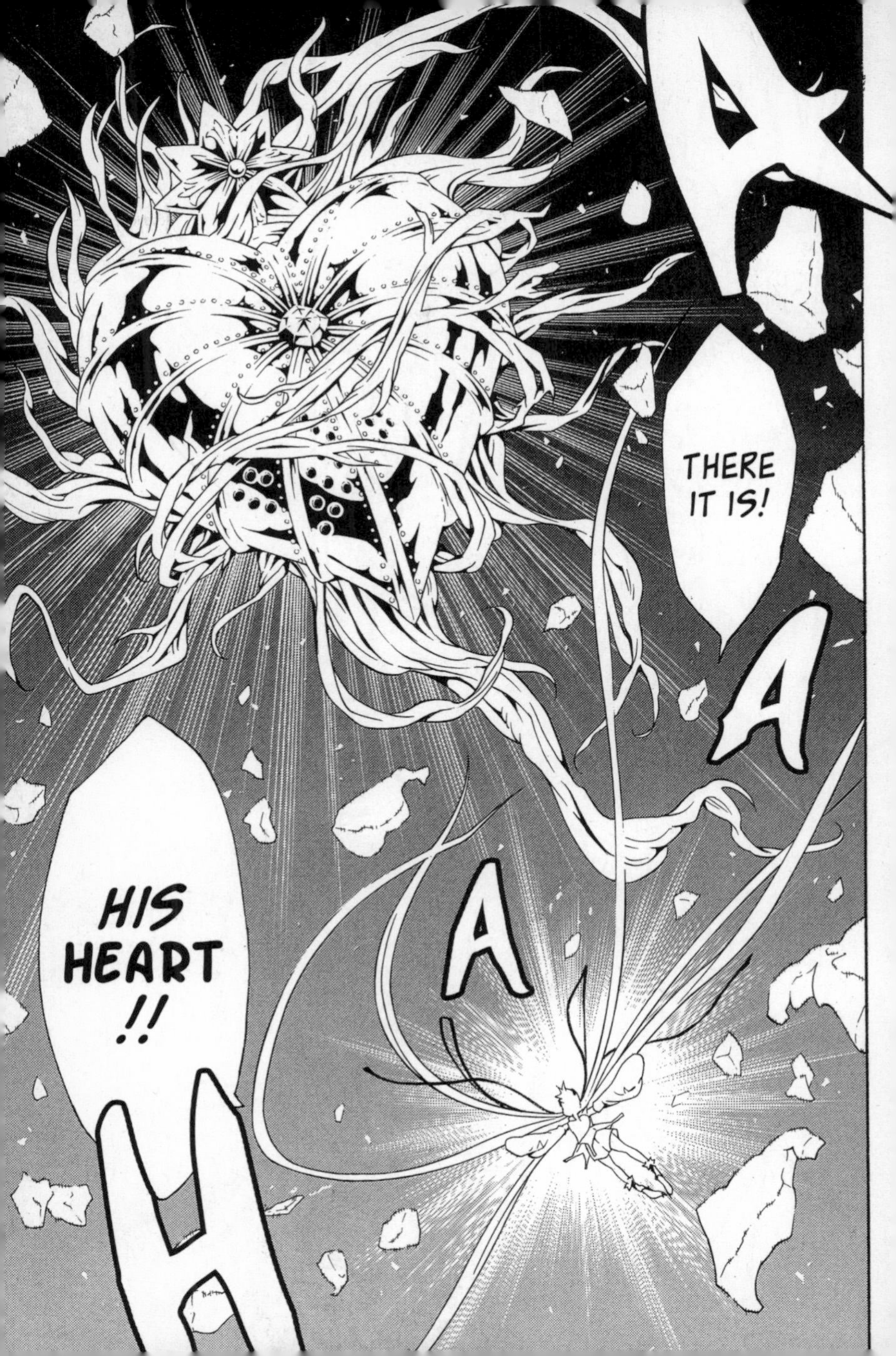
THERE IT IS!
HIS HEART!!
HAAAA

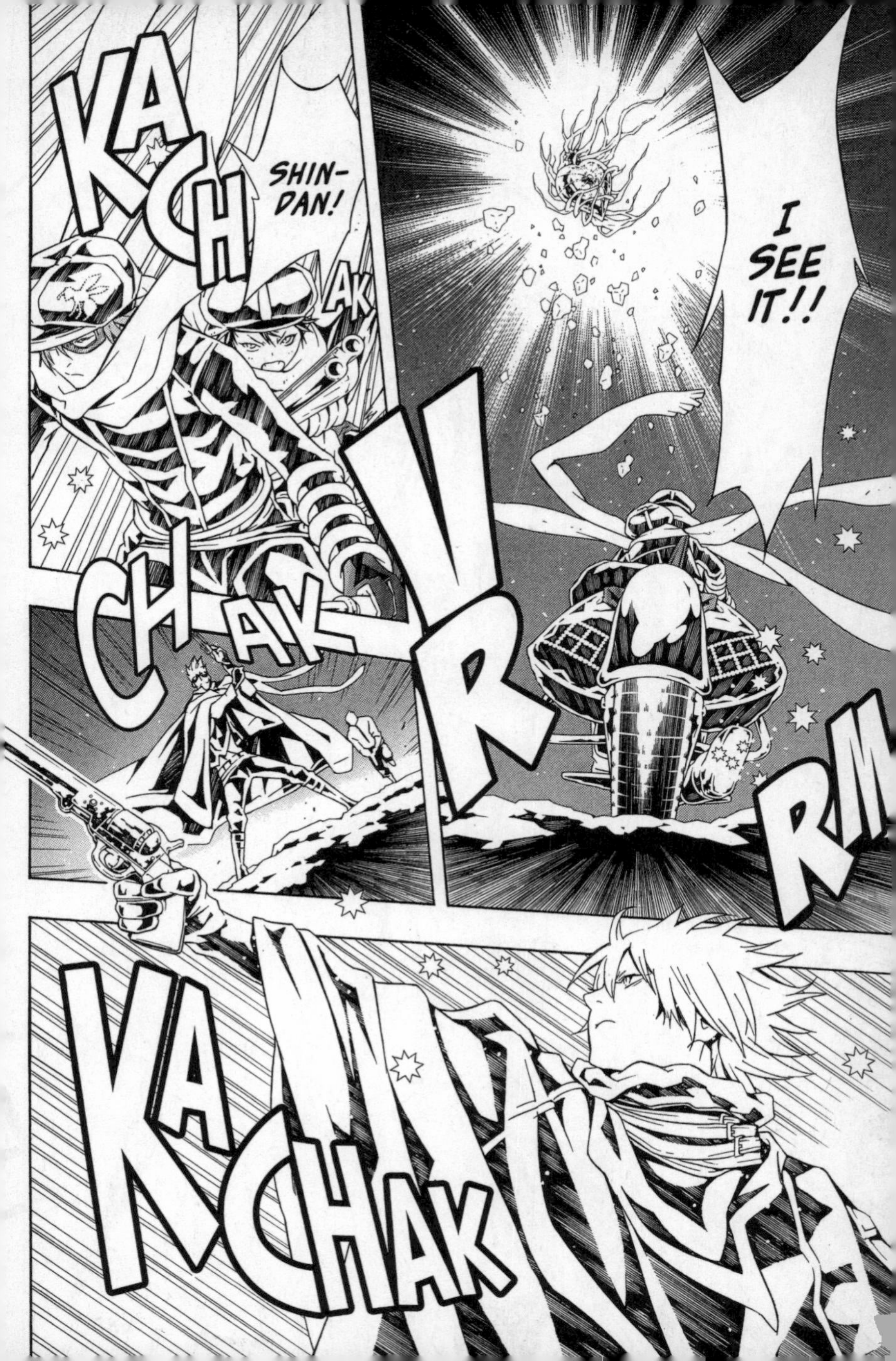

I SEE IT!!
VRRM
KACHAK
SHIN-DAN!
CHAK
KACHAK

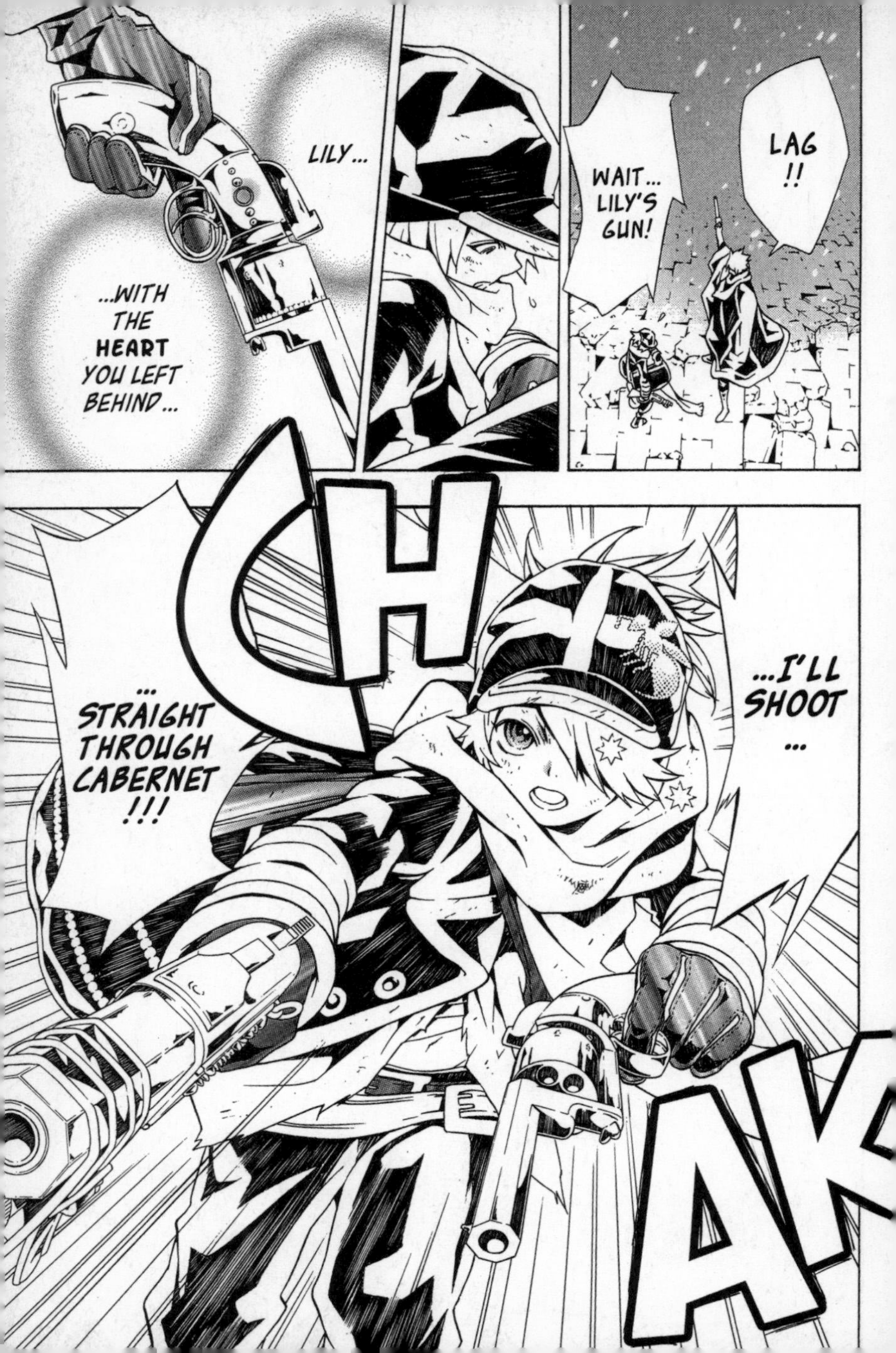
LAG !!
WAIT... LILY'S GUN!
LILY...
...WITH THE HEART YOU LEFT BEHIND...
...I'LL SHOOT ...
CH
AK
... STRAIGHT THROUGH CABERNET !!!

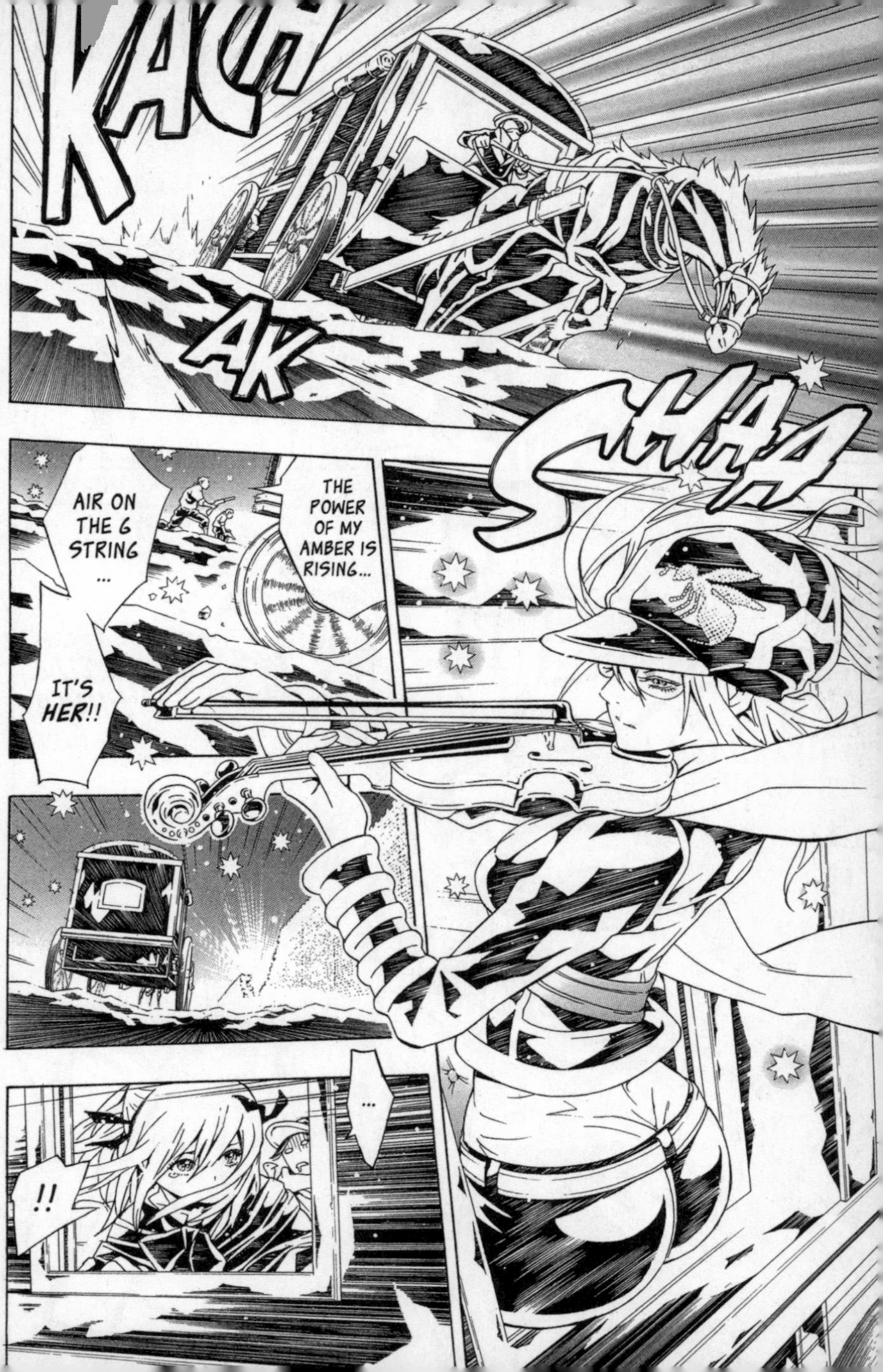
KACH
AK
SHAA
THE POWER OF MY AMBER IS RISING...
AIR ON THE G STRING ...
IT'S HER!!
...
!!

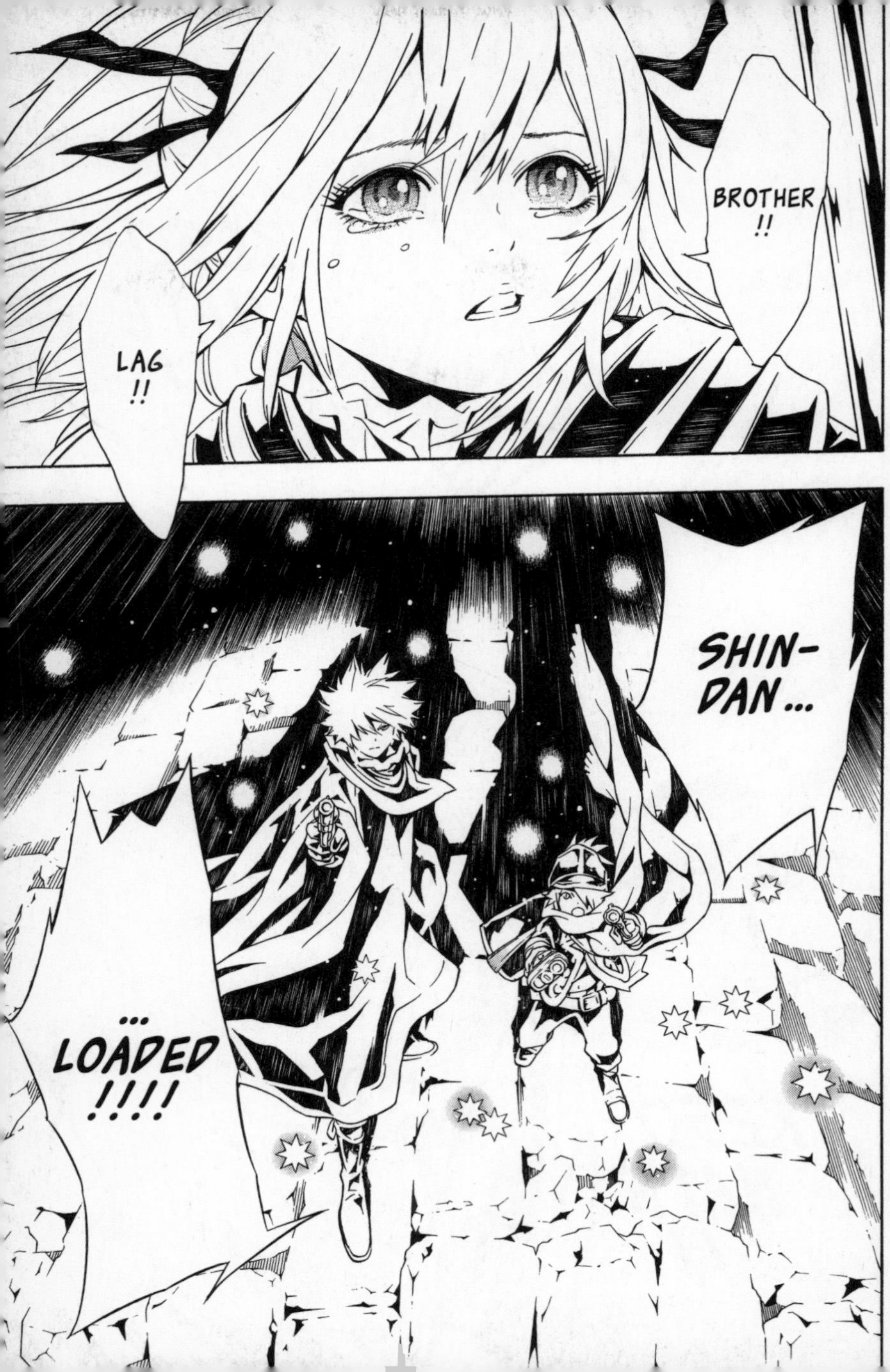
BROTHER !!
LAG !!
SHIN-DAN...
...LOADED !!!!

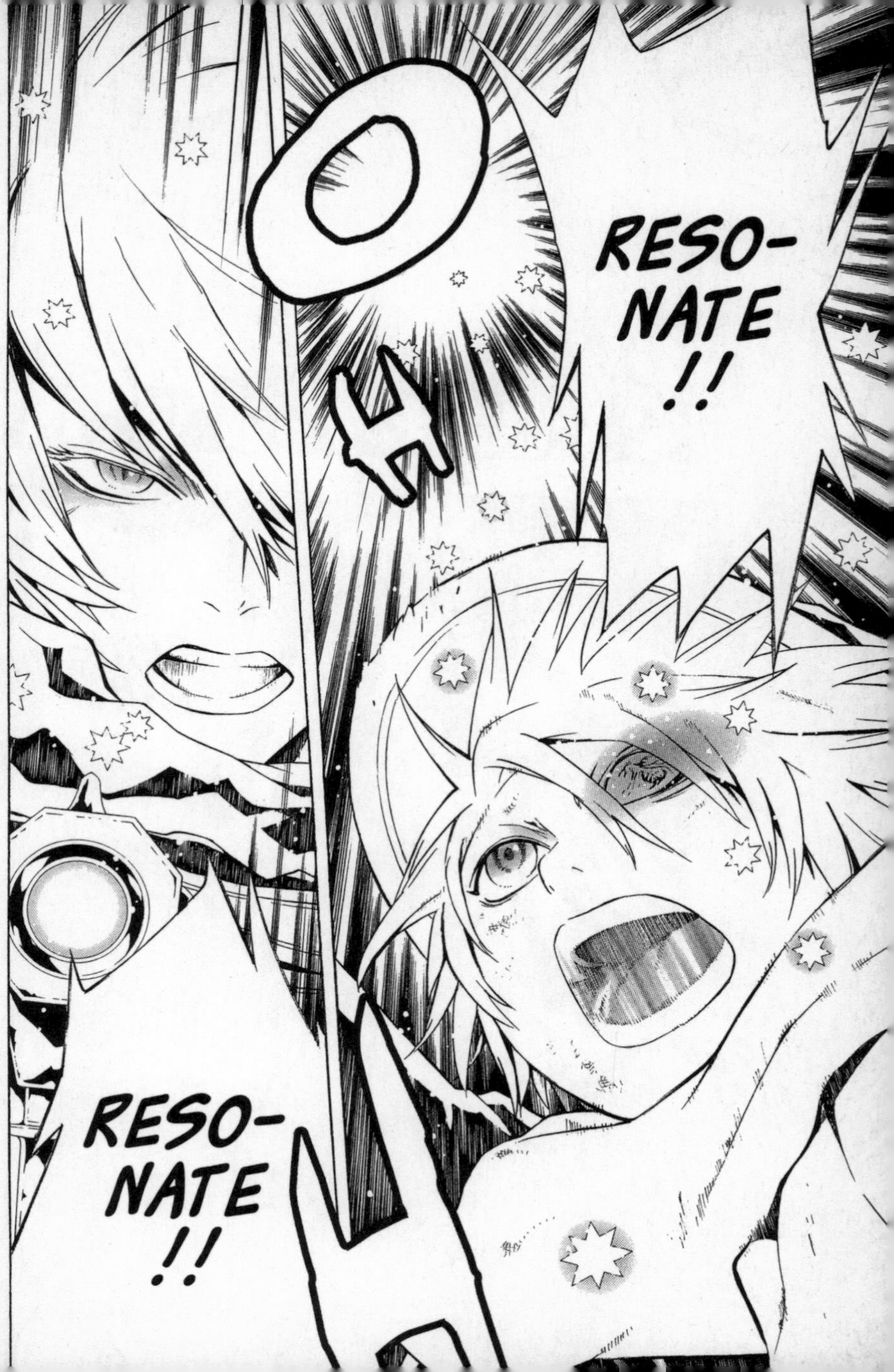

RESO-NATE!!
OH
RESO-NATE!!

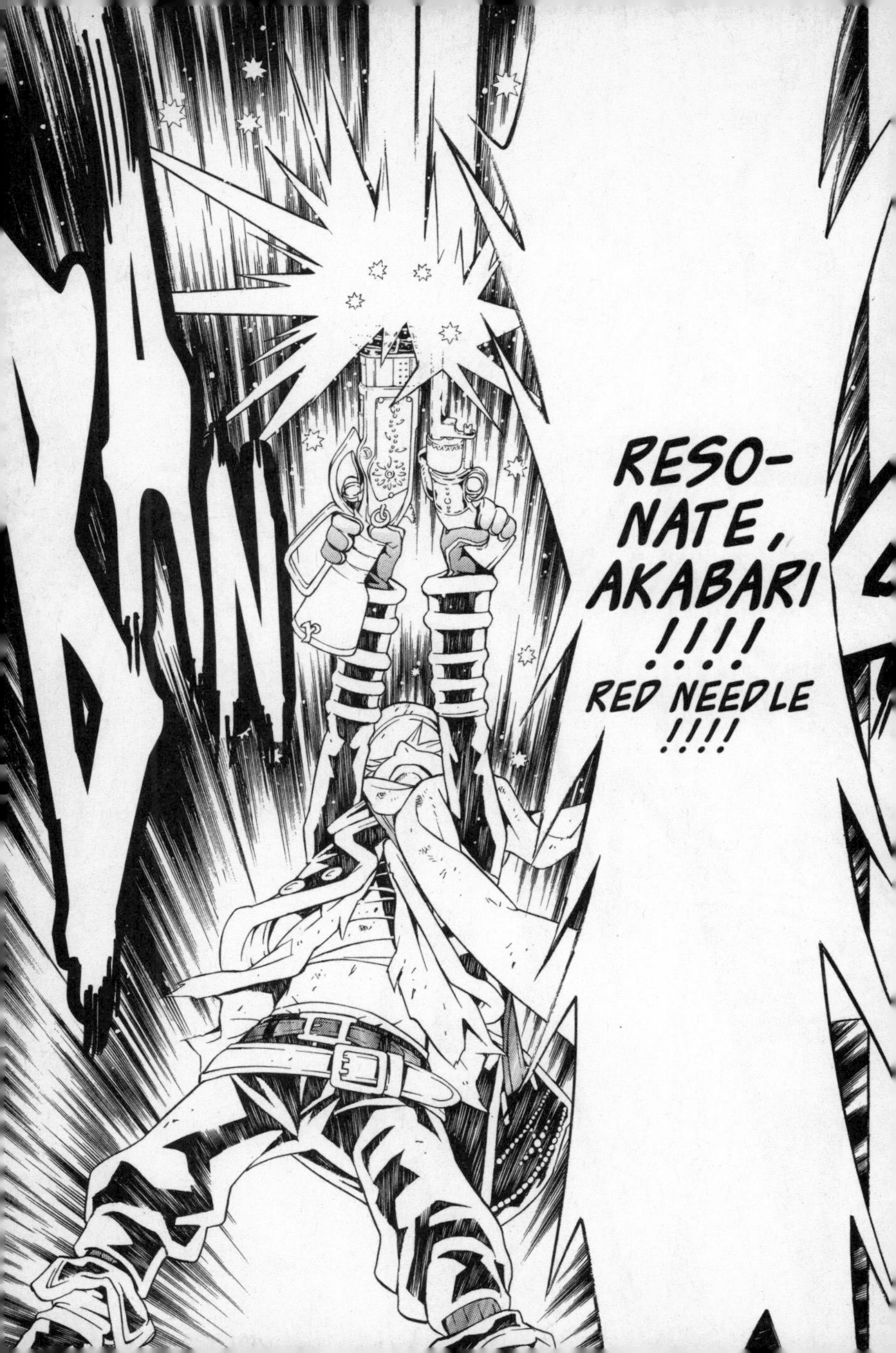
RESO-NATE, AKABARI!!!!
RED NEEDLE!!!!

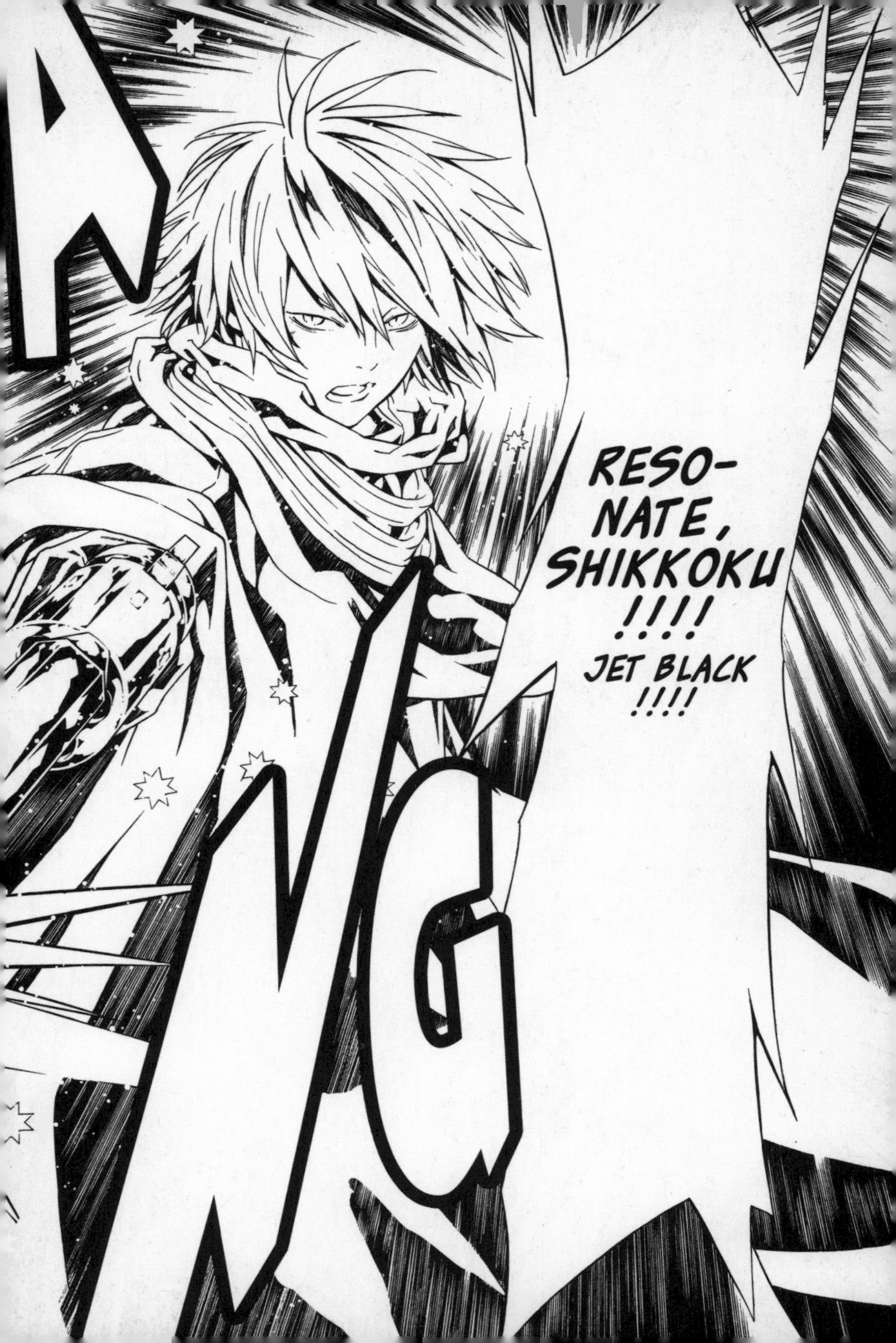
RESO-NATE, SHIKKOKU !!!!
JET BLACK !!!!

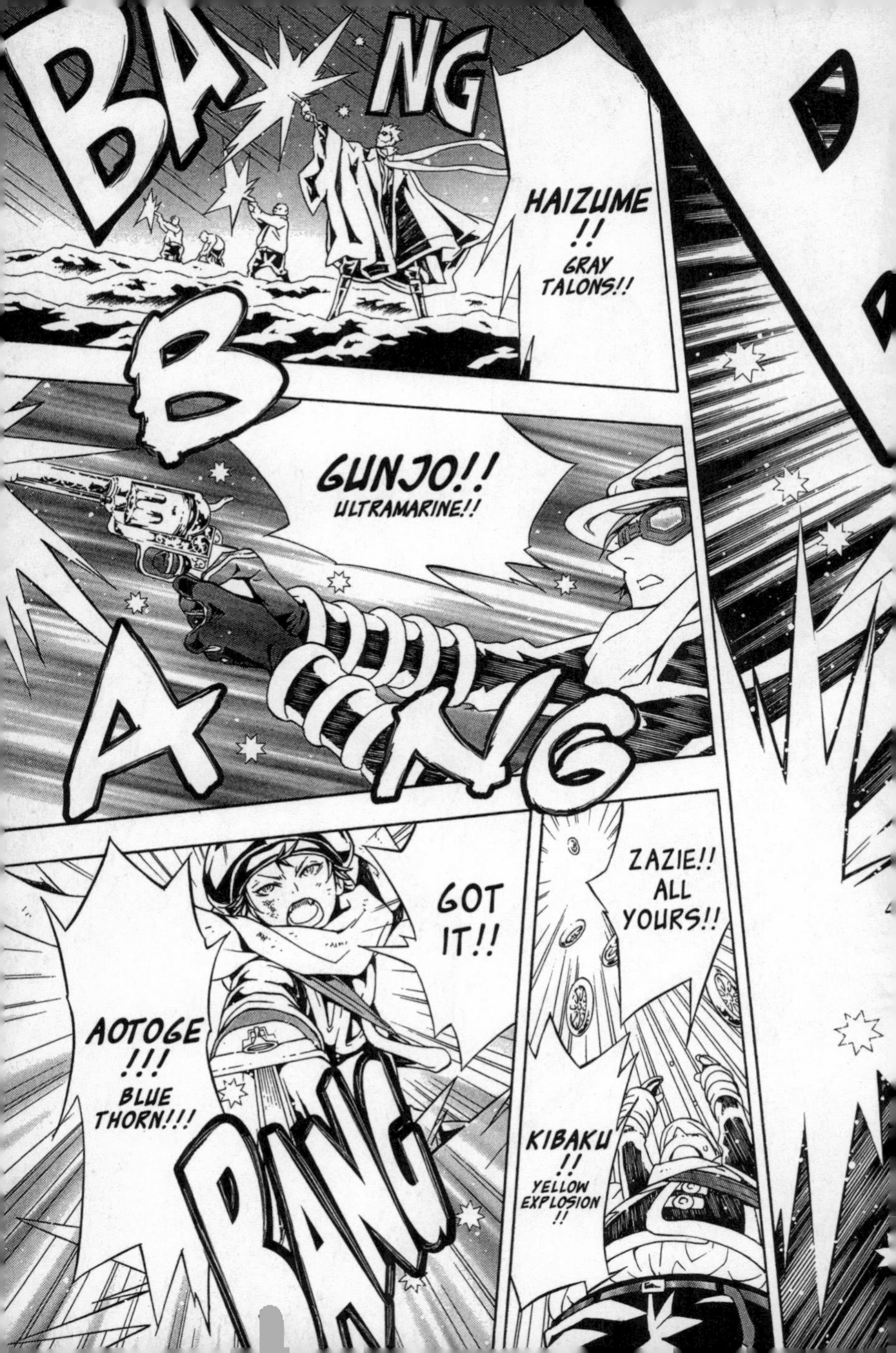
BANG
HAIZUME!! GRAY TALONS!!
BANG
GUNJO!! ULTRAMARINE!!
ZAZIE!! ALL YOURS!!
KIBAKU!! YELLOW EXPLOSION!!
GOT IT!!
AOTOGE!!! BLUE THORN!!!

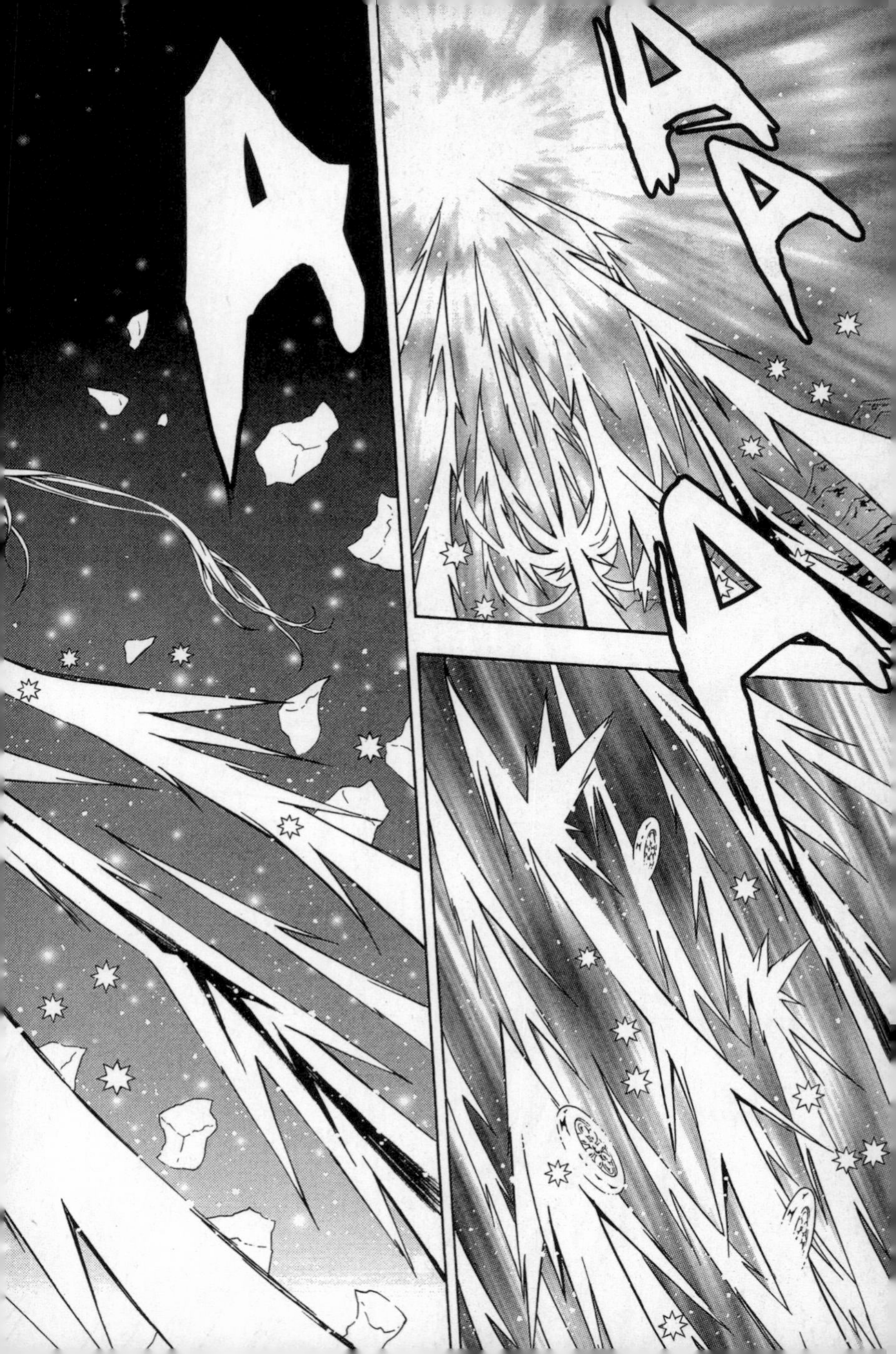

AA
A
A

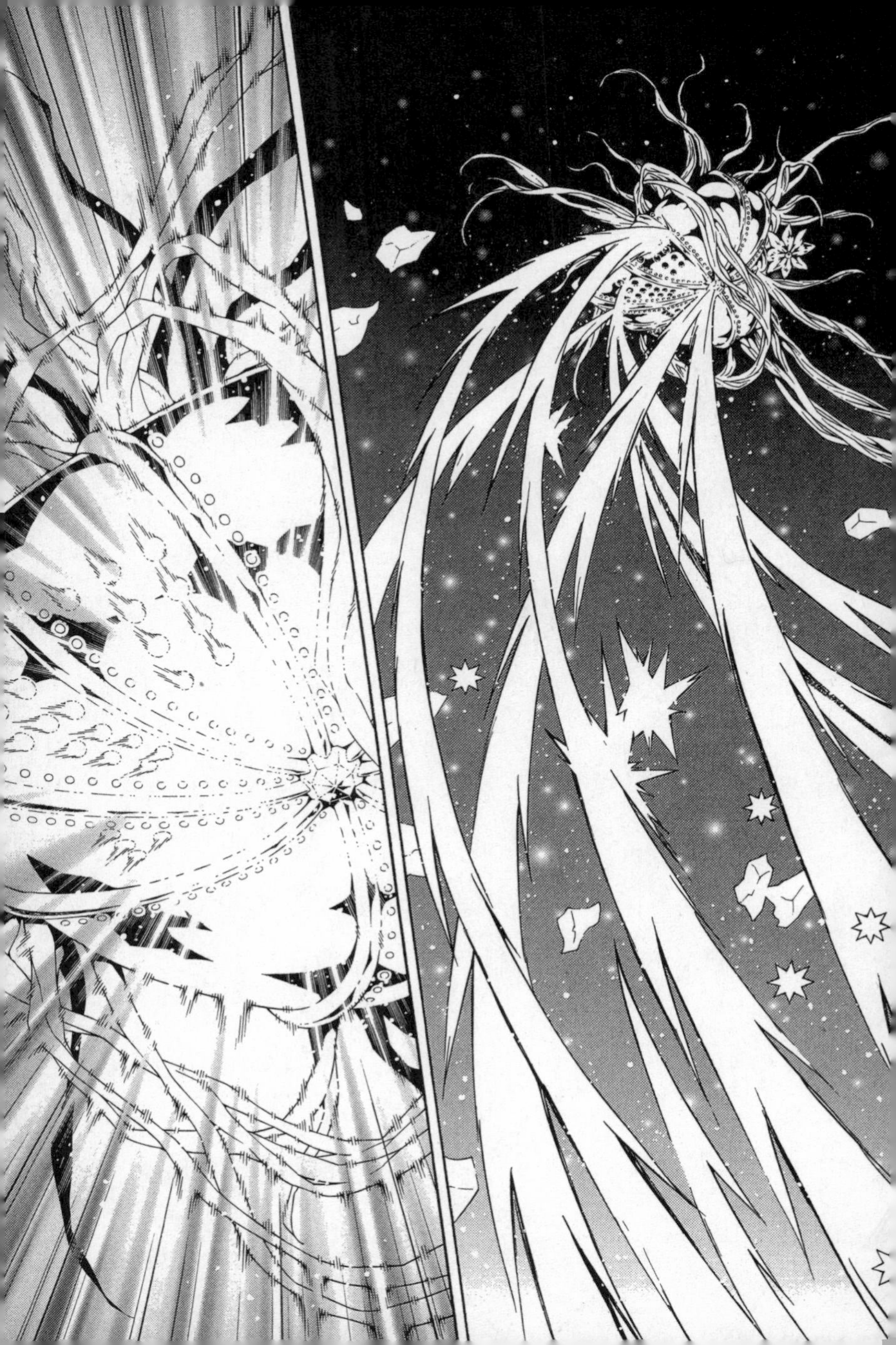

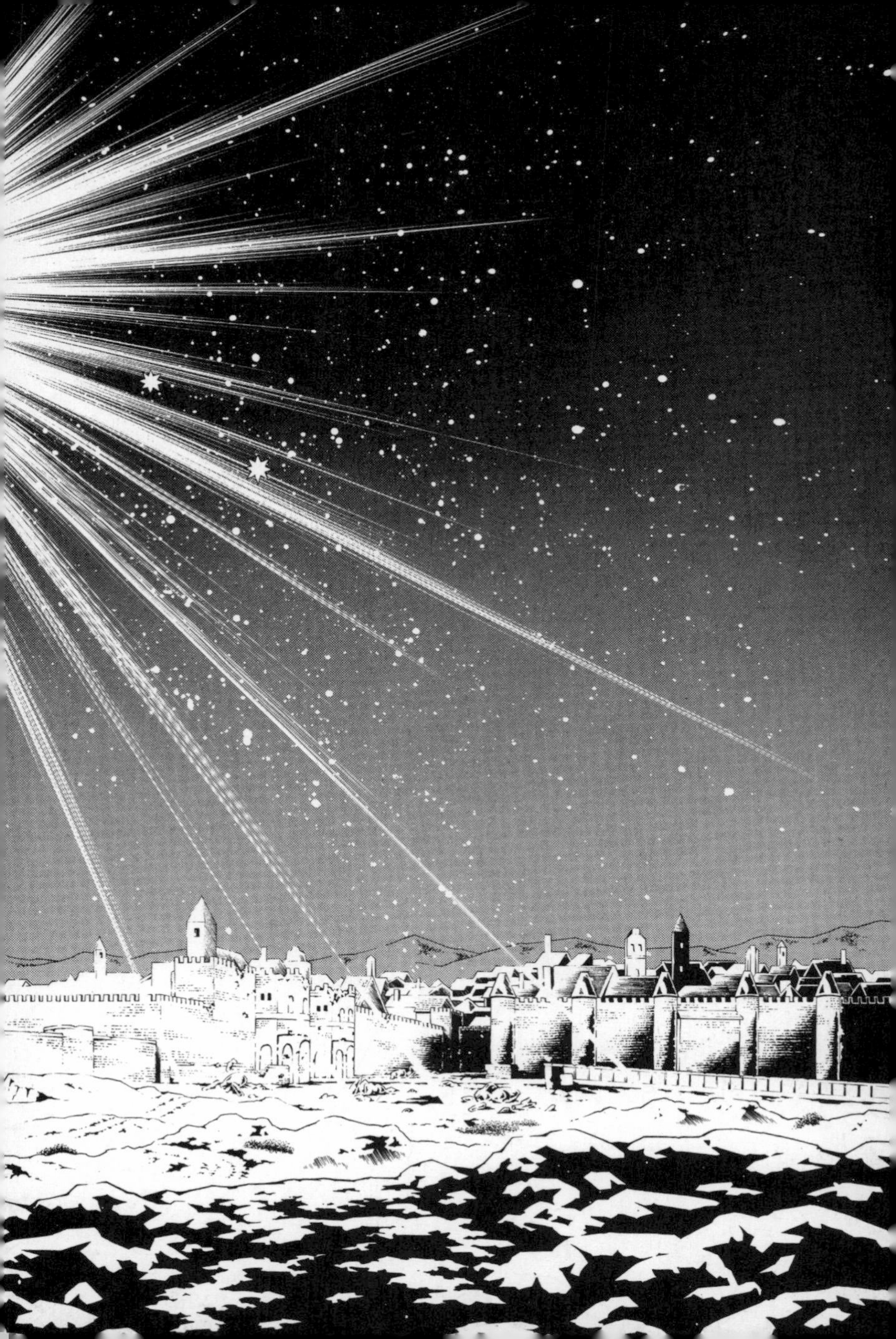

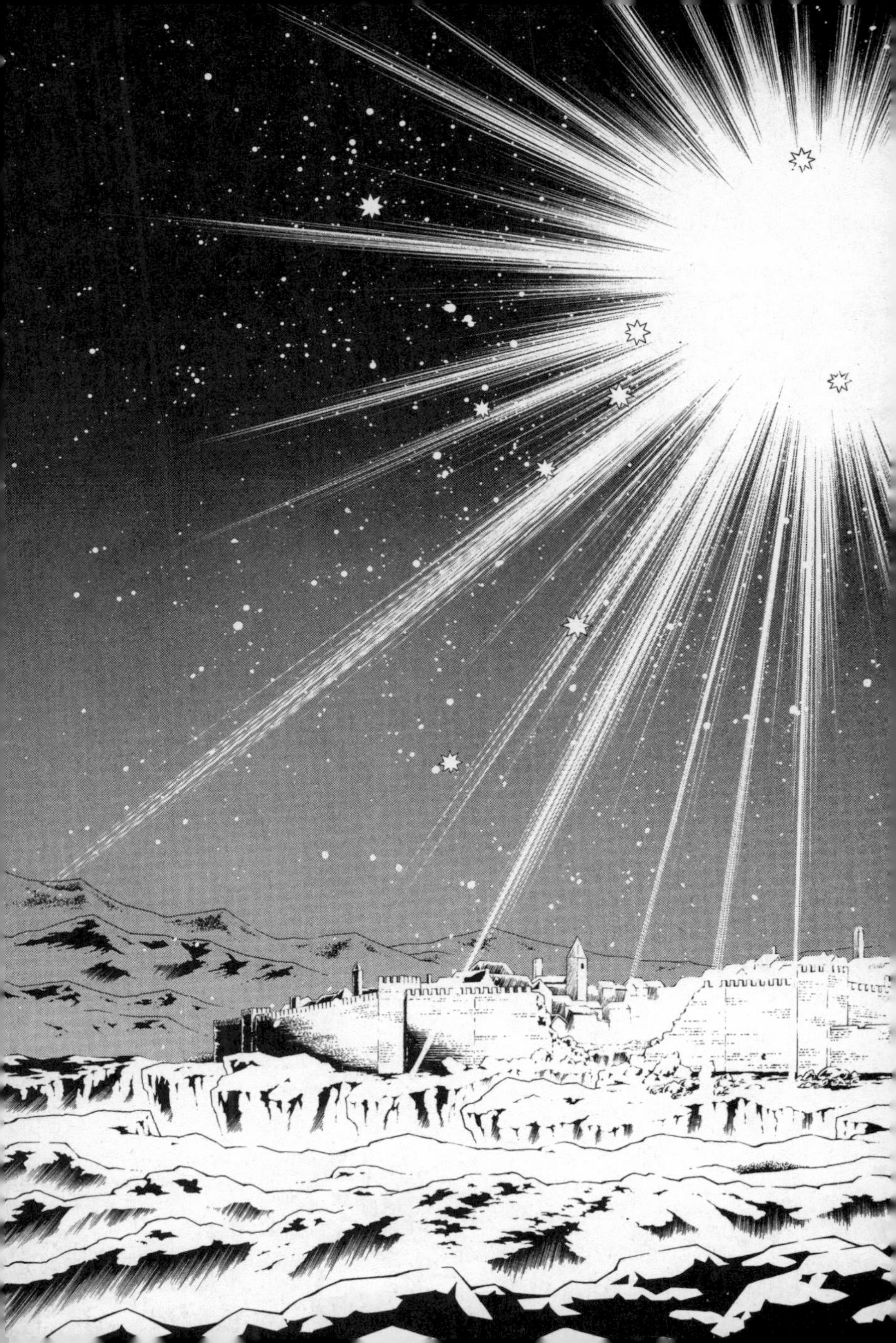

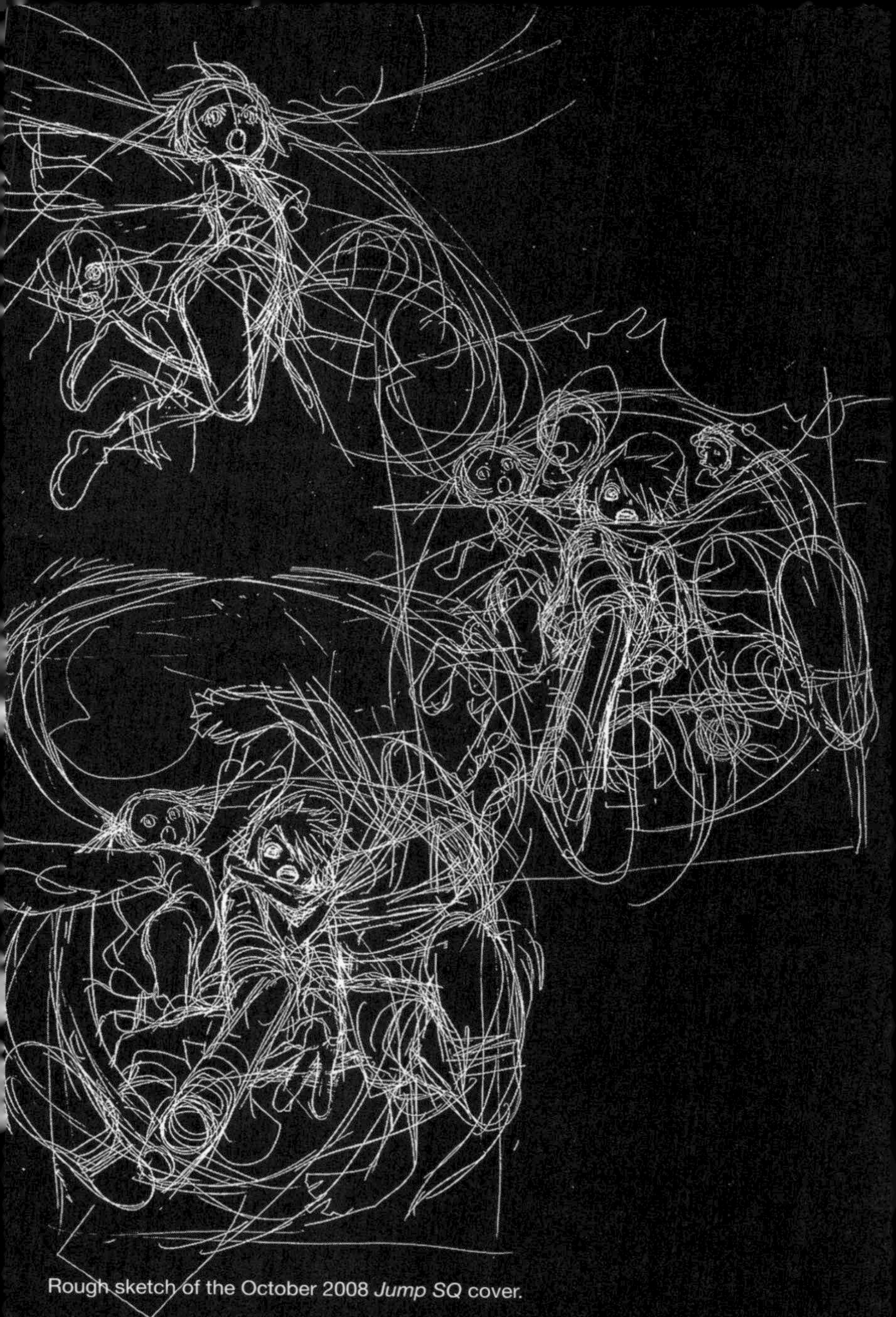

Rough sketch of the October 2008 *Jump SQ* cover.

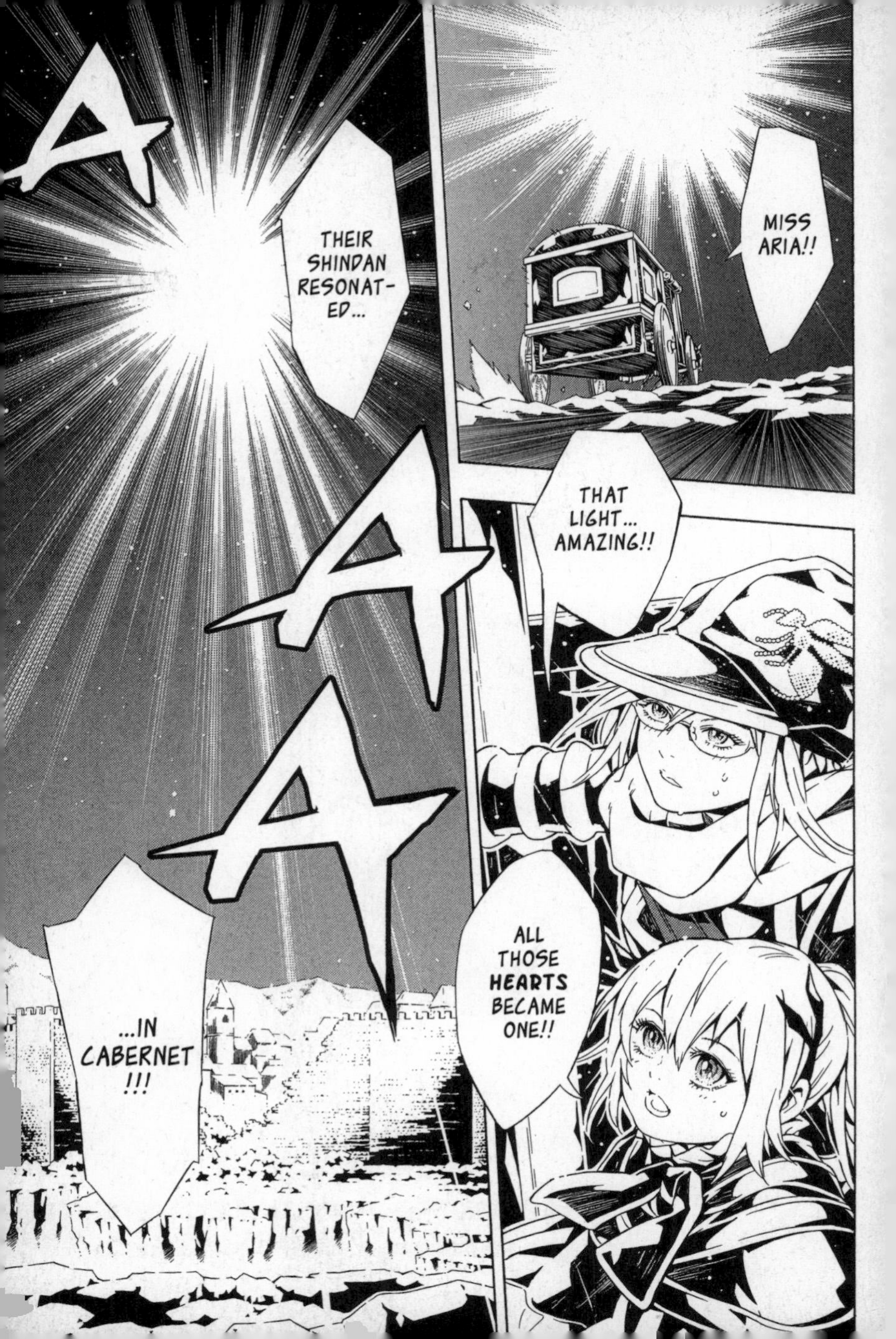
MISS ARIA!!
THAT LIGHT... AMAZING!!
ALL THOSE HEARTS BECAME ONE!!
AAA
THEIR SHINDAN RESONATED...
...IN CABERNET!!!

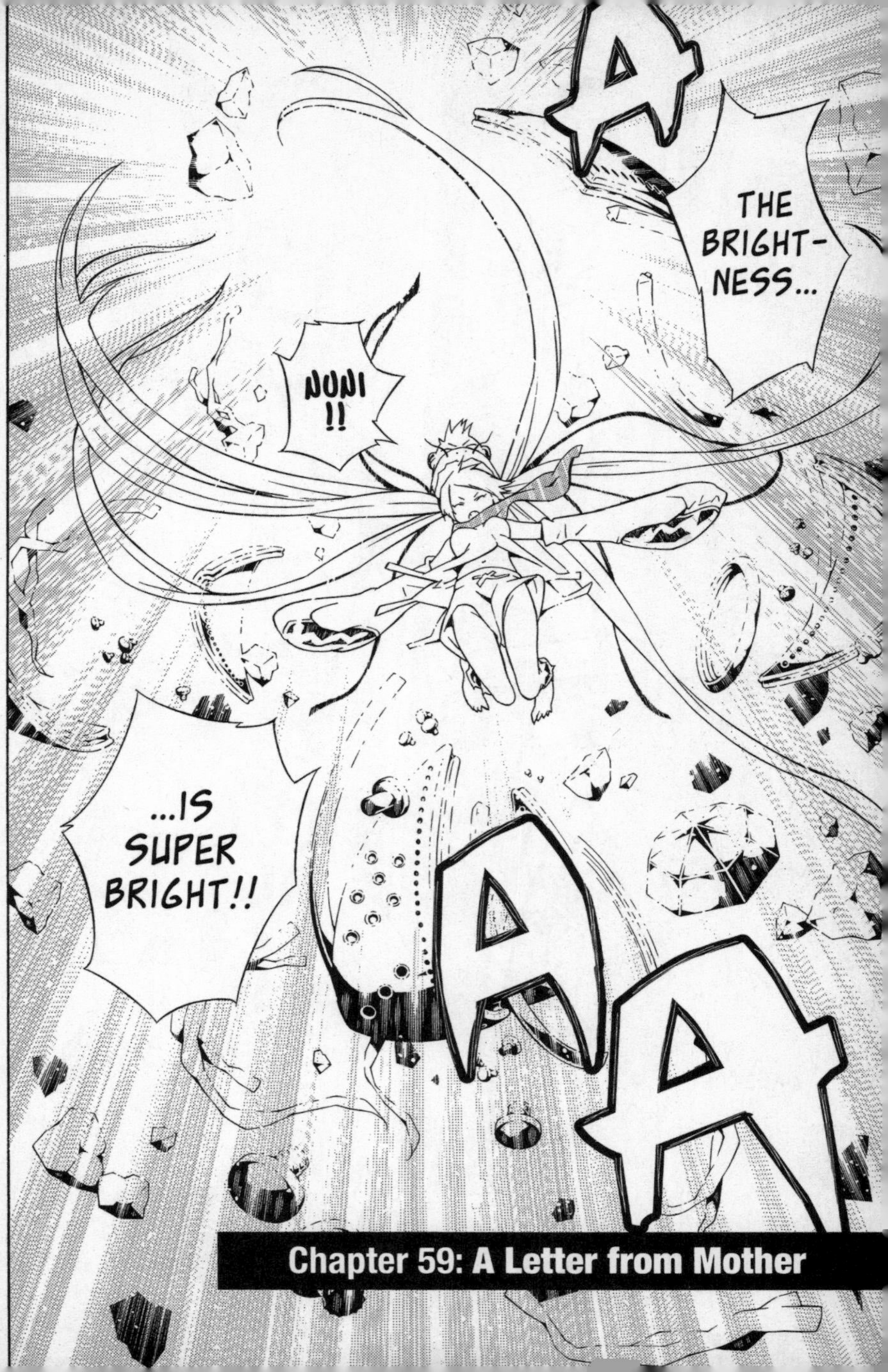
AAA
THE BRIGHT-NESS...
NUNI !!
...IS SUPER BRIGHT!!

Chapter 59: A Letter from Mother

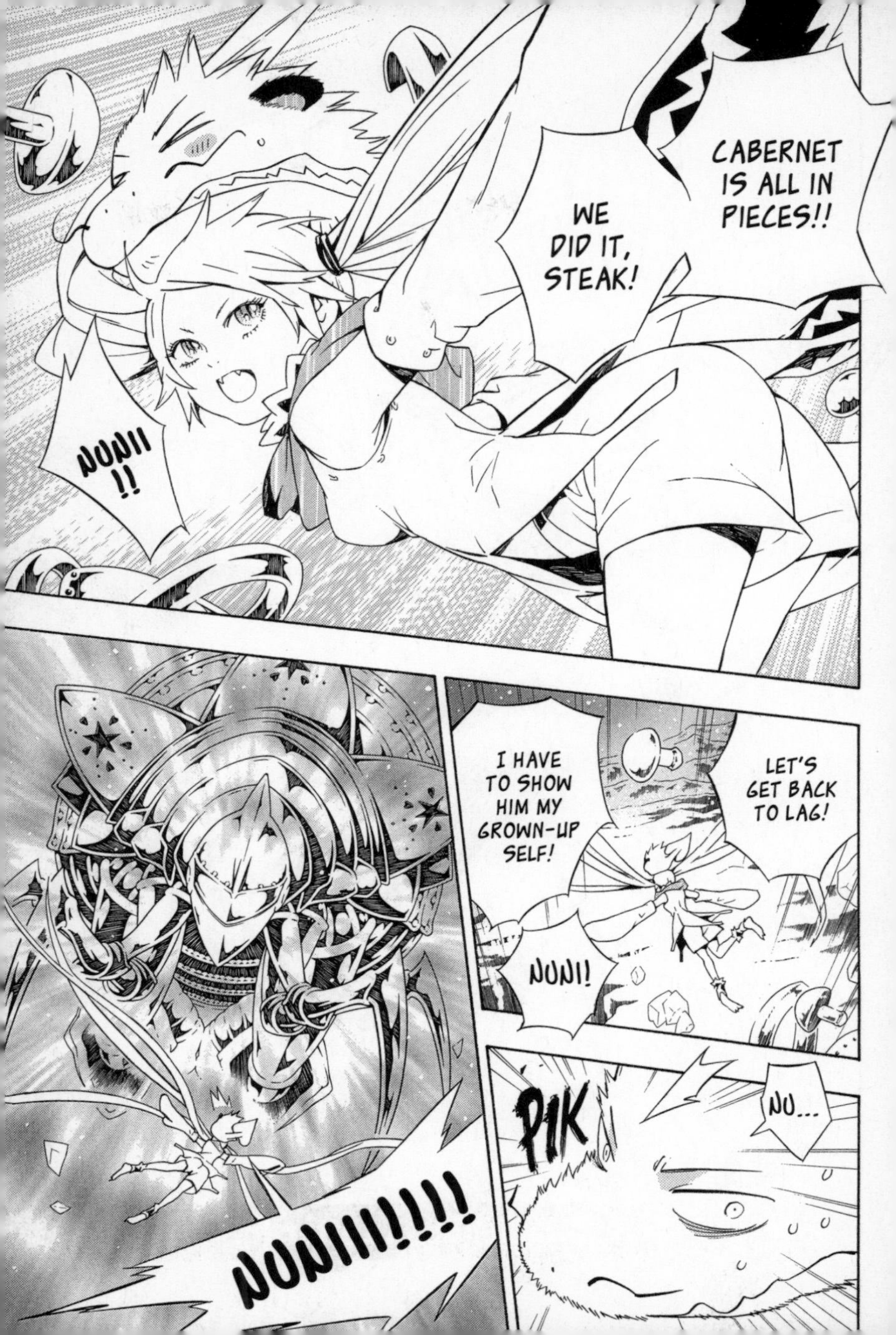
CABERNET IS ALL IN PIECES!!
WE DID IT, STEAK!
NUNI !!
LET'S GET BACK TO LAG!
I HAVE TO SHOW HIM MY GROWN-UP SELF!
NUNI!
NU...
PIK
NUNIII!!!!

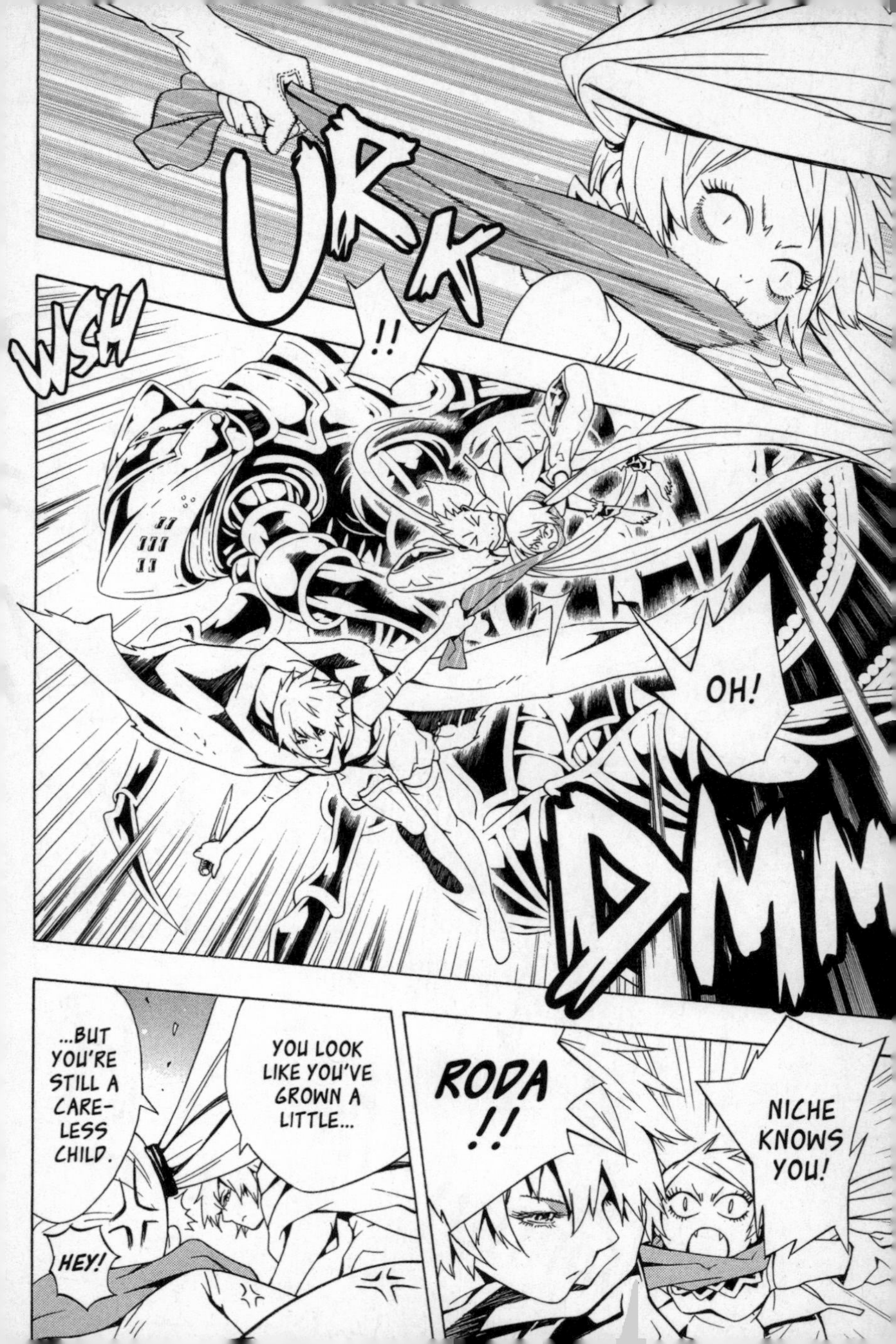
URK
!!
WSH
OH!
DMM
NICHE KNOWS YOU!
RODA !!
YOU LOOK LIKE YOU'VE GROWN A LITTLE...
...BUT YOU'RE STILL A CARE- LESS CHILD.
HEY!

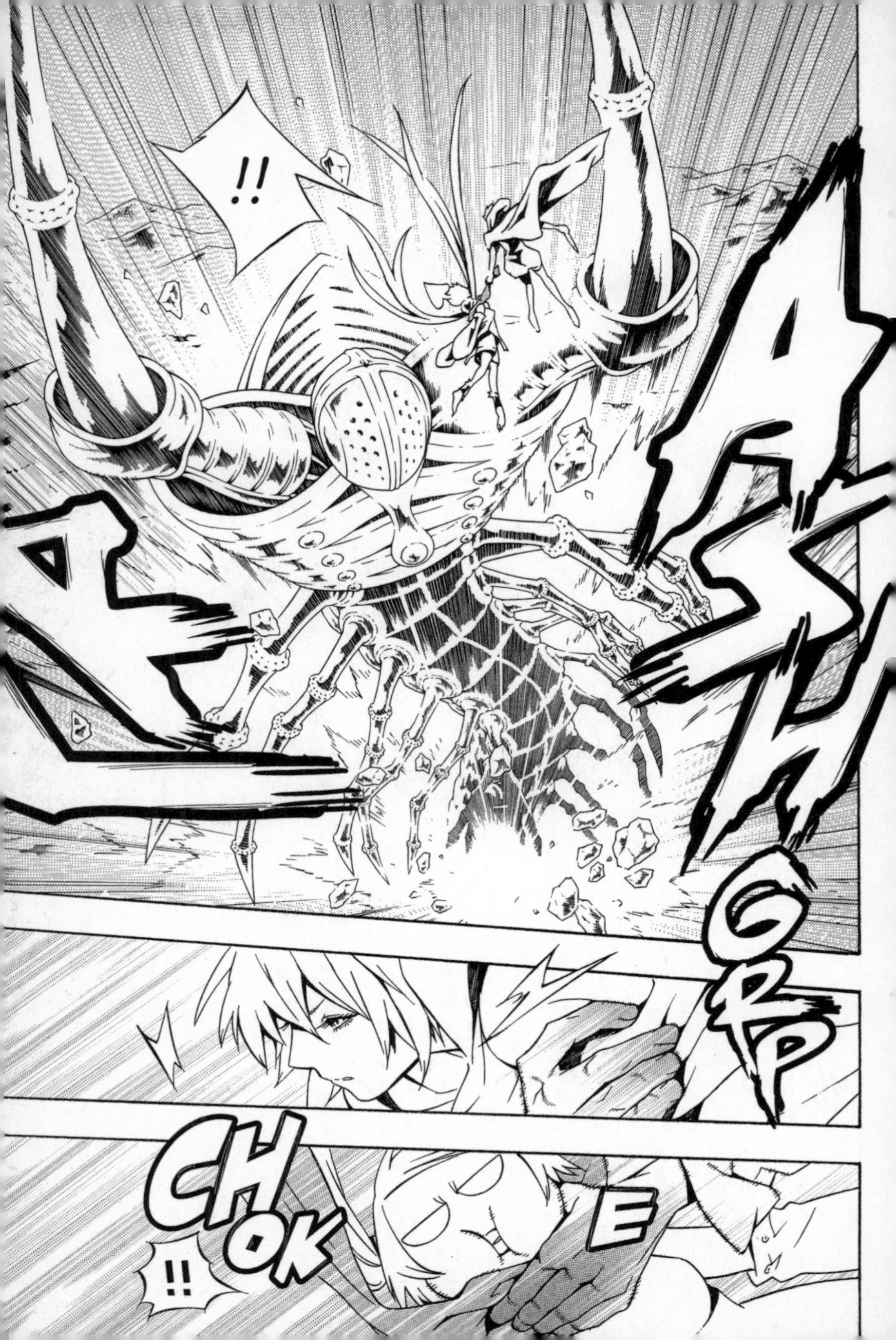
!!
GRP
CHOKE
!!

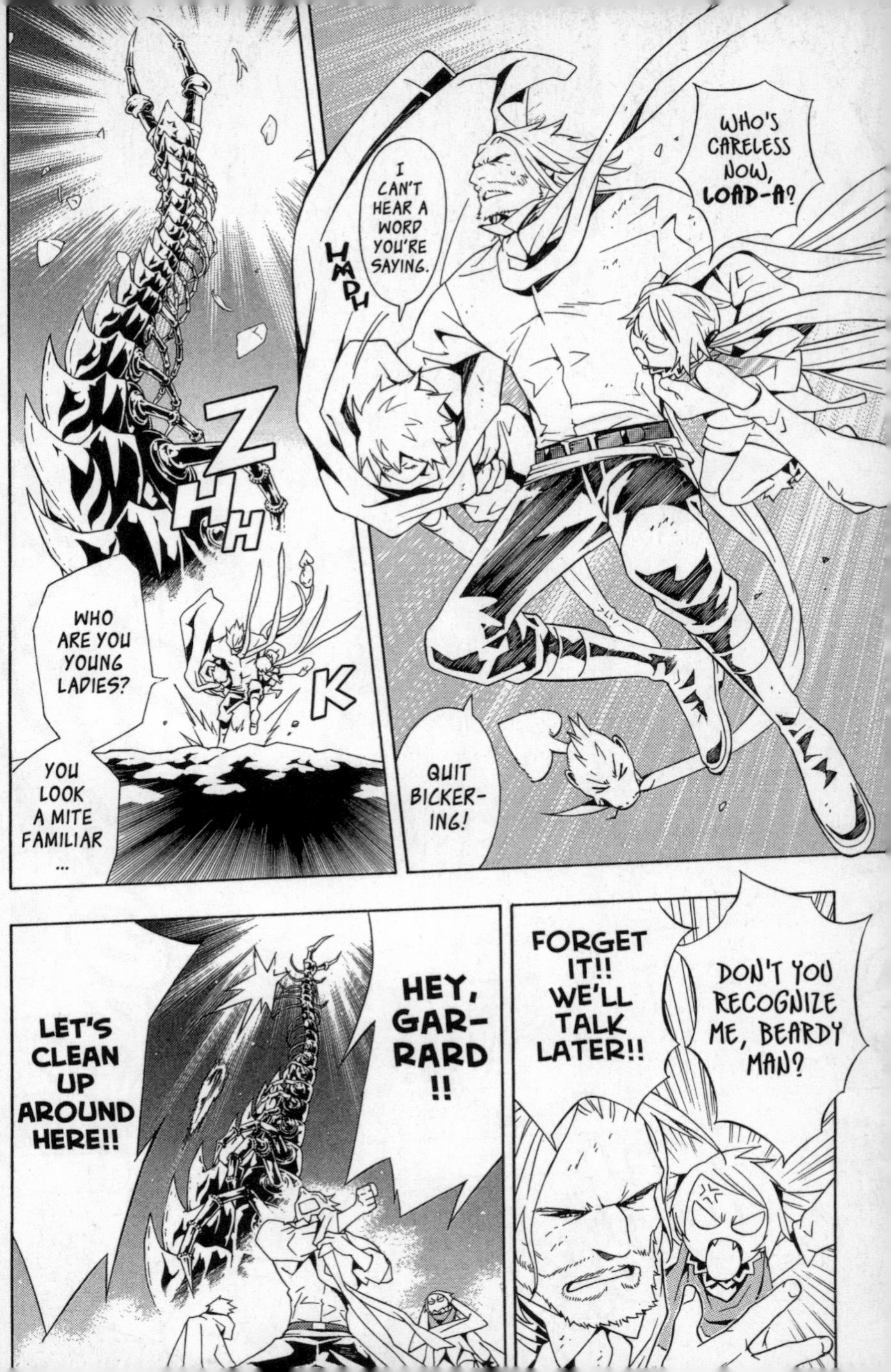

WHO'S CARELESS NOW, LOAD-A?
I CAN'T HEAR A WORD YOU'RE SAYING.
HMPH
QUIT BICKER-ING!
ZHHH
K
WHO ARE YOU YOUNG LADIES?
YOU LOOK A MITE FAMILIAR ...
DON'T YOU RECOGNIZE ME, BEARDY MAN?
FORGET IT!! WE'LL TALK LATER!!
HEY, GAR-RARD!!
LET'S CLEAN UP AROUND HERE!!

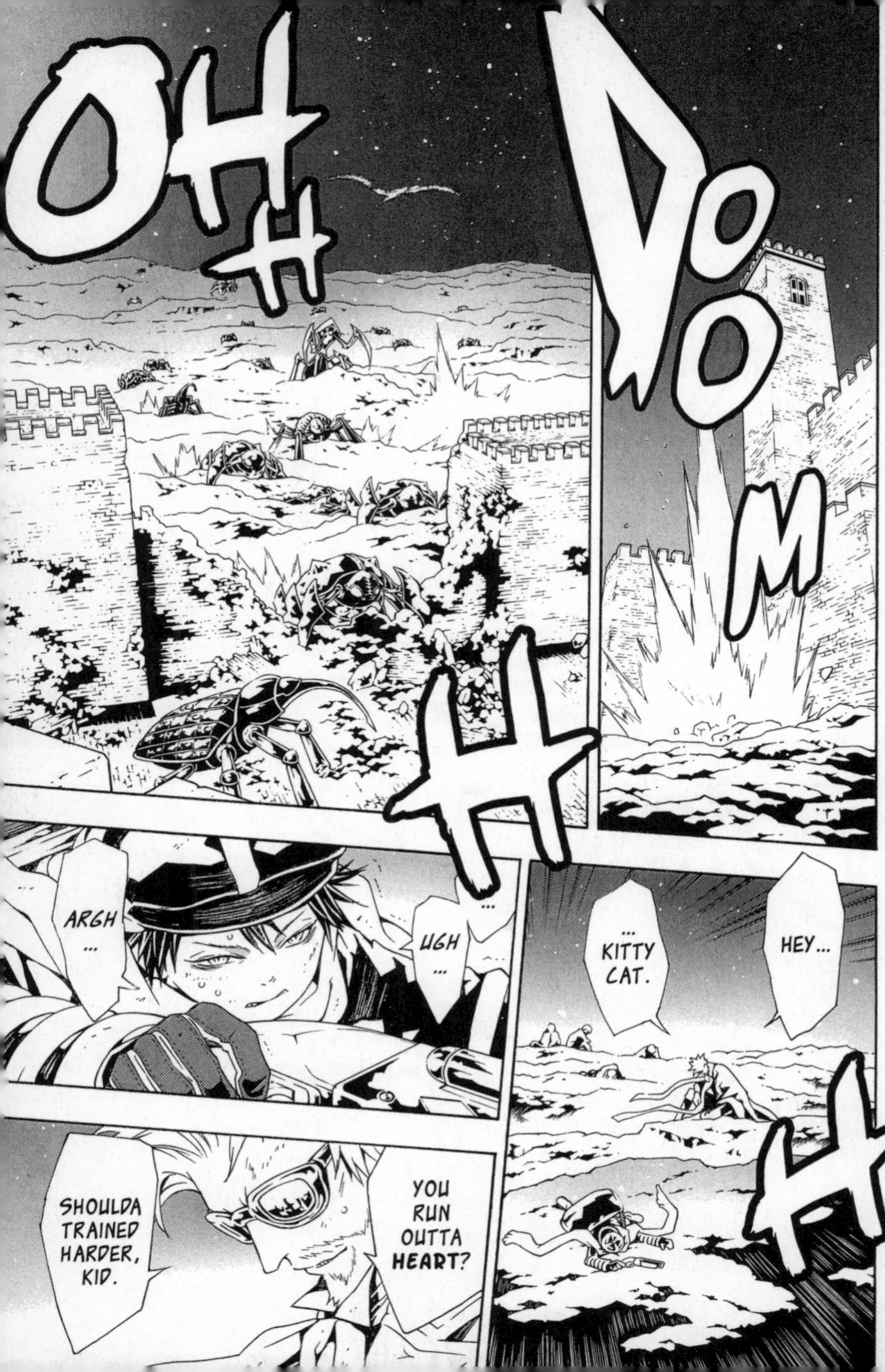

DOOM
OHHH
HH
HEY...
...KITTY CAT.
...
UGH ...
ARGH ...
YOU RUN OUTTA HEART?
SHOULDA TRAINED HARDER, KID.

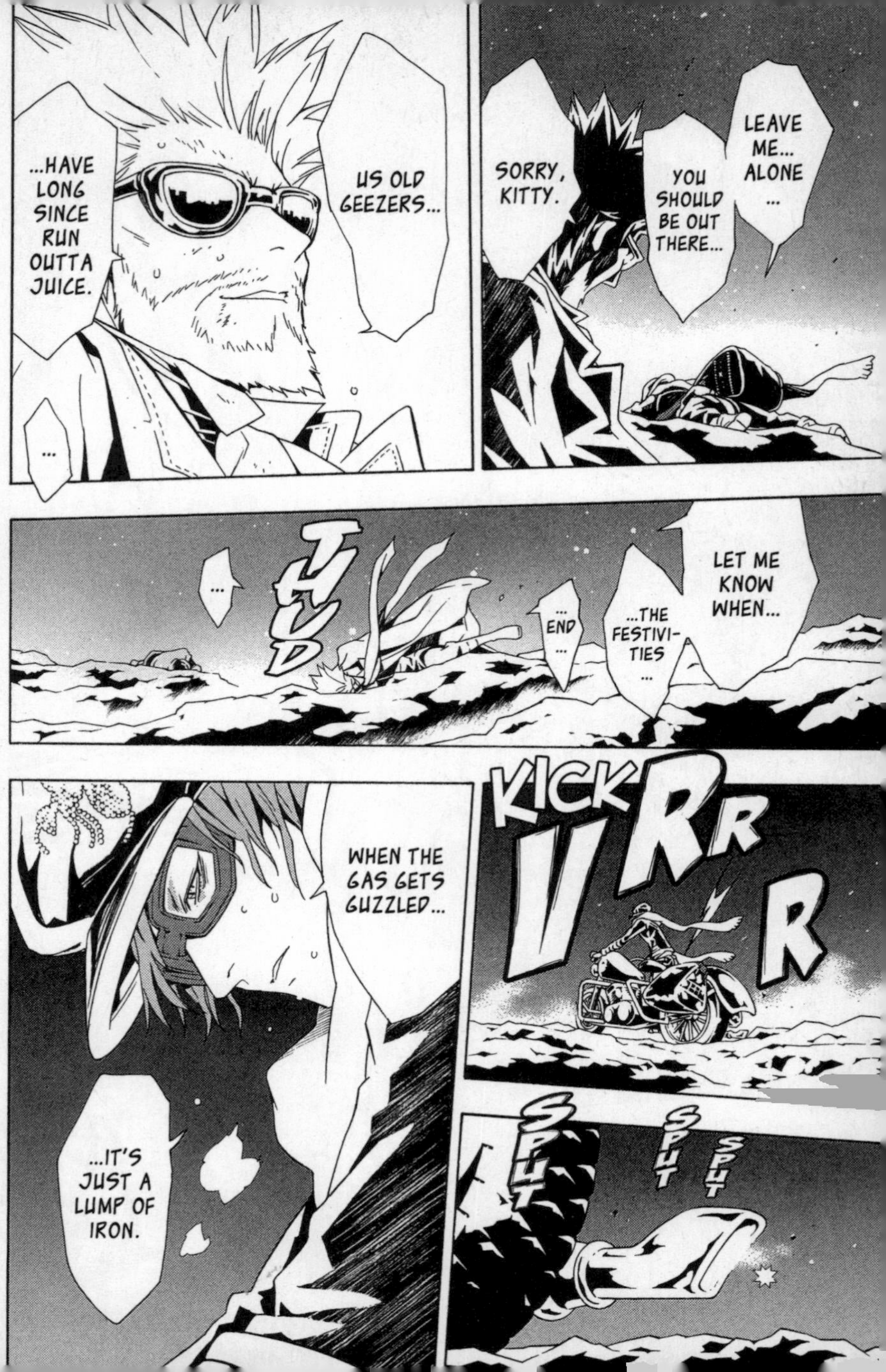
LEAVE ME... ALONE ...
YOU SHOULD BE OUT THERE...
SORRY, KITTY.
US OLD GEEZERS...
...HAVE LONG SINCE RUN OUTTA JUICE.
...
LET ME KNOW WHEN...
...THE FESTIVITIES ...
... END ...
...
THUD
KICK
VRRR
R
SPUT
SPUT
SPUT
WHEN THE GAS GETS GUZZLED...
...IT'S JUST A LUMP OF IRON.

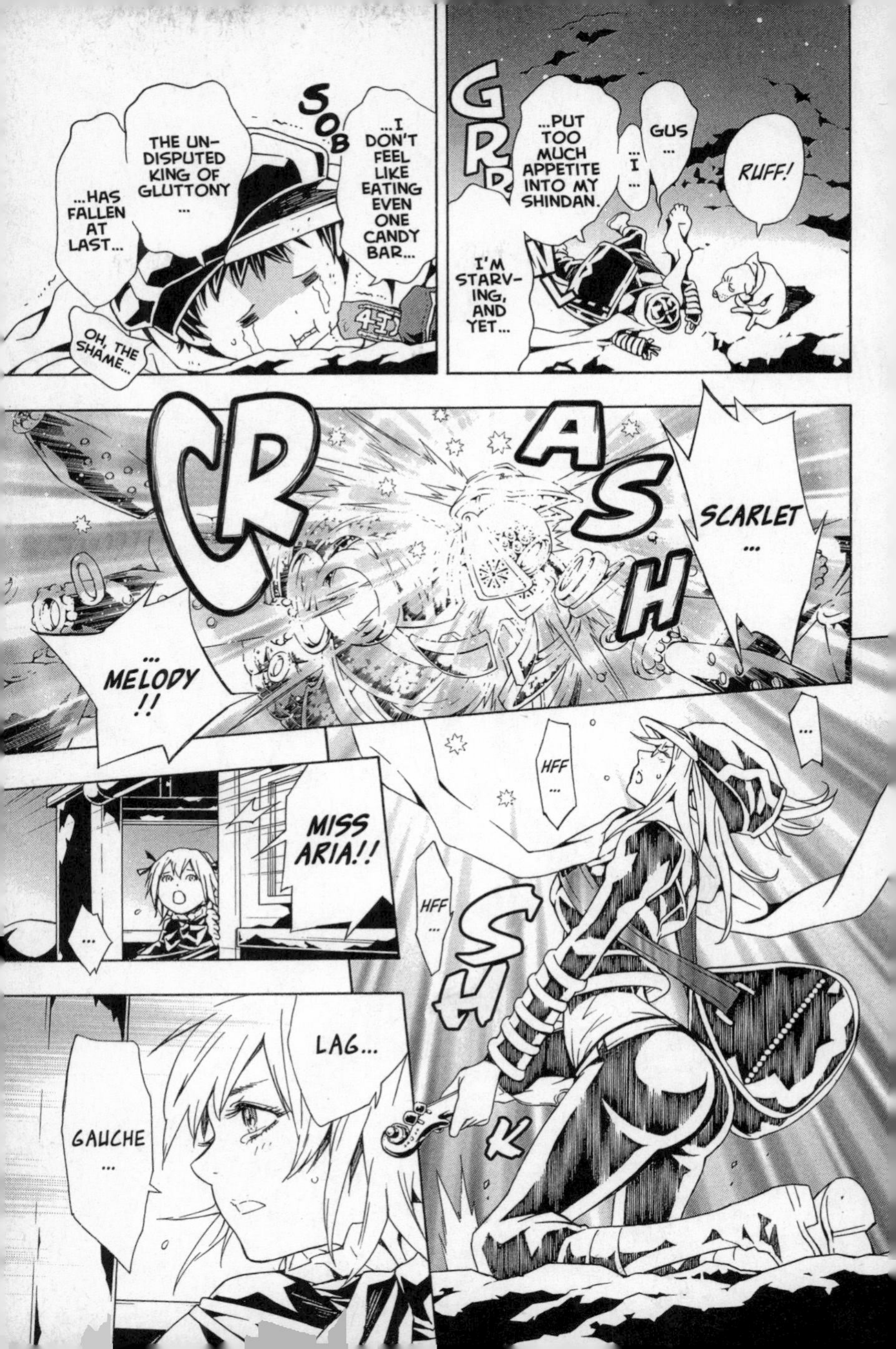
RUFF!
GUS...
...I...
...PUT TOO MUCH APPETITE INTO MY SHINDAN.
GR
I'M STARVING, AND YET...
...I DON'T FEEL LIKE EATING EVEN ONE CANDY BAR...
SOB
THE UNDISPUTED KING OF GLUTTONY...
...HAS FALLEN AT LAST...
OH, THE SHAME...
CRASH
SCARLET...
...MELODY!!
...
HFF...
MISS ARIA!!
...
HFF...
SH
LAG...
GAUCHE...
K

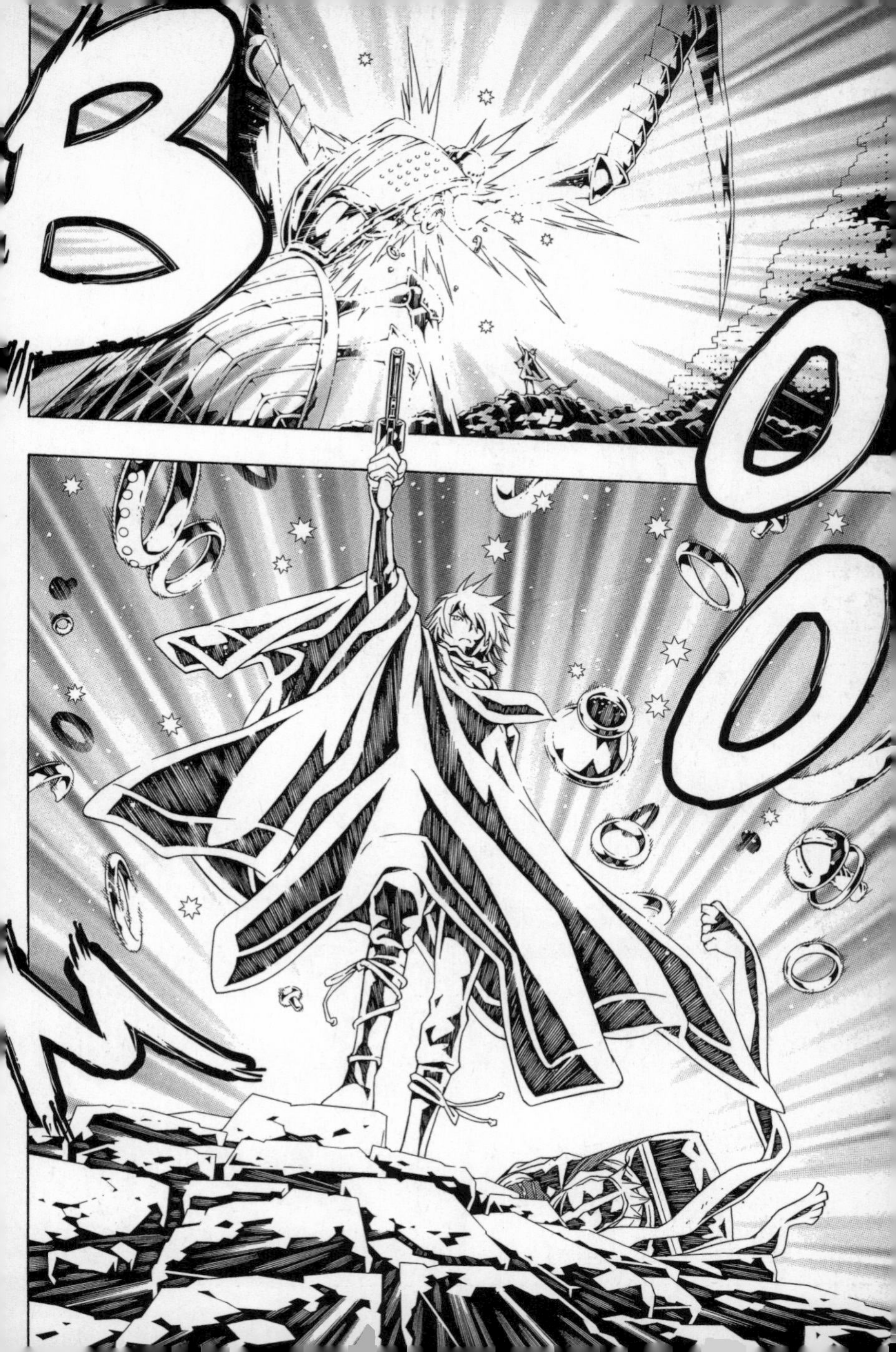
BOOM

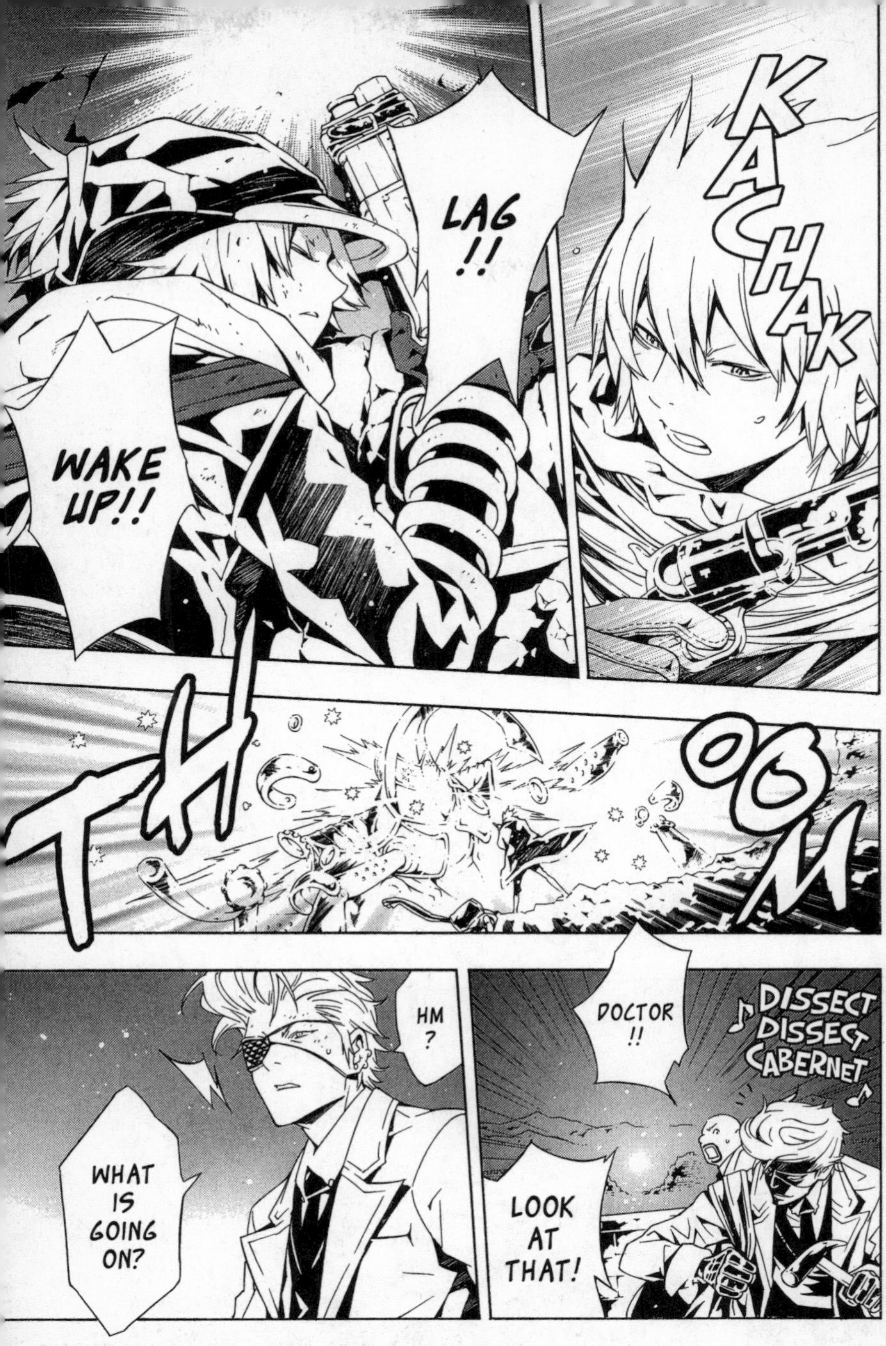
KACHAK
LAG!!
WAKE UP!!
THOOM
DISSECT DISSECT CABERNET
DOCTOR!!
LOOK AT THAT!
HM?
WHAT IS GOING ON?

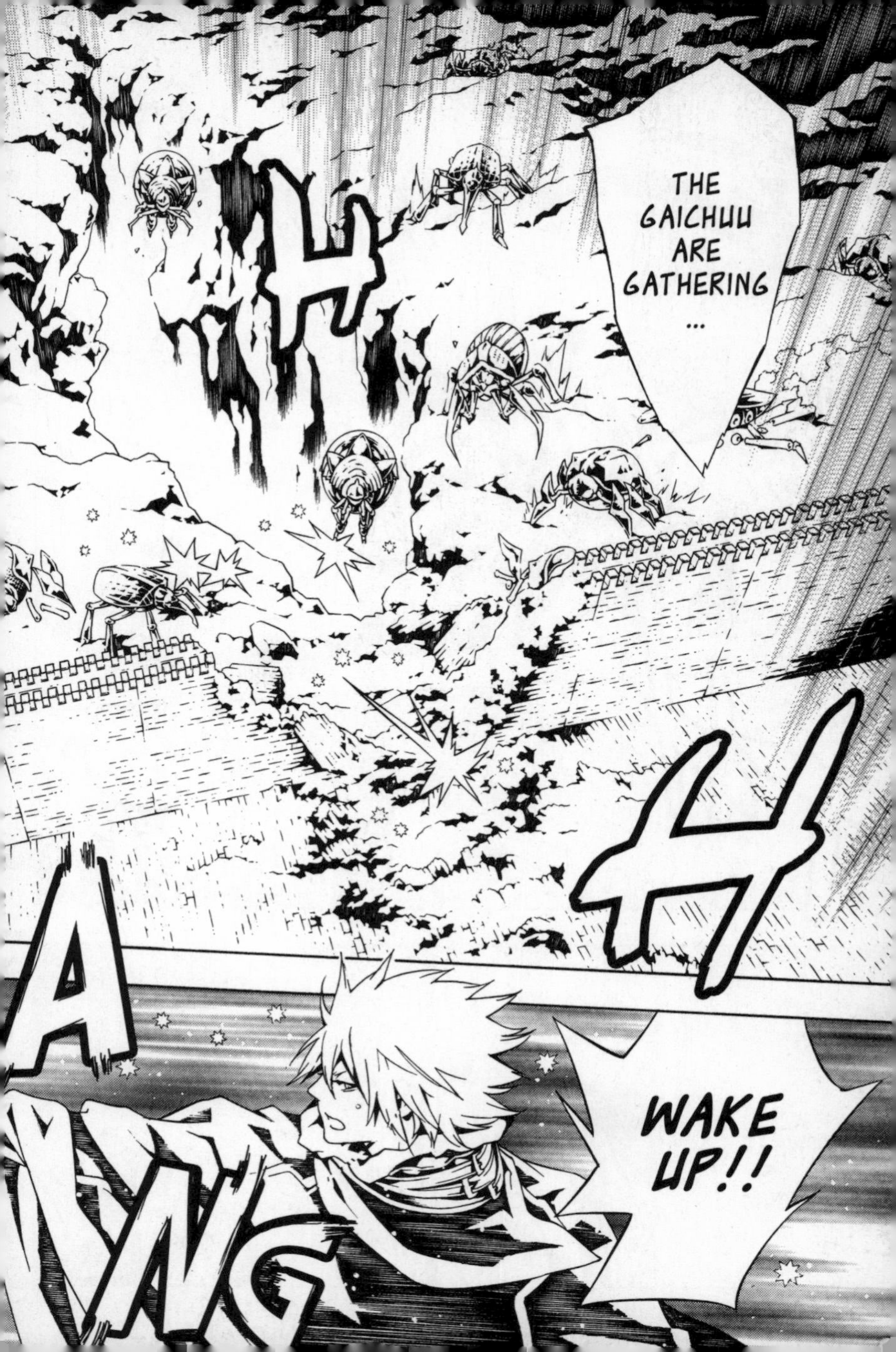
THE GAICHUU ARE GATHERING ...
WAKE UP!!

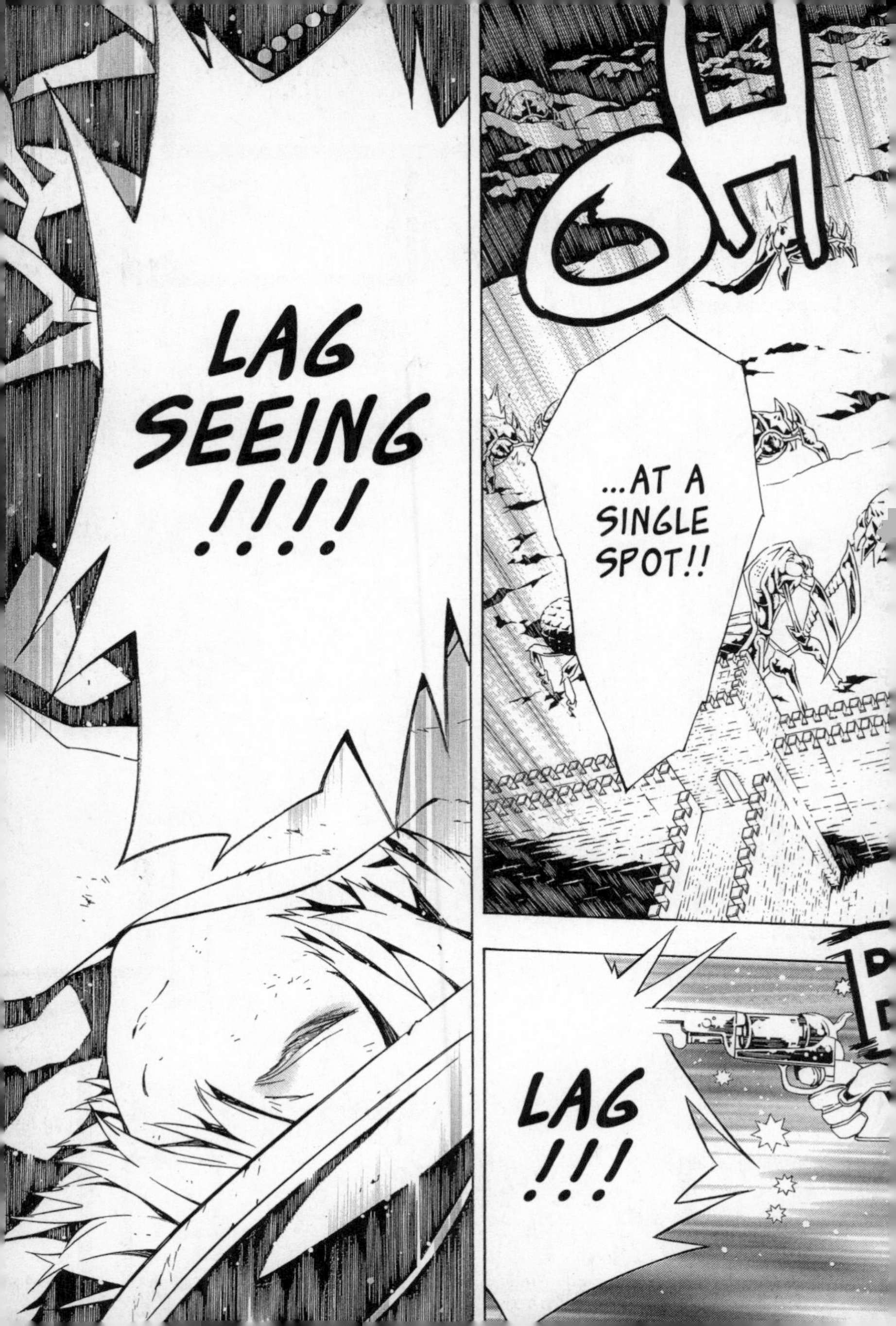
...AT A SINGLE SPOT!!
LAG!!!
LAG SEEING!!!!

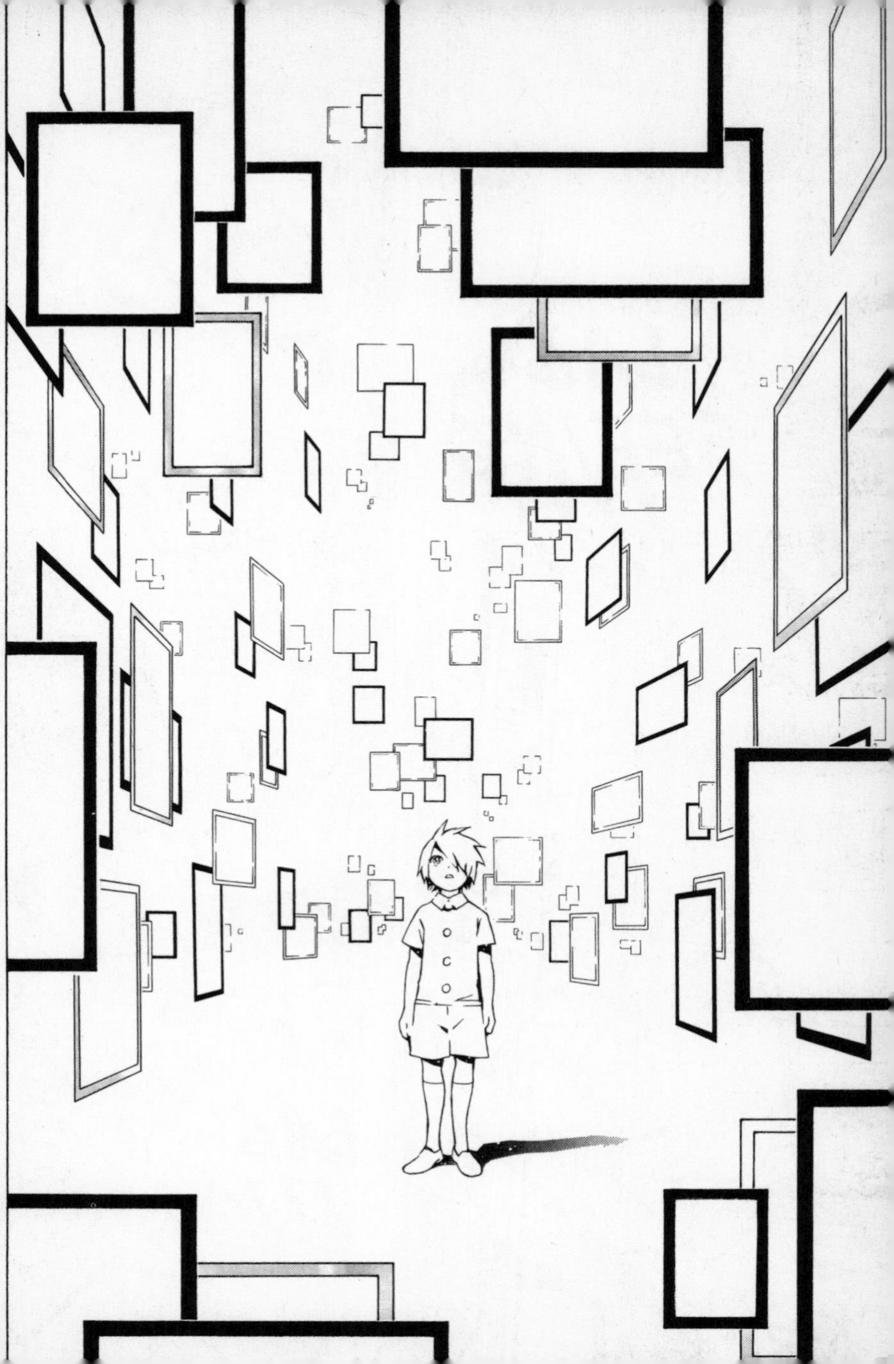

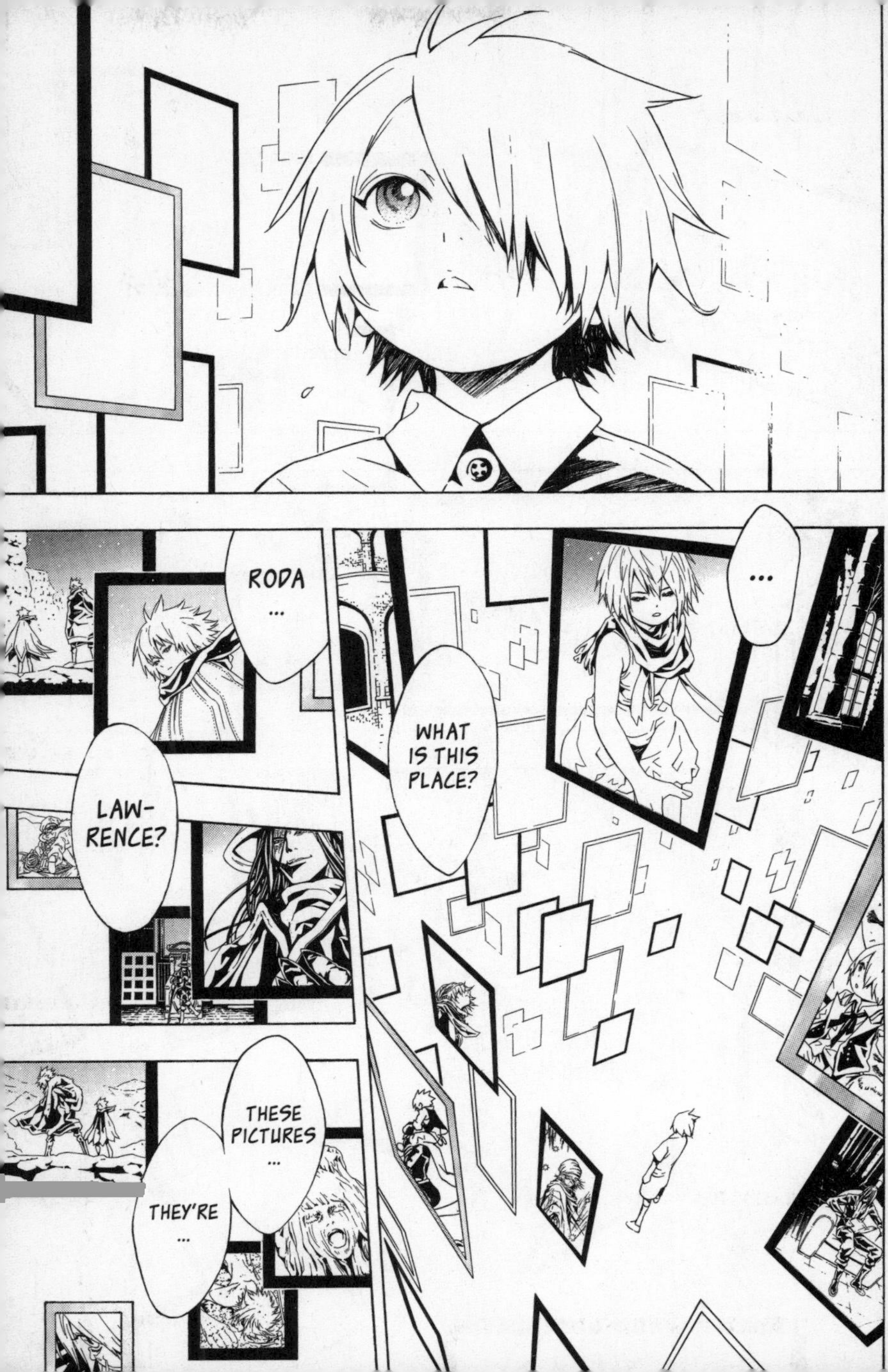
...
WHAT IS THIS PLACE?
RODA ...
LAW-RENCE?
THESE PICTURES ...
THEY'RE ...

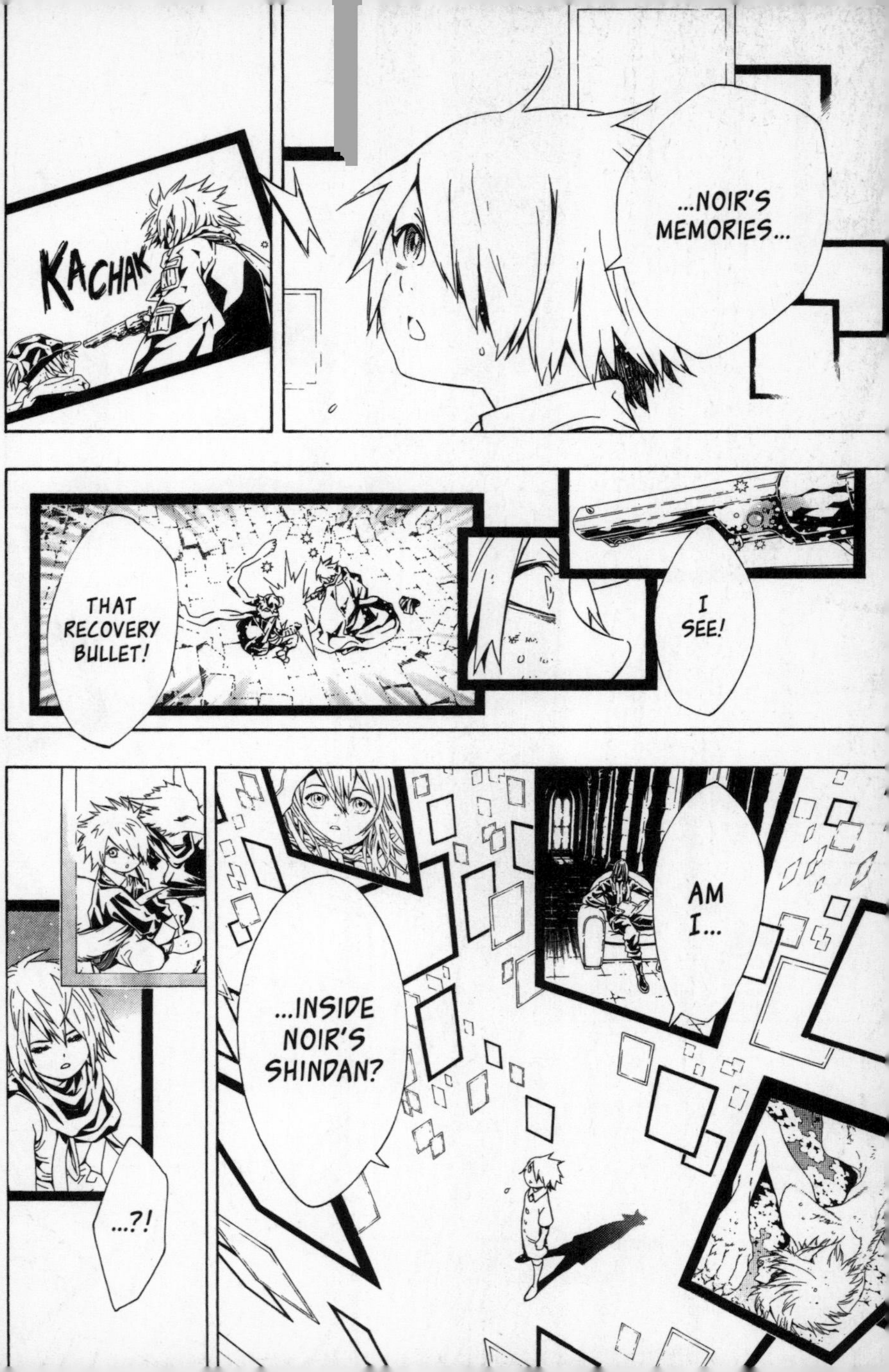
...NOIR'S MEMORIES...
KACHAK
I SEE!
THAT RECOVERY BULLET!
AM I...
...INSIDE NOIR'S SHINDAN?
...?!

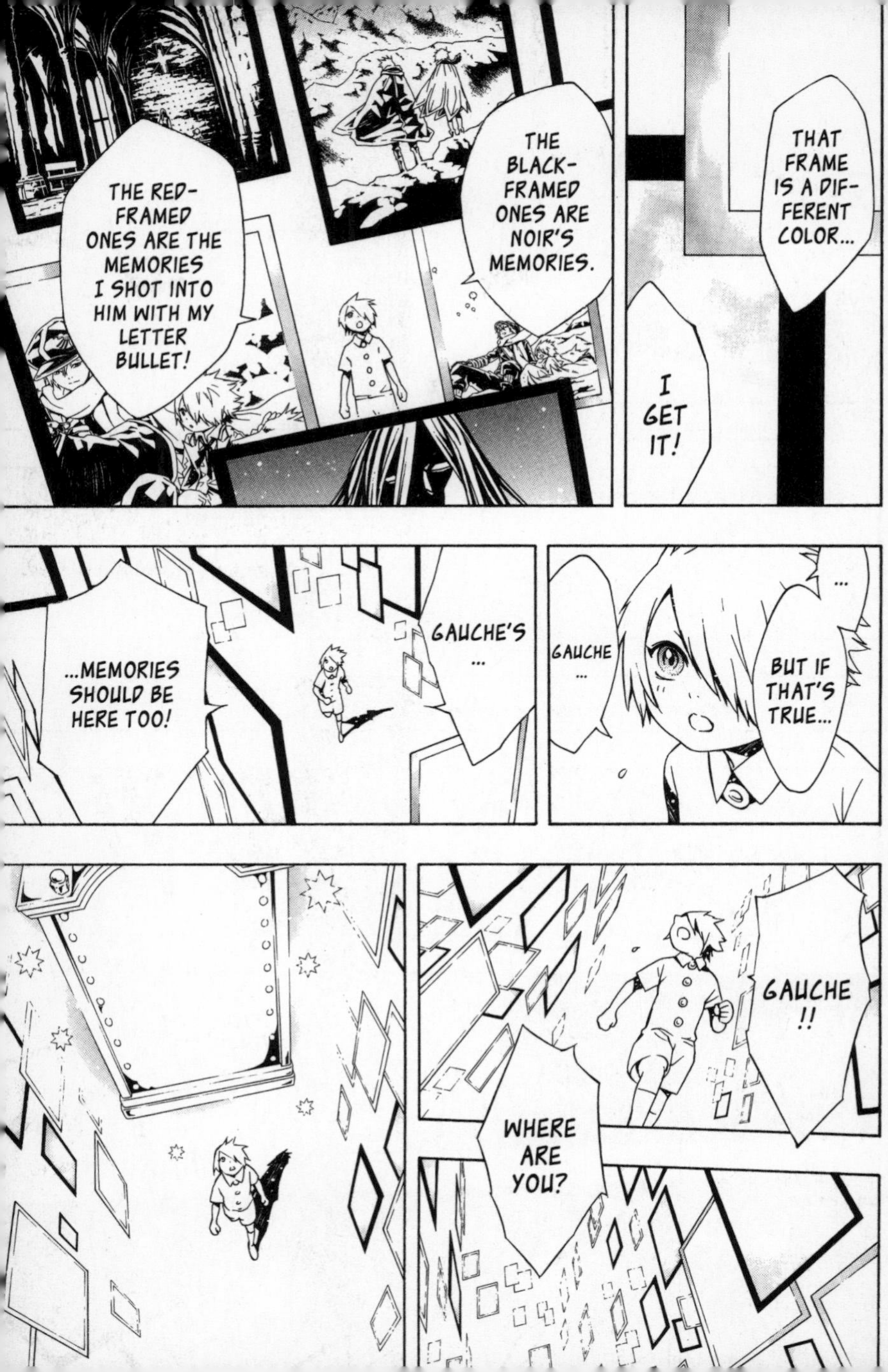
THAT FRAME IS A DIF-FERENT COLOR...
I GET IT!
THE BLACK-FRAMED ONES ARE NOIR'S MEMORIES.
THE RED-FRAMED ONES ARE THE MEMORIES I SHOT INTO HIM WITH MY LETTER BULLET!
...
BUT IF THAT'S TRUE...
GAUCHE...
GAUCHE'S...
...MEMORIES SHOULD BE HERE TOO!
GAUCHE!!
WHERE ARE YOU?

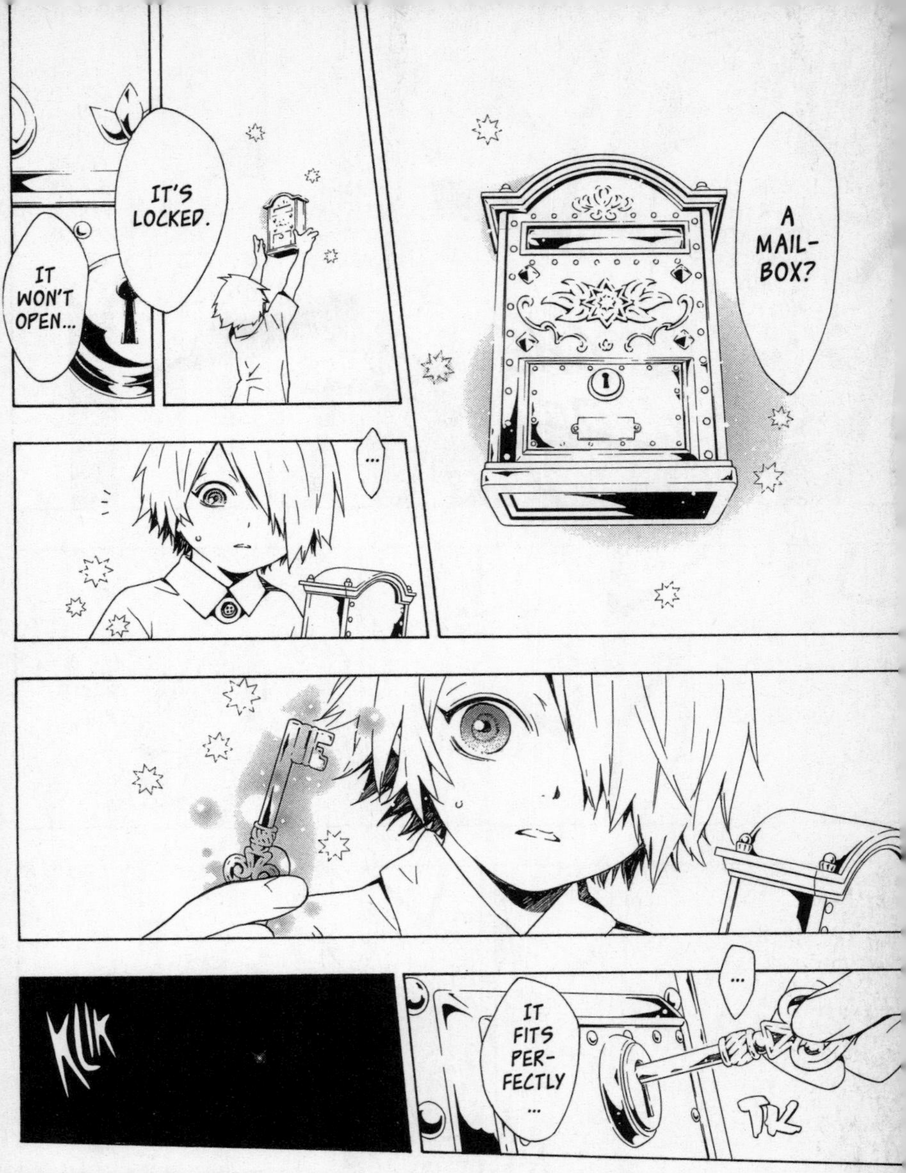
A MAIL-BOX?
IT'S LOCKED.
IT WON'T OPEN...
...
...
IT FITS PER-FECTLY...
TK
KLIK

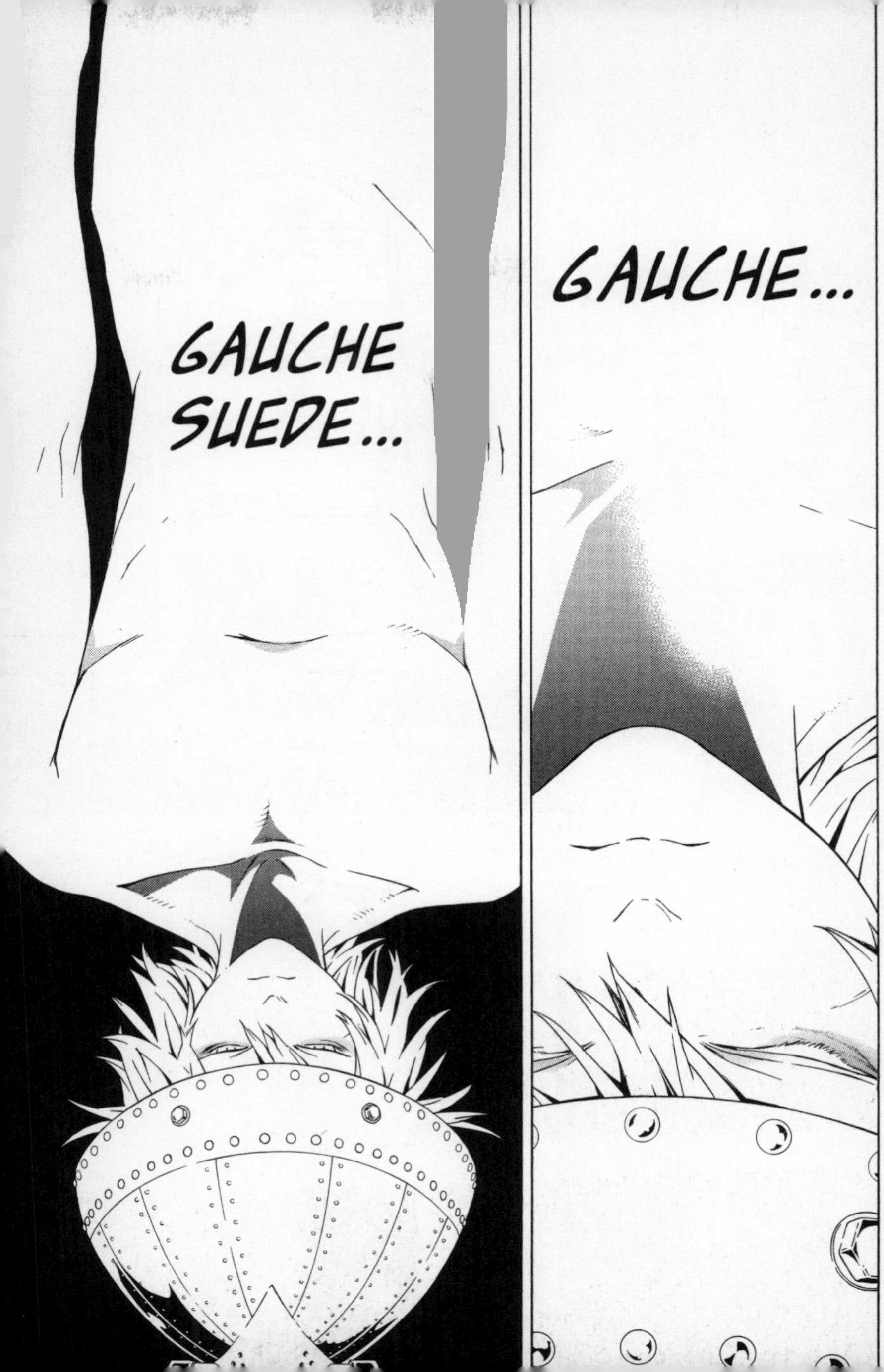
GAUCHE...
GAUCHE SUEDE...

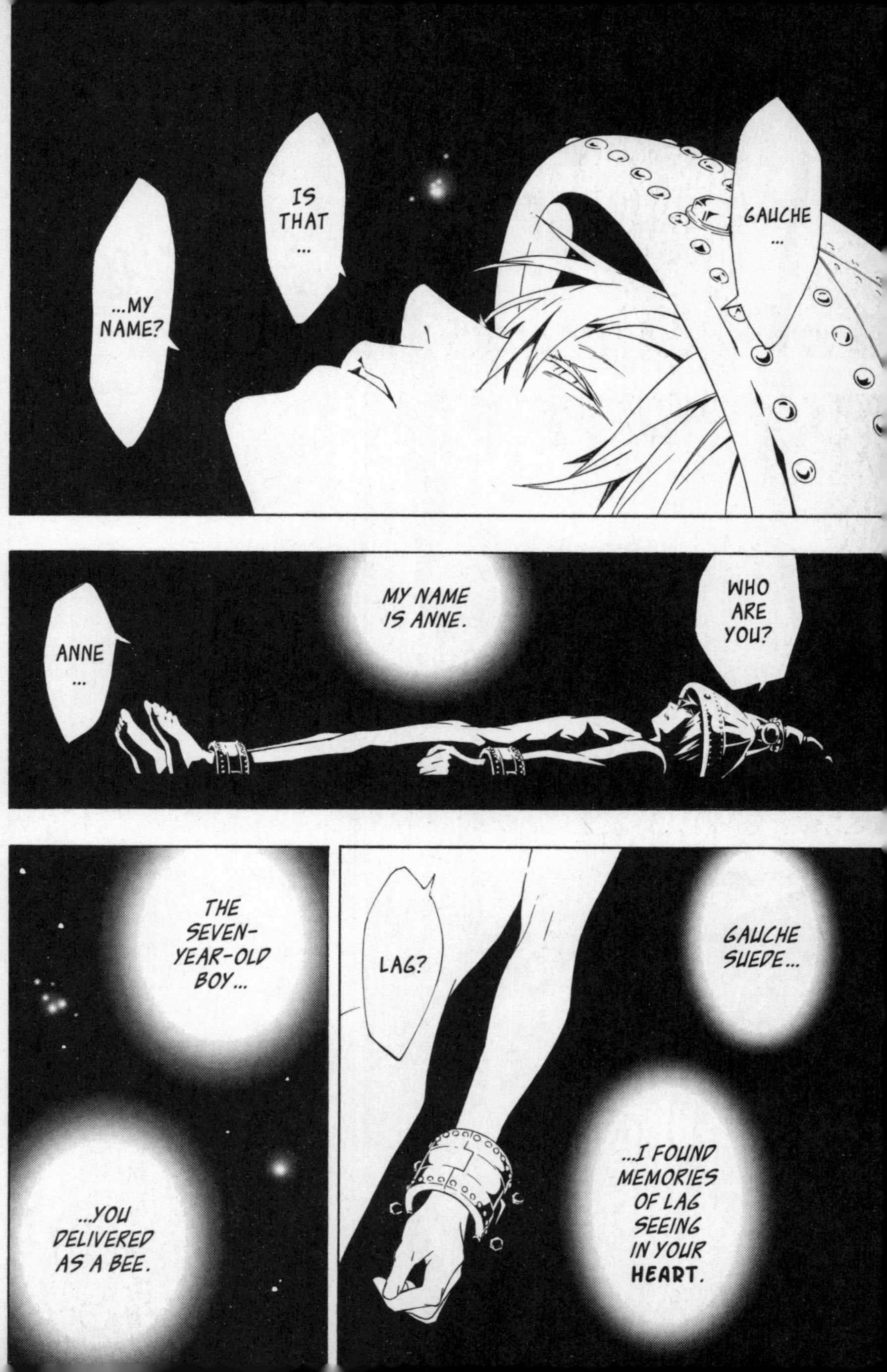
GAUCHE ...
IS THAT ...
...MY NAME?
WHO ARE YOU?
MY NAME IS ANNE.
ANNE ...
GAUCHE SUEDE...
LAG?
...I FOUND MEMORIES OF LAG SEEING IN YOUR HEART.
THE SEVEN-YEAR-OLD BOY...
...YOU DELIVERED AS A BEE.

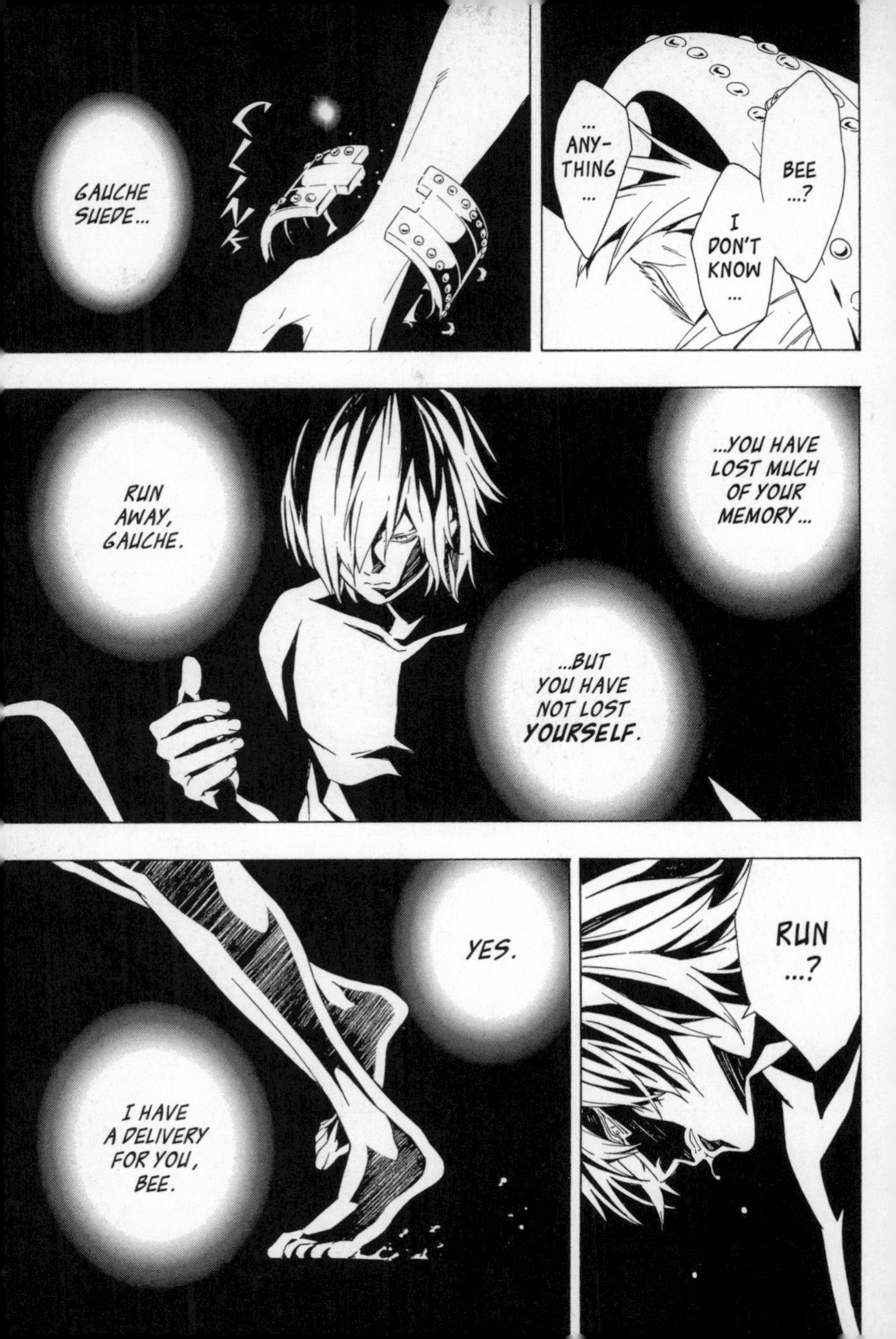
BEE ...?
I DON'T KNOW ...
... ANY-THING ...
CLINK
GAUCHE SUEDE...
...YOU HAVE LOST MUCH OF YOUR MEMORY...
...BUT YOU HAVE NOT LOST **YOURSELF**.
RUN AWAY, GAUCHE.
RUN ...?
YES.
I HAVE A DELIVERY FOR YOU, BEE.

DELIVER THIS MEMORY...
...TO LAG SEEING.
LAG...
...I CAUSED YOU A LOT OF SORROW, DIDN'T I?
AND YET I'M SURE YOU'VE GROWN INTO A STRONG, UPRIGHT YOUNG MAN.
I HOPE YOU'RE READY TO LEARN THE TRUTH.
LISTEN TO WHAT SABRINA MARY IN CAMPBELL HAS TO SAY.
LAG...

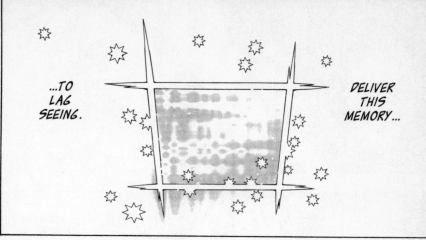

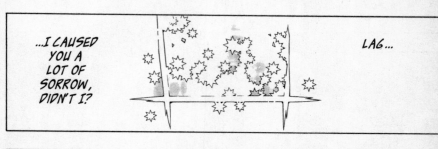

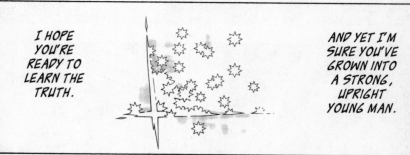

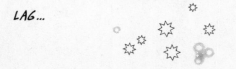

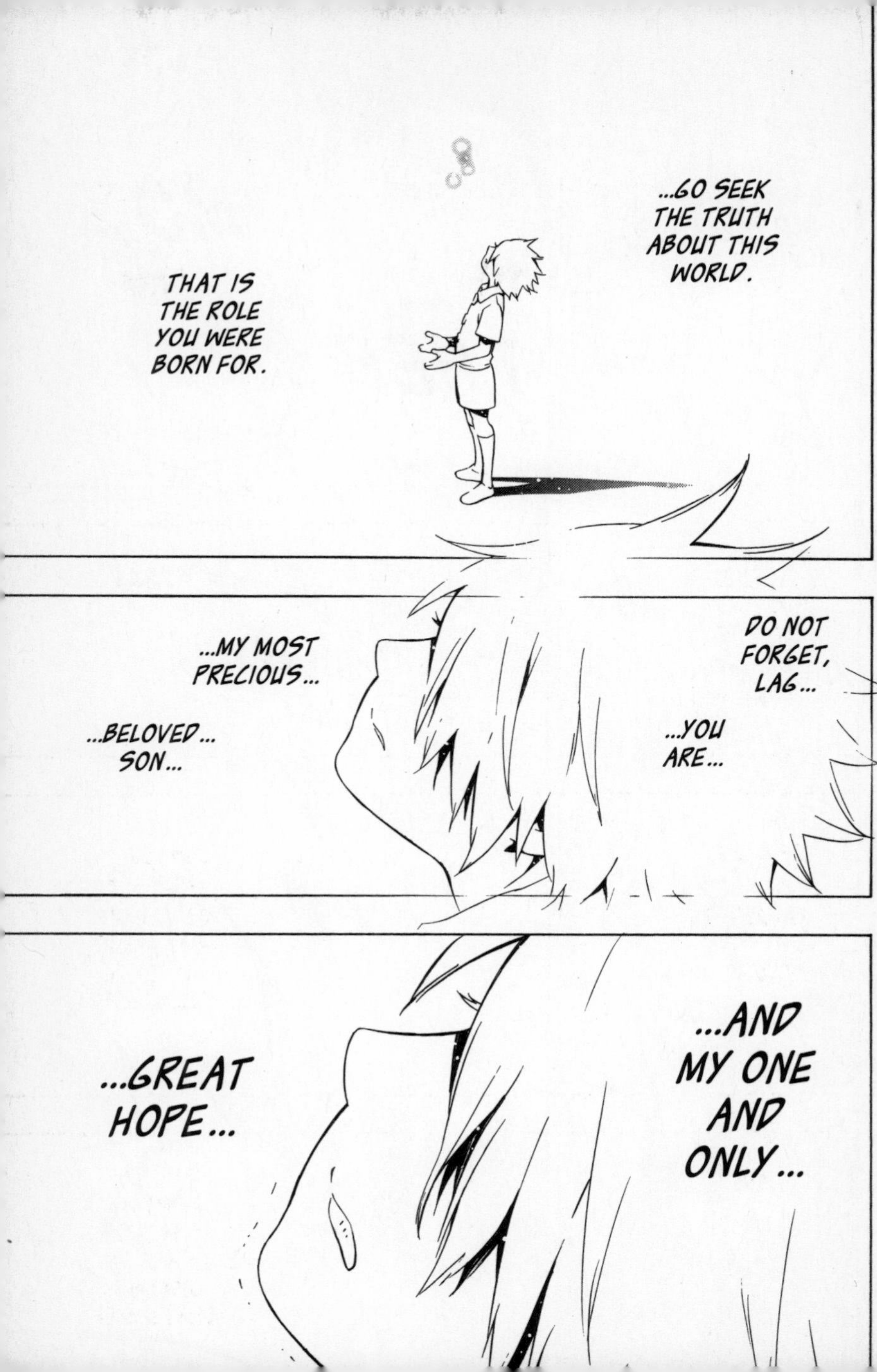
...GO SEEK THE TRUTH ABOUT THIS WORLD.
THAT IS THE ROLE YOU WERE BORN FOR.
DO NOT FORGET, LAG...
...YOU ARE...
...MY MOST PRECIOUS...
...BELOVED... SON...
...AND MY ONE AND ONLY...
...GREAT HOPE...

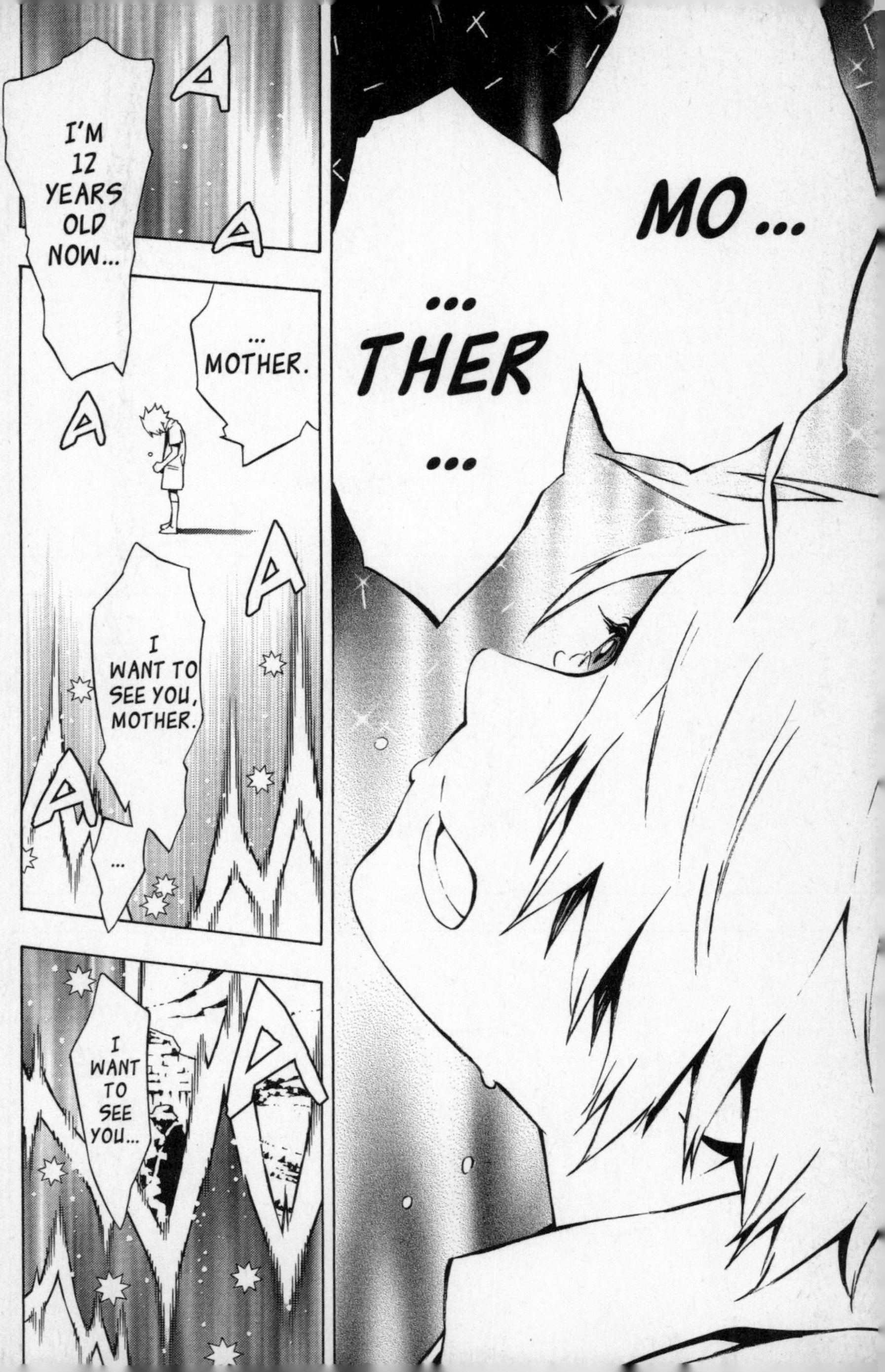
MO...
...THER...
I'M 12 YEARS OLD NOW...
A
A
...MOTHER.
A
A
I WANT TO SEE YOU, MOTHER.
A
...
I WANT TO SEE YOU...
A

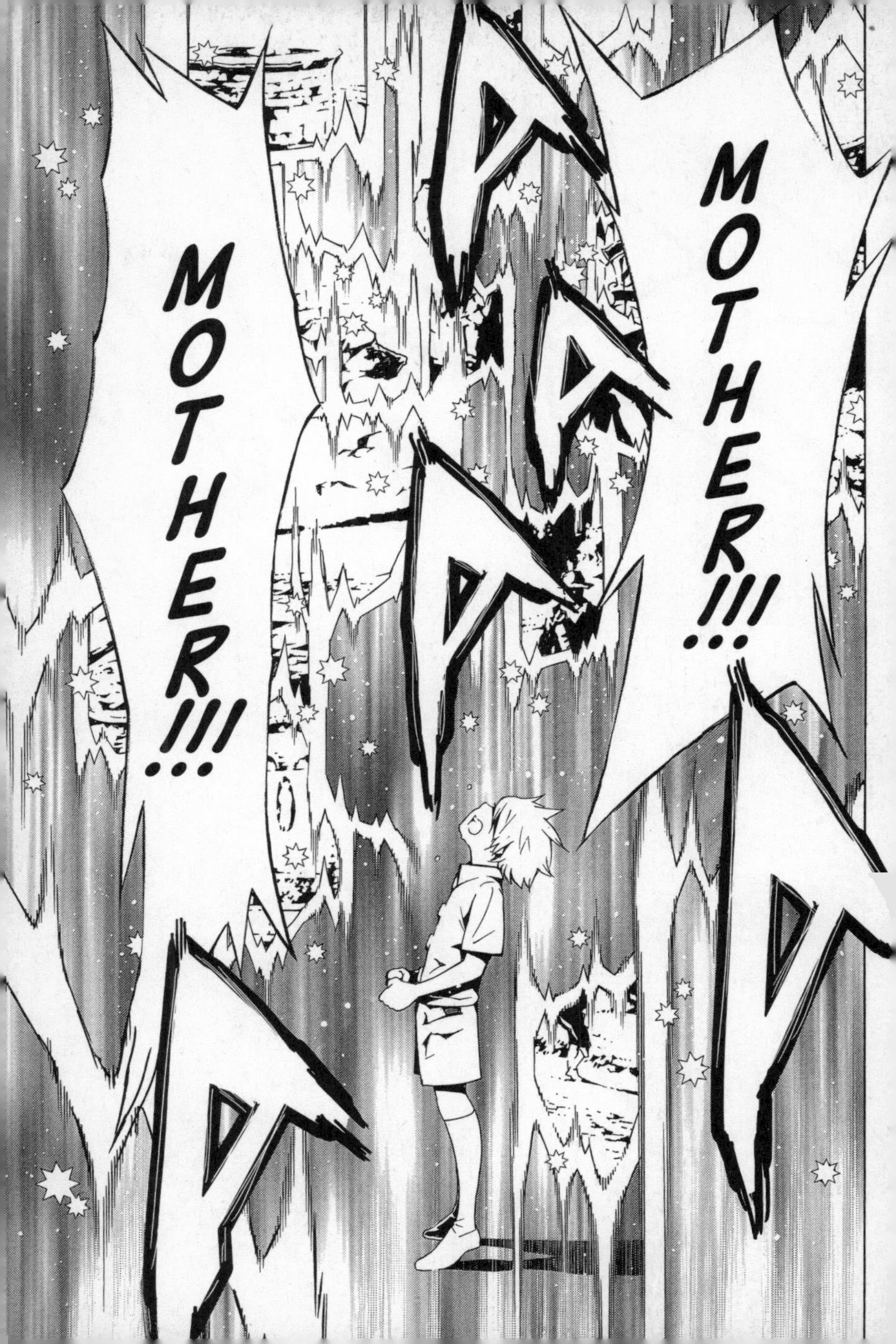
MOTHER!!!...
MOTHER!!!...

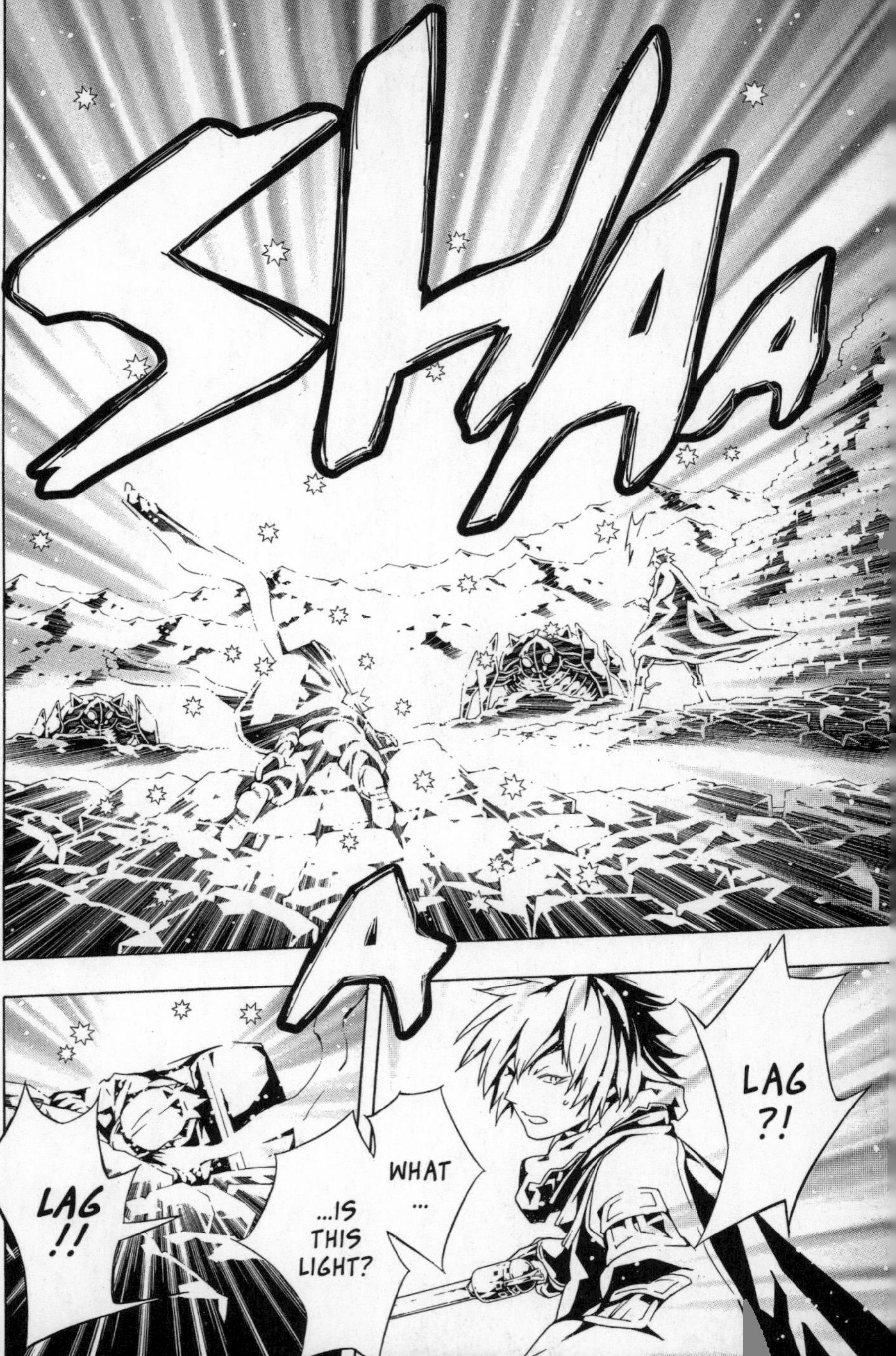
SHAAA
LAG ?!
WHAT ...
...IS THIS LIGHT?
LAG !!

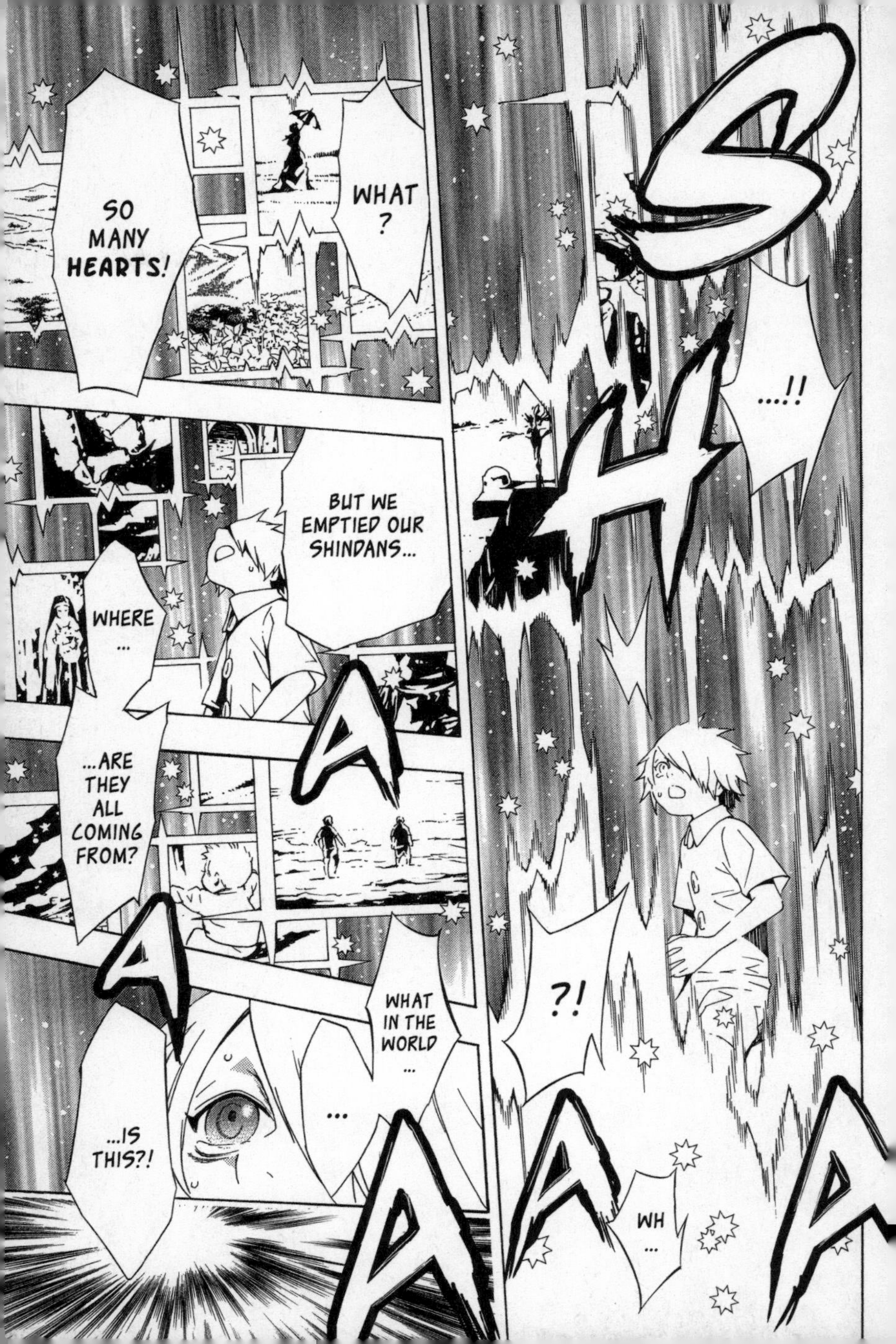
SHAAAAAA
...!!
?!
WH ...
WHAT ?
SO MANY HEARTS!
BUT WE EMPTIED OUR SHINDANS...
WHERE ...
...ARE THEY ALL COMING FROM?
WHAT IN THE WORLD ...
...
...IS THIS?!

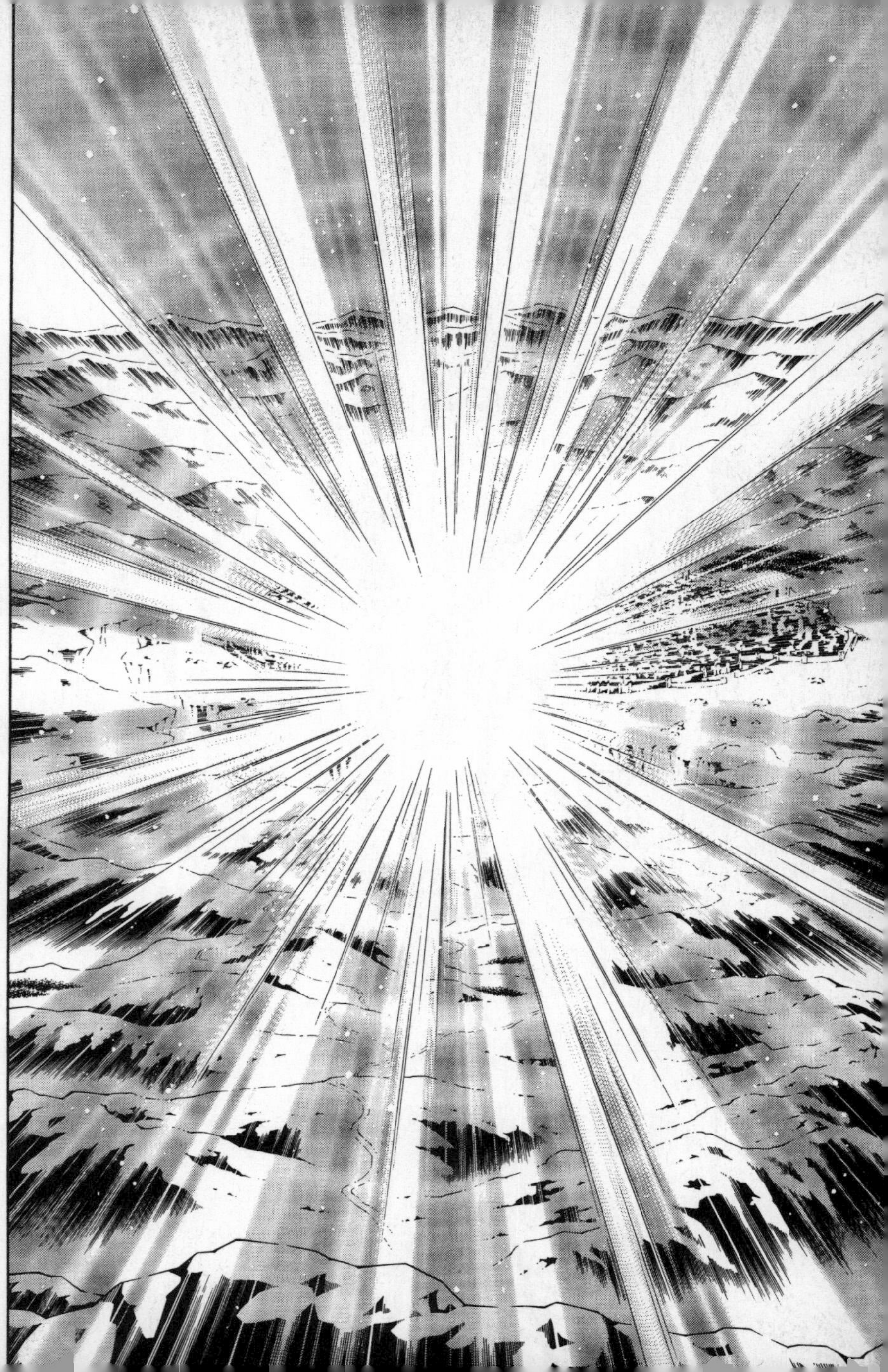

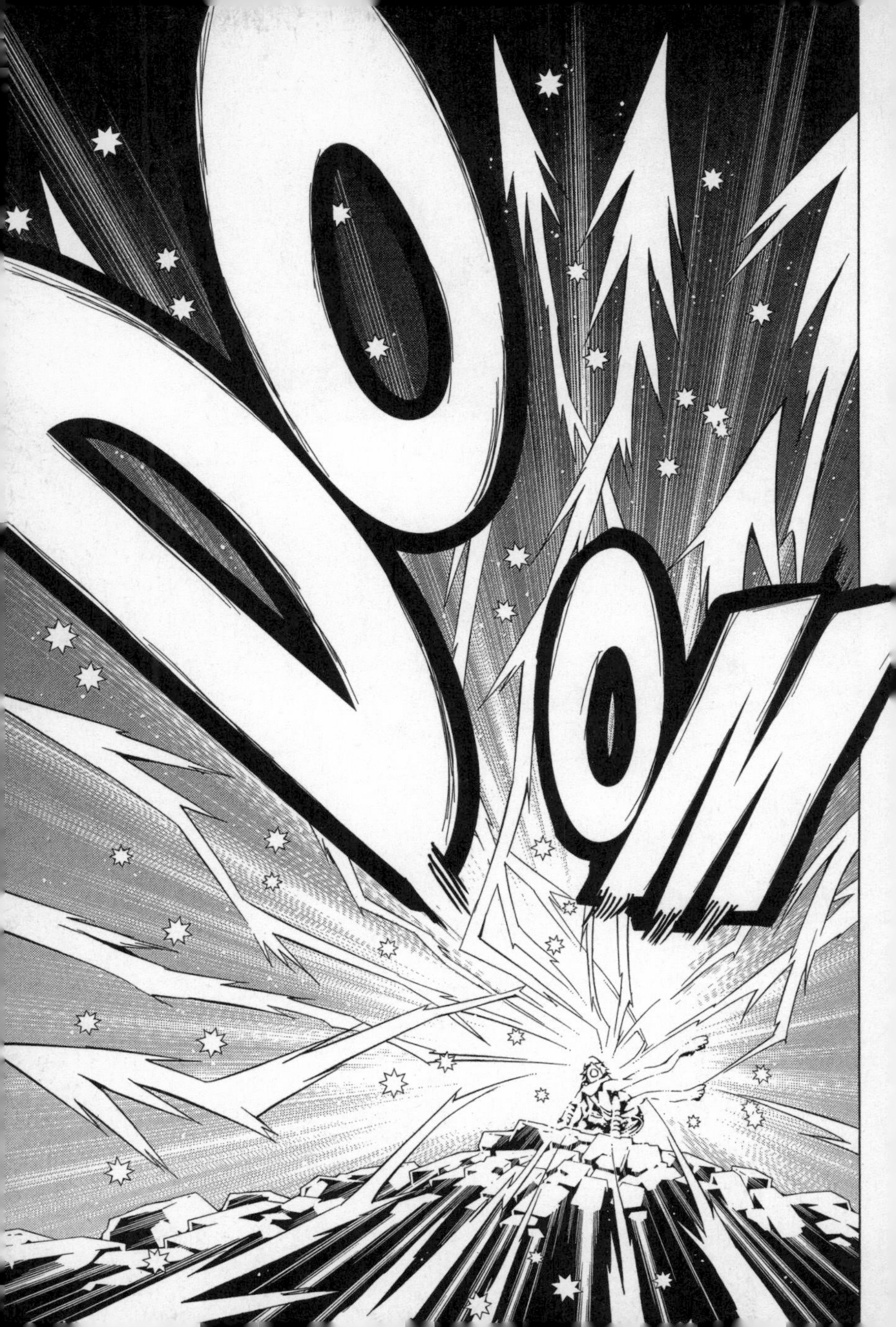

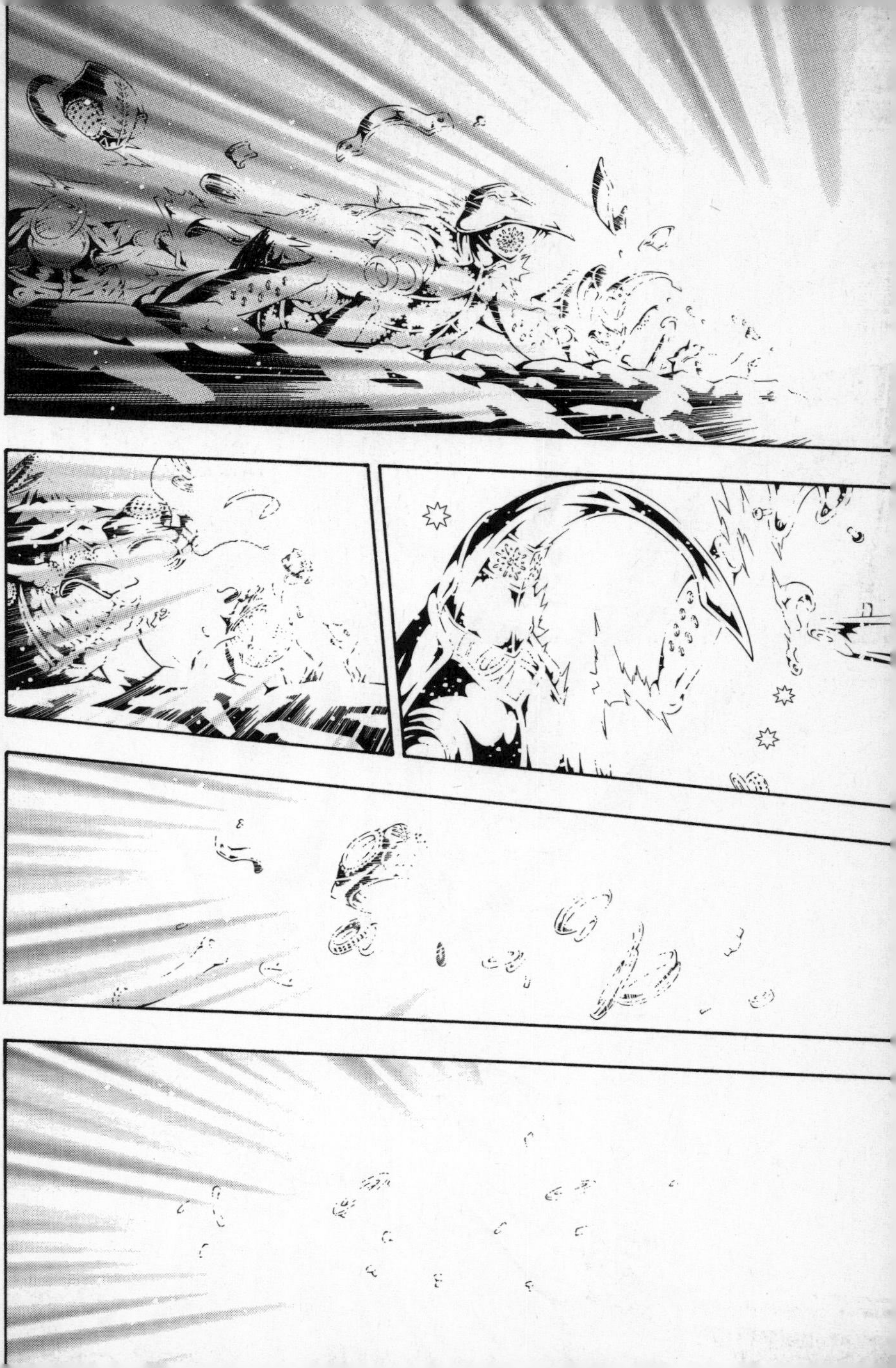

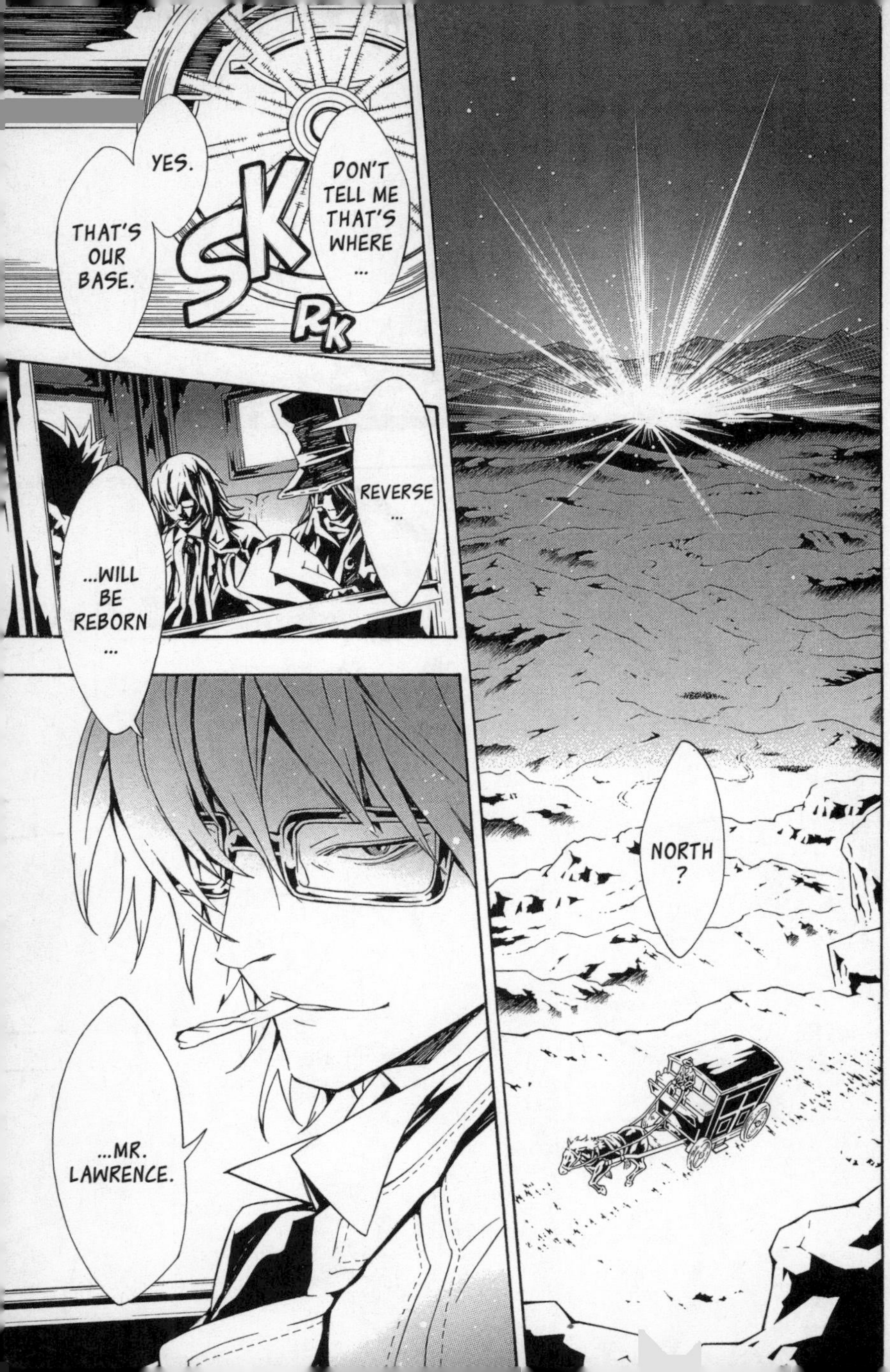
NORTH ?
DON'T TELL ME THAT'S WHERE ...
SKRK
YES.
THAT'S OUR BASE.
REVERSE ...
...WILL BE REBORN ...
...MR. LAWRENCE.

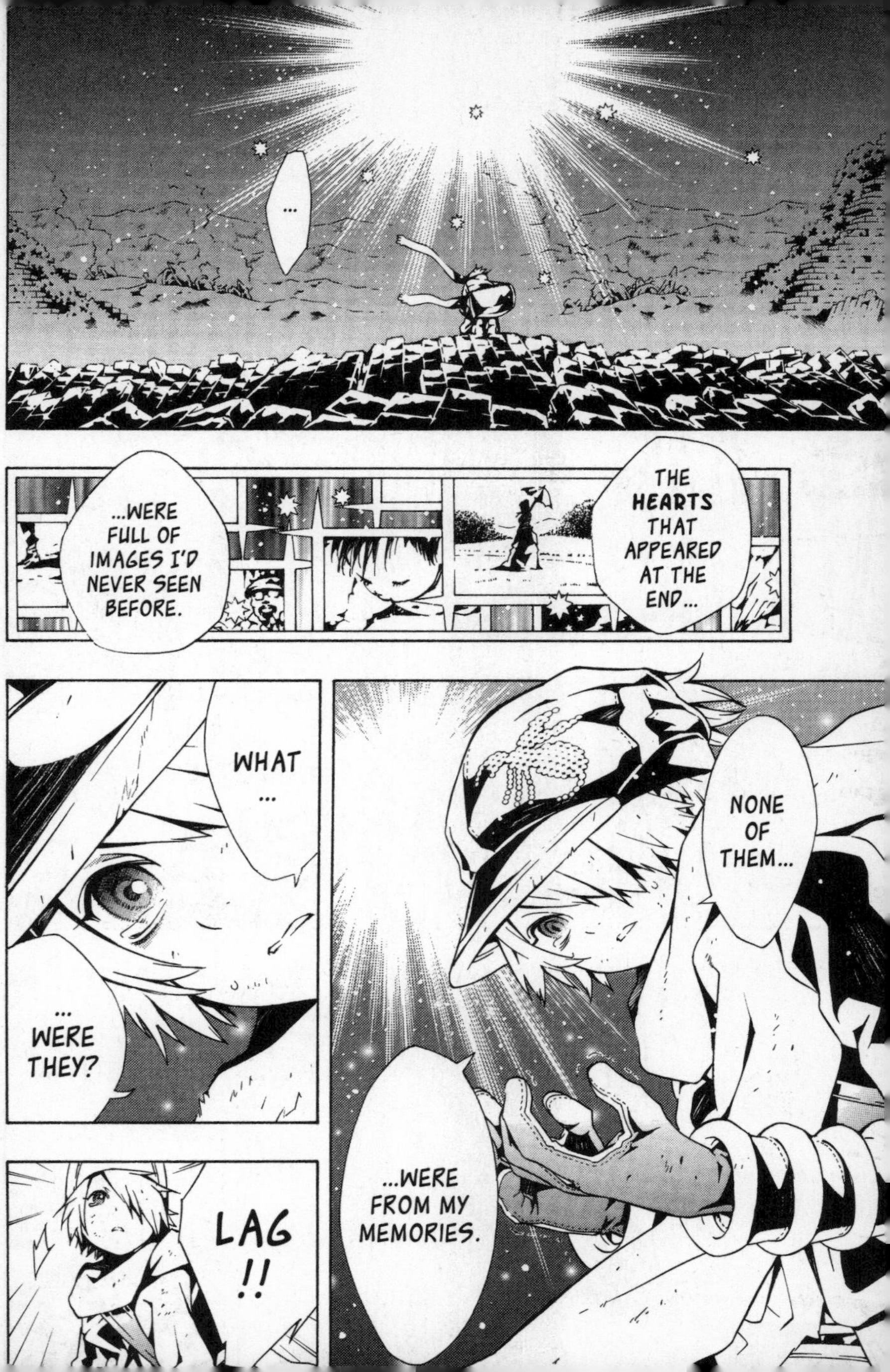
...
THE HEARTS THAT APPEARED AT THE END...
...WERE FULL OF IMAGES I'D NEVER SEEN BEFORE.
NONE OF THEM...
...WERE FROM MY MEMORIES.
WHAT ...
... WERE THEY?
LAG !!

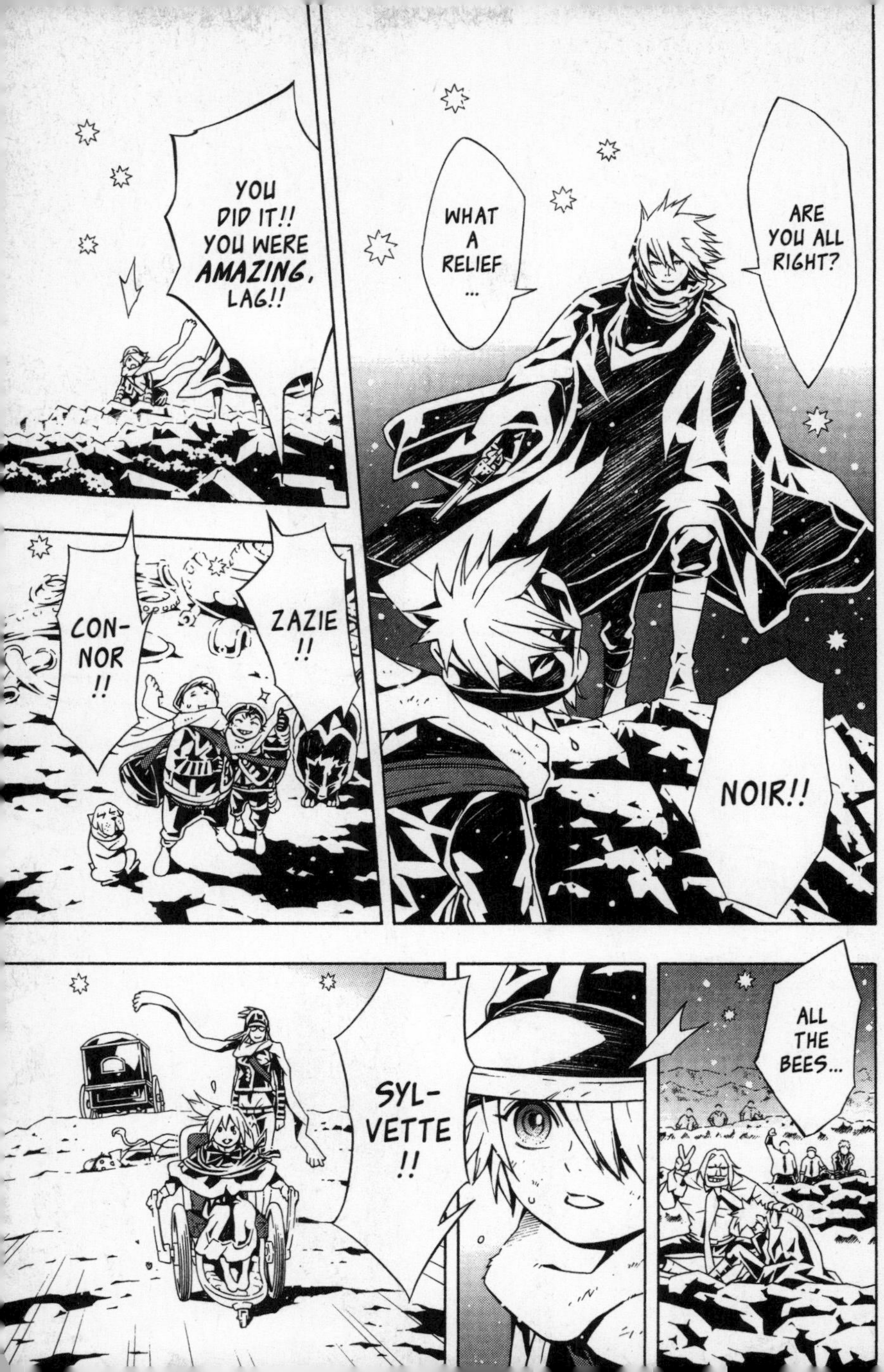
ARE YOU ALL RIGHT?
WHAT A RELIEF ...
NOIR!!
YOU DID IT!! YOU WERE AMAZING, LAG!!
ZAZIE !!
CON-NOR !!
ALL THE BEES...
SYL-VETTE !!

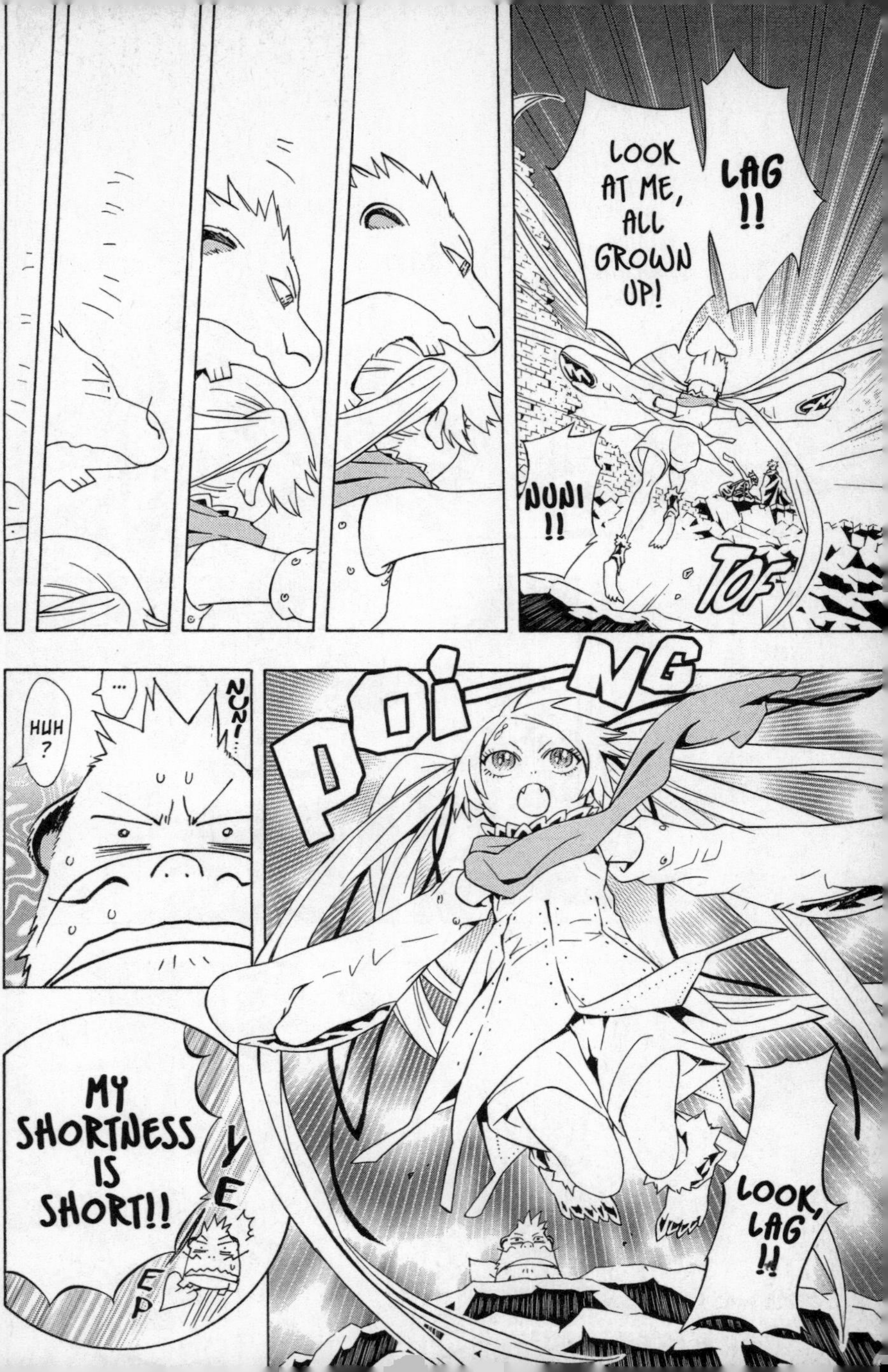
LAG!!
LOOK AT ME, ALL GROWN UP!
NUNI!!
TOF
POING
LOOK, LAG!!
NUNI...
...
HUH?
MY SHORTNESS IS SHORT!!
YEEP

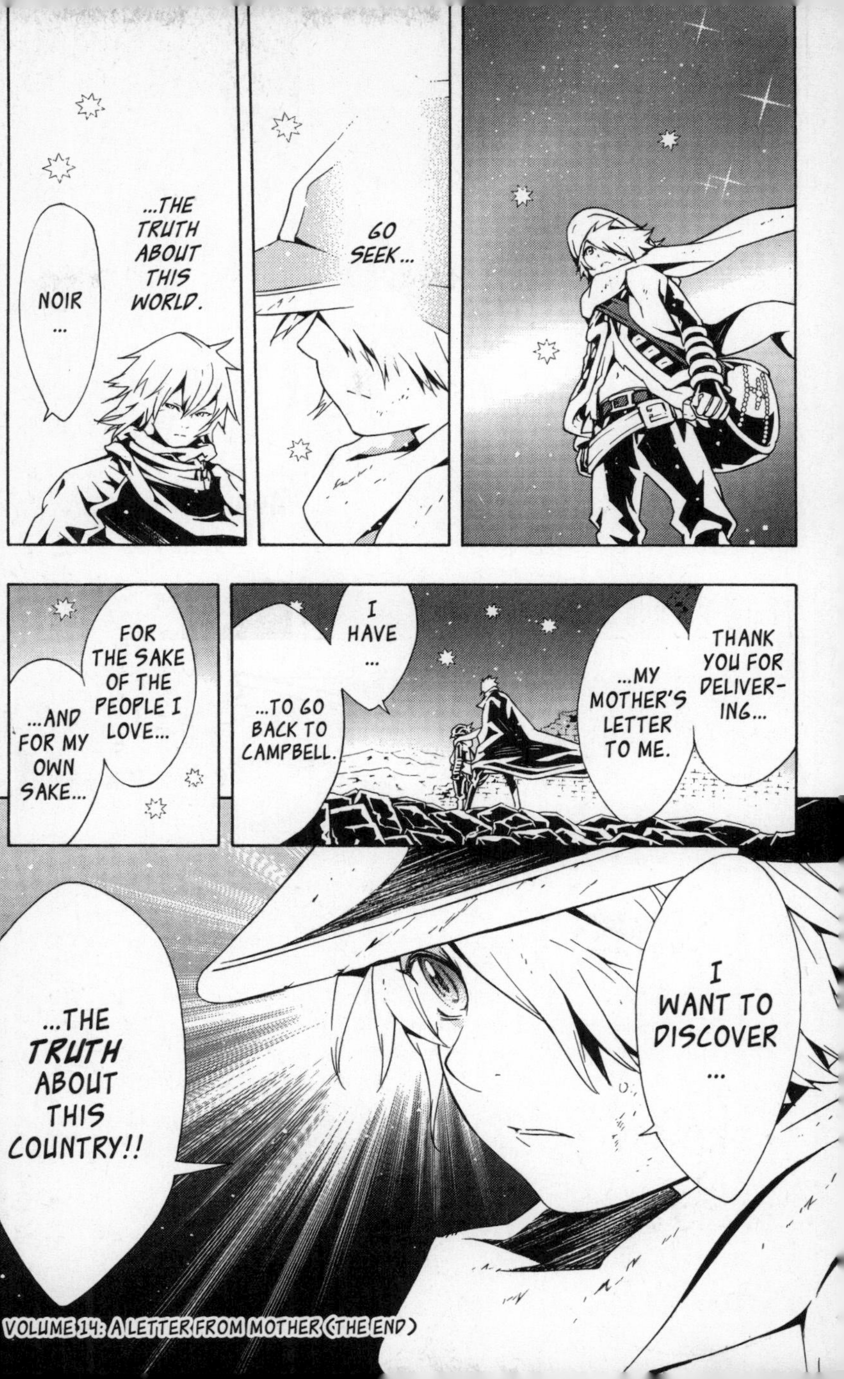
GO SEEK...
...THE TRUTH ABOUT THIS WORLD.
NOIR ...
THANK YOU FOR DELIVERING...
...MY MOTHER'S LETTER TO ME.
I HAVE ...
...TO GO BACK TO CAMPBELL.
FOR THE SAKE OF THE PEOPLE I LOVE...
...AND FOR MY OWN SAKE...
I WANT TO DISCOVER ...
...THE TRUTH ABOUT THIS COUNTRY!!
VOLUME 14: A LETTER FROM MOTHER (THE END)

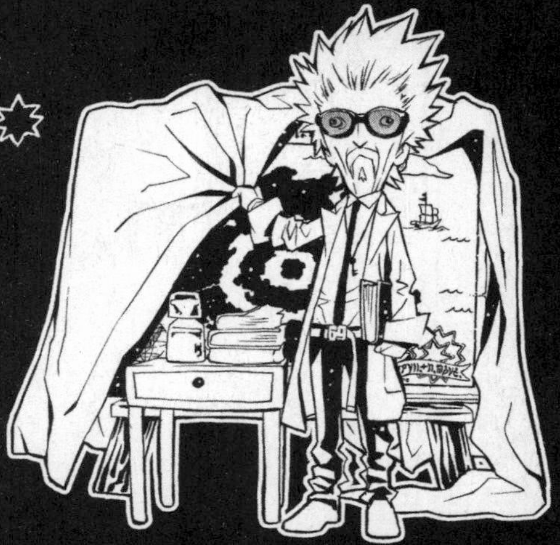

Dr. Thunderland's Reference Desk

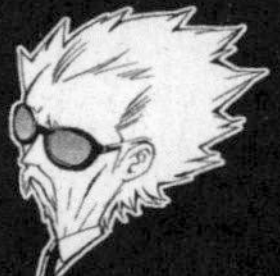

That Cabernet never gives up, does he? *Bah!* How long I've waited…how very long…and yet my cue still has yet to be called! They probably ran out of pages for me because Cabernet wouldn't die!! That bugger used up the pages that would show me in action!! *Waah!!*

I work at the Beehive in Yuusari, researching this and that, but my scenes in this manga always get cut. Every volume I tirelessly share facts about the world of Amberground, but nevertheless my scenes get cut. Where have I disappeared to? Give me back my stolen scenes…***Wanted!!*** ♪

■ NICHE GROWS UP

Well…that was startling. Thinking it over, in previous volumes Niche always reacted strongly whenever Lag was injured. Still, it seems she didn't mature completely. That leaves me relieved in some ways, but disappointed in others. And she reverted right back! I wonder if there's a time limit on it or something. I must research this phenomenon.

What's more, Niche's already staggering strength seemed to double in might! What if they develop this into a battle plan where Lag is turned into a human sacrifice to rile Niche up every time he gets into a pinch?

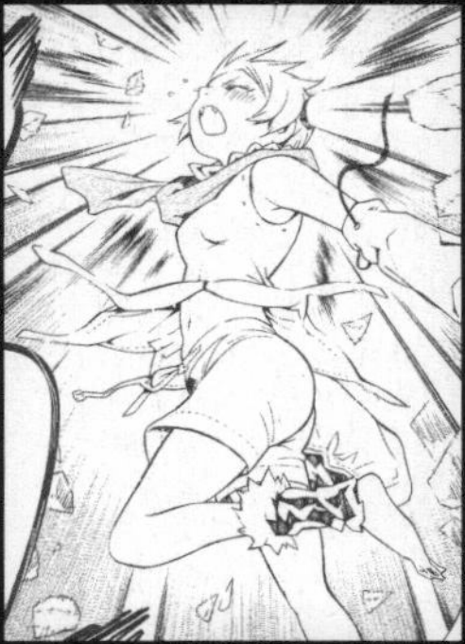

■ CABERNET: HUMAN FORM

That was startling too! Cabernet took on humanoid form! Thanks to the collective *heart* of the Bees and Noir, it was finally destroyed…but it made me realize again how great a threat these creatures are. I can only pray that no Gaichuu more powerful than Cabernet ever appears. Think of the scenes it could steal from me…a nefarious threat indeed!

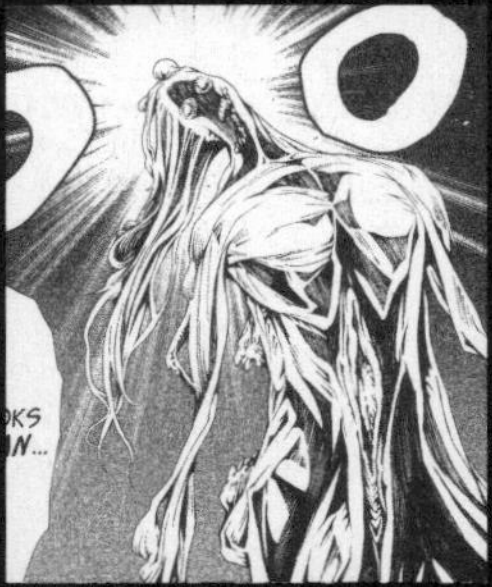

■ THE LETTER FROM MOTHER

Still more startling! Lag's mother, Anne Seeing, may still be alive in Akatsuki! Hmm…intriguing. And she hid a message to her son in Noir's *heart*. The memory was locked in a mailbox that opened to reveal the "letter" only after Lag's *heart* touched it. So Lag himself was the key to the box. Hmm…this is a new form of letter I've never seen before. And this means that Noir…I mean Gauche…carried out his duty as a Bee without realizing it.

But were you listening closely, everyone? Lag's mother told Noir, "You have lost much of your memory." Does that mean he still has some memory left? Heh heh heh! I'm such a genius for noticing that! Come on, tell me I'm a genius! Shower me with praise!

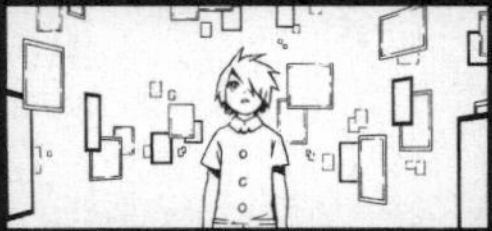

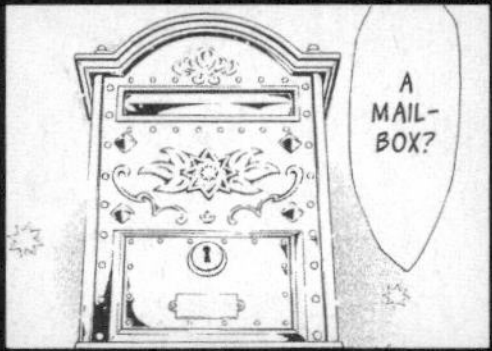
A MAIL-BOX?

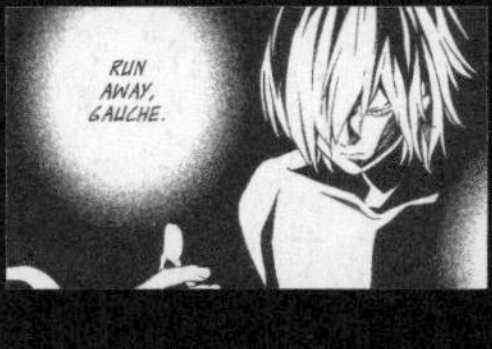
RUN AWAY, GAUCHE.

Now, it's too early to say anything for sure, but it looks like Lag will be busy finding out about his mother, himself and the past in the next volume. What secrets have been hidden? I hope it's not anything painful. After all, Lag is still so young. I'm worried about him. Maybe I should go with him? Eh? Eh?

■ LAG'S MEMORIES
Most startling of all! Lag seemed to have used up all his *heart*, and yet, when all seemed lost, massive *heart* flooded out from somewhere within! And it included memories Lag had never seen before.

That reminds me of something. Do you remember back in volume 8, chapter 30, when Cabernet attacked Lag after he'd run out of *heart*? I've always thought that was odd. Remember? Gaichuu are attracted to people's shining *hearts*, and they don't bother to attack anyone whose *heart* level is on empty. So if Cabernet attacked Lag...get it? Somehow, beneath Lag's ordinary *heart*, there must be a massive store of *heart* he knows nothing about lying dormant!

But how could someone else's *heart* get into Lag? I'm sorry. At this point I'm as clueless as you are. But it's the perfect mystery for a certain scientific genius to solve in his long-awaited debut in the main story...Yes! Finally! Woo-hoo!

■ NEW REVERSE BASE
Hmm...it's somewhere in the north. That reminds me of the land where Niche's sister...no, surely not...

Shall I reinvent myself as well? As someone who's *in the darn book?* Sorry to be blunt, but I'm tired of pussyfooting around! The new me will come straight to the point!

NORTH ?

Route Map

Finally, I am including a map, indicating Lag's route and Cabernet's flight path, created at Lonely Goatherd Map Station of Central Yuusari.

A: Akatsuki B: Yuusari C: Yodaka

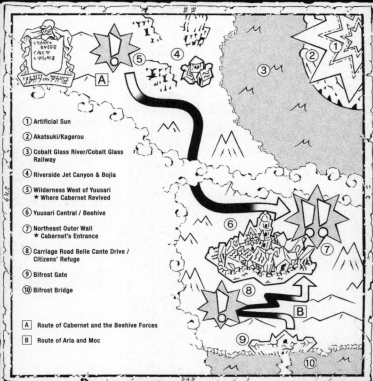

① Artificial Sun

② Akatsuki/Kagerou

③ Cobalt Glass River/Cobalt Glass Railway

④ Riverside Jet Canyon & Bojia

⑤ Wilderness West of Yuusari
　★ Where Cabernet Revived

⑥ Yuusari Central / Beehive

⑦ Northeast Outer Wall
　★ Cabernet's Entrance

⑧ Carriage Road Belle Cante Drive / Citizens' Refuge

⑨ Bifrost Gate

⑩ Bifrost Bridge

A　Route of Cabernet and the Beehive Forces

B　Route of Aria and Moc

The new me won't mess around! He'll take to the mound and stare down the batter's box! He'll be a real man!!

...Then he'll get thrown out of the game for beaning players, his bonus will be cut and he'll be drummed out of the league. So much for that. Good night.

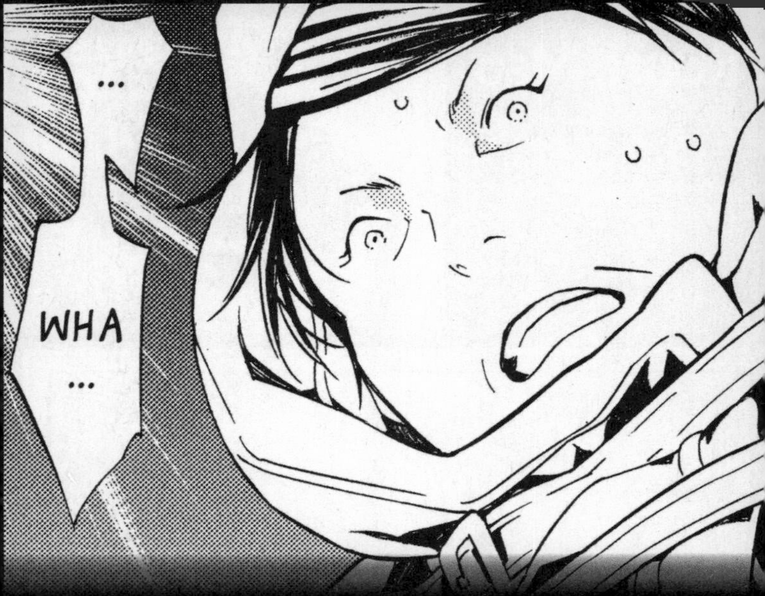
...
WHA
...

In the next volume...

To the Little People

Following the message from his mother, Lag returns to his hometown, the little village of Campbell. But is he ready to learn the truth about his own past...and Amberground?

Available **November 2013!**